GABRIEL HERMAN
215-740-5441

D1257792

THE LAW OF DEBTORS AND CREDITORS
2013 CASEBOOK SUPPLEMENT

EDITORIAL ADVISORS

Vicki Been
Elihu Root Professor of Law
New York University School of Law

Erwin Chemerinsky
Dean and Distinguished Professor of Law
University of California, Irvine, School of Law

Richard A. Epstein
Laurence A. Tisch Professor of Law
New York University School of Law
Peter and Kirsten Bedford Senior Fellow
The Hoover Institution
Senior Lecturer in Law
The University of Chicago

Ronald J. Gilson
Charles J. Meyers Professor of Law and Business
Stanford University
Marc and Eva Stern Professor of Law and Business
Columbia Law School

James E. Krier
Earl Warren DeLano Professor of Law
The University of Michigan Law School

Richard K. Neumann, Jr.
Professor of Law
Maurice A. Deane School of Law at Hofstra University

Robert H. Sitkoff
John L. Gray Professor of Law
Harvard Law School

David Alan Sklansky
Yosef Osheawich Professor of Law
University of California at Berkeley School of Law

Kent D. Syverud
Dean and Ethan A. H. Shepley University Professor
Washington University School of Law

THE LAW OF DEBTORS AND CREDITORS
Sixth Edition
2013 Casebook Supplement

Elizabeth Warren
Leo Gottlieb Professor of Law Emeritus
Harvard University

Jay Lawrence Westbrook
Benno C. Schmidt Chair of Business Law
University of Texas

Katherine Porter
Professor of Law
University of California, Irvine

John A. E. Pottow
Professor of Law
University of Michigan

Wolters Kluwer

Law & Business

Copyright © 2013 Elizabeth Warren, Jay Westbrook, Joel M. Westbrook, Katherine Porter, and John Pottow.

Published by Wolters Kluwer Law & Business in New York.

Wolters Kluwer Law & Business serves customers worldwide with CCH, Aspen Publishers, and Kluwer Law International products. (www.wolterskluwerlb.com).

No part of this publication may be reproduced or transmitted in any form or by any means, electronic or mechanical, including photocopy, recording, or utilized by any information storage or retrieval system, without written permission from the publisher. For information about permissions or to request permissions online, visit us at www.wolterskluwerlb.com, or a written request may be faxed to our permissions department at 212-771-0803.

To contact Customer Service, e-mail customer.service@wolterskluwer.com, call 1-800-234-1660, fax 1-800-901-9075, or mail correspondence to:

Wolters Kluwer Law & Business
Attn: Order Department
PO Box 990
Frederick, MD 21705

Printed in the United States of America.

1 2 3 4 5 6 7 8 9 0

ISBN 978-1-4548-3769-5

SFI
Certified Chain of Custody
Product Line Contains At Least
20% Certified Forest Content
www.sfiprogram.org
SFI-00756

About Wolters Kluwer Law & Business

Wolters Kluwer Law & Business is a leading global provider of intelligent information and digital solutions for legal and business professionals in key specialty areas, and respected educational resources for professors and law students. Wolters Kluwer Law & Business connects legal and business professionals as well as those in the education market with timely, specialized authoritative content and information-enabled solutions to support success through productivity, accuracy and mobility.

Serving customers worldwide, Wolters Kluwer Law & Business products include those under the Aspen Publishers, CCH, Kluwer Law International, Loislaw, ftwilliam.com and MediRegs family of products.

CCH products have been a trusted resource since 1913, and are highly regarded resources for legal, securities, antitrust and trade regulation, government contracting, banking, pension, payroll, employment and labor, and healthcare reimbursement and compliance professionals.

Aspen Publishers products provide essential information to attorneys, business professionals and law students. Written by preeminent authorities, the product line offers analytical and practical information in a range of specialty practice areas from securities law and intellectual property to mergers and acquisitions and pension/benefits. Aspen's trusted legal education resources provide professors and students with high-quality, up-to-date and effective resources for successful instruction and study in all areas of the law.

Kluwer Law International products provide the global business community with reliable international legal information in English. Legal practitioners, corporate counsel and business executives around the world rely on Kluwer Law journals, looseleafs, books, and electronic products for comprehensive information in many areas of international legal practice.

Loislaw is a comprehensive online legal research product providing legal content to law firm practitioners of various specializations. Loislaw provides attorneys with the ability to quickly and efficiently find the necessary legal information they need, when and where they need it, by facilitating access to primary law as well as state-specific law, records, forms and treatises.

ftwilliam.com offers employee benefits professionals the highest quality plan documents (retirement, welfare and non-qualified) and government forms (5500/PBGC, 1099 and IRS) software at highly competitive prices.

MediRegs products provide integrated health care compliance content and software solutions for professionals in healthcare, higher education and life sciences, including professionals in accounting, law and consulting.

Wolters Kluwer Law & Business, a division of Wolters Kluwer, is headquartered in New York. Wolters Kluwer is a market-leading global information services company focused on professionals.

Summary of Contents

Contents

Preface

At the core of U.S. bankruptcy law is the fresh start, and this supplement is a fresh start to the consumer bankruptcy section of this textbook. Since our first edition in 1985, personal bankruptcy filings have skyrocketed, and Congress has amended the bankruptcy laws repeatedly to try to keep up, most dramatically in 2005. The consumer debt market also changed markedly during this time period, with "innovation" in financial services resulting in more consumers having more kinds of debts. With that explosion of debt came the risk of more financial distress, especially as the public safety net weakened. Somewhat paradoxically, this run-up in consumer debt fueled economic growth in this country, which is driven by consumer spending, but whatever the benefits of that growth, it is undeniable that more debt has brought more bankruptcy. As the bankruptcy has boomed, lawyers in practice have tried to keep up, embracing new technologies for case management—just as consumer lenders have harnessed new technologies to develop sophisticated credit scoring and marketing systems. In sum, it's a Brave New World.

This supplement reflects both these longer-term structural changes to the consumer bankruptcy system and the more recent developments in the field: Supreme Court cases interpreting the 2005 amendments, the consequences of the Great Recession, and the creation of the Consumer Financial Protection Bureau. The basic teaching structure has stayed the same. We start with nonbankruptcy law as the backdrop, then divide bankruptcy law for individuals into liquidation (chapter 7) and payout (chapter 13), tracking mostly chronologically a typical case. The big difference from the latest edition—driven by legal changes and developments in practice—is postponing the "means test" (the cornerstone of the 2005 amendments) until after the assignments working through Chapters 7 and 13. The means test is nominally a mechanical screen that applies at the front of a case when a petition is filed, but as we have watched the cases play out in the first decade after the amendments and talked with lawyers in the field, we have become convinced that this means test is something more. Namely, it is a broad and complex part of the most critical decision a consumer debtor will make (and the debtor's lawyer will advise): under which chapter to file for bankruptcy. This chapter choice has always been in our view one of the most fundamental issues in bankruptcy, so the supplement has been reorganized to reflect that, leaving its consideration to the end.

The Preface to the sixth edition provides an overall description of how this book approaches the law of debtors and creditors. Generations of students have found it helpful, and we continue to recommend it.

Perhaps the biggest change reflected in the supplement is that we are now four authors. The two additional authors are Professors Katherine Porter and John Pottow from the University of California, Irvine and the University of Michigan, respectively. They share the founding authors' love of teaching and their commitment to pragmatic, problem-based learning. As wee ones when the 1978 Bankruptcy Code was passed, Porter and Pottow differ from Warren and Westbrook in their sense of what is "new," but all four share a sense of what is important about bankruptcy law and its impact on people and society. We hope this supplement reflects that shared vision.

Cambridge		Warren
Austin		Westbrook
	And introducing	
Irvine		Porter
Ann Arbor		Pottow
		Professors of Law

Acknowledgments

We are indebted to many people for our continued evolution of this book over six and a half editions. Samuel Bufford, Dan Keating, Jaime Dodge, and Steven Ware have sent us corrections and suggestions of great value (and occasional embarrassment). Angelica Ornelas and Bruce Markell provided helpful ideas on ethics problems. We have received superb research help from law students Suzanne Lawson (UC Irvine 2013), Sarah Coleman (Texas 2014), Mathew Driscoll and Jaaron Sanderson (both Texas 2013), Joshua Clark, Hyung Seok Kang, Meredith Morgan (all Michigan 2013), and Katherine Roller (Michigan 2014). We give a special thanks to outstanding staff who worked on this project: Lynh Tran (UC Irvine), Margaret Klocinski (Michigan), Helen Klein (UC Irvine), and Thor Quick (Texas). We owe a special thanks to the law students at Texas and Michigan who tested the beta version in the first term of 2013.

Two of us have young kids, and the other two have young grandkids, so we are all also grateful to families who endured nights and weekends when we were immersed in this supplement. We hope all of you enjoy using it as much as we did creating it.

Cambridge

Austin

Irvine

Ann Arbor

Warren

Westbrook

Porter

Pottow

Professors of Law

We also thank the following authors and copyright holders for permission to use their materials:

Collection Agency Headed by "Thugs" Helps Merchants, The Daily Iowan, April 12, 1982. Reprinted with the permission of United Press International, Inc.

Deadbeat Dad Who Owed Nearly $700k is Off to Prison, May 20, 2008. Copyright 2008 by wftv.com.

Ditzen, Lawyer's Methods, Debtors' Nightmare, Philadelphia Inquirer, June 12, 1994. Used with permission of Philadelphia Inquirer Copyright © 2013. All rights reserved.

Drennan, Insolvency applicants who can get bus won't be allowed a car. 24 March 2013. Reprinted by permission of The Independent.ie.

Feibelman, "Defining the Social Insurance Function of Consumer Bankruptcy." Reprinted from the Spring 2005 issue of the ABI Law Review, Vol. 13, No. 1, with the permission of the American Bankruptcy Institute (www.abiworld.org).

Gross, Failure and Forgiveness: Rebalancing the Bankruptcy System, Yale   Law Press, 1997.

Hall, More Hoopla at Simpson Home Auction, Los Angeles Times, July 15, 1997. Copyright © 1997. Los Angeles Times. Reprinted with Permission.

Jackson, The Fresh Start Policy in Bankruptcy Law, 98 Harv. L. Rev., 1393 (1985).

Jones and Zywicki, It's Time for Means-Testing, 1999 BYU L. Rev. 177, 1999.

Kale, Dressed for Success, Chicago Tribune, April 20, 1982. All rights reserved. Photograph used by permission and protected by the Copyright Laws of the United States. The printing, copying, redistribution, or retransmission of this Content without express written permission is prohibited.

Lawless, The Paradox of Consumer Credit, 2007 U. Ill. L. Rev. 347.

Mayer, Caroline E. Bankrupt and Swamped with Credit Offers, From The Washington Post, © April 15, 2005. The Washington Post. All rights reserved. Used by permission and protected by the Copyright Laws of the United States. The printing, copying, redistribution, or retransmission of the Material without express written permission is prohibited.

McKnight, Joseph, Protection of the Family Home from Seizure by Creditors: The Source and Evolution of a Legal Principle, 86 Southwestern Historical Quarterly 369 (1983). Reprinted by permission of the Texas State Historical Association.

Moor, Tom, Tribune Staff Writer. Repo man relies on timing, skills, The South Bend Tribune, Oct. 31. 2008. Reprinted by permission of the South Bend Tribune.

Norris, Basking in Islands of Legalism, From The New York Times, 1/22/2010 © 2010. The New York Times. All rights reserved. Used by permission and protected by the Copyright Laws of the United States. The printing, copying, redistribution, or retransmission of the Material without express written permission is prohibited.

Rao, Debt Buyers, Rewriting of Rule 3001: Taking the Proof out of the Claims Process," by John Rao. Reprinted from the July/August 2004 ABI Journal, Vol. 23, No. 6, with the permission of the American Bankruptcy Institute (www.abiworld.org).

Simpson House Available for $3.9 Million, The New York Times, August 6, 1997. Used with permission of the Associated Press Copyright © 2013. All rights reserved.

Son Can't Pay, So Father's Body is Returned, The New York Times, October 14, 1992. Used with permission of The Associated Press Copyright © 2013. All rights reserved.

Whitford, A Critique of the Consumer Credit Collection System, 1979 Wis. L. Rev. 1047. Copyright 2012 by The Board of Regents of the University of Wisconsin System; Reprinted by permission of the Wisconsin Law Review.

World Bank, Report on the Treatment of the Insolvency of Natural Persons (2013). Reprinted by permission of the World Bank.

NOTE

The problems in this book are filled with debtors, creditors, lawyers, trustees, and others who are the products of our imaginations. Any resemblance to any real person, solvent or insolvent, is purely coincidental.

We have edited cases and articles for the sake of smoother reading. Citations and footnotes have been deleted without indication. Footnotes that were not eliminated retain their original numbers; asterisks indicate editors' footnotes. Formatting has been altered liberally.

The Bankruptcy Code is referred to as ''the Code,'' and citations to it are by section number only. ''The Act'' refers to the Bankruptcy Act of 1898. Citations to various federal consumer law acts may be to the USCA or the original public law number as appropriate.

THE LAW OF DEBTORS AND CREDITORS
2013 CASEBOOK SUPPLEMENT

PART I

INTRODUCTION

Assignment 1.

An Introduction to Debtor-Creditor Law

This is a book about debtors and creditors. It deals with the laws governing debtor and creditor behavior, laws that prescribe when obligations must be paid, how unpaid obligations can be collected, and how bankruptcy law can change those legal obligations. Not surprisingly, this is a book laden with rules, regulations, common law doctrines, state codes, federal statutes, and enough other "law" to challenge even the most diligent student.

Although there is much law in this book, there is also much that relies on bookkeepers, accountants, and actuaries. For unlike most courses you have taken so far in law school, where you read cases with facts not in dispute but with complex analysis of what those facts mean to an evolving common law or whether, for example, a collection of undisputed facts give rise to a lack of reasonable care, here you will find parties fighting frequently and heatedly over specific facts, such as the value of an asset. So upping the intellectual ante, we will have to consider both complex law *and* disputed facts. (It's not too late to drop, but you will never know what you're missing.)

But it would be a mistake to think you will find here a musty cupboard filled with rules and numbers. Bankruptcy law is ultimately about human conduct in the charged context of financial distress. It is one thing to fight hard to win a lawsuit; when there is not enough money to go around, people fight even harder. "*And may the odds be ever in your favor!*" This text is thus equally filled with stories of tragic circumstances and shrewd uses of leverage. It is sometimes about people who wear pin-striped suits and live without passion, but it is also about rugged self-help and self-defense in a very tough world. Don't believe us? Take a look at this story; we couldn't have made this up had we tried.

Son Can't Pay, So Father's Body Is Returned

Richmond, Tex.—The body of a man who died Friday was dumped on his son's doorstep by a funeral home on Monday evening because the son had been unable to pay the full price of cremation.

The bizarre episode, in this town 30 miles southwest of Houston, began Saturday morning when the body of George Bojarski, who had died of esophageal cancer at the age of 66, was picked up by the Evans Mortuary.

Mr. Bojarski's son, Larry, paid the funeral home $299 of the $683 cremation fee and was told that if he failed to pay the balance, the body would be returned.

Gary Geick, the Justice of the Peace for Fort Bend County, quoted Larry Bojarski today as saying that he had not had the money to pay the balance and that he had not believed that the funeral home would follow through with its threat....

But on Monday evening, George Bojarski's body, covered only by a sheet, was found at the door of his son's apartment.

It was unclear why the Evans Mortuary had not given the son more time to pay the fee; a telephone call today seeking comment from the funeral home was not returned. The town's Police Chief, Butch Gore, said there had been no decision on whether to bring criminal charges.

The Hernandez Funeral Home in the nearby town of Rosenberg has now agreed to provide the cremation services at no cost.

"My father's been in the business for 50 years," said one of the owners, Joe Hernandez, "and he's never heard of a case like this. The son was kind of like in shock. Here your dad is laying there on the floor after being dead for three days." [*New York Times*, October 14, 1993, at A16, col. 1.]

Beyond stark tales like this one are larger questions about the role of debt in society. Debt lies at the heart of every modern economy. It is commonly agreed that the invention of a permanent national debt through the "gilt" bonds of the Bank of England in the Eighteenth Century was the foundation for the Industrial Revolution. If any cultural tool deserves a comparison with fire, it is debt: essential, yet dangerous.

In American society, and increasingly in every country around the world, the bankruptcy process lies at the heart of the evolving role of debt in both the global economy and lives of ordinary people. At the macro level, the central place of debt is epitomized by the bankruptcy of Lehman Brothers in 2008. At $600 billion, it was not just the largest bankruptcy in the history of the galaxy, it was part of a financial collapse of interconnected debt instruments that was a major precipitating cause of the Great Recession. At the micro level, debt's prevalence has been seen in the numerous studies documenting how widespread consumer debt financing has become: we now know that more adults have major consumer debt than go to church, have college degrees, or vote in major elections.

While the debt loads of today (at both the macro and micro level) may seem terrifying to many, prophecies of financial collapse are not new. Societies for thousands of years have struggled with debt.

"On Bankruptcy" [1]
Simone Weil (1937)

A rapid glance at history is enough to show the subversive role consistently played, ever since money existed, by the phenomenon of debt. The cancellation of debts was the principal feature of reforms of both Solon and Lycurgus. And later on the small Greek cities were more than once shattered by movements in favor of another cancellation. The revolt by which the Roman plebeians won the institution of the tribune ship had its origin in a widespread insolvency, which was reducing more and more debtors to the condition of slavery; and even if there had been no revolt a partial cancellation of debts had become imperative, because with every plebeian reduced to a slave Rome lost a soldier. . . .

The payment of debts is necessary for social order. The non-payment of debts is quite equally necessary for social order. For centuries humanity has oscillated, serenely unaware, between these two contradictory necessities. Unfortunately, the second of them violates a great many seemingly legitimate interests and it has difficulty in securing recognition without disturbance and a measure of violence.

A. THE STRUCTURE OF DEBTOR-CREDITOR LAW

The law in the United States relating to debts can sometimes be framed as a series of dichotomies: debtors and creditors; state and federal law; secured and unsecured credit; in-court and out-of-court resolution; liquidation vs. payout; and more. Perhaps the most fundamental distinction as a matter of practical social policy is the one between the debts that arise from the daily lives of consumers and those that are created by the operation of a business. A human who is broke raises many similar concerns to a corporation that is floundering, but there are even more differences. A second major distinction is the one between collection of a specific debt by a single creditor (for example, by the seizure of the debtor's wages) and the resolution of all debts in a collective proceeding, such as a bankruptcy petition. One creditor's pursuit of a debtor for recovery on a debt

---

1. French title: Esquisse d'une apologie de la banqueroute.

raises different concerns from ten creditors' pursuit of ten debts in a single proceeding.

In this book, we first divide the materials between consumer debtors and business debtors. Then we divide each section between single-debt enforcement and the collective-debt enforcement of bankruptcy. Finally, we divide the bankruptcy materials between liquidation ("sellout") and reorganization ("payout"). Although we do not spend equal time on each area, we use this analytical framework to underscore how bankruptcy is an *overlay* upon a rich fabric of pre-existing collections law. We start the consumer section with a creditor's attempt to collect a single debt, sampling the jungle warfare of debt collectors, credit reports, and repossessions that are the main enforcement mechanisms against consumers. Then we turn to consumer bankruptcy with its policy pendulum swinging between enforcing an individual's promises to repay on the one hand and providing cancellation of debts as a "fresh start" for the debtor on the other.

The business section is also divided into collection of single debts and a collective resolution in bankruptcy. It starts with the ancient writs commanding a sheriff to seize the debtor's property and contrasts them with the modern use of secured creditor repossessions under Article 9 of the Uniform Commercial Code. The business section then moves on to the fascinating world of chapter 11 where some contenders, like Lehman, simply collapse into liquidation but others, like all the major airlines, seem to fly through in (relative) health. Sometimes success means forgiveness of parts of debts or extensions of repayment terms by lenders, sometimes success means merging into a strategically similar former rival (like those airlines), and sometimes success can mean a combination of the two.

The basic consumer-business distinction is not a sharp line. A large empirical study of bankruptcy has shown that many individuals who file for bankruptcy do so as their small businesses collapse. Elizabeth Warren and Jay L. Westbrook, Financial Characteristics of Businesses in Bankruptcy, 73 Am. Bankr. L.J. 499 (1999) (hereafter cited as *Financial Characteristics*); see also Robert Lawless and Elizabeth Warren, The Myth of the Disappearing Business Bankruptcy, 93 Calif. L. Rev. 745 (2005); Douglas G. Baird & Edward R. Morrison, Serial Entrepreneurs and Small Business Bankruptcies, 105 Colum. L. Rev. 2310 (2005). That said, the great majority of cases are clearly either business or nonbusiness, and a grasp of the two distinct operating systems is critical to understanding the actual operation of the bankruptcy laws.

B. A BRIEF INTRODUCTION TO BANKRUPTCY THEORY (AND DATA)

If the field of bankruptcy had produced a generally accepted Grand Theory, with perhaps some details disputed, it might make sense to begin with that so a student could analyze each part of the material in the appropriate pigeonhole of the theory and gauge its fit. Alas, it has not. On the contrary, bankruptcy law has sprouted a spirited theoretical discourse that we will explore a bit in time. It also occurs to us that a student has little basis for critique and comparison at the start of a course, especially one such as bankruptcy that has many moving parts. Thus, we intentionally postpone a full-blown discussion of bankruptcy theory until the last chapter in this book.

In lieu of a full discussion at the outset, we present a quick sketch showing some of the different theories—sometimes just arguments—of what bankruptcy law should be. As you move through the book and find yourself mired in the complexities of the statute, this summary of bankruptcy theory may help you hear the music behind the madness.

In the consumer realm, it is fair to say that many if not most American theorists accept, albeit with varying degrees of enthusiasm, that bankruptcy is largely about a "fresh start" for individual debtors. See, e.g., Local Loan Co. v. Hunt, 292 U.S. 234 (1934). It would be hard to argue otherwise in a country whose central myths are captured in Ellis Island and in the Conestoga wagon setting out across the plains to a new life. Comparatively, the United States has always been, and remains, more committed to the fresh start idea for consumers who file bankruptcy than any other country in the world.

Some theorists explain the fresh start in economic terms, noting the insurance-like function of bankruptcy's discharge and advocating a contractual approach. See, e.g., Barry E. Adler, Bankruptcy Primitives, 12 Am. Bankr. Inst. L. Rev. 219 (2004). Others look to more morality-based grounds of the discharge, noting the deep-seated norm of forgiveness in many Western cultures. Heidi M. Hurd & Ralph Brubaker, Debts and the Demands of Conscience: The Virtue of Bankruptcy (Oxford Univ. Press forthcoming 2013). We can therefore say as a high-level theoretical matter that most believe consumer bankruptcy is about a fresh start, but then we quickly dissolve into disagreement about just why a fresh start is important. Similarly, when critiquing legislative policy, these different theoretical approaches lead to different arguments. Take, for example, the intermittent cries for less generous relief to consumers (i.e., restricting the fresh start). They are sometimes grounded in considerations of ethics ("Easy discharge is more proof that we are going to heck in a handbasket!"), but are sometimes grounded by economic concerns ("Easy discharge drives up the price of unsecured consumer credit!"). Moreover, both of these theoretically based arguments themselves contain implicit empirical suppositions. *Are* we going to heck in a handbasket? *Does* ease of bankruptcy discharge affect the price of consumer credit? If so, how much? (They also raise epistemic questions: *how do we know* whether we are going to heck in a handbasket?).

Thus, in addition to theoretical debates about how to think about the consumer bankruptcy system, on which scholars have not reached consensus, we also have rich second-order debates on empirical matters. Whether and to what extent bankruptcy law affects the cost of consumer credit is hotly debated by hard-working scholars and policymakers on all sides, but that empirical debate is of greater interest to those who are grounded in an economic theory of justification of the fresh start. And just to make your head truly spin, sometimes people of the same theoretical orientation toward bankruptcy law arrive at opposite conclusions of what the law should be. Take a moral philosopher's approach to bankruptcy. One might say that easy bankruptcy discharge results in laxity that is undesirable for our collective conception of the good and so the discharge should be constrained. But one might also say that an eroding social safety net requires on the contrary that the bankruptcy discharge be loosened up just to preserve the moral status quo, lest members of our society fall into greater indignity.

Business bankruptcy, at least from a creditor's perspective, addresses the problem of the "common pool," which is the difficulty of acting collectively and cooperatively to maximize the value of a debtor's assets (and thus the creditors' aggregate return). Think of it this way: individually, each creditor faces an incentive to break one of the debtor's fingers to encourage him to pay up and redouble his efforts at earning income. If ten creditors, however, each break a finger, then the debtor may not be able to work *at all* for a bit, and so there will be less wage income than if the creditors had just done nothing. (Taken to an extreme of course, a dead debtor can't pay anything; in fact, worse than that, a dead debtor actually incurs burial costs, which economists might bemoan as deadweight loss.) One prominent theory suggests that a huge collective action problem means bankruptcy law rests upon a "Creditors' Bargain," which means bankruptcy law should be built around what creditors would theoretically put into a kind of Rawlsian contract to achieve the best collective result for creditors.

The Creditors' Bargain approach assumes, however, that only creditors' interests matter in bankruptcy, not those of the owners of the business or its employees. In response, a number of scholars have argued that bankruptcy law reflects an enormous complex of conflicting social and economic goals that cannot be over-simplified. Elizabeth Warren, Bankruptcy Policymaking in an Imperfect World, 92 Mich. L. Rev. 336 (1993). This "complex policies" crowd also notes that bankruptcy law, in reallocating assets in circumstances of scarcity, serves a necessarily distributive function, which often makes the "just-solve-collective-action" types want to curl up into a ball and cry. While there has been spirited debate between these two constituencies, at a certain point matters reduce to axiomatic first principles of what one believes bankruptcy law *should* be about—principled differences that may be irreconcilable. Douglas G. Baird, Bankruptcy's Uncontested Axioms, 108 Yale L.J. 573 (1998).

A related and significantly correlated theoretical dichotomy divides "contractualists," who believe the best way to decide these hypothetical bargains of creditors is to allow them actually to sit down and decide (with the debtor) what their bankruptcy law should be, case-by-case, subject to some state-enforced ground rules, versus "collectivists," who believe that a mandatory bankruptcy code protects the interests of non-participating third parties and more efficiently tracks the likely outcome obtained by such envisioned negotiations without wasting all the time and expense.

One point is conceded by all: A major goal of bankruptcy is to preserve value. Bankruptcy preserves economic value, even in liquidation. The collective approach to orderly liquidation of assets is more value-preserving than the often chaotic process of seizure and sale by a host of competing creditors. Second, "reorganization bankruptcy" preserves the "going concern" value of a continuing business, reflecting the simple economic fact that businesses, like people, are often worth more alive than dead. Bankruptcy helps to preserve social values as well. Bankruptcy liquidation is an orderly and efficient way to bury a failed business, while bankruptcy reorganization offers the hope of saving jobs and the communities that depend on them, as well as ameliorating the inevitable social pain of business failure.

When you go through the business materials, keep these theoretical debates in your head, just as you should think about the fresh start issues on the consumer side.

For our part, we will defer jumping into these theoretical skirmishes for now, but we do want you to think about the empirical suppositions that are behind many policy recommendations purportedly flowing from these theories, and sometimes immanent in the theories themselves. Accordingly, throughout the book we reference studies that present data on how the bankruptcy system actually works as a *descriptive* matter, because only then can we engage, at least in our opinion, in an intelligent discussion of where the law should evolve as a *normative* matter.

The most comprehensive empirical studies are the four iterations of the Consumer Bankruptcy Project, in some or all of which each of us joined as investigators. The data collections for these studies occurred in 1981, 1991, 2001, and 2007, and have been the foundation of over a hundred published works. Some of the key work includes: Teresa A. Sullivan, Elizabeth Warren, and Jay L. Westbrook, As We Forgive Our Debtors: Bankruptcy and Consumer Credit in America (Oxford 1989) (hereafter cited as *As We Forgive*); Teresa A. Sullivan, Elizabeth Warren and Jay L. Westbrook, The Fragile Middle Class: Americans in Debt (Yale 2000) (hereafter cited as *Fragile Middle Class*); Robert M. Lawless, Angela K. Littwin, Katherine M. Porter, John A.E. Pottow, Deborah K. Thorne, and Elizabeth Warren, Did Bankruptcy Reform Fail?: An Empirical Study of Consumer Debtors, 82 Am. Bankr. L.J. 349 (2008) (hereafter cited as *Reform*), and Katherine Porter (Ed.), Broke: How Debt Bankrupts the Middle Class (Stanford University Press, 2012) (hereafter cited as *Broke*).

Empirical studies of business bankruptcy encompass examinations of both large, public companies and small businesses and individual entrepreneurs. A comprehensive look at the entirety of business cases can be found in *Financial Characteristics*. More recent work includes: Elizabeth Warren and Jay L.

Westbrook, Contracting Out of Bankruptcy: An Empirical Intervention, 118 Harv. L. Rev. 1197 (2005); and Elizabeth Warren and Jay L. Westbrook, The Success of Chapter 11: A Challenge to the Critics, 107 Mich. L. Rev. 603 (2009).

A number of more discrete studies, both consumer- and business-oriented, have also added important insights, and we point to those data at relevant places in the book too. We also draw on data from the Administrative Office of the Courts and other sources of national data on credit and finance.

Today, there are opportunities for students to dip their toes into the empirical bankruptcy seas using two handy websites. The UCLA-LoPucki Bankruptcy Research Database, available at no cost to all researchers, contains data on public company bankruptcies with large assets. It is available at http://lopucki.law.ucla.edu/index.htm. The Bankruptcy Data Project at Harvard offers a free database of bankruptcy filings by date and jurisdiction. The site, http://bdp.law.harvard.edu/, also contains a large bibliography of empirical papers on bankruptcy.

C. A *VERY* BRIEF HISTORY OF U.S. BANKRUPTCY LAW

Although ancient civilizations had laws regulating the treatment of defaulting and insolvent debtors, those antecedents are murky and their connection with modern bankruptcy law is more proclaimed than demonstrated. It is said that in Roman times the creditors did not merely divide the debtor's possessions, but took the debtor to the plaza and divided him.[2] Whether or not it was so (and whether or not "bankruptcy" derives from the Italian "banca rotta" or "broken [merchant's] table"), the clearest origins of United States bankruptcy law are to be found in England.

From the original English bankruptcy statute, adopted in the reign of the first Elizabeth, until the time of the American Revolution, "bankruptcy" was an involuntary creditor's collection device—a sort of super-attachment of all the debtor's property for equal division among creditors. Generally, it could be used only against traders or merchants. The benefit to bankrupts was release from the unpaid portion of their debts, the "discharge." A separate and later development was "insolvency" law, designed for the relief of debtors. Insolvency was always voluntary. Debtors who placed all their property in the hands of their creditors and the court were "discharged" from debtors' prison but not released from their debts in the modern sense of the word. Their obligations to pay remained, and creditors could still use collection devices other than imprisonment.[3]

In the United States, combining bankruptcy and insolvency elements into a unified debtor-creditor statute was a difficult process marked by various

---

2. Theodor C. Albert, The Insolvency Laws of Ancient Rome, 28 Cal. Bankr. J. 365, 368 (2006).
3. See generally, Emily Kadens, The Last Bankrupt Hanged: Balancing Incentives in the Development of Bankruptcy Law, 59 Duke L.J. 1229, 1236 (2010).

unsuccessful attempts. Notwithstanding specific constitutional recognition that a uniform national bankruptcy law was vital to national interests, United States Const., art. I, §8, cl. 4, more than a century passed before our legal ancestors could fashion a permanent federal bankruptcy statute acceptable to competing constituencies. For history buffs and students of social class, Bruce H. Mann's book, A Republic of Debtors, provides an outstanding analysis of bankruptcy, morality, and the economy in early America. It methodically shows how the most basic questions about the morality of bankruptcy relief and about the economic consequences of discharge provoked sharp debates in our government—debates that echo still today.

Throughout the nineteenth century, there were periodic struggles between mercantile and borrower interests over enactment of "bankruptcy" or "insolvency" laws. The farmers of the South and West detested the idea of involuntary bankruptcy, while the Northern and Eastern merchants wanted a discharge to be contingent on creditor agreement by specified majorities. Many believed that the two bodies of law, insolvency and bankruptcy, could not stand together ("a bill to serve God and Mammon"). As we said, the debates were sharp; the intensity of feeling generated by what is regarded by many as a dry and technical subject was quite remarkable:

> [The proposed bankruptcy law] comes from the class of men who are grinding the face of the poor…[and from] the same spirit that hung and killed and drew and quartered women for witchery.

31 Cong. Rec. S2362 (daily ed. March 1, 1898) (statements of Senator Stewart, Nev.).

Insolvency and bankruptcy were brought together only fleetingly, in a series of short-lived acts. See generally, David A. Skeel, The Genius of the 1898 Bankruptcy Act, 15 Bankr. Dev. J. 321 (1999). The bankruptcy "system" for the first 109 years after the adoption of the federalization of bankruptcy in the Constitution was thus little more than a series of brief legislative fiats, alternately pro-creditor or pro-debtor, accompanied by a growing awareness that a uniform compromise law would better serve everyone. (In the meantime, various states enacted their own insolvency laws, which were permitted to stand in the absence of congressional legislation.)

The interests of "God and Mammon" were at last accommodated in the Bankruptcy Act of 1898 (the "Act"), in the aftermath of an economic "panic." The panic jolted both creditors and debtors into compromise, realizing their needs for legal order in financial failure, and so both constituencies gave more ground than they had in the past. The benefit to debtors of this compromise was obvious, providing debt relief through discharge, a concept that creditors had repeatedly fought. Creditors for their part accepted that a workable bankruptcy system, providing orderliness to the collection process and encouraging debtors to make at least some payments, was worth the cost of permitting debtors a discharge. The legislation enacted in 1898 thus represented a series of fine compromises on a host of difficult issues. With its passage, the first enduring American bankruptcy law took shape.

The Act was amended a number of times in the following years, but it was not revised extensively until the 1930s, following the greatest economic collapse of them all, the Great Depression. The Chandler Act, encompassing the most extensive of these changes, was adopted in 1938. From a modern perspective, the two most important innovations of the Chandler Act were the adoption of new procedures for the reorganization of businesses and the scheduled payment of debt over time by financially troubled wage earners. The details of the evolution of reorganization—today's chapter 11—are discussed later in the section on business bankruptcy. The wage earner's scheduled payment plan—today's chapter 13—provided a way to reorganize a family's finances in much the same way a business could reorganize its obligations. It effectively introduced into federal bankruptcy the debt compositions and extensions[4] of state law, but more importantly it added the federal law power of a discharge of remaining debt upon payment plan completion. After the Depression, many sought refuge there.

Bankruptcy law enjoyed a quiet period for several decades thereafter. By the early 1970s, however, Congress had come to realize the bankruptcy laws were badly out of date. It created a National Bankruptcy Commission to propose reforms. Its report to Congress in 1973 offered recommendations for both consumer and business bankruptcy that were the foundations of the Bankruptcy Code adopted in 1978. That law, while subject to some important revisions, is still basically the law today. The bankruptcy community often refers to this law as the "Code," and contrasts it with old precedents decided under the "Act." The Code also retained the famous "chapter" system of bankruptcy, including liquidation procedures in chapter 7 for businesses and consumers, reorganization for businesses in chapter 11, and repayment bankruptcy for individuals in chapter 13. (If you ever see Roman numerals—such as Chapter XIII—the reference relates to the Act; we use some important old precedents, so look at the date of the case you are reading.)

In the 25 years after 1978, Congress enacted modest amendments, most of which responded to pressures of interest groups or specific concerns. In 1984, for example, Congress added sections benefiting grain farmers and shopping center landlords, among others. In 1986, Congress added a new type of bankruptcy, chapter 12, especially for family farmers. It also created a new U.S. Trustee's office in the executive branch of government to provide assistance to the courts and to serve various administrative functions.

---

4. A "composition" is a reduction in the amount of debt, while an "extension" provides more time to pay.

The consumer credit industry, which grew tremendously with deregulation in the 1980s and 1990s, began to press Congress for bigger changes to consumer bankruptcy law. A new National Bankruptcy Review Commission was convened and issued a report in 1997 that contained a large and comprehensive set of proposals for changes to consumer and business bankruptcy law. There were strong dissents on a number of issues, primarily on whether the existing consumer system was unduly generous.

Unhappy with the Commission Report, the credit industry took its case to Congress, drafting the basics of a bill to reform the consumer bankruptcy system in a manner more to its liking. The amendments came close to passing several times between 1998 and 2005, when Congress finally enacted the Bankruptcy Abuse Prevention and Consumer Protection Act ("BAPCPA"). With respect to consumer bankruptcy, these 2005 Amendments contained the most far-reaching changes since the adoption of the Code. The amendments reflect a view that bankruptcy law needed to be rebalanced in favor of creditors because it was too often being abused by debtors. Most bankruptcy specialists believe that the basic premise of BAPCPA is wrong, that most debtors who file for bankruptcy do so in the aftermath of a serious economic shock such as a job loss or medical problem, and that a change in the laws will not change the underlying economic realities facing people in serious financial trouble. Although the system is still adjusting to the new law—and equilibrium is tough to gauge given the foreclosure crisis that began in 2007—it seems that most of the fundamental components of the prior system remain unchanged.

D. BANKRUPTCY COURT ORGANIZATION

No introduction to bankruptcy would be complete without a discussion of procedure. (You thought you left procedure behind in the first year? Quell naïve!) Bankruptcy cases are filed in special federal courts. This is more the exception rather than the rule if we look at other systems, and so many a foreign lawyer is confused about these special tribunals when working on cross-border disputes. The legal basis of these courts' jurisdiction, putting matters delicately, is complex and uncertain. That topic is covered in detail in the chapter on jurisdiction. At this early point, however, understanding the practical operation of the courts is important.

Again, a little history will help. Before 1978, there were no specialized bankruptcy judges. But even under the nineteenth century bankruptcy statutes, federal district judges usually had specialized help with bankruptcies. Full-time or part-time officials handled much of the work in such cases. Under the Act, these officials were called "referees," and they made many of the everyday decisions in bankruptcy matters. Their position was roughly equivalent to that of a specialized "master" who served on a regular basis. The referees were appointed by the district judges.

One of the principal reforms of the Code in 1978 was to expand greatly the bankruptcy jurisdiction of the district courts (and hence, indirectly, the power of these judicial helpers, who by this point were being called, although not without controversy, "bankruptcy judges"). 28 U.S.C. §1336. This expanded jurisdiction was to be exercised primarily by the bankruptcy judges as part of the district court organization. The new bankruptcy judges continued to be non-Article III judges, appointed for fourteen years, unlike their Article III counterparts on the federal bench. The Supreme Court took the wind out of these jurisdictional sails by declaring the new system unconstitutional, albeit in a fractured decision with no clear majority. See Northern Pipeline Construction Co. v. Marathon Pipe Line Co., 458 U.S. 50 (1982). Moreover, the Court subsequently held unconstitutional related but lesser aspects of the Code's jurisdictional provisions (pertaining to jury trial rights).

Congress responded to *Marathon* in 1984 with a crazy quilt of jurisdictional provisions that make the bankruptcy court now a "unit" of each district court under the supervision of the district judges. The courts of appeals were given the responsibility of appointing bankruptcy judges to solve other constitutional problems raised by *Marathon*, but the job of overseeing the functioning of the bankruptcy court was given largely to the district courts. The biggest post-*Marathon* change to buttress the constitutionality of the bankruptcy courts was to divide the universe of bankruptcy matters into "core" and "noncore" proceedings, with different jurisdictional treatment of each. Congress delegated jurisdiction over "core" proceedings in bankruptcy to the bankruptcy judges directly (subject to district court discretion); their decisions are final judgments by a court of law, although they can be appealed to a district court. With regard to "noncore" proceedings, a bankruptcy judge can hear them only as a "master" who submits *proposed* findings to the district court (unless the parties involved consent to a binding decision by the bankruptcy judge); these are not final judgments and can be reviewed de novo by the district court upon timely party objection.

Under this congressional scheme, therefore, bankruptcy judges' decisions on matters within their core jurisdiction can be appealed to the district court, which reviews their factual findings on a "clearly erroneous" basis. If a party is dissatisfied with the district court's resolution of an appeal, it may appeal further to the court of appeals, as with any other district court decision. The Code also permits any of the circuit courts to adopt a special appellate procedure whereby the first appeal from a bankruptcy court decision is to a panel of bankruptcy judges instead of to a district judge. Code §158(c). These alternatives to the district courts are called "BAPs," referring to their statutory names: Bankruptcy Appellate Panels. While an appeal to a BAP sidesteps the district court, panel jurisdiction is consensual; any party can insist that the appeal be heard by the district court. Parties disgruntled with the bankruptcy court's proposed findings of fact and conclusions of law in a *noncore* proceeding simply object and the district court is required to conduct a de novo review (with further appeal as usual to the circuit).

Since 1984, the Supreme Court has twice pronounced these provisions constitutionally tainted, although with twists and caveats that left the situation highly (some would say increasingly) confused. In the spring of 2011, the Supreme Court achieved the apogee of its confusion in deciding Stern v. Marshall, 131 S. Ct. 2594 (2011). The case was the usual boring technical problem in a bankruptcy case, a dispute over many millions of dollars between a famous Playmate (Anna Nicole Smith), and the children of her deceased billionaire husband—more suitable for reality TV than the lofty chambers of the Supreme Court (at least until the inevitable reality TV show about the Supreme Court). There is now a brisk, sometimes frantic debate whether this decision threatens the entire jurisdictional structure of the Code. Stern has left in its wake great confusion over the powers of the approximately 350 bankruptcy judges who preside each year in over a million consumer cases and business cases involving billions of dollars. The Supreme Court may well have to weigh in again soon; stay tuned.

Incidentally, the Supreme Court also has a more pedestrian job, promulgating the Rules of Bankruptcy Procedure, in much the same way it does the Federal Rules of Civil Procedure. The rules must defer to any controlling provision of the Code. In general, these rules, and the accompanying official forms, prescribe the procedures for administration of the bankruptcy estate, the filing of claims by creditors, the forms and schedules to be completed by each petitioning debtor, the giving of notice to creditors of particular developments in the case, and the like.

The taxonomy of disputes in the Rules is noteworthy, particularly for understanding the posture of many cases included in this book. Part VII of the Rules governs "adversary proceedings," which are defined in Rule 7001. Such proceedings include, for example, actions to invalidate a lien on the debtor's property and actions that have been removed to bankruptcy court from state court. Adversary proceedings are full-blown federal lawsuits within the larger bankruptcy case, so they typically carry two captions: the "In re" bankruptcy caption of the broader case and the more familiar "A v. B" caption of the specific dispute. Part VII of the Bankruptcy Rules virtually incorporates the Federal Rules of Civil Procedure. The Federal Rules of Evidence are also applicable to adversary proceedings. Disputes other than adversary proceedings are denominated "contested matters" and are subject to the less elaborate procedures described in Rule 9014. Those that are reported will appear as motion decisions with only the "In re" caption.

E. A SPECIFIC INTRODUCTION TO THE CODE

Title 11 of the U.S. Code is devoted wholly to the Bankruptcy Code. It is divided into "chapters." For historical reasons, all but one of the chapters are odd-numbered: 1, 3, 5, 7, 9, 11, 12, 13, and 15. Chapters 1, 3, and 5 are general provisions that are applicable in all proceedings in bankruptcy unless explicitly made inapplicable in a specific context. Chapters 7, 9, 11, 12, 13, and 15 each govern a different type of bankruptcy proceeding. Except for certain situations in chapter 15 (which covers multinational bankruptcies), a debtor can be in only one of these chapters at any given time.

Chapter 1 is devoted to structural subjects such as definitions, rules of construction, general powers of the bankruptcy court, and the debtor eligibility requirements for each of the types of proceedings available. Chapter 3 governs case administration, including appointment and compensation of someone called "the trustee," whom we will discuss soon, and of other professional persons such as attorneys and accountants. It also contains the provisions governing the operation of a bankrupt estate. Chapter 5 provisions include regulation of the claims and distribution process, discharges, and special bankruptcy-specific powers to trump certain pre-existing legal rights.

The next chapters house the specific rules for each type of bankruptcy. Chapter 7 governs the classic "straight" bankruptcy liquidation for both consumers and businesses. Chapter 9 has the special provisions for the bankruptcy of a municipality or other governmental unit. Chapter 11 is the chapter most often used by reorganizing businesses. Chapter 12 governs reorganization bankruptcies filed by family farmers or fishermen. Chapter 13, which excludes corporations, is the reorganization procedure discussed above that allows consumers to make payments to their creditors over time without having to relinquish their assets. A chapter 15 case is a special "ancillary" proceeding in which the United States court assists a foreign court that has primary bankruptcy jurisdiction over a foreign debtor.

The jurisdictional and procedural provisions governing bankruptcy are found in Title 28 of the U.S. Code. The criminal provisions, which define and establish sanctions for offenses such as bankruptcy fraud, are in Title 18 of the U.S. Code.

Certain provisions of Title 11 are not covered in depth in these materials. For example, there will be only a summary discussion of chapter 9 municipal bankruptcies—exemplified by the huge bankruptcy filed by Jefferson County (Birmingham) Alabama amidst the stench of the financial maneuvers used to finance its new sewer system. There is also no coverage of Subchapters III and IV of chapter 7, which provide special rules for the bankruptcies of stockbrokers and commodity dealers respectively. These are highly specialized and technical areas of an already-technical law.

F. BEYOND LAW: WHY BANKRUPTCY?

Filing bankruptcy is a wrenching decision for virtually all the people and businesses that seek relief. The motivations vary, but perhaps two forces prevail above all others. One is the debtors' need for relief, and indeed, the filing of a bankruptcy petition triggers something not ironically called the "order for relief." Debtors from exhaustion or other reasons feel the need to halt once and for all the collection activity that is grinding away at them to gain some control over their lives or the operating of their business. We discuss these pressures more in the next chapter, in the consumer context, and later on, in the business context. The second motivation for filing is a desire to preserve one's assets. For consumers, this sometimes is as much sentimental as financial, such as trying to hold on to a home with a mortgage the debtor is struggling to pay. For businesses, the calculus is more likely to be purely economic. Haste makes waste, and allowing a creditor to seize and sell assets at a forced sale is nearly always a loss of value. As with so many of life's important lessons, O.J. Simpson illustrates the point with verve.

More Hoopla at Simpson Home Auction
Carla Hall, July 15 1997

The traveling circus that is the O.J. Simpson affair loaded up its wagons and made one more spectacular pass through L.A. County—this time in a modest, glamour-free swatch of suburbia.

Simpson's fabled Brentwood estate was put on the auction block Monday—it's estimated he owed well over $100,000 in back mortgage payments—on the steps of the county courthouse in Norwalk. At last, Norwalk citizens had their own moment to bask in the reflected glare of television cameras, as the bank that has held title to the home turned in the winning bid of about $2.6 million.

"It's the only O.J. event on the Eastside—and it took 'em three years to get here," said Dick Whitrock, who left his South Whittier home to observe.

As rudimentary public auctions of property in foreclosure go, this one set a standard for excitement. The action unfolded before a sprawling array of a hundred-some reporters, television cameras from around the world and another couple hundred curious onlookers. The bidding itself was done in a matter of minutes.

. . .

"We've been filmed before—but it's usually because someone is going to sue us," said Renee Patrick, vice president of Trustee's Assistance Corp., which set up the auction on behalf of winning bidder Hawthorne Savings, the bank holding the trust to the house.

The mere fact that the auction was so open and ritualized gave it a certain riveting rawness—kind of like a flogging in a town square.

Dutifully, an official polled those cordoned behind police tape in the courtyard, calling out several times for bidders. "Any other qualified bidders? Please, please come forward," said Patrick Dobiesz, the gray-suited, bespectacled head of the company that took care of the foreclosure proceedings for the bank. Without blinking—or laughing—he uttered this to a crowd mostly composed of tense reporters and curious members of the public, some in shorts and T-shirts drinking coffee, munching cookies and looking more in the market for groceries than multimillion-dollar Brentwood property.

"Melrose" Larry Green, the perpetual call-in hound to the Howard Stern radio show, signaled the official that he wanted to bid, producing a financial statement showing a balance of $933,799.26 in an investment account he said was his. But that wasn't good enough, and he was turned away.

In fact, nothing less than a cashier's check for $2,531,259—or the cool cash itself—would have gotten you a chance to bid in the bright sunlight. That's the amount owed to the bank.

Auctioneer Garth Russell opened the bidding at $1.875 million, but within minutes the house was sold at $2,631,259. To the bank. There were two other qualified bidders. One never opened his mouth and slipped out in the post-auction pandemonium.

The other bidding party consisted of Glendale investor Steve Whitlock and Pasadena investor John Hall, who routinely buy properties at auction and turn around and sell them. But they quickly discovered there was nothing routine about their bid Monday.

. . .

"STEVE Whitlock, the LOSING bidder...," intoned a television reporter corralling Whitlock into a stand-up interview.

A tall, lanky gray-haired man in a plaid shirt and dark green slacks, Whitlock shrugged off the attention.

"It just looked like a good deal," he said. "The fact that it was O.J.'s house—we're here three times a week bidding on property."

Neither Whitlock nor Hall had any intention of moving into the house. "We'd have sold it fast,' said Whitlock, who figures the residence could fetch $4 million.

Whitlock bid one dollar over the full sum that Simpson owed the bank and brought several checks to cover various potential bid amounts. 'I would have gone to $2.6 million," he said. The winning bid was only about $31,000 more than that, and the two investors were peppered with inquiries about why they didn't try to top the bank's last offer.

"You set the amount you're willing to pay," Whitlock said. "If it goes over that, you move on to the next thing."

Now that the bank has bought the house, it essentially pays itself back the $2.5 million it is owed by Simpson. (Hawthorne Savings initiated foreclosure proceedings in late March, when Simpson had fallen $86,000 in arrears in mortgage payments.) It will pay the extra $100,000 to one or more of the many lien holders on the property.

Now that the bank has the property, it can turn around and try to sell the house for a handsome profit.

"They'll probably do what you and I would do if we wanted to sell our houses," said Dobiesz, whose T.D. Service Co. took care of the foreclosure proceedings and represented the bank at the auction. "They might hire brokers.'

Dobiesz also figured the bank wouldn't be standing on Simpson's lawn that afternoon to throw him out. "I think they'll turn it over to their attorneys and let them go through the proper procedures,' he said, estimating that would take two to three months.

. . .

Simpson House Available, for $3.9 Million

LOS ANGELES, Aug. 5 (AP)—The bank that foreclosed on O.J. Simpson's. Rockingham home and then bought it last month has listed the property for sale. And potential buyers have been invited to have a look, if they have enough money.

Mr. Simpson's gated property at 360 North Rockingham Avenue, the nation's best-known celebrity house during his trial on murder charges, has $3.95 million asking price, the Los Angeles Times reported today.

Hawthorne Savings listed the property with Fred Sands Estates on Monday, the newspaper said, citing unidentified sources. Mr. Sands said he was confident that the 6,400-square-foot, seven-bedroom home in the city's Brentwood section would sell quickly.

Three agents have been assigned to the sales team, and an elaborate process has been set up to separate potential buyers from the curious. The agents will require proof that people have sufficient money on deposit for a down payment—a minimum 25 percent, or $1 million, in most cases.[5]

As a final twist, the person who finally bought the house for almost $4 million bulldozed it and built a new one. Why would a house that sold at a creditor's sale for only $2.6M be put on the market a month later for $3.9M? One element might be the rule that permits the bank lender to Simpson to "credit bid," which means that it can "bid" its debt and has to put up cash only for the $31,000 that it bid in excess of what it is owed. The Supreme Court has held that the

---

5. We have no evidence that Melrose Green came back with his financial statement.——Eds.

statute gives a creditor a right to credit bid in most cases. RadLAX Gateway Hotel, LLC v. Amalgamated Bank, 132 S. Ct. 2065 (2012).

This acquisition allowed the bank to pocket a quick million-plus by getting the house at a forced sale and then being able to sell it at its leisure. Yet Messrs. Whitlock and Hall were also there, willing to bid a similar amount to—but not much more than—the outstanding debts on the property, and Whitlock predicted the ultimate sale price almost exactly. So what kept them from bidding more? Maybe this profit was not such a sure thing for the bank or maybe bidders at forced sales are only interested in a great bargain.

A central purpose of modern bankruptcy law is to preserve value and eliminate, or at least mitigate, the fact that forced sales destroy value. To improve the results at forced sales, or better still, avoid them, is a goal upon which almost all scholars agree. More importantly, consumer and businesses alike recognize that bankruptcy has the potential to prevent the loss of value.

G. CONCLUSION

Over a million households file for bankruptcy each year. The vast majority of these cases are either under chapter 7 or chapter 13. Who are these people? Perhaps not who you might think, which brings us to some empirical data. Research shows that when measured by enduring social criteria—education, occupation, homeownership—these families in bankruptcy represent a broad cross-section of the middle class, from doctors and lawyers to salesclerks and fast-food workers. Elizabeth Warren & Deborah Thorne, A Vulnerable Middle Class: Bankruptcy and Class Status, in *Broke*. Although many of them have poverty-level incomes when they file for bankruptcy, few of them are from the long-term poor. They may be down at the moment of filing, but the debtors are solidly in the middle of American society. Along with these families, who share many characteristics with our neighbors and co-workers, is a star-studded cast that has included Stephen Baldwin, Kim Basinger, Peter Bogdanovich, Jose Conseco, M.C. Hammer, Larry King, Burt Reynolds, Mike Tyson, Michael Vick, Dionne Warwick, and the group TLC.

The corporate list has its own stars, including mega-busts Lehman Brothers, Enron, and Worldcom (MCI), as well as the less headline-grabbing but still culturally significant downfalls (and sometimes rebirths) of such commercial icons as Borders Books, Kodak, Trump Casinos, General Motors, Chrysler, Marvel Entertainment, Barney's, Frederick's of Hollywood, two major league ball clubs (the Texas Rangers and the L.A. Dodgers), Circuit City, K-Mart, both Popeye's and Boston Chicken, Einstein's Bagels, Interstate Bakeries (Twinkies), and, most sadly, a number of law firms. In some industries, bankruptcy verges on a rite of passage. (Can you name the major airline carrier that has *not* filed bankruptcy? Hint: LUV). Other companies land in bankruptcy when their entire industry collapses, with bankruptcy becoming the graveyard to bury the former industry leaders; the subprime mortgage industry (the former subprime mortgage industry?) is a recent example. Still other companies look to bankruptcy to solve specific problems, such as tort liability for asbestos exposure. The management of most companies file chapter 11 to try to reorganize themselves as a going concern—who wants to admit defeat at the start?—but a good chunk of these companies will eventually wind up liquidating.

At the intersection of the statutes, the doctrine, the cases, the empirical data, and a host of normative convictions lies a system that powerfully affects the lives of millions of our fellow citizens and the economic futures of thousands of businesses each year. As you go through the materials in this book, feel free to flip back to this introduction, both for its explanatory "cheat notes" on, for example, the different chapters in the Code as well as for its theoretical overview of what this important legal system is trying to do.

Problem Set 1

1.1. After graduation from law school you spent two years in a big firm doing SEC securities registration statements. You began to feel like an idiot savant, and you decided that there had to be more variety and interest to the practice of law. So you and two old classmates (one who had hibernated in the library for a litigation department and one who had taken rich people to lunch for a trusts and estates department) opened up a general practice firm.

The firm has been in existence for over a year now, and it is becoming solidly established. Over lunch one day, you and your partners reflect on the nature of your practice. It seems that the bulk of your clients are not disputing whether money is owed (ah, those lovely contract and tort hypos you mastered in law school); instead they are engaged in either trying to make someone pay money or trying to avoid paying money themselves. You recognize that much of your time is spent guiding clients in coercing or avoiding payment.

Chatting over lunch today, the three of you are once again exchanging horror stories (as all lawyers do) about what the client didn't tell you and how terrible your legal advice turned out to be because of the key fact the client didn't reveal. You tell of hearing in a deposition for the first time that your debtor-client had a huge asset his creditors could grab or that your creditor-client was about to push a debtor into a bankruptcy, not realizing bankruptcy would invalidate an important security interest your client held in one of the debtor's assets.

This conversation leads you and your partners to revise your standard interview form. Your current form includes a typical question asking debtors to list assets and liabilities. You believe your clients really intend to make a full disclosure to you, but you find that many people do not recognize immediately where they may owe money or where they may have unrealized assets. You conclude that a more particularized list might trigger more complete information from your clients, so you and your partners decide to compile checklists of potential debts and assets for both consumer and business clients. What is on each list?

1.2. You work for a major firm in a large city. One of the firm's most important clients is Security Bank. Security is having trouble with collection of an unsecured loan of $183,366 from a local physician, Janille Talis. The firm has asked you to help the bank determine the wisest course of action with Talis.

Talis is a pathologist employed by Community Hospital. Her take-home salary is $12,500 per month. She owes $1,200 per month to your client. She spends about $1,800 on food, utilities, dry cleaning, and other day-to-day essential expenses. Her other monthly payments are listed below. Her credit report has no late payments, except to Security Bank.

Central Bank, home mortgage	$4200
USA Savings, car loan	$650
Young Professionals Fitness Centre (2 year contract)	$450
Amon Kwart (dentist)	$675
Robbie Reich, co-worker	$150
Farmington Country Club, Initiation Fee	$300
MasterCard & Visa	$1050
Fancy Nancy's Boutique Clothing Store	$850
John South, alimony payment	$2325

Before exploring possible legal actions you try to evaluate Security's leverage as it compares with other creditors' positions. Of the creditors on this list, who is Talis most likely to pay? Why? How can Security try to improve its relative position?

1.3. Kim Sung-joo owns a home that he bought in 2005. He paid $15,000 down and signed a mortgage obligation for $190,000, which he has now paid down to $180,000. His salary as a convention planner was ample to cover the monthly payments, but he was laid off last year and has now missed three payments. His current job as a sales clerk ("only temporary, of course") will not support the mortgage payments. He has talked to the mortgage servicer, a bank in another city, about waiting just a little longer until the upturn in the local economy gets him his old job back or, alternatively, about just selling the house now. The servicer has so far been vague about what it could or would do, but said it might consider foreclosure and a foreclosure sale.

A similar house in a nearby subdivision sold three months ago for about $170,000, after being put on the retail market for two or three months and listed with a real estate broker, who charged a six percent commission. A similar house sold in a foreclosure sale last month for $129,428. It was bought by the creditor for whom the sale was being held for exactly the amount of the debt owed the creditor. The creditor was the only one who showed up at the sale. A lawyer friend told Mr. Sung-joo he will owe personally any shortfall on the mortgage debt above the money received at a sale.

Should Mr. Sung-joo propose to the bank to employ a broker to sell the house? As the bank loan officer, should you approve such a "short sale," assuming that you have been given the power to do that by the actual owner of the note and mortgage? If not, should the bank foreclose or wait a few months more? Would any of those answers change if Mr. Sung-joo lived in a state with an "anti-deficiency" statute that blocks collection of any shortfall following a forced sale?

If you were a tax appraiser for the county where Mr. Sung-joo lives, what would you list as the value of his home?

1.4. You enjoyed law school but the war stories about practice scared you straight back into your former profession of journalism. Your law degree did have the effect of landing you the job of Chief Legal Correspondent for a widely circulated newsmagazine. Your first cover story is to be about the bankruptcy system.

The impetus for the story was a modest uproar between Congress and the judicial branch that arose after someone took a hard look at the federal budget and figured out that a sizeable chunk of the entire federal judiciary is funded from the filing fees paid by bankruptcy debtors. You have the data on the filing fees per case and approximately how many cases were filed in each chapter in 2011.

Case	Fees	Number of Petitions
Chapter 7	$306	965,679
Chapter 9	$1046	16
Chapter 11	$1046	11,438
Chapter 12	$246	630
Chapter 13	$281	401,696
Chapter 15	$1046	61

You are working an angle for the story. Do these fees seem outrageous or reasonable? What do you need to know to evaluate that? What distinctions might be important? What might be the explanation for the fee differences? Why would some members of Congress be pushing to lower these fees, while others have a newly discovered interest in the bankruptcy system as a source of revenue?

Make a list of at least three types of people that you would want to interview for your story. For each type of person, write two specific questions about the bankruptcy system for them. Be prepared to share.

PART II

CONSUMERS OUTSIDE BANKRUPTCY

Assignment 2.

Consumer Nonbankruptcy Collection Law

Consumer debt collection has formal legal procedures, both in-court for unsecured creditors and out-of-court for secured creditors. But equally if not more important are the informal collection efforts creditors undertake to encourage debtors to repay. That informal world also is regulated by laws. Some directly set the divide between permissible and impermissible persuasion; others exert indirect effects by regulating areas likely to be of interest to creditors and debtors jockeying for leverage.

A.   LEVERAGE

1.   Competing Concerns

As we saw with Dr. Talis (Assignment 1), the debtor-creditor payment process can best be viewed as a constant balancing. A debtor who has bills to pay makes a series of decisions about the costs and benefits of paying each bill. The process may be explicit or unarticulated, but either way debtors decide when to pay, which bills to pay first, or whether to pay at all.

Creditors engage in another balancing process. A creditor tries to determine how, at the lowest cost, to make it more attractive for the debtor to pay the money owed. The creditor looks for means to enhance its leverage in convincing the debtor to pay the obligation.

Collection Agency Headed by "Thugs" Helps Merchants

Davenport, Ia. (UPI)—Quad Cities' businessmen, burdened with bundles of bad checks by the faltering economy, are turning to an unconventional collection agency with a pair of tough-looking hombres at the helm.

Dressed in leather jackets over Harley-Davidson T-shirts, Kenneth Fitzpatrick and Maurice Holst don't look like modern entrepreneurs.

But just let someone dare to not pay up on a rubber check. That's when Fitzpatrick, better known as Doc, pushes back the bandanna tied around his head, reaches into his jacket and whips out a worn copy of the Iowa Code.

While he explains the state's penalties for passing bad checks, Holst, who prefers to be called Trammp, scowls and looks menacing. A person might easily get the impression that they'll knock the garbage cans over on the way out.

But they don't. They may look like "Easy Riders," but they never use violence or threatening language. Folks seem to be scared of them anyway and cough up the requested money.

"One person even ran next door to borrow the money to make good on a check," Trammp said.

Local businessmen have welcomed the crusty, street-smart pair with open arms. In less than two months, 2 Outlaws Check Collecting Service has grown into a thriving business.

"They're happy to see us," Doc said of the clients. "They say we're just what they're looking for. It's a crazy world out there where people are scared to collect money for themselves."

"They have to manage their business," Trammp said. "They don't have time for collecting bad checks."

Doc got the idea for the business while working for a liquor store in California, where he made a little extra money collecting the store's bad checks.

Then when he moved to Iowa and ran into money problems with a broken leg, he bounced a few checks of his own.

"I noticed that all these people (collection agencies) do is call you," he said. "That didn't scare me."

Doc and Trammp decided they could do better. After checking the legalities of such an enterprise, the pair registered their trade name with the Scott County Recorder's Office, printed up business cards and went to work.

"We gave one business card to an alderman and I guess he was pretty shook up about it," Trammp said, describing the reaction of Davenport councilman Larry d'Autremont, who runs a medical supply store.

"They didn't do anything to me," d'Autremont confided. "But they scared the hell out of me."

Doc said the pair started out collecting a $5 check for a local restaurant, but since then, "things started to snowball." About 10 friends have joined the business, which blossomed into rent collection and unpaid charge accounts.

"We work in pairs," Doc said. "That protects us as well. We don't want anybody saying we threatened them."

The collectors begin with a courteous telephone call.

"Most of the time the people say they'll pay up and send a check in the mail," he said. "Maybe 15 to 20 percent will pay just on a phone call. But sometimes you have to investigate them, if they've skipped town or something."

If a phone call doesn't work, Doc and Trammp show up on the offender's doorstep for a personal visit. Sometimes it takes more than one visit, or more than two people.

If that fails, they may institute legal action by filing a suit in small claims court or—if there is a large amount of money involved—talk the county prosecutor into filing criminal charges.

For their services, 2 Outlaws receives half of whatever they collect, whether it is a $5 check or a $1,000 charge account.

"Most people are happy to give it to us," Trammp said. "Half is better than nothing."... [*Daily Iowan*, Apr. 12, 1982, at p. 8B.]

If the 2 Outlaws are not available, creditors must turn to other tools to increase the odds of repayment. Harassing phone calls or including the debtor's name and picture in a "Deadbeat of the Month" advertisement in the local paper might be an inexpensive—but effective—means of encouraging debtor repayment. Of course, debtors can try to discourage creditor collection efforts. Keeping a pack of large dogs, having an unlisted phone number, or even moving every few weeks might deter certain collection activities. At a certain point, creditors give up.

Leverage is thus important both to debtors and creditors. Yet the exercise of this leverage is cabined by legal and social constraints. Legally, there is both restriction (no assault, regardless of debt amount) and channeling (court orders are required for garnishment). Socially, a debtor may have emotional motivations, such as loyalty in paying back a family member who stood by with financial support during tough times or fear that that a doctor who is not repaid may withhold future service. There is also baseline variation in moral beliefs whether debts "should" be repaid driven by cultural norms and plain old personal preference. The content of law and norms affects leverage.

2.   *The Role of Law*

Most money owed is repaid without resort to any legal process. Even when there is a dispute whether a debt is payable, or when a debtor is unable to repay on time, resort to legal devices to coerce (or avoid) payment is rare. Formal proceedings are a sizeable fraction of state and federal court cases, but they still are a tiny fraction of the universe of potential debt collection "events."

Professor William Whitford explains in an empirical study that one reason for this infrequent resort to formal law is that many creditors are unlikely to use courts because they see litigation as loaded with unnecessary costs and risks:

> A risk inherent in almost all litigation is that one party will net nothing by losing the case entirely. For the creditor in consumer credit collection, this risk takes the form either that the debtor will be judgment proof or that the creditor will be judged not to own a valid debt. The creditor can avoid the risk that the debt may be declared invalid by obtaining voluntary debtor payment. Moreover, when the debtor is judgment proof, it does not usually mean that he or she is assetless, but rather that available assets are exempt [from collection] or encumbered [with a security interest]. Nothing in the exemption laws, however, prevents the debtor from making a voluntary payment from otherwise exempt assets. Alternatively, a judgment proof debtor can attempt to borrow from a friend or relative, or to obtain a consolidation loan from a finance company, in order to settle a debt. These sources of payment cannot be reached directly by a creditor through coercive execution, of course, and hence create additional incentives to the creditor for voluntary settlement.

Whitford, A Critique of the Consumer Credit Collection System, 1979 Wis. L. Rev. 1047, 1055.

In our own empirical studies of people in bankruptcy, we too found remarkably little use of the formal collection process against consumers prior to bankruptcy. In the 2001 Consumer Bankruptcy Project study, about two-thirds of bankruptcy debtors had no legal actions filed against them before bankruptcy despite the fact that many had been struggling financially for years. Measured another way, less than five percent of all debts owed by bankruptcy debtors are the subject of lawsuits.

You might conclude that you can close up this book right now because mastery of the legal system is therefore irrelevant. Nice try. The most obvious point, of course, is that there is still the other one-third of bankruptcy cases, and attorneys are frequently called to aid in resolving those disputes. A lawyer who is unfamiliar with the rules of debtor-creditor law is not in a position to provide effective help. The less obvious point is that formal law matters for bankruptcy debtors who have not been the targets of legal actions for two reasons. First, the formal rules of collection provide the backdrop against which parties reach informal, negotiated agreements (how procedurally difficult and expensive it is to compel payment through a court will dictate the discount a creditor may offer in voluntary settlement). Second, as mentioned above, the legal system also sets ground rules of what parties can do in those informal negotiations primarily through statutory enactments.

Not all creditors and debtors follow the law. Indeed, they often do not. Nor do debtors or creditors always seek legal advice before they engage in various collection activities.

B. INFORMAL REMEDIES FOR NONPAYMENT OF DEBT

Laws create negotiating endowments for informal debtor-creditor negotiations. The universe of laws that could affect these negotiations is vast. Some laws do so intentionally, either by expressly setting rules on what counts as permissible persuasion, such as the Fair Debt Collection Practices Act, or by implicitly affecting the process by regulating areas likely to have a profound effect on these repayment negotiations, such as the Fair Credit Reporting Act. Still other laws are a step removed from regulating the negotiating world but nevertheless have an equally important effect on leverage: if you can't get your driver's license renewed until you pay your child support, your ex-spouse has strong leverage as your creditor, even though the driving certification laws ostensibly have nothing to do with debtor-creditor law. We examine each of these types of laws in turn.

1. The Rules of the Game: Fair Debt Collection Practices

One of the oldest restrictions on collection was blunt and direct: usury laws. If a creditor charged more than a specified rate of interest, the loan would be deemed usurious. This meant the interest, and under some statutes the principal itself, would be deemed uncollectible and sometimes the creditor's conduct deemed criminal. Usury laws regulate the debt itself and thus sit at the core of debtor-creditor law. While usury has ancient foundations, and remains in use in most nations, it has limited applicability in the United States. A series of Supreme Court cases and statutes has effectively "deregulated" interest rates for most common consumer transactions, such as credit cards and mortgages, allowing creditors to shop for favorable state law. See Marquette National Bank v. First Omaha Service Corp., 439 U.S. 299 (1978).

Freed from interest rate restrictions, lenders charged higher rates and fees and lent to riskier customers. These practices, along with the usual bumps in the economy such as recessions, led to a burgeoning debt collection industry. Technological advances, such as automated phone dialing, and social changes, such as an increased proclivity to post identifying information on the Internet, have concomitantly lowered collection costs. (Other new technologies, however, such as mobile phones and caller ID, have hampered debt collection, so the net technology effect remains unclear.)

The law struggles to keep up with the inventiveness of the parties, especially the repeat-player debt collectors. In the 1970s, Congress adopted the Fair Debt Collection Practices Act, ("FDCPA"). The act provides a federal remedy for debt collection abuses. Even with the FDCPA firmly in place, some debt collectors continue the quest for innovation.

Lawyer's Methods, Debtors' Nightmare

Edwina Rizzo vividly remembers the day her husband was on life support waiting for a heart transplant and Steven B. Zats called demanding payment of an overdue cable television bill.

Rizzo, of Havertown, says she explained her husband's critical condition and the bill collector replied: "Hey, people get sick and die every day. That's not my problem."

Zats told her in another conversation, she says, to bring payment to his office without delay. "You crawl, you walk, you get a bus," Rizzo remembers him saying, "you do whatever you can to get here."

And that, according to many who have dealt with him, is vintage Steven Zats.

A slender man who dresses in sneakers, blue jeans and T-shirts, Zats, 33, is perhaps the most aggressive—and some say the most unmerciful—small debt collector in the Philadelphia region.

Many of the debtors Zats pursues are poor, unemployed or disabled. Their debts often involve a single unpaid bill—usually a disputed payment for medical services. Most of his 600 clients are doctors, dentists or health-care firms.

Zats, a lawyer, routinely obtains judgments against them, freezes their bank accounts, and adds his own fees to their debts, driving up costs hundreds of dollars....

"I was gullible, all right?" says Viola Hartman, of Kensington [a Legal Services client]. "They called and said it was a survey on banks and all this."

Hartman is 63 and a widow. She works as a part-time housekeeper in a Philadelphia public school.

She owed $1,500 for a laser surgery bill which she believed her insurance was supposed to pay.

It didn't.

Zats sued to collect.

When someone from [Zats' corporation] called earlier this year [posing as a telephone survey company], Hartman disclosed that she banked at CoreStates Bank.

In February, Zats froze her account there and cleaned it out.

Hartman bounced checks for her water and telephone bills.

"I didn't even know that they could do such a thing to you," she said. "I'm two months behind on everything now because of it. I'm behind in my mortgage, my gas bill...."[*Philadelphia Inquirer*, June 12, 1994, at pp. A1 and A8.]

Mr. Zats declined to be interviewed for this story, but one of the debtors furnished a letter from Mr. Zats. He wrote: "My goal in business is to please my clients, not to please the debtors. Debtors don't like to have their bank accounts frozen and their personal belongings sold to satisfy the debts. Since the debtors have not been concerned with paying the bill . . . my office cannot be concerned if the debtors can't pay their rent because of a frozen bank account."

Debt collection abuses are not rare. One reason is that many Americans are in debt trouble. A 2007 poll found that one in seven Americans was contacted by a debt collector in the preceding year, and that was in good financial times. In each recent year, the Federal Trade Commission has received more complaints about debt collectors than any other industry and has obtained civil fines of $1 million or more for widespread abuses. The new Consumer Financial Protection Bureau has authority to enforce the FDCPA.

Some brief excerpts from the statute are reproduced below. It will be useful to look through the key provisions more than once to identify which practices are prohibited and which parties are controlled by the statute. The prohibitions in the statute did not come out of thin air. Congress was responding to documented abuses.

——————— **FAIR DEBT COLLECTION PRACTICES ACT** ———————
15 U.S.C.A. 1692 et seq.

§1692a. DEFINITIONS

. . .

(3) The term "consumer" means any natural person obligated or allegedly obligated to pay any debt.

(4) The term "creditor" means any person who offers or extends credit creating a debt or to whom a debt is owed, but such term does not include any person to the extent that he receives an assignment or transfer of a debt in default solely for the purpose of facilitating collection of such debt for another.

(5) The term "debt" means any obligation or alleged obligation of a consumer to pay money arising out of a transaction in which the money, property, insurance, or services which are the subject of the transaction are primarily for personal, family, or household purposes, whether or not such obligation has been reduced to judgment.

(6) The term "debt collector" means any person who uses any instrumentality of interstate commerce or the mails in any business the principal purpose of which is the collection of any debts, or who regularly collects or attempts to collect, directly or indirectly, debts owed or due or asserted to be owed or due another. Notwithstanding the exclusion provided by clause (F) of the last sentence of this paragraph, the term includes any creditor who, in the process of collecting his own debts, uses any name other than his own which would indicate that a third person is collecting or attempting to collect such debts. . . . The term does not include—

(A) any officer or employee of a creditor while, in the name of the creditor, collecting debts for such creditor;

(B) any person while acting as a debt collector for another person, both of whom are related by common ownership or affiliated by corporate control, if the person acting as a debt collector does so only for persons to whom it is so related or affiliated and if the principal business of such person is not the collection of debts;

(C) any officer or employee of the United States or any State to the extent that collecting or attempting to collect any debt is in the performance of his official duties;

(D) any person while serving or attempting to serve legal process on any other person in connection with the judicial enforcement of any debt;

(E) any nonprofit organization which, at the request of consumers, performs bona fide consumer credit counseling and assists consumers in the liquidation of their debts by receiving payments from such consumers and distributing such amounts to creditors; and

(F) any person collecting or attempting to collect any debt owed or due or asserted to be owed or due another to the extent such activity (i) is incidental to a bona fide fiduciary obligation or a bona fide escrow arrangement; (ii) concerns a debt which was originated by such person; (iii) concerns a debt which was not in default at the time it was obtained by such person; or (iv) concerns a debt obtained by such person as a secured party in a commercial credit transaction involving the creditor.

§1692d. HARASSMENT OR ABUSE

A debt collector may not engage in any conduct the natural consequence of which is to harass, oppress, or abuse any person in connection with the collection of a debt. Without limiting the general application of the foregoing, the following conduct is a violation of this section:

(1) The use or threat of use of violence or other criminal means to harm the physical person, reputation, or property of any person.

(2) The use of obscene or profane language or language the natural consequence of which is to abuse the hearer or reader.

(3) The publication of a list of consumers who allegedly refuse to pay debts, except to a consumer reporting agency or to persons meeting the requirements of section 603(f) or 604(a)(3) of this Act.

(4) The advertisement for sale of any debt to coerce payment of the debt.

(5) Causing a telephone to ring or engaging any person in telephone conversation repeatedly or continuously with intent to annoy, abuse, or harass any person at the called number.

(6) Except as provided in section 804, the placement of telephone calls without meaningful disclosure of the caller's identity. . . .

§1692e. FALSE OR MISLEADING REPRESENTATIONS

A debt collector may not use any false, deceptive, or misleading representation or means in connection with the collection of any debt. Without limiting the general application of the foregoing, the following conduct is a violation of this section:

(1) The false representation or implication that the debt collector is vouched for, bonded by, or affiliated with the United States or any State, including the use of any badge, uniform, or facsimile thereof.

(2) The false representation of—

(A) the character, amount, or legal status of any debt; or

(B) any services rendered or compensation which may be lawfully received by any debt collector for the collection of a debt.

(3) The false representation or implication that any individual is an attorney or that any communication is from an attorney.

(4) The representation or implication that nonpayment of any debt will result in the arrest or imprisonment of any person or the seizure, garnishment, attachment, or sale of any property or wages of any person unless such action is lawful and the debt collector or creditor intends to take such action.

(5) The threat to take any action that cannot legally be taken or that is not intended to be taken.

(6) The false representation or implication that a sale, referral, or other transfer of any interest in a debt shall cause the consumer to

(A) lose any claim or defense to payment of the debt; or

(B) become subject to any practice prohibited by this title.

(7) The false representation or implication that the consumer committed any crime or other conduct in order to disgrace the consumer.

(8) Communicating or threatening to communicate to any person credit information which is known or which should be known to be false, including the failure to communicate that a disputed debt is disputed.

(9) The use or distribution of any written communication which simulates or is falsely represented to be a document authorized, issued, or approved by any court, official, or agency of the United States or any State, or which creates a false impression as to its source, authorization, or approval.

(10) The use of any false representation or deceptive means to collect or attempt to collect any debt or to obtain information concerning a consumer. . . .

§1692f. UNFAIR PRACTICES

A debt collector may not use unfair or unconscionable means to collect or attempt to collect any debt. Without limiting the general application of the foregoing, the following conduct is a violation of this section:

(1) The collection of any amount (including any interest, fee, charge, or expense incidental to the principal obligation) unless such amount is expressly authorized by the agreement creating the debt or permitted by law.

(2) The acceptance by a debt collector from any person of a check or other payment instrument postdated by more than five days unless such person is notified in writing of the debt collector's intent to deposit such check or instrument not more than ten nor less than three business days prior to such deposit.

(3) The solicitation by a debt collector of any postdated check or other postdated payment instrument for the purpose of threatening or instituting criminal prosecution.

(4) Depositing or threatening to deposit any postdated check or other postdated payment instrument prior to the date on such check or instrument.

(5) Causing charges to be made to any person for communications by concealment of the true purpose of the communication. Such charges include, but are not limited to, collect telephone calls and telegram fees.

(6) Taking or threatening to take any nonjudicial action to effect dispossession or disablement of property if—

(A) there is no present right to possession of the property claimed as collateral through an enforceable security interest;

(B) there is no present intention to take possession of the property; or

(C) the property is exempt by law from such dispossession or disablement.

(7) Communicating with a consumer regarding a debt by post card.

(8) Using any language or symbol, other than the debt collector's address, on any envelope when communicating with a consumer by use of the mails or by telegram, except that a debt collector may use his business name if such name does not indicate that he is in the debt collection business.

The omitted provisions include, *inter alia,* a requirement that collection agencies verify the accuracy of debt information and a restriction on the ability of collection agencies to bring lawsuits in fora far from the debtor. The act also provides for both administrative and private enforcement, with the recovery for violations of actual damages, costs, and $1,000 in statutory damages. State law provides a useful supplement to the FDCPA. Crucially, most state statutes encompass more entities than the FDCPA's list. Many state laws also provide for larger penalties and longer statutes of limitation.

Attorneys' cool observation of the application of various consumer protection laws, including the FDCPA, became a little less detached in 1995, when the Supreme Court announced that attorneys themselves were included as one of the groups from which the public would be protected. See Heintz v. Jenkins, 514 U.S. 291 (1995). A number of cases against lawyers who collect consumer debts followed. The following is a piquant example of the modern lawyer's exposure to the FDCPA.

—— McCOLLOUGH v. JOHNSON, RODENBURG & LAUINGER ——
637 F.3d 939 (9th Cir. 2011)

THOMAS, Circuit Judge:

. . .

Tim McCollough, a former school custodian, opened a credit card account with Chemical Bank sometime around 1990. Chemical Bank merged with the Chase Manhattan Bank ("Chase Manhattan") in 1996 and continued business under the Chase Manhattan name. McCollough continued to make purchases on the account.

McCollough and his wife fell behind on their credit card bills after he allegedly suffered a brain injury at work and she underwent surgery. When McCollough made his last payment on the Chase Manhattan account in 1999, an unpaid balance of approximately $3,000 remained. In 2000, Chase Manhattan "charged off" the account on its books.

Collect America, Ltd. ("Collect America"), through its subsidiary, CACV of Colorado, Ltd. ("CACV"), is a purchaser of bad debt portfolios—typically, debts that have been charged off by the primary lender. CACV purchases the debts; Collect America attempts collection.

In 2001, CACV purchased McCollough's delinquent account from Chase Manhattan. CACV sued McCollough in 2005 for $3,816.80 in state court to collect the debt. Acting pro se, McCollough replied that the "statute of limitations is up." Two weeks later, CACV dismissed the case. CACV documented service of the complaint and McCollough's response in its electronic files.

In 2006, Collect America retained JRL [Johnson, Rodenburg & Lauinger], a law firm specializing in debt collection, to pursue collection of McCollough's outstanding debt. . . . Charles Dendy was the JRL attorney who handled the law firm's collection cases for Montana. During the period from January 2007 through July 2008, JRL filed 2,700 collection lawsuits in Montana. On an average day, JRL filed five lawsuits in the state; on one day, JRL filed 40 lawsuits. JRL attorney Lisa Lauinger testified that approximately 90% of the collection lawsuits resulted in a default judgment.

The contract between JRL and Collect America contained the following disclaimer: "Collect America makes no warranty as to the accuracy or validity of data provided." In addition, the contract expressly made JRL "responsible to determine [its] legal and ethical ability to collect these accounts." CACV transmitted information about McCollough's account to JRL using debt collection software. CACV also sent the law firm the electronic file.

The law firm's screening procedures flagged a statute of limitations problem with McCollough's debt. On January 4, 2007, JRL account manager Grace Lauinger wrote to CACV: "It appears that the Statute of Limitations has expired on this file as of August 21, 2005. If you can provide us with an instrument in writing to extend the Statute of Limitations." The next day, JRL recorded in the electronic file that " * * * NO DEMAND HAS GONE OUT ON THIS FILE * * * THIS IS THE COLLECT AMERICA BATCH THAT WE ARE HAVING PROBLEMS W[ITH]."

On January 23, 2007, CACV responded to JRL attorney Lisa Lauinger in an email entitled "sol extended" that McCollough had made a $75 partial payment on June 30, 2004, and inquired: "Do you need any info from me on this one?" Based on that payment date, the five-year statute of limitations on the claim against McCollough would not have expired until 2009.

However, the information was incorrect: McCollough had not made a partial payment on June 30, 2004. . . .

On April 17, 2007, JRL filed a collection complaint signed by JRL attorney Charles Dendy against McCollough in Montana state court. The complaint sought judgment for an account balance of $3,816.80, interest of $5,536.81, attorney's fees of $481.68, and court costs of $120.00.

...

On June 13, 2007, McCollough filed a pro se answer to the complaint, asserting a statute of limitations defense:

FORGIVE MY SPELLING I HAVE A HEAD INJURY AND WRITING DOSE NOT COME EASY

(1) THE STACUT OF LIMITACION'S IS UP, I HAVE NOT HAD ANY DEALINGS WITH ANY CREDITED CARD IN WELL OVER 8 1/2 YEARS

(2) I AM DISABLED I GET 736.00 A MONTH S.S.I. ....

(3) WHEN WORKERS COMP STOPED PAYING I RAN OUT OF MONEY, CHASE WOULD NOT WORK WITH ME, THEY PASSED IT ON TO COLLECTOR'S. . . .

(4) THIS IS THE THIRED TIME THEY HAVE BROUGHT ME TO COURT ON THIS ACCOUNT, ... WHEN WILL IT STOP DO I HAVE TO SUE THEM SO I CAN LIVE QUIETLY IN PAIN

One month later, McCollough also telephoned Dendy and left a message indicating that he would be seeking summary judgment on the basis of the statute of limitations.

Dendy noted on July 11, 2007, "[w]e need to get what the client has for docs on hand." . . .

On August 6, 2007, CACV informed Grace Lauinger that McCollough had not made a partial payment on June 30, 2004, as previously stated; rather, the entry on that date "was actually unused costs by another office, not payment." . . .

In October 2007, Dendy served on McCollough a list of twenty-two requests for admission that included the following: [All statements in the Complaint are true and correct. Defendant McCollough made a payment on the Chase credit card on or about June 30, 2004 in the amount of $75.00.].

On December 7, 2007, Dendy sent to CACV an email marked "URGENT." The email read:

An attorney has appeared in this action and has served discovery requests. . . . The attorney is one who is anti purchased debt and who attempts to run up costs in an attempt to secure a large cost award against plaintiff. . . . Please provide me with copies of everything you can get for documentation as soon as possible. . . .

. . . CACV instructed Dendy to dismiss the suit "asap" because of the "SOL problem." JRL then moved for dismissal with prejudice and the state court dismissed the action.

McCollough sued JRL in federal district court alleging violations of the FDCPA. . . .

The case was then tried to a jury over the course of three days. At trial, lay witnesses Keri Henan and Ken Lucero testified about their experiences being sued by JRL. Michael Eakin, a consumer law attorney with Montana Legal Services, testified about the rapid growth of debt-collection lawsuits in Montana and about JRL's role in that trend; he also testified that "a vast majority" of JRL's lawsuits against debtors result in default judgments because JRL tries its cases without consideration for the pro se status of most of its defendant-debtors. James Patten, a Montana collection lawyer, described the importance of reasonable pre-suit investigation and testified that it was JRL's "factory" approach of "mass producing default judgments," rather than any mistake, that caused JRL to prosecute the time-barred debt. . . .

The jury found in favor of McCollough . . . and awarded him the $1,000 statutory maximum for violations of the FDCPA; $250,000 for emotional distress; and $60,000 in punitive damages.

. . .

II.

The district court properly granted summary judgment against JRL on the FDCPA claims. The FDCPA prohibits debt collectors from engaging in various abusive and unfair practices. See Heintz v. Jenkins, 514 U.S. 291 (1995). The statute was enacted to eliminate abusive debt collection practices; to ensure that debt collectors who abstain from such practices are not competitively disadvantaged; and to promote consistent state action to protect consumers. 15 U.S.C. §1692(e). The statute defines a "debt collector" as one who "regularly collects ... debts owed or due or asserted to be owed or due another," 15 U.S.C. §1692a(6), and covers lawyers who regularly collect debts through litigation, Heintz, 514 U.S. at 293– 94, 115 S. Ct. 1489.

A.

Although the FDCPA is a strict liability statute, it excepts from liability those debt collectors who satisfy the "narrow" bona fide error defense. Reichert v. Nat'l Credit Sys., Inc., 531 F.3d 1002, 1005 (9th Cir. 2008) (quotation omitted). That defense provides that:

A debt collector may not be held liable in any action brought under [the FDCPA] if the debt collector shows by a preponderance of evidence that the violation was not intentional and resulted from a bona fide error notwithstanding the maintenance of procedures reasonably adapted to avoid any such error.

15 U.S.C. §1692k(c). "The bona fide error defense is an affirmative defense, for which the debt collector has the burden of proof." Reichert, 531 F.3d at 1006 (citing Fox v. Citicorp Credit Servs, Inc., 15 F.3d 1507, 1514 (9th Cir.1994)). Thus, to qualify for the bona fide error defense, the defendant must prove that (1) it violated the FDCPA unintentionally; (2) the violation resulted from a bona fide error; and (3) it maintained procedures reasonably adapted to avoid the violation.

The district court correctly concluded that JRL's bona fide error defense failed as a matter of law. JRL argues that it maintained adequate preventive procedures by utilizing a system to flag potential statute of limitations problems. However, the procedures that support a valid bona fide error defense must be " ' "reasonably adapted" to avoid the specific error at issue.' " Reichert, 531 F.3d at 1006 (quoting Johnson v. Riddle, 443 F.3d 723, 729 (10th Cir.2006)). JRL's error in this case was not its failure to catch time-barred cases; indeed, JRL initially spotted the limitations period problem and sent a letter to CACV requesting "an instrument in writing to extend" the limitations period. Instead, JRL erred by relying without verification on CACV's representation and by overlooking contrary information in its electronic file. JRL thus presented no evidence of procedures designed to avoid the specific errors that led to its filing and maintenance of a time-barred collection suit against McCollough.

. . .

The undisputed evidence established that JRL's reliance on CACV's email was unreasonable as a matter of law. First, Collect America's contract with JRL expressly disclaimed "the accuracy or validity of data provided" and instructed that JRL was "responsible to determine [its] legal and ethical ability to collect" the account. Second, the electronic file confirmed that the event that took place on June 30, 2004, was the return of "unused costs" rather than a partial payment. Third, the electronic file also indicated that McCollough had asserted a statute of limitations defense to a collection action filed against him in 2005 over the same debt. Finally, McCollough informed JRL that the debt fell outside the limitations period both in his answer to JRL's complaint and in a phone call. . . .

[With respect to the request for admissions,] JRL contends that the FDCPA should not be read to cover discovery procedures such as requests for admission, although JRL concedes that the FDCPA covers both the filing of complaints and the service of settlement letters during the course of litigation, Our precedents do not support such a distinction. Rather, the FDCPA "applies to the litigating activities of lawyers." Heintz, 514 U.S. at 294, 115 S. Ct. 1489. . . .

The district court correctly held that JRL's service of false requests for admission violated the FDCPA as a matter of law. . . .

JRL's requests for admission asked McCollough to admit facts that were not true: that he had never disputed the debt, that he had no defense, that every statement in JRL's complaint was true, and that he had actually made a payment on or about June 30, 2004. JRL had information in its possession that demonstrated the untruthfulness of the requested admissions.

The requests for admission did not include an explanation that, under Montana Rule of Civil Procedure 36(a), the requests would be deemed admitted if McCollough did not respond within thirty days. Because we consider the debt collector's conduct from the standpoint of the least sophisticated debtor, we must conclude that the service of requests for admission containing false information upon a pro se defendant without an explanation that the requests would be deemed admitted after thirty days constitutes "unfair or unconscionable" or "false, deceptive, or misleading" means to collect a debt. Here, JRL effectively requested that McCollough admit JRL's entire case against him and concede all defenses. The least sophisticated debtor cannot be expected to anticipate that a response within thirty days was required to prevent the court from deeming the requests admitted. The district court properly granted summary judgment on this claim. . . .

Affirmed.

Lawyers continue to complain about the penetration of the FDCPA into routine legal work, but with mixed success. The Seventh Circuit has held, by a vote of 6–4 *en banc*, that when the law firm's first "communication" with the debtor was a summons and complaint in a lawsuit, the firm was obligated as a debt collector to furnish a "debt validation notice" (a statutory notice that advises consumers of certain rights). Thomas v. Simpson & Cybak, 392 F.3d 914 (7th Cir. 2004) (en banc). On the other hand, a district court has held that a firm whose consumer debt collection activities were less than five percent of its cases is not a "debt collector" within the FDCPA. Camara v. Fleury, 285 F. Supp. 2d 90 (D. Mass. 2003).

When the FDCPA was being debated, lawyers pressed Congress for an exception for litigation. In 1998, a bill made it to the Senate that would have made such an adjustment but it died there. Lawyers continue to sweat out the FDCPA, except for the oblivious or wrongheaded who think that a person with a law degree is surely several degrees of separation from someone as pernicious-sounding as a "debt collector."

2. The Trump in the Game: Credit Reporting System

Creditors have long exercised as a primary source of leverage the power to refuse new credit to debtors who did not pay prior debts to them. The problem, of course, is that debtors may find it easy to walk away from a single creditor. Creditors know that their leverage will be stronger if there is nowhere else for the debtor to walk. In other words, if a creditor can influence *other* providers of goods and services (and credit) to withhold future credit from a deadbeat debtor, the unpaid creditor gains much greater leverage in encouraging repayment.

To maximize this leverage effect, creditors need an inexpensive, fairly accurate method of tracking and reporting debtors' payment behavior. Well established credit reporting agencies in the United States do the trick. The three largest entities are Experian, Equifax, and TransUnion. Creditors participate in two ways with the bureaus. They are both "furnishers," because they provide information on their borrowers, and "users," who access bureau data to evaluate applicants' creditworthiness (and also to obtain names for credit card solicitations).

The credit reporting companies gather extensive information. Such information nearly always includes things such as the number of credit accounts the debtor has, the credit limits for each account, the timeliness and amounts of the debtor's payments, and the number of times a debtor has been delinquent in repayments. It also includes information from public records, such as foreclosures and other lawsuits, and most relevant to this book, whether a person has filed bankruptcy. Here is a redacted excerpt of the account information from a TransUnion report pulled in 2011. Note how far back one's credit life goes.

CITICARDS CBNA

701 E 60TH ST N SIOUX FALLS , SD 57104 Phone number not available	Balance:	$0	Pay Status:	Paid or Paying as Agreed	
	Date Updated:	10/2002	Account Type:	Revolving Account	
	Credit Limit:	$2,400	Responsibility:	Individual Account	
	Past Due:	$0	Date Opened:	11/1993	
			Date Closed:	09/2002	

Loan Type: Credit Card
Remark: Account closed by consumer

Late Payments
30 months   Last 24
30 60 90   Months   OK X X X X X X X X X X X X X X X X X X X X OK OK OK OK
0 0 0   sep aug jul jun may apr mar feb '02 dec nov oct sep aug jul jun may apr mar feb '01 dec nov oct

DIRECT LOAN SVC SYSTEM

PO BOX 5609 GREENVILLE , TX 75403-5609 (800) 848-0979	Balance:	$0	Pay Status:	Paid or Paying as Agreed	
	Date Updated:	02/2011	Account Type:	Installment Account	
	High Balance:	$59,705	Responsibility:	Individual Account	
	Past Due:	$0	Date Opened:	07/2001	
	Terms:	$646 for 121 months	Date Closed:	02/2011	

Loan Type: Student Loan
Remark: Closed

Late Payments
48 months   Last 48
30 60 90   Months   OK OK OK OK OK OK OK OK OK OK OK OK OK OK OK OK OK OK OK OK OK OK OK OK
0 0 0   '11 dec nov oct sep aug jul jun may apr mar feb '10 dec nov oct sep aug jul jun may apr mar feb
                         OK OK OK OK OK OK OK OK OK OK OK OK OK OK OK OK X OK OK OK OK OK OK OK
                         '09 dec nov oct sep aug jul jun may apr mar feb '08 dec nov oct sep aug jul jun may apr mar feb

Although their data are extensive, credit reporting agencies sometimes have been criticized for not collecting some information, such as income, employment history, and payment records for rent or utilities. This skew in collected data ironically gives those who eschew credit cards and other traditional forms of credit a thin file, which is interpreted adversely.

Information in a credit report is also used to calculate a "credit score," a numerical estimate of a consumer's credit risk. The most well-known is the FICO score, whose acronym reflects the name of the industry leader in such scores, the Fair Isaac Company. Five data categories make the following relative contributions to a FICO score: Payment history: 35%; Amounts owed: 30%; Length of credit history: 15%; Recent credit use: 10%; Types of credit in use: 10%. The credit agencies, and many creditors, have different proprietary algorithms for creating their own scores, but FICO score is frequent shorthand. Experian and VISA even have a "BankruptcyPredict" score that purports to gauge the likelihood of a future bankruptcy filing. The precise nature of the inputs into these scores and the formulas are tightly guarded, proprietary secrets.

The information in credit reports is refreshed on a daily basis. Each month the consumer reporting agencies enter an estimated 4.5 billion pieces of information into their databases. Creditors make widespread use of credit reporting, asking bureaus to pull about three million files every day. In recent years, the use of credit reports has expanded beyond marketing credit products or checking a loan applicant's creditworthiness. Despite some controversy, credit reports are now used for employment and insurance purposes.

The system is far from perfect. A 2004 study by the Public Interest Research Group found that 79% of credit reports contained errors, and that 25% contained errors big enough to change the person's credit scores. Errors can go in either direction, positive or negative. Errors of omission are a particular concern for consumers trying to improve a score. A 2002 Consumer Federation study found that 78% of files were missing a revolving account that was in good standing, and 31% of files were missing a mortgage account that had never been delinquent. These errors are troubling, because as one Congressman explains, "A poor credit history is the 'Scarlet Letter' of 20th century America." 136 Cong. Rec. H5325-02 (daily ed. July 23, 1990 (statement of Rep. Annunzio)).

This creates a paradox of sorts. On the one hand, creditors should care about data accuracy because they are users of credit reports. On the other hand, as furnishers, creditors care much more about tattling on delinquent debtors because of the leverage this creates in collections (it is no accident the collections script starts "Protect Your Credit Rating") than they do about updating files on customers who are current, which incurs direct costs for diffuse benefits. The Fair Credit Reporting Act, 15 U.S.C. sec. 1681 et seq., provides procedures to which a reporting agency must adhere when the accuracy of a creditor's report is questioned. The agency cannot defend itself by blaming the creditors for any misinformation; both are responsible and both often find themselves as co-defendants when something goes awry. The remedies are quite limited, however, and as with much of consumer law, the substantive law is hollow without enforcement.

3. *All Part of the Game: Other Laws Affecting Leverage*

While creditors can sue when a debtor has not paid, the process is expensive and fraught with the possibility of mistake. Creditors are delighted to offload this risk by getting others to encourage the debtor to repay; it's a free leverage enhancement. Sometimes the government steps into that role.

Deadbeat Dad Who Owed Nearly $700k Is Off to Prison

For the first time in Central Florida, a deadbeat parent has been sentenced to prison for not paying child support. Robert Abraham owed $697,000. His children and ex-wife have been trying to collect for the last 17 years.

Abraham was handcuffed, fingerprinted and carted off to state prison, Tuesday. He'll spend two years behind bars. "It wasn't only money they were cheated out of," said his ex-wife Sandi Pinkham. "He cheated them out of being a father and not once did he ever say, 'Sorry.'"

Pinkham has spent years in courtrooms fighting her ex-husband for the money he owes. In March, Abraham pleaded guilty to being a deadbeat dad. Today, he told the judge he had no money.

"I was in jail for six months," said Abraham. "If I had the money don't you think I would've purged myself out. I got a staph infection, got sick, I almost died. Don't you think I would've gotten out if I could?"

But prosecutors pointed out that Abraham bought expensive watches, took trips to Europe and at one time owned two homes. His son testified against him.

"He didn't live the way we did," said his son Reed Abraham. "I can't tell you how many times we'd have mac and cheese for dinner and my mom wouldn't eat."

Because Abraham has continuously ignored court orders for 17 years, the judge said leniency was not an option.

As he was being taken out of the courtroom, Abraham looked at his ex-wife and son, frowned, and shook his head. After prison, he will have three years of community control and probation. And, he'll have to account for every dollar earned and every dime spent.

Abraham is the first man in Central Florida to face third degree felony charges for non-payment of child support. Usually, the state comes up with other ways to make deadbeat parents pay. That can include suspending driver's licenses, taking tax refunds or lottery winnings. The state can even file liens against homes owned by the deadbeat parents. Copyright 2008 by wftv.com. All rights reserved.

The Florida statute that brought down Father Abraham was clearly intended to coerce payment, but other laws may achieve that incentive more obliquely. For example, a bank that has not been repaid may report the debtor to the IRS for "income" from the forgiveness of debt.[6]

Dozens of similar provisions in the state and federal laws indirectly reallocate the leverage between debtors and creditors. Few would show up in an index of debtor-creditor laws, but many have powerful effects on the leverage a party can exercise in collecting a debt.

C. FORMAL REMEDIES FOR NONPAYMENT OF DEBT

Some debtors do not pay in response to the usual tools of persuasion. At this point, creditors can invoke formal legal remedies. The classic process is a lawsuit to obtain a judgment, but some creditors enjoy self-help rights or can intervene in relationships the debtor has with third parties to collect. We cover these topics only briefly because collection, apart from the constraints of the FDCPA, is generally governed by state law, meaning that there are local twists and terminologies. These are crucial for the practitioner but overwhelming for the student. You're welcome.

1. Secured Creditors: Repossession

For students who have had a course in Article 9 of the Uniform Commercial Code ("UCC"), this section will be a quick review of what they have already learned about personal property security. Students without such a course should pay close attention.

When it comes to collection remedies, the most important question is whether a creditor is "secured." A secured creditor is one who holds a *lien* (or *security interest*) on certain property belonging to the debtor that will serve as *collateral* to secure the debt. Some liens are granted as a matter of law by statute; others are offered by the debtor voluntarily. The term "security interest" is usually reserved for the subset of voluntary liens on personal property (a voluntary security interest in real property is called a mortgage). Why do debtors offer security? Sometimes it is the only way the lender will agree to the loan. Offering collateral also tends to make the loan cheaper than borrowing on an unsecured basis, which is part of the reason that home mortgage rates are lower than credit card rates. Creditors without security are "general" or "unsecured" creditors.

---

6. If a creditor forgives a debt—that is, releases the debtor from the obligation to pay—tax law treats that release as the functional equivalent of receiving income, on which, of course, tax is due. 26 U.S.C. §61(a)(12). "Cancellation of debt" income is conceptually logical, but the results can be awkward, to say the least.

A security interest in personal property is created by complying with the state law requirements derived from Article 9 of the UCC and usually stems from execution of a security agreement. (Creation of liens on real property, which Article 9 excludes, is the subject of much less uniform state law.) A lien may be a "purchase-money security interest"—*PMSI* in the trade—which is a lien that arises when funds are loaned to purchase the collateral itself, such as a car loan. A non-PMSI loan arises when the collateral is already owned by the debtor before borrowing, such as when a homeowner taps his home equity for an aptly named "home equity loan," or simply when a borrower offers a watch to a pawnbroker. If there is a PMSI and non-PMSI encumbering the same piece of collateral, generally the PMSI will have priority, meaning it will have to be satisfied in full first as a "first" or "senior" lien, with the non-PMSI being a "second" or "junior" lien. This system of lien priority is a major part of a secured credit course, and not surprisingly, it has consequence for repayment in bankruptcy.

When a lien is created, we say it *attaches* to the collateral. An attached lien can also be *perfected*, which usually entails the creditor registering it in a public record in a state office, thereby giving notice of the lien to the world, much the same way mortgages are often *recorded* at the title registry in their appropriate county office. Perfection is a smart move because it cements a lien's power. For example, an unperfected lien can lose out to a subsequently perfected lien, reversing the general rule that first in time is first in right with liens. (Possession of tangible collateral perfects liens too, so the pawnbroker's lien both attaches and is simultaneously perfected when the borrower turns over the watch.)

Secured creditors rely on their collateral to improve the chances that they will be repaid. If the debtor defaults on the debt, the secured creditor may repossess the collateral. Taking possession of the debtor's property tends to have a focusing effect on the need to comply with payment obligations, especially if that car was how the debtor was planning on getting to work tomorrow. If the debtor remains in default, the secured creditor can even sell the repossessed collateral, use the proceeds to repay its outstanding loan, and sue the debtor for a *deficiency judgment* for any balance remaining after sale. (In real estate, this process is called *foreclosure*.)

Because secured creditors will look to the collateral to be repaid, they try to keep track of it. Lenders to big commercial borrowers often send agents around to conduct periodic checks to make sure the inventory securing a loan is indeed as plentiful as the debtor represents. Loan documents also often restrict the debtor's disposition of the property, which is why a homeowner's mortgage holder ("mortgagee") must sign off before the home is sold. Tradesfolk specializing in repossession are a colorful lot called "Repo Men." The eponymous 1984 film warrants attention.

Repo man relies on timing, skills

MISHAWAKA—Ron Brunkel has seen the great lengths people will go to avoid having their cars repossessed. He's seen guns on the front seat as a warning to stay away . . . dogs chained to the bumpers . . . vehicles parked in the neighbor's garage. Not to mention verbal—sometimes even physical—confrontations. "We get threatened all the time," said Brunkel, vice president of Mishawaka-based SS Recovery. "But when we get that threat, we either leave the car or talk the person out of it. We get training on what to say, and on what not to say." Brunkel said some of his employees have had guns pulled on them, while others have been assaulted. A 23-year-old Mishawaka man was taken to Memorial Hospital Oct. 24 after he was assaulted while attempting to repossess a car in the 1800 block of East Randolph Street in South Bend. While the man and a co-worker were preparing to remove the vehicle, a man at the address jumped in the car and started driving away. The man drove the vehicle into the repo worker, who flew across the hood and struck his head on the windshield, cracking the glass, the co-worker told police. The worker clung to the vehicle for two blocks before he slipped off near the intersection of Randolph and Sampson streets. A Niles man was arrested. As of Thursday afternoon, charges were being prepared in the case but had not been filed, said Catherine Wilson, a spokeswoman for the St. Joseph County prosecutor's office. The 23-year-old, who has since been released from the hospital, did not return several phone calls this week seeking comment. But in March 2002, repossession turned deadly when 43-year-old Gary McCracken was shot to death in the 1300 block of North College Street while repossessing a vehicle for Affordable Auto. No arrests were ever made in the case. . . "We try and keep our average up to 95 percent when it comes to avoiding any altercations," Brunkel said. "We do that based upon good timing and actual training. We do a little bit of background work to see if this person has been in trouble before. So basically we profile the person we're going to get the car from." Workers often will confiscate the car in the middle of the night to avoid disputes; they do not knock on doors to alert the person they are taking a car. "We try and outsmart them," Brunkel said. [South Bend Tribune, October 31, 2008.]

The foregoing excerpt demonstrates why secured status of a creditor is so important. If you are behind on your Visa bill and Visa sends some guy to take your car to "square things up," that's called theft. But if you get behind on your auto loan and Ford Credit sends some guy around to take your car, that's called repossession. It's the ultimate creditor self-help tool and is almost entirely outside the judicial process. Given this extra-judicial nature and high-friction environment, UCC §9-609 codifies the common law rule that prohibits a repossessor from committing a "breach of the peace." The case law is all over the place on what constitutes a breach of the peace, and the fact patterns are, shall we say, memorable. Generally, the standard is permissive; a repossession agent cannot use fists, weapons, or otherwise threaten violence. Telling lies or entering someone's driveway is fair game. A threat by the *debtor* to breach the peace (for example, by pulling a gun when she sees the tow truck) means the creditor has a duty to back off, even though the debtor is the party stirring up trouble.

Repossession's self-help system is a rough and tumble world. If the secured creditor cannot stomach such brusquerie, it can invoke the formal legal process by using its secured status to seek a writ of replevin or sequestration, which ends with the sheriff taking the property. Resort to formal legal process is more likely in the real estate realm, where about half of all states require a mortgagee to file a lawsuit to foreclose a mortgage. Secured creditors' remedies are cumulative: they get the neat repo trick, but if that is dangerous or daunting, they can follow the lesser route of their unsecured cousins and sue on the debt, a process to which we now turn.

2. *Unsecured Creditors: Judgment and Execution*

Unsecured creditors (or secured creditors opting for this route) can sue to collect from a debtor that refuses to pay. When a creditor pursues judicial collection, the first step is to establish in court that the debt is owed. This may involve a complex trial, rich with factual disputes and legal questions of contract, tort, and the like, or it may be the more banal and abbreviated suit under Article 3 of the UCC on a check or other like instrument. Even quicker, and more common in the consumer context, the court process may be nothing more than the entry of a default judgment following the debtor's failure to appear. Default judgments sometimes occur because the debtor has no defense to the debt, but even with a valid defense, cash-strapped consumers who are not paying their debts can ill-afford to hire an attorney. The procedural requirements of defending a lawsuit, even in a small claims process, may overwhelm them, or they may have been the victims of so-called "sewer service" and not even realize a lawsuit is occurring. Furthermore, many consumer contracts require arbitration of debt disputes, so many court judgments are really just summary entries of arbitration orders.

Still, the paradigm is the civil trial, and attorneys (at least in the popular mind) exult in the litigation process. Yet those same attorneys, once victorious in litigation, may have no idea what to do in real life if the losing defendant fails to write out a check for the judgment. Defendants who pay as they are leaving the courthouse after an unfavorable verdict are unheard of; let us know if you encounter one in practice. The judgment gives the successful plaintiff no priority in any of the debtor's property or income. Without further action, it is a piece of paper suitable only for framing. The victorious plaintiff, now a *judgment creditor*, is still just a plain old unsecured creditor, one who has now incurred legal fees to boot. It is the attorney's next job—arguably the one the client cares more about—to translate that paper judgment into paper money, usually a check or cash.

The postjudgment collection process begins with procuring a writ, which is simply a court order. The most basic writ for debt collection is variously called a writ of *execution* or *attachment* or even *fi. fa.* (pronounced "fi fay," from *fieri facias*). (The terms are arcane, vary from state to state, and sometimes are used interchangeably.) The clerk of court will issue such writs as a routine matter upon request of the judgment creditor showing a copy of the judgment.

The writ directs the sheriff or marshal to look for non-exempt property of the judgment debtor, seize it, sell it, and pay the proceeds to the judgment creditor until the judgment is fully paid. Physically hunting for the debtor's property can be a tough job. In practice, the lawyer for the judgment creditor will often tell the sheriff where to look and may even go along. Ordinarily the sheriff will take physical possession of any property found (e.g., a stereo or some tools) and lock it up back at the courthouse. If personal property cannot be seized immediately (e.g., because it is too big for sheriff's pick-up), the sheriff may tag it with a notice of seizure. Since real property can never be physically hauled off, it is always seized by posting notice of seizure and sale or some similar method. The entire process of seizure is often called a *levy*, and what the sheriff does is "levy upon" the property. The whole process, from writ issuance to seizure, is often called an *execution*.

Once the sheriff has levied upon a specific piece of the debtor's property, a lien attaches (and is perfected simultaneously) by operation of law, rendering the judgment creditor a *judicial lien creditor* ("lien creditor" for short). A judicial lien is just as valid and as helpful as a voluntarily created secured interest, but it takes much longer to create, as this cumbersome procedure reveals. There are two other drawbacks. First, in part because the lien creditor has a non-consensual property interest, it must sell its property via a formal procedure. It cannot just retain the property in satisfaction of the debt or sell it using a commercially reasonable procedure, both options available to Article 9 secured creditors. Instead, the sheriff will advertise the property for public sale and sell it to the highest bidder, remitting the proceeds (after fees) to the judicial lien creditor. (Any remaining proceeds will be paid back to the judgment debtor, unless some subsequent judgment creditor levied symbolically upon the property while it was stored at the courthouse.) After sale and distribution, an entry is made in the judgment record noting the partial or complete satisfaction of the judgment. If the proceeds are insufficient to pay the judgment in full, then the sheriff will be commanded to look for more of the debtor's property to seize, and the process will start over.

Second, each state has laws exempting certain types of property from creditor execution. These *exemption* laws vary widely across states and will be studied in more detail in Assignments 4 and 5. What is important to note for now is that these exemptions only protect against sheriff levy, i.e., involuntary seizure by an unsecured creditor. A secured creditor, by contrast, can have a debtor grant it a voluntary lien against property that would otherwise be exempt from levy. If the debtor defaults on such a secured loan, nothing in the state's exemption laws prevents the collateral's seizure.

3.   *Involving Third Parties: Garnishment*

Law generally follows practical necessity, and nowhere is that more evident than in the law of collections. Not all property is physically in the hands of the true owner. (Think of the coin collection in a safety deposit box at the bank or even a dented car sitting overnight at an auto shop.) In addition, some property exists only in the abstract. The most common example is a debt owed to the debtor by a third party. (Think of wages in the period after the employee has done the work but before the employer has issued a paycheck, or think about an account receivable for goods already delivered.) The law has developed a means by which creditors can direct these third parties to turn over the debtor's property or to divert payments that otherwise would go to the debtor in satisfaction of intangible property like an account receivable.

To seize property held by a third party or intangible property requires writs that are different from the standard execution ones. The most common is a writ of *garnishment*, which, despite its name, does not involve adorning the judgment with a sprig of parsley. Instead, a garnishment writ is typically used to attach debts owed to the debtor for the benefit of the debtor's judgment creditor. A creditor may garnish a debtor's wages by obtaining a writ directing the employer to pay the wages to the creditor rather than to the employee. Similarly, a creditor might garnish a bank to obtain funds in a checking account or the contents of a safety deposit box.

The garnishment writ has two parts: (1) a set of questions designed to determine whether the party served with the writ—the "garnishee," e.g., the employer or the bank—owes any money to the debtor or has any property belonging to the debtor, and (2) a command to the garnishee to withhold payment or return of the debtor's property pending further order of the court. If the garnishee answers the questions falsely or disobeys the command to withhold payment or delivery, it may be liable to the judgment creditor. For example, the employer who pays wages to the debtor after service of the writ of garnishment (which would violate the writ's command) may owe the judgment creditor an amount equal to the wages wrongly paid. The same may be true of the bank that honors the debtor's checks after service of the writ.

As a procedural matter, a garnishment is an ancillary lawsuit against the third-party garnishee. If, for example, the third party denies owing anything to the debtor (e.g., the debtor missed the last two weeks of work), a trial may be held on that issue. It more often happens that the garnishee asserts a defense to the writ in the form of some superior right in the debtor's property (e.g., the employer has a right of setoff against a salary advance the debtor had previously drawn). The judgment debtor receives notice of this process and may well participate in it. If the garnishee is found to owe money to the debtor or to have the debtor's property without any superior rights therein, a judgment will be entered against the garnishee. This judgment is satisfied when the garnishee delivers the debtor's property or pays the debt to the judgment creditor. The delivery or payment simultaneously satisfies the garnishee's obligation to the debtor.

While garnishment procedures vary widely, in most states the garnishing creditor gets a temporal "net"—the time between service of the garnishment writ and the garnishee's answer—during which the creditor gets to "catch" obligations arising in favor of the debtor. Thus garnishment of a bank account will let a creditor obtain not only the amount on deposit on the date the writ was served, but also funds deposited thereafter up until the time that the answer to the garnishment writ is due. By contrast, a few states use a "spear" approach, where a writ only catches whatever is available at the moment of service.

Wage garnishments present a special issue of concern about abusive practices. If a garnishing judgment creditor could seize the entire salary or wages that an employer owed to a judgment debtor, a person's ability to survive might be seriously jeopardized. Surely the debtor's incentive to work would be sharply reduced, resulting in hardship to the debtor's family and increased social costs. Moreover, such garnishment power would give the creditor excessive leverage to strike a new bargain with a defaulting debtor. A debtor facing garnishment of all wages might well offer the creditor property that the law protects from seizure as exempt or promise to pay a much higher interest rate on the debt. In response to such concerns, Congress limited the amount of wages that creditors may garnish. 15 U.S.C. §1671 et seq. One impetus for the federal law is the enormous variation that existed among states. Some states prohibit garnishments altogether (with the frequent exception of efforts to collect family support obligations), while other states have no restrictions. Many states are scattered between these extremes. The federal garnishment restrictions act as a floor, creating a minimum protection.

In the next case, the family support creditors got their garnishment order in first, leaving the other creditors to fight over what was left. The others were willing to fight, but they had some trouble figuring out exactly how much was left to fight over.

——————— **COMMONWEALTH EDISON v. DENSON** ———————
144 Ill. App. 3d 383, 494 N.E.2d 293, 98 Ill. Dec. 859 (Ill. App. 1986)

Justice STOUDER delivered the opinion of the court:

Employer-Appellant, Caterpillar Tractor Company (Caterpillar) appeals from two separate judgments of the circuit court of Will County....

The first action was originally brought by plaintiff-appellee, Commonwealth Edison (Com Ed) to collect monies due and owing to it by defendant, Willie Denson. On June 27, 1984, the circuit court entered judgment in favor of Com Ed and against Denson for $629.54 plus costs. Summons was issued pursuant to an affidavit for a wage deduction order in the amount of the outstanding judgment and Com Ed served interrogatories upon Caterpillar, Denson's current employer....

Caterpillar responded to the interrogatories and forwarded a check to Com Ed in the amount of $139.32. Caterpillar declined to deduct the full 15 percent of Denson's gross earnings, in accordance with the order, as it was already withholding $60 per week from his wages pursuant to a previously filed support order.

The second action was originally brought by plaintiff-appellee, Newsome Physical Therapy Clinic (Newsome) to collect monies due and owing to it by defendant, Dwight Morgan. On October 31, 1984, the circuit court entered judgment in favor of Newsome and against Morgan for $748.19 plus costs. Summons was issued pursuant to an affidavit for a wage deduction order in the amount of the outstanding judgment and Newsome served interrogatories upon Caterpillar, Morgan's current employer....

Caterpillar contends under Illinois law no garnishment is allowed which would exceed the lesser of 15 percent of gross earnings, or the amount by which the weekly disposable earnings exceed 30 times the Federal minimum hourly wage which was $3.35 per hour at all times relevant to this case....

From our review of the Acts and Regulations involved we have determined the trial court erred and therefore its judgment must be reversed. The contention that payroll deductions required under a support order should not be included when computing the percentage reduction of a debtor's disposable earnings is not a legally supportable interpretation and application of these statutes.

We initially examine the Federal law. Under the Supremacy Clause (Article VI, U.S. Constitution) the garnishment restriction provision of the Consumer Credit Protection Act (CCPA) (15 U.S.C., Sec. 1671 et seq.) pre-empts state laws insofar as state laws would permit recovery in excess of 25 percent of an individual's disposable earnings. The cardinal provision of the Act is 15 U.S.C., Sec. 1673. . . .

The Federal Act does not pre-empt the field of garnishment entirely, but provides that in those instances where state and federal laws are inconsistent, then the courts are to apply the law which garnishes the lesser amount. (15

U.S.C., Sec. 1677.) In Illinois, Section 12-803 of the Code of Civil Procedure (Ill. Rev. Stat. 1985, Ch. 110, par. 12-803) provides:

> 12.803. Maximum wages subject to collection. The maximum wages, salary, commissions and bonuses subject to collection under a deduction order, for any work week shall not exceed the lesser of (1) 15% of such gross amount paid for that week or (2) the amount by which disposable earnings for a week exceed 30 times the Federal Minimum Hourly Wage prescribed by Section 206(a)(1) of Title 29 of The United States Code, as amended, in effect at the time the amounts are payable. This provision (and no other) applies irrespective of the place where the compensation was earned or payable and the State where the employee resides. No amounts required by law to be withheld may be taken from the amount collected by the creditor. The term "disposable earnings" means that part of the earnings of any individual remaining after the deduction from those earnings of any amounts required by law to be withheld.

The Federal Act does not seek to establish any order of priority among garnishments. There being no other Federal statutory provision setting priorities as between support order garnishments and creditor garnishments, the matter of priority is thus determined by Illinois law. Pursuant to Illinois statute, it is clear and unequivocal that as between garnishments of the same type, the prior in time is to be satisfied first. As between judgment creditor garnishments and support order garnishments, Illinois gives priority to those for support regardless of the timing of those garnishments.

. . . Thus, when garnishments are sought only by judgment creditors, no more than the lesser of 25 percent of disposable earnings, or 15 percent of gross earnings, or the amount by which disposable earnings exceed 30 times the Federal minimum wage may be withheld for that purpose; when garnishments are sought only to enforce support orders, as much as 65 percent of disposable earnings may be withheld for that purpose. The interrelationship, however, between the general rule and the exception, when both creditor and support garnishments are sought, is less clear. Plaintiffs in this case argue support garnishments should be considered entirely independent of judgment creditor garnishments, and that the Acts should be construed under the facts of the case as reserving 15 percent of the employees' earnings for attachment by judgment creditors after the satisfaction of family support orders. We find no basis for this argument either in the language of the statutes or in their legislative history.

Our conclusion is reinforced by the manner in which 15 U.S.C., Sec. 1673 has been construed by the Secretary of Labor. . . . ". . . (iv) If 25% or more of an individual's disposable earnings were withheld pursuant to a garnishment for support, and the support garnishment has priority in accordance with State law, the Consumer Credit Protection Act does not permit the withholding of any additional amounts pursuant to an ordinary garnishment which is subject to the restrictions of section (1673(a))." 29 C.F.R., Sec. 870.11. . . .

We are mindful of the plaintiff's argument that the statutes as thus construed may help debtors to evade payment of their debts if they collusively procure orders of support that exceed the statutory maximums. This point was considered and indeed vigorously debated in Congress prior to the passage of the Act. . . . Thus, we hardly feel free to tamper with the way in which Congress has chosen to balance the interests of the debtor, his family, and his creditors.

Reversed and remanded with directions.

———————

The employer-garnishee, Caterpillar, was defending its employees' interests in the last case but often the garnishee is defending its own interest against a garnishing creditor. A bank account is often the source of this kind of dispute between garnishee and judgment creditor. The law regards the account as a debt the bank owes to the depositor, so garnishment is the way to reach the asset. The account, with its ready liquidity, is attractive to the judgment creditor as an easy way to satisfy the judgment debt. But banks often have multiple relationships with their depositors. It is not uncommon for a business or individual to maintain a checking account with the same bank where one or more loans are outstanding. The customer then becomes the bank's creditor for the deposit account and bank's debtor on the loan accounts. When the deposit account is garnished, the bank rapidly switches hats, agreeing as account debtor that the money is owed to the customer but arguing that as loan creditor it is owed offsetting amounts that must be settled before any garnishor is paid. The bank then offers to satisfy the writ only the net amount—if any—left in the account after the bank's own *setoff*. Of course, there is often a dispute between the judgment creditor and the bank on whose debt has priority, with the creditor claiming that its writ was served and a lien attached before the bank had properly accelerated and offset the debtor's obligation to it, and the bank claiming the converse. For the moment, it is enough to say that the bank almost always wins.

Problem Set 2

2.1. The senior partner of your big Wall Street firm explains that one of the pension funds the firm advises is considering a sizeable investment in a payday loan company, but in order to assess the investment, it wants an opinion from your firm that the practices of the company are generally in accordance with the law.

The partner hands you a copy of a May 31, 2000, story in the *Christian Science Monitor* that begins: "Kesha Gray needed $100 fast. Her credit-cards were at their limit, she had no home equity to fall back on, and her daughter's day-care bill was due. She saw only one alternative. She went to a 'payday lender' and wrote a check for $162, post-dated for two weeks—when she was due to get a paycheck. When two weeks rolled around, more-pressing bills gobbled up her paycheck, and she couldn't muster the $162 she owed. Instead, she paid a $15 fee to roll over the loan. Two weeks later, she paid the debt. Total annualized interest rate 924 percent." Although fourteen states outlaw payday loans, the industry reports 20,000 outlets and $40 billion in loans outstanding.

Another publication quoted a typical collection letter: "WE HAVE CONTACTED THE CITY OF CHICAGO POLICE DEPARTMENT. THEY ARE AWARE OF YOUR BAD CHECK WITH NATIONWIDE BUDGET FINANCE. IT IS A FELONY TO WRITE A BAD CHECK IN THE STATE OF ILLINOIS. YOUR FAILURE TO RESPOND TO THIS NOTICE WITHIN 72 HOURS WILL RESULT IN US APPLYING FOR A WARRANT FOR YOUR ARREST."

The senior partner knows that you will want to review individual practices in detail, but she asks first for your general assessment. See FDCPA §§1692a; 1692e and 1692f.

2.2. You decided to forsake the lure of the big firm and go with a small practice in Columbus. You like the eight partners in the firm and are eager to make yourself useful. The firm has carved out a niche in what the partners call "Main Street" law—real estate closings, car accidents, contract disputes, unpaid bills for local businesses, etc.

Last month you received an assignment for Condoleezza Chalmers, who owns a small rental house. She is upset that a tenant moved out and left about $2,000 worth of damages beyond the security deposit. You reviewed the case and sent out one of the firm's standard form letters outlining the damages claimed by the client, demanding a quick resolution, and indicating that you will take immediate legal action, including a lawsuit, if the outstanding amount isn't paid promptly. You were shocked to receive a letter this morning from the former tenant claiming violations of the FDCPA and agreeing to settle the matter if Ms. Chalmers will drop all claims. You do a little investigating and discover that the former tenant is a third-year law student. (It now occurs to you why no one wanted to rent to you when you were in law school.) Advice?

2.3. Sean Smythe and Mona Morris used to live together. Despite working as a bank teller, Mona frequently was short of funds. Her habit was to "borrow" $100 from Sean every two weeks but never repay him. The last time she asked for money, Sean made her sign a written I.O.U., promising to repay the money in thirty days. When that time elapsed, Sean and Mona began to bicker; eventually Mona moved out. She left behind her computer. Sean has called you, his former college roommate, for help. He apologizes for bothering you, explaining that he tried to find the answer on the Internet (using Mona's computer, of course) but all he learned is that your state has a law that allows debtors to exempt computers.

Does Sean have the right to keep the computer in satisfaction of the debt? Does he have other effective collection remedies?

2.4. Bruno Holtry is one of your company's best repossession agents. He's quick at his work, which limits the potential for violent responses from debtors. Bruno just called you to report on his last job of the night. He says that he was headed to the employer of Isabel Fury to repossess her 2000 Honda Accord when she passed him headed home from work. He followed her. She stopped the car in front of a modest ranch house and went to the door. He verified that the address was not her home based on your records but figured since it was a few blocks away that he would repo the car and let her walk home. The job was easy, he reported, because Isabel left the keys in the car and the windows rolled down. He heard her yelling and chasing after him when he was a half-block away, but he knew better than to stop and invite trouble.

At this point, you are wondering why you got the call when Bruno says that he better call you back "because a helicopter's landing out back." You are nonplussed but can't put the pieces together. Waiting for Bruno to call you back, you flip on the office TV. Across the bottom of the screen is an "Amber Alert" for a missing two-year old, Jermaine Fury. When the telephone rings back, it is a police detective, who explains that when Bruno took the car, Jermaine was asleep in his car seat. Apparently, Bruno did not notice him, but Isabel called 911 to report a stolen child. After launching an intense missing child protocol, the police called Bruno and had him check the car. When the police and Isabel arrived on the scene, Bruno was giving the toddler his first root beer. Is your company in legal trouble based on the day's events? Is Bruno? Is Isabel? Is Jermaine? See UCC §9-609.

2.5. Mark Watkins has had continuing difficulties with credit charges on his account at Highland Department Store. Apparently, Highland transposed two numbers in recording monthly charges sometime last spring, and it billed Watkins for $4,000 in goods Watkins did not purchase. Watkins notified a call center representative of the error, but Highland continued to issue bills. After three months and two letters, Watkins decided he had done all he could do, tossing all subsequent bills.

Watkins recently decided to purchase a condominium and hired you to handle the transaction. When he applied for a mortgage, however, he was turned down. The mortgage company sent him a form letter explaining that he was not "within the range of applicants" to whom the mortgagee made loans. Having a good job and timely bill payments, he is outraged and thinks Highland is to blame. How can he confirm his suspicions? See Fair Credit Reporting Act (§§1681b, i, m, n, o). Would it matter if Watkins's dispute were for $40 instead?

2.6. Cash2U, Inc. makes small-dollar, unsecured consumer loans. It obtained a $30,000 judgment against one of its borrowers, Wayne Smettles. On February 1, Cash2U delivered a writ of garnishment to the sheriff for service on Amos State Bank, where Wayne has his checking account. On that date the account was overdrawn by $10. On February 5, Wayne's employer direct deposited his $5,000 paycheck into the account. The sheriff served the writ of garnishment on the bank on February 9. Ignorant of the writ, Wayne wrote a check for $500 to the telephone company on February 9, which the bank paid on February 10. The bank answered the writ on February 15, the day before Wayne's direct deposit wages of $300 arrived, and five days before the writ's answer was due. You are the bank's junior counsel. Who gets what?

2.7. NCP Homebuilders, Inc. employs a sales staff of 18 to 22 people to market their new homes. These employees are salaried and they work with individual homebuyers to help them purchase NCP homes. The employees must work with the homebuyers' family budgets, mortgage and tax rates, employment plans, etc., to help both the company and the buyer determine what the buyer can afford.

Carlos Valdez is the sales force supervisor. He monitors the work of his employees and keeps close tabs on any "image" factors that might reflect poorly on NCP. He trains and educates his staff, advises them on clothing, indicates when haircuts are appropriate, and so on. He fires employees who are not productive enough in sales or whose appearance or sales tactics are not approved by the company.

Valdez consults you on a new matter. He has just received a notification of a garnishment of the wages of one of the sales employees, Wilkins Micawber. Valdez would like to fire Mr. Micawber. What do you advise? If Valdez wrongfully fires him what are the possible consequences? Are there any risks besides an employee suit? See §304 of the Consumer Credit Protection Act, 15 U.S.C. §1674.

PART III

CONSUMER BANKRUPTCY

Section 1:
The Foundation

Assignment 3.

The Bankruptcy Estate and the Automatic Stay

A.   INTRODUCTION

Bankruptcy is technically an *in rem* proceeding, meaning that it affects property. We say "technically" because its main practical consequence is to discharge a consumer from all ongoing obligations, which means enjoining all creditors from collecting on their erstwhile debts. §524. That sounds pretty personal to us. And we suspect it does as well to the creditors who have kissed their obligations goodbye. Nevertheless, as good lawyers, we acknowledge the formalism of the bankruptcy process and note that bankruptcy's *in rem* proceeding starts with something called the bankruptcy *estate*.

Remember first year property law (and you thought it was just Civ Pro you would have to remember)? Remember when a rich uncle wants to give his spendthrift nephew some property (like cash or Blackacre) but does not want him to get full control of it for fear he will blow it all fast and foolishly? The solution was to create a trust, into which uncle (settlor) would put the property (res). Legal title in control would go to a trusted friend (trustee), who would shepherd the property for the benefit of nephew (beneficiary). Although nephew enjoyed the *benefits* of the property and perhaps got periodic disbursements from the trustee, he could never demand money out of the trust because he did not *own* the property. Nor could uncle, because once he divested himself of ownership of property to the trustee, he could not change his mind and take it back; the trustee was now in control of a traditional inter vivos trust and became legal owner of the property for the benefit of nephew.

Filing bankruptcy creates a similar trust—albeit a poor man's trust—with all the same elements. Here, upon filing the bankruptcy petition, the debtor settles the trust, the *res* of which is called "the estate." The trust's beneficiaries are all the debtor's creditors. Who gets to be the trustee? Appropriately enough, someone the Bankruptcy Code calls "the trustee." Just as the anxious nephew cannot access any property without the trustee's permission, so too the creditors of a debtor can do nothing on their own; the trustee is in control of the estate. And just as the rich uncle cannot take property back from the trust, so too does the debtor lose all control of what was formerly his property. The trustee runs the show. To reinforce this control, the trustee is assisted by a legal *stay* (injunction) that arises automatically upon filing bankruptcy. The stay enjoins any creditor from trying to seize estate property or otherwise pursue collection against the debtor. This automatic stay gives most debtors their first relief from months of creditor dunning, a welcome price to pay to cede control to a trustee.

The trustee, sometimes called the "trustee-in-bankruptcy" ("TIB"), is usually a local lawyer. The selection of a trustee depends on the chapter of bankruptcy at issue, and in some instances, on the creditors' level of participation in the case. The trustee in a particular case is different from the federal employees called "U.S. Trustees," apparently to confuse bankruptcy students; you should not conflate the two. The U.S. Trustees work for the U.S. Department of Justice and largely do oversight and administration. Their tasks are quite different from the rank-and-file lawyers who serve as the trustees who control the more than one million consumer bankruptcy cases each year. The vast majority of debtors are so broke they have no distributable assets with which to create their estates. See David T. Stanley and Marjorie Girth, Bankruptcy: Problem, Process, Reform 87 (1971); Herbert and Pacitti, Down and Out in Richmond, Virginia: The Distribution of Assets in Chapter 7 Bankruptcy Proceedings Closed in 1984-1987, 22 Rich. L. Rev. 303 (1988). This makes the job of trustee hardly a glamorous one, but yeoman's service in the trustee ranks helps chances for appointment when a high-ticket liquidation finally rolls into the district.

The trustee administers the debtor's estate by gathering all the estate assets. In a liquidation case, the trustee sells the assets; in a reorganization case, the trustee administers the bankruptcy case. The trustee has a special obligation, by custom and common law, to unsecured, general creditors and therefore is especially charged with scrutinizing the debtor's reports to locate any concealed property or to discover any wrongdoing that might result in a failure to get a discharge. The trustee is also careful to be sure that no one creditor tries to take more than its share and thus challenges security interests or claims to special priority treatment. The trustee is thus both the creditors' friend and nemesis. He stands for the proposition that equity is equality. That maxim means that unless a creditor can clearly demonstrate that it deserves some priority in the bankruptcy payout, the trustee will assume all creditors are equal and try to maximize the pot for that collective. Also, the trustee fees are calculated in part as a percentage of the funds distributed and that distribution is primarily to unsecured creditors. §§326, 330.

These two features of a bankruptcy case filing—(1) the creation of an estate and concomitant vesting of all control over that estate in a trustee, and (2) the automatic imposition of a stay against all creditor action—are the most important consequences of commencing a bankruptcy case, and so we examine each in more detail below. Before we proceed, however, we should mention just briefly some preliminaries involved in filing for bankruptcy. We think there are four things worth noting.

First, nearly all bankruptcy cases start voluntarily, with a debtor filing a *petition* to initiate the case. Petitions are often filed when a debtor is finally fed up with being hounded by creditors ranging from anxious to belligerent. (In making this filing decision, the debtor is guided more often than not by a lawyer.) The petition is the basic request for bankruptcy relief and is signed by the debtor, on penalty of perjury, as certification that all the information contained in the filing is true. The completed petition and required fee are filed with the clerk, who will date-stamp the minute, hour, and day of filing. In a voluntary case, this is the instant at which the bankruptcy estate is created and the automatic stay on all collection actions arises. The mere filing of that petition thus has the effect of the entry of a judicial order and so is called the *order for relief.* §301.

Second, filing a bankruptcy case requires a ton of initial paperwork. A bankruptcy debtor must pull together copious information on assets, debts, and income to complete the bankruptcy petition's *schedules*. Even a diligent lawyer with a fairly well organized client may get some of the pieces wrong, and heaven help the lawyer with a client whose recordkeeping is spotty. Current bankruptcy law puts significant pressure on lawyers to verify the accuracy of the debtor's records; the attorney must sign the debtor's petition. In consumer cases, by signing the petition, the attorney certifies the completion of a "reasonable investigation" into that accuracy and the absence of knowledge that the information in the schedules is incorrect. §707(b)(4)(C), (D). A lawyer who fails to do that may forfeit fees in the case, or, even worse, become subject to sanctions. §§526, 707(b). Pro se debtors flounder under the paperwork requirements, even those who can juggle octuplets. See Order and Notice of Dismissal, In re Suleman, No. 8:12-bk-15375-CB, (Dkt. 10) (Bankr. C.D. Cal. May 15, 2012) (Docket Entry 10). Cases filed without the assistance of an attorney are several times more likely to be dismissed for paperwork problems or other technical reasons than those filed by lawyers. See Angela K. Littwin, The Do-It-Yourself Mirage, in *Broke*.

Third, the debtor doesn't just get to file the petition and quietly await the benefits of the order for relief without ever confronting creditors. All debtors must attend a first meeting of creditors, often called the *341 meeting*, in reference to the Code section that mandates it, within 40 days of the petition. Think of it as the Confrontation Clause of bankruptcy. The primary function of the meeting is to permit an examination of the debtor by the trustee and any interested creditors, although it is a rare consumer case where an especially diligent or hostile creditor actually shows up. But other than that, in the absence of motions practice or some other sort of litigation fight, a debtor can generally avoid court (and the creditors) altogether.

The fourth and final note is the most significant. A consumer debtor will generally have to decide whether to file for relief under chapter 7 or chapter 13, an important decision with serious effects on debtors and their creditors. We defer scrutinizing the mechanics and consequences of that crucial choice until those chapters have been studied. We flag it now to note that the commencement of a case requires strategic and legal decision-making, not just the physical legwork of compiling documents.

B. THE ESTATE

At the instant of filing the bankruptcy petition, all the property owned by the debtor becomes "property of the estate," a deliberately expansive concept, with only a few specific exceptions set forth in section 541 of the Code. There is a small set of policy-based exceptions, such as 541(b)(5) for retirement accounts, as well as some that appear more lobbying-based (Anyone wish to explain the special treatment of liquid or gaseous hydrocarbons under 541(b)(4)?). But on the whole 541(a)'s reach is broad.

The most important exception to this expansive scope is for "services performed by an individual debtor after the commencement of the case." §541(a)(6). For typical consumer debtors, this means that wages, commissions, and the like earned after the petition is filed will not become property of the estate and do not have to be surrendered to creditors. This is the first benefit of the "fresh start."

This naturally raises questions about what is the debtor's old property (and hence the estate's) and what is new property (and hence the debtor's). If the debtor gets a present from a friend three days after filing bankruptcy, that sounds like new property. If the same friend pays back an I.O.U. three days after the bankruptcy, that sounds like old property, because the I.O.U. note (assuming it were more than three days old) would be property that went into the estate, and the cash from the friend's payment would be a traceable back to that property. While it is easy to say in the Code the estate contains "all property" of the debtor, courts still struggle with these relation-back sorts of issues.

—— **PROCHNOW v. APEX PROPERTIES, INC. (D/B/A REMAX)** ——
467 B.R. 656 (C.D. Ill. 2012)

MYERSCOUGH, District Judge.

STATEMENT OF FACTS

Prochnow was at all relevant times a duly licensed salesperson—also referred to as a realtor or realtor associate – [of] Apex Properties Inc., d/b/a Remax Choice of Bloomington, Illinois (ReMax) [and] was at all relevant times a duly licensed real estate broker. In August 2006, Prochnow and ReMax, through its predecessor, entered into a Broker–Realtor–Associate Contract (Associate Contract). The compensation paid to Prochnow and other realtor-associates licensed with ReMax was arranged on a commission basis.

. . .

On August 3, 2009, Prochnow filed his Chapter 7 bankruptcy petition. Prochnow was at that time still a realtor-associate with ReMax and continued in that capacity until January 8, 2010. On his Schedule B, Prochnow affirmatively represented that he had no accounts receivable, no liquidated debts owed to him, and no contingent or unliquidated claims of any nature. On January 8, 2010, Prochnow ceased working as a realtor-associate with ReMax. On February 23, 2010, Prochnow's bankruptcy case was closed. On June 16, 2010, Prochnow, represented by new counsel, filed a Motion to Reopen Case. In the Motion, Prochnow alleged that he became entitled to the payment of compensation from ReMax for real estate commissions from [certain] closings occurring after August 3, 2009, the date Prochnow filed his bankruptcy petition. . . .

The bankruptcy court granted ReMax's Motion for Summary Judgment... First, the bankruptcy court found that Prochnow had earned the . . . contract commission pre-petition and that it was part of the bankruptcy estate. Because Prochnow failed to disclose his interest in a share of the . . . contract commission on his schedules, the bankruptcy court [also] found he was judicially estopped from claiming an interest in those funds. This appeal followed.

ANALYSIS

Prochnow argues . . . said commission was earned post-petition and was not an asset of the bankruptcy estate. . . . Prochnow asserts the commission was earned post-petition, when the real estate closing occurred. In support thereof, Prochnow relies on the language of the Associate Contract which specifically provides: "No commissions shall be considered earned or payable to Realtor-Associate until the transaction has been completed and the commission has been collected by the Broker."

. . .

1. The Commission Was Part of the Bankruptcy Estate

The bankruptcy court found that the . . . contract commission was part of the bankruptcy estate. "Whether property is included in the bankruptcy estate is a question of law." In re Parsons, 280 F.3d 1185, 1188 (8th Cir.2002). "To determine the nature of a debtor's interest in property, we look to state law; to determine whether that interest counts as property of the debtor's estate, we look to federal bankruptcy law." In re Krueger, 192 F.3d 733, 737 (7th Cir.1999). Section 541(a) of the Bankruptcy Code defines "property of the estate" to include "all legal or equitable interests of the debtor in the property as of the commencement of the case." 11 U.S.C. §541(a)(1). This definition of property of the estate is broad—"including interests of all types and degrees of contingency"—but is generally limited to interests in existence at the time of the commencement of the case. In re Taronji, 174 B.R. 964, 967 (Bankr. N.D. Ill. 1994). "Section 541(a)(6) expands this basic definition of property of the estate to include certain property interests that are acquired after the commencement of the case." Id. "However, Section 541(a)(6) contains an express exception, exempting 'earnings from services performed by an individual debtor after the commencement of the case." In re Jokiel, 447 B.R. 868, 871 (Bankr. N.D. Ill. 2001) (quoting 11 U.S.C. §541(a)(6)).

On appeal, Prochnow essentially argues that he earned the commission post-petition because the Associate Contract provided that commissions were not earned until the transaction (i.e. the closing on the property) had been completed and the commission was collected by ReMax. This Court first notes that the provision in the Associate Contract merely made Prochnow's interest contingent. Under Illinois law, a broker (which in this case would be ReMax), is entitled to a commission for the sale of real estate when he procures a buyer who is ready, willing, and able to purchase the real estate on the terms prescribed by the seller. As the bankruptcy court noted, "once the Hudson [c]ontract was signed and the financing contingency set forth in the contract was met, ReMax, as the broker in the transaction, had earned its commission." In re Prochnow, —— B.R. at ——.

. . .

"A debtor's contingent interest in future income has consistently been found to be property of the bankruptcy estate." In re Yonikus, 996 F.2d 866, 869 (7th Cir. 1993). In fact, "[a] contingency is no bar to [a] property interest becoming property of the bankruptcy estate, even if the contingency requires additional postpetition services, and even if the right to enjoyment of the property may be defeated." In re Allen, 226 B.R. 857, 865 (Bankr. N.D. Ill. 1998). Moreover, the test for determining whether post-petition income is property of the bankruptcy estate depends on whether the income accrues from pre-petition or post-petition services. *See* In re Laflamme, 397 B.R. 194, 199 (Bankr. D.N.H. 2008) (commissions received postpetition are property of the estate if "all acts of the debtor necessary to earn it are rooted in the pre-bankruptcy past") (internal quotation marks omitted). As stated by the Seventh Circuit, in a case involving a tax refund, "[t]he background rule under the old Bankruptcy Act, to which courts still refer in the era of the Bankruptcy Code, defines the bankruptcy estate to include property that is 'sufficiently rooted in the pre-bankruptcy past and so little entangled with the bankrupts' ability to make an unencumbered fresh start.' " In re Meyers, 616 F.3d 626, 628 (7th Cir.2010) (quoting Segal v. Rochelle, 382 U.S. 375, 380, 86 S. Ct. 511, 15 L. Ed. 2d 428 (1966)).

Although Prochnow's right to the commission may have vested post-petition, the payment was actually for pre-petition services. *See* In re Jokiel, 447 B.R. at 872 (noting that the key issue to determining whether a post-petition severance payment was property of the bankruptcy estate was "whether the severance payment was rooted in pre- or post-petition services"). When Prochnow filed his petition for bankruptcy, the amount of the commission was clearly established. In addition, Prochnow had done all he needed to do to receive the commission even though the commission was contingent on the transaction actually being completed. *See, e.g.,* In re Dzielak, 435 B.R. 538, 546 (Bankr. N.D. Ill. 2010) (finding that the debtor's potential interest in a 401(k) plan was property of the estate even though the divorce court had not yet issued an order distributing an interest in the property; the debtor had "a claim for, or a contingent interest in, all or part of the retirement account"). Prochnow has not identified any services performed post-petition which would suggest the need to allocate the commission between pre- and post-petition services. *See, e.g.,* In re Bagen, 186 B.R. 824, 829 (Bankr. S.D.N.Y. 1995) (finding that the debtor's "pre[-]petition contingent contractual rights to postpetition property is property of the estate" but allocating the sum between pre- and postpetition services), *aff'd* 201 B.R. 642 (S.D.N.Y. 1996). Therefore, this Court finds that the bankruptcy court properly found that Prochnow's portion of the commission for the Hudson contract was property of the bankruptcy estate. . . .

Prochnow is [in the alternative] judicially estopped from pursuing the commission. *See* Cannon–Stokes v. Potter, 453 F.3d 446, 448 (7th Cir. 2006) (noting that "[j]udicial estoppel is an equitable doctrine, and it is not equitable to employ it to injure creditors who are themselves victims of the debtor's deceit"). . . . Prochnow was required to disclose any assets on his schedule when he filed his bankruptcy petition. *See* 11 U.S.C. 521(a)(1)(B)(i) (requiring that a debtor file a schedule of assets); 11 U.S.C. §101(5)(A) (defining a claim to include a "right to payment, whether or not such right is reduced to judgment, liquidated, unliquidated, fixed, contingent, matured, unmatured, disputed, undisputed, legal, equitable, secured, or unsecured").

. . .

The Seventh Circuit has held that "a debtor in bankruptcy who denies owning an asset, including a chose in action or other legal claim, cannot realize on that concealed asset after the bankruptcy ends." Cannon–Stokes, 453 F.3d at 448 (citing cases). That is precisely what Prochnow is attempting to do here. The bankruptcy court did not therefore abuse its discretion by finding Prochnow was judicially estopped from pursuing the commission.

THEREFORE, the decision of the Bankruptcy Court is AFFIRMED.

Do you think this was a close case, given the contract's language saying the commission was not earned until closing? If so, does the fact the court was inclined to stop Prochnow from claiming the funds (for being sneaky in his bankruptcy filings) predetermine how it was going to rule? Sneaky debtors make poor test cases. For another arguably closer case that went the other way (with a less sneaky debtor), consider Sharp v. Dery, 253 B.R. 204 (E.D. Mich. 2000) (reversing bankruptcy court and holding that debtor's annual bonus for the fiscal year completed prepetition—but issued two months into the next year—was *not* property of the estate because the debtor had to remain employed "in good standing" to be entitled to the prior year-end bonus).

Conceptually, disputes about the inclusion of certain expectancies in "property of the estate" under section 541 can be divided into three main categories: future interests, restrictions on transfer, and degree of legal entitlement. The first, illustrated by *Prochnow* and *Sharp*, involves timing: legal interests that are not enforceable at the date of bankruptcy but may be enforceable at a future time. The question is whether they are sufficiently matured and certain to be included in the estate. Knowing in your heart of hearts you had a great year at work does not give you a legally enforceable right to demand a bonus from your boss. Nor does her saying, "What a great year you've had!" at the office Christmas party. Sidestepping estoppel doctrines, mere expectations or hopes are not property. These "ripening" disputes also raise ancillary questions of allocation when some but not all rights are enforceable. For example, the *Sharp* court declined an interesting argument to try to pro-rate the bonus as without legal basis. But see Stoebner v. Wick (*In re* Wick), 276 F.3d 412 (8th Cir. 2002) (pro-rating, between trustee and debtor based on pre- and post-petition labor of the debtor, the value of stock options that were unvested at time of bankruptcy filing).

The second type of dispute involves restrictions on transfer. Suppose the debtor owns a small family cottage, but the deed contains a restriction that it cannot be sold to someone outside the debtor's family. The cottage is surely the debtor's property, but if the restriction were valid in bankruptcy, then it could not pass to the trustee (a trustee related to the debtor would be disqualified) and hence to the bankruptcy estate, leaving the debtor's creditors out in the cold. For that reason, such restrictions are not generally favored in bankruptcy as a policy matter, and provisions such as section 541(c)(1) make most of them unenforceable. Congress has allowed only a few exceptions, the most important is the section 541(c)(2) protection of bona fide spendthrift trusts validly created under applicable law. As the case below shows, however, that exception is construed narrowly.

————— **In re CHAMBERS** —————
451 B.R. 621 (Bankr. N.D. Ga. 2011)

MULLINS, Bankruptcy Judge.

The issue before the Court is whether campaign contributions made to a candidate for public office ("campaign funds"), who files bankruptcy without incorporating the campaign, are property of the bankruptcy estate. Debtor alleged that a garnishment order froze certain bank accounts, including her State Representative Campaign Account (a Wachovia government checking account) containing the subject campaign funds, in violation of section 362 of the Bankruptcy Code. The Court held an expedited hearing on October 26, 2010, and thereafter entered an Interim Order requiring the campaign funds be held in trust by the Chapter 13 Trustee [pending this opinion on the merits].

FACTUAL BACKGROUND

On October 6, 2010, the Debtor filed a chapter 13 petition. At the time of filing, the Debtor was running a campaign for re-election as a Georgia State Representative. The Debtor did not incorporate her campaign. Prior to the bankruptcy filing, Miami Circle filed a garnishment order on Wachovia Bank, which froze Debtor's bank accounts, including her campaign funds account. The Debtor filed chapter 13 in an attempt to free the campaign funds from garnishment, make them available to her campaign, and shield them from the reach of her personal creditors, including Miami Circle.

CONCLUSIONS OF LAW

The scope of section 541(a) of the Bankruptcy Code is intentionally broad. It not only includes property in which a debtor has an equity interest, it includes all property in which a debtor has *any* interest. 11 U.S.C. §541(a); United States v. Whiting Pools, Inc., 462 U.S. 198, 103 S. Ct. 2309, 76 L. Ed. 2d 515 (1983). The United States Supreme Court stated that section 541(a) sweeps in, as property of the estate, even a debtor's equitable right of redemption. Whiting

Pools, 462 U.S. at 204–05, 103 S. Ct. 2309. Following this decision, Whiting Pools has had a talismanic presence in bankruptcy law, affecting a wide range of subject matter and guiding courts in nearly all circuits. Although the scope of section 541(a) is broad, it is limited to the rights debtor had prepetition. Section 541(a) cannot alter the pre-petition interest a debtor had in the property; the estate merely steps into a debtor's prepetition shoes. Whiting Pools, 462 U.S. at 205, 103 S. Ct. 2309.

This attribute is commonly seen in the context of security interests. For example, if there are liens attached to account funds prepetition, the inclusion of the funds as property of the estate does not destroy the liens; the secured creditors would be entitled to adequate protection of their interest. *See* Butner v. United States, 440 U.S. 48, 55, 99 S. Ct. 914, 59 L. Ed. 2d 136 (1979) ("Property interests are created and defined by state law. Unless some federal interest requires a different result, there is no reason why such interests should be analyzed differently simply because an interested party is involved in a bankruptcy proceeding."). Section 541(a) does nothing other than characterize property of the estate. It does not determine which creditors are entitled to the estate property.

The breadth of the concept of property of the estate is reinforced by section 541(c)(1)(A) which states, "an interest of the debtor in property becomes property of the estate under section (a)(1) ... notwithstanding any provision in ... applicable nonbankruptcy law ... that restricts or conditions transfer of such interest by the debtor." 11 U.S.C. §541(c)(1)(A). Section 541(c)(1)(A) is commonly referred to as the "anti-alienation provision."

An exception to the anti-alienation provision is found in section 541(c)(2) of the Bankruptcy Code which excludes from the bankruptcy estate a debtor's interest in a spendthrift trust. 11 U.S.C. §541(c)(2); Patterson v. Shumate, 504 U.S. 753, 758, 112 S. Ct. 2242, 119 L. Ed. 2d 519 (1992). Section 541(c)(2) states, "a restriction on the transfer of a beneficial interest of the debtor in a trust that is enforceable under applicable nonbankruptcy law is enforceable in a case under this title." 11 U.S.C. §541(c)(2). Applying the canon of statutory construction that the express mention of one thing excludes all others *(expressio unius est exclusio alterius)* to an integrated reading of sections 541(a), (c)(1)(A), and (c)(2), leads to the conclusion that creating a spendthrift trust is the only state law property transfer restriction that allows a debtor's interest in property to escape the reach of section 541(a).

LEGAL ANALYSIS

The issue before the Court is a matter of first impression. Application of section 541 to the facts directs the Court to conclude that the campaign funds are property of the estate.

The Debtor has a property interest, however restricted by state law, in the campaign funds. Therefore, per section 541(a) and Whiting Pools, the campaign funds constitute property of the estate. 11 U.S.C. §541(a)(1). Nothing more []or less than the Debtor's prepetition interest in the campaign funds becomes property of the estate. Whiting Pools, 462 U.S. at 205 n.8, 103 S. Ct. 2309 ("§541(a)(1) does not expand the rights of the debtor in the hands of the estate..."). All section 541(a) does is define the estate and what the estate is comprised of; it does not address which creditors have rights to estate property. Because section 541(a) does nothing more than characterize what constitutes property of the estate, the Court does not reach the issue of whether certain creditors (e.g. campaign creditors) have priority claims with respect to the campaign funds. Section 541(a) including the campaign funds as property of the estate is comparable to the funds being held in the hands of a fiduciary.

Section 541(c)(1) provides further support for this inclusion by affirmatively invalidating any use restriction state law places on the campaign funds. [Georgia elections law] limits what campaign funds may be spent on:

> Contributions to a candidate, a campaign committee, or a public officer holding elective office and any proceeds from investing such contributions shall be utilized only to defray ordinary and necessary expenses.

[This law] describes how a candidate may *not* treat the campaign funds: "[c]ontributions and interest thereon, if any, shall not constitute personal assets of such candidate or such public officer." Although [the state law] restricts use of the campaign funds, the anti-alienation provision prevents the state law from excluding the funds from becoming property of the estate.

Additionally, the spendthrift trust exception to the anti-alienation provision does not apply here because the campaign funds are not held in a spendthrift trust under Georgia law. There is no evidence of a writing creating an express trust, let alone an express trust containing a valid spendthrift provision. *See* O.C.G.A. §53–12–80(a); In re Hipple, 225 B.R. 808 (Bankr. N.D. Ga. 1996) (Cotton, J.). Even if the campaign funds were held in a trust, the writing creating that trust would have to unequivocally state the spendthrift provision and the Debtor would have to lack access to the funds. In Hipple, Judge Cotton noted, ". . . the purpose of a . . . spendthrift trust is to protect the beneficiary from himself and his creditors . . . such a trust fails when the beneficiary exercises 'absolute dominion' over trust property." In re Hipple, 225 B.R. at 814. The Debtor presented no evidence of her lack of access to the campaign funds, because Georgia's campaign finance law does not restrict *access*. In contrast to a spendthrift trust, Georgia's campaign finance law theoretically allows candidates to be lavish and irresponsible in spending their campaign funds, it simply restricts the *kinds* of expenses that can be paid from the campaign funds.

Without a valid trust, the spendthrift trust exception to the anti-alienation provision does not apply.

CONCLUSION

The campaign funds are property of the estate pursuant to section 541 of the Bankruptcy Code and Whiting Pools and its progeny. If this outcome has political implications, they are simply a derivative, necessary consequence of the Court's adherence to the Bankruptcy Code and controlling case law.

IT IS ORDERED.

Introducing a third law school course you took earlier—constitutional law—note that the Supremacy Clause makes clear section 541(c)(1) brushes aside Georgia elections law. One wonders how the Republican campaign supporters of Representative Chambers would feel knowing their contributions are helping satisfy the debts of a credit card company whose chairman runs a Democratic Super-PAC (hypothetically, of course). This gives a flavor of the difficult policy balances—more precisely, policy overrides—presented by the broad-reaching scope of the Bankruptcy Code. (Sadly, Jill Chambers (R-Atlanta) did not succeed in her quest for re-election. Local pundits made much of the fact that she was the financial watchdog of the Atlanta public transit system while her own financial chaos led to bankruptcy.)

The third and final type of dispute regarding "property of the estate" involves entitlement. It raises the tricky question whether certain legal prerogatives are sufficiently alienable to qualify as private *property*. (The distinction between a "property" right and a mere "license" right of contract is analogous to the constitutional distinction between a "right" and a mere "privilege.") The problem often arises as to new kinds of property, like the licenses for television stations or a new internet entitlement. The trustee in the bankruptcy of Casey Anthony has asked the court for permission to sell Ms. Anthony's life story. As of press time, bidders have already emerged.

C.   THE AUTOMATIC STAY

Filing a bankruptcy petition not only creates a new estate, it also triggers an automatic stay that prohibits any creditor's attempt to continue to collect from the debtor or the debtor's property. The automatic stay is often likened to "closing the windows and locking the doors" to prevent any property from leaving the newly formed estate. Eventually the court will oversee the gathering and distribution of the assets, but until that time or until the stay is lifted, creditors are generally precluded from taking any individual action against the debtor or the debtor's bankruptcy estate. Section 362(a) details the prohibitions of the stay, while section 362(b) provides exceptions that permit certain types of actions against the debtor to continue.

In many respects, bankruptcy law is about control, a point that we will explore in more depth in the business section. For now, it is enough to emphasize that it is the automatic stay that puts the court in full control of the debtor's assets instantly, all over the United States (and, to some extent, all over the world). The automatic stay is also the first intrusion of federal bankruptcy laws into the state actions that a creditor would ordinarily be entitled to take. As the following cases illustrate, the power of the automatic stay is broad and the consequence of not respecting it severe.

——————— **In re GREEN** ———————

2011 WL 5902502 (Bankr. E.D.N.C.)

DOUB, Bankruptcy Judge.

. . . The Debtor filed a voluntary petition for relief under Chapter 7 of the Bankruptcy Code on August 10, 2009.

BACKGROUND

The Debtor attended ECU [East Carolina University] for a number of semesters including the Fall of 2007. The evidence presented at the hearing shows that the Debtor received grants and scholarships from various sources to fund her education. In the Fall of 2007, one of these sources was a Federal Perkins Loan in the amount of $750.00. Federal Perkins Loans are managed by the Office of Student Loans at ECU. The letters and invoices ECU sent the Debtor regarding payment of the Perkins Loan are the subject of the alleged willful violations of the automatic stay the Debtor asserts against ECU.

Another source of the Debtor's financial aid was a North Carolina Department of Health and Human Services, Division of Services for the Blind grant, which paid the remainder of any unpaid tuition not covered by other sources of financial aid, such as federal grants and loans, or institutional grants and loans. [An administrative error resulted in an overpayment by the Division of Services for the Blind of approximately $1,949.83 that ECU was required to refund. As such, the Debtor became liable to ECU for $1,949.83 plus interest because ECU repaid the Division of Services for the Blind on her behalf.]

Subsequent to the petition date, the Debtor continued attending ECU. Specifically, Debtor attended two Summer Sessions at ECU in the Summer of 2010. The Debtor withdrew from school during one of these sessions, causing her to become ineligible for some of her financial aid. As such, a portion of the financial aid for which the Debtor had not earned by finishing the session was returned to its originator by ECU. This resulted in the Debtor owing ECU $3,212.00. After the Debtor's discharge was entered, ECU began billing the

Debtor for the unpaid $3,212.00 and the $1,949.83 overpayment from the Fall of 2007 plus interest totaling $5,344.50. . . .

The Debtor appeared pro se at the September 29, 2011 hearing. The Debtor introduced evidence tending to show ECU attempted to collect on an outstanding pre-petition debt while the automatic stay was in place. More specifically, the Debtor proffered letters and invoices sent by the ECU Office of Student Loans in an attempt to collect on the $750.00 debt that were mailed after the automatic stay was in effect and after ECU received notice of the filing of the bankruptcy petition.

. . .

In the Response, ECU asserts that it did not engage in any actions that warrant the imposition of sanctions. At the hearing, ECU stipulated to the previously mentioned invoices and letters sent by the Office of Student Loans. However, ECU argued at the hearing that the collection attempts were not willful violations of the automatic stay because they were inadvertently sent to the Debtor as a result of a lack of communication between the various departments at ECU. ECU presented evidence through the testimony of Debra Bailey. . . . Ms. Bailey further explained that the letters and invoices were printed and mailed through an automated process on a thirty-sixty-ninety day interval. Therefore, any mailing of them was not an intentional act but an error produced because the Office of Student Loans was not informed of the bankruptcy petition. Furthermore, Ms. Bailey testified that ECU has since taken steps to institute a procedure whereby the different departments within the university are required to check a software system to ensure no student has filed a bankruptcy petition prior to attempting to collect on a debt.

DISCUSSION

Section 362(a) of the Bankruptcy Code imposes a stay on "any act to collect, assess, or recover a claim against the debtor that arose before the commencement of a case under" title 11. 11 U.S.C. §362(a)(6). The Bankruptcy Code also provides that any "individual injured by any willful violation of a stay provided by this section shall recover actual damages ... and in appropriate circumstances, may recover punitive damages." 11 U.S.C. §362(k)(1). This Court has held that "willfulness does not refer to the intent to violate the automatic stay, but the intent to commit the act which violates the automatic stay." Lofton v. Carolina Fin. LLC (In re Lofton), 385 B.R. 133, 140 (Bankr. E.D. N.C. 2008) (citing Citizens Bank v. Strumpf, 37 F.3d 155 (4th Cir.1994), overruled on other grounds 516 U.S. 16, 11 (1995)). . . .

[B]ecause the Office of Student Loans caused the letters and invoices to be sent and such actions were a violation of the automatic stay, ECU willfully violated the automatic stay.

. . .

In the Debtor's case, ECU has stipulated that violations of the stay occurred and has recognized the significance of the automatic stay by correcting internal practices to allow for notification of any bankruptcy petition between departments. However, ECU is a large state supported university with a Cashier's Office and Office of Student Loans. The collection of tuition, fees, and loans is big business involving millions of dollars. ECU is to be commended for curing its deficiencies in collection procedures, but should have done so long before 2010. For having failed to do so prior to 2010, the imposition of punitive damages is merited. No actual damages were proven by the Debtor.

Based on the foregoing, the Court finds that ECU's willful acts of sending four letters or invoices to the Debtor after receiving notice of the bankruptcy were in willful violation of the automatic stay. The Debtor is entitled to recover sanctions in the amount of $500.00 per violation of the automatic stay, totaling sanctions of $2,000.00.

Therefore, the Motion for Sanctions is GRANTED. . . .

This case nicely illustrates the power and the breadth of the automatic stay barring any attempt to collect any debt, as well as the courts' unwillingness to permit a large organization to plead bureaucracy as a defense, even when it has prospectively cleaned up its act. The next case, which features a bureaucracy defense that stretches credulity, adds in the question of just what counts as "an act to collect" in violation of the stay.

——— **NISSAN MOTOR ACCEPTANCE CORP. v. BAKER** ———
239 B.R. 484 (N.D. Tex. 1999)

KENDALL, District Judge.

This is an appeal from a judgment entered by the United States Bankruptcy Court for the Northern District of Texas, Dallas Division, on February 6, 1996. The Bankruptcy Court held that various actions of Appellant-Creditor Nissan Motor Acceptance Corporation ("Appellant") violated the terms of the automatic stay provided by 11 U.S.C.A. §362(a) (West 1998). The Bankruptcy Court awarded actual and punitive damages for Appellees Debtors ("Appellees") in the amount of $23,000, and reasonable attorneys' fees and expenses in the amount of $4,981.75. The Bankruptcy Court granted Appellant the option of satisfying the actual and punitive damages portion of the judgment by delivering to Appellees a new 1996 Nissan Pickup Truck B, Model SE, together with its title free and clear of any liens. For the reasons stated below, the judgment of the Bankruptcy Court is affirmed.

I. FACTUAL BACKGROUND

Appellees filed a Chapter 7 bankruptcy petition on December 30, 1993. At the time of filing, Appellees listed their 1991 Nissan Pickup ("Vehicle"), for which Appellees were in arrears to Appellant by more than two monthly payments. In their Statement of Intentions submitted with their petition, Appellees stated an intent to reaffirm the debt to Appellant for the Vehicle. On January 4, 1994, Appellant, without knowledge of Appellees' bankruptcy, repossessed the Vehicle. Both sides admit that Appellees' counsel contacted Appellant following the repossession to inform Appellant of Appellees' bankruptcy. Appellant disputes Appellees' assertion that they requested the return of the Vehicle. Nonetheless, the Bankruptcy Court found that as of January 4, 1994, Nissan had notice of Appellees' bankruptcy.

Appellant did not turn over the Vehicle upon notice of Appellees' bankruptcy, but retained possession of the Vehicle. On February 23, 1994, almost two months after the bankruptcy was filed and over six weeks after Appellant received notice of the bankruptcy, Appellant filed its motion for relief from stay, or, in the alternative, adequate protection [a motion seeking bankruptcy relief for secured creditors whose collateral is depreciating (see Assignment 10). However, while this motion was pending before the Bankruptcy Court, Appellant sold the Vehicle on March 16, 1994. The Bankruptcy Court, which did not know of the sale of the Vehicle, eventually granted Appellant's motion on June 1, 1994.

In November 1994, Appellees filed the adversary proceeding subject to this appeal seeking damages for violation of the automatic stay provided by §362....

II. ANALYSIS

The bankruptcy court's findings are reviewed under the clearly erroneous standard, and its legal conclusions are reviewed de novo. See Fed. R. Bankr. P. 8013.

Nissan's first assertion on appeal is that the Bankruptcy Court erred in holding that Appellant's exercise of control over the Vehicle after notice of the automatic stay was a willful violation of the stay. Interwoven in Nissan's argument is the issue of adequate protection—whether a secured creditor is required to turn over its collateral, which is property of the estate, without first receiving adequate protection....

...At particular issue here is §362(a)(3), which states that the automatic stay prohibits "any act to obtain possession of property of the estate or of property from the estate or to exercise control over property of the estate."

Numerous cases have held that a creditor's continued retention of estate property after notice of a bankruptcy filing constitutes an "exercise of control" over property of the estate in violation of the automatic stay....

...There is nothing in §363(e) that grants a creditor like Appellant the authority to engage in self-help to retain estate property as adequate protection, which is exactly what Appellant did in this case. Moreover, contrary to Appellant's argument, §542(a) provides that a creditor like Appellant "*shall* deliver to the trustee, and account for, [estate] property or the value of such property" (emphasis added). Section 542(a) has been construed to establish an affirmative obligation on the creditor to return estate property unless it is of inconsequential value to the estate, and nothing in §542(a) requires the debtor to provide the creditor with adequate protection as a condition precedent to turnover. Appellant's action is a violation of its obligation under §542(a) to turn over estate property, and subverts the authority of the Bankruptcy Court as specified in §363(e) to order adequate protection when the Bankruptcy Court, not the creditor, deems such protection necessary.

Appellant's second issue on appeal is whether Appellant's sale of the Vehicle was a willful violation of the stay.... Appellant knew that the stay was in effect when it filed its motion on February 23, 1994. Appellant cannot "play dumb" and rely on its "records," which inexplicably indicated to Appellant that the stay had lifted on March 5, 1994, when there was no order from the Bankruptcy Court relating to Appellant's motion until June 1, 1994. Appellant's disregard of the Bankruptcy Court's authority is inexcusable, and the Bankruptcy Court did not err in finding that Appellant's sale of the Vehicle was a willful violation of the stay....

Appellant's fourth issue on appeal is whether there was sufficient evidence to award actual damages.... Appellant ignores the ample testimony offered by Appellees on their actual damages. In addition to Appellees' testimony that they paid their daughter-in-law to drive them when necessary, Appellees testified that the Vehicle was the only reliable source of transportation that they had, that Appellee Baker's daily commute to and from his work was ninety miles, that Appellees struggled to secure reliable transportation after the Vehicle was repossessed by Appellant, and that Appellees had to purchase and finance a used Honda Civic in May 1994, as a replacement for the Vehicle. This evidence belies Appellant's contention that there was no other proof of actual damages. Thus, the Bankruptcy Court's award of actual damages was not clearly erroneous.

Appellant's fifth issue on appeal is whether the Bankruptcy Court erred and abused its discretion in awarding punitive damages.... In light of Appellant's willful violation of the stay by exercising self-help to possess and sell estate property, the Bankruptcy Court did not err, nor did it abuse its discretion, in awarding punitive damages....

Finally, Appellant's seventh issue on appeal is whether there is sufficient evidence to support the Bankruptcy Court's award of "excessive" attorneys' fees under §362(h).... Under the facts and circumstances of this case, the Court finds that the Bankruptcy Court's award of $4,860.00 in attorneys' fees per §362(h) is not clearly erroneous.

III. CONCLUSION

For the reasons stated above, the judgment of the bankruptcy court...is AFFIRMED.

Notice that the court was willing to lift the stay, which means that Nissan could have gotten the car. But when Nissan acted on its own without approval from the bankruptcy court, it ran up nearly $30,000 in damages. There's a message here, and it is not a subtle one.

The ability to lift the stay also shows that bankruptcy is not just a debtor-protective device. While a debtor's life may be greatly changed at the moment the bankruptcy petition is filed by the breathing room accorded by the automatic stay, that respite may be short-lived. Some creditors may be entitled to relief from the stay, and an even greater number will claim that they are entitled to relief (or at least posture so).

Finally, pause to reflect how many different actions can violate the automatic stay. In *Nissan*, merely "doing nothing" in the context of an obligation to turn over the car violated the stay. In a case likely to be of interest to students, Andrews University v. Merchant, 958 F.2d 738 (6th Cir. 1992), the court considered whether it was a violation of the automatic stay for a school to refuse to turn over a transcript requested by foreign-national alumnus—as required for his U.S. nationalization petition—until an outstanding tuition bill was paid. What do you think it held?

Problem Set 3

3.1. You have just been appointed trustee for the estate of Donald Lapman, whose flaky other-worldliness has long charmed his friends and has now brought him into Chapter 7 bankruptcy. Donald had some connection with the following property on the day he filed his bankruptcy petition:

[a] his parakeet, Toto;

[b] a 2010 Ford Focus he bought used, which is still subject to a purchase-money security interest in an amount exceeding its value;

[c] candid snapshots of hundreds of his friends, some of them quite intimate;

[d] two tickets to an upcoming Björk concert;

[e] household furniture, including dishes, pans, chairs, a couch, and the like;

[f] 25 shares of Monumental, Inc. left to him by his Uncle Rufus;

[g] an undivided 3/48ths interest in a big-game hunting preserve, also left by Rufus;

[h] 3,214 bubble gum baseball cards, some dating back to 1948;

[i] an arrangement with his younger brother: When Donald left home for college years ago, he lent his brother his catcher's mitt, with the understanding Donald could get it back whenever he wanted it;

[j] a bank account on which Donald is the named trustee for the benefit of his little niece Sherry, in the amount of $2,750;

[k] his salary for the month prior to the petition, which he received just hours after filing;

[l] his retirement account, which he cannot touch until he retires.

A month after the petition was filed, the parakeet unexpectedly laid two eggs, which have since become two little parakeets. Seven months later, Donald received from Monumental an annual dividend in the amount of $225. In addition, in the two months since the petition was filed Donald continued working and was paid his salary; his employer also made a contribution to his retirement fund. Which of the above items are "property of the estate" under §541(a)? See also §541(d).

3.2. Your client is Bartholomew Harrington Moss IV. He is broke and owes more than $100,000 to various creditors. His only income is $2,500 per month from a $450,000 trust that his mother established for him. He can get only the income from the trust until she dies, at which time he will get the corpus of the trust. The trust instrument says that his rights to the income and corpus are not assignable. His mother is quite ill. The doctors say she may last six months, but almost certainly not a year. What do you advise?

3.3. On March 1 a local farmer, Frances Alleta, contracted to sell her winter wheat crop of 10,000 bushels to a local grain warehouse for the market price prevailing on May 1. Unable to make it financially, Frances filed a bankruptcy petition April 1. The immature wheat had no market value at that moment. On March 1 the market price for wheat was $10 a bushel, but a severe drought in Argentina raised world prices so that it was worth $15 a bushel on April 1 and $20 a bushel on May 1, when Frances harvested it. When the buyer pays the $200,000, who gets what?

3.4. Sydney Leavens has done her best to pay her bills, but the combination of medical problems and a cutback at work has left her in a deep financial hole. On Monday, Advanta Bank seized her car. She was desperate to get it back, so she cashed out the money in her retirement account, and she wrote a check to

Advanta to pay off the car loan. The company said they would return the car when the check cleared. Recognizing that she was in a financial mess, Sydney decided on Tuesday to see a bankruptcy lawyer, who filed a petition that afternoon. On Wednesday, Advanta deposited Sydney's check. On Thursday, the check cleared, but Advanta has called you for advice before they return the car. What do you tell them? §§362(a), (h); 521(a)(2).

3.5. Joe Weiner has come to see you about getting some help with his staggering debt burden. Joe makes about $34,000 per year as a meat cutter, but he hurt his arm last year and was out of work for nearly eight months. His current wages are reduced by $100 per week because they have been garnished in an action by a finance company. Joe owes about $68,000 in unsecured debt, including gasoline credit cards, medical bills, credit union loans, finance company loans, past due alimony and child support, store credit cards, and overdue utility bills. He also owes $4,500 on his car loan and another $750 to an auto repair garage. Joe adds that he has been receiving dunning letters and phone calls, his doctor's collection agency has threatened legal action if he doesn't come up with some money by tomorrow, the utility company has sent a notice that service will be discontinued at midnight, and both the car lender and the garage have threatened repossession.

To try to hold things together, Joe takes each paycheck and makes small payments to each creditor. When the car lender threatened to repossess his car, Joe wrote him a check for the balance due even though he had only $44.12 in the bank. He has just received a summons from the district attorney to appear in court tomorrow morning on a bad check charge. Joe is late on his rent again, and his landlord has threatened to evict him if he doesn't pay his past-due rent by Friday. His credit counselor has run out of suggestions.

Joe's assets consist of his car, clothing, kitchen utensils, and small pieces of furniture. He will get paid tomorrow morning for the two-week pay period that ended yesterday. He has filled out all the necessary paperwork and produced the required documentation. You have satisfied yourself that he is qualified for a chapter 7, which he has asked you to file later today. Joe wants to know what he can expect to happen in the next few weeks. He especially wants to know if he will get his full paycheck, undiminished by the garnishment, tomorrow and every two weeks thereafter. See §§362(a), (b)(2), (b)(22), (b)(23), 366.

3.6. Puja Seam arrives in your office in tears. She shows you a notice that her house has been posted for sale by foreclosure at noon tomorrow. She explains that she has been in the middle of a divorce, and that her ex-husband claimed that he was making mortgage payments when he was not. She had called him about the earlier notices, but he had said that the notices were "mistakes" and he would "straighten them out." For the past month she has been unable to find him, and she fears he has fled the state. She tried calling the mortgage company, but her loan modification efforts keep ending in lost paperwork and disconnected phone calls. Now the sheriff's department says the sale is going forward. You know that if it does, she and her children will lose their home.

Puja has filled out all the schedules in your conference room today, but she did not know to bring paycheck stubs, tax returns, or any other paperwork with her; nor has she sought credit counseling. She lives an hour away and isn't sure where all that paperwork is at home. What can you do for her today? Make a list of what you need from Puja and how you can get it. See 11 U.S.C. §§521(a), (b), (i); 101(12A); 109(h); 526; 707(b)(4)(C), (D). When your paralegal points silently to the value listed for the car ($250), does that raise an issue beyond asking her if she is sure of it?

Section 2:
Chapter 7 Liquidation

Assignment 4.
Property Exempt from Seizure

A. INTRODUCTION

If you have ever seen a cartoon of a skinny little guy who is broke and wearing only a barrel, you may have wondered why the creditors left the barrel. The law in every state makes at least some property exempt from execution and other legal process so that no debtor can be reduced to absolute destitution. The policy reasons include a desire to avoid results so draconian as to threaten the social fabric of the community, which for similar reasons precludes the pledging of a pound of flesh as collateral. In addition, exemption policies also express a healthy dose of self-interest by non-debtors. The concern that a creditor not leave the debtor with so little property that the debtor and the debtor's family will become a charge on the community means that exemption laws are often directed toward making certain that every debtor retains enough basic property to have a chance to get out of the hole and make a fresh start. (Applicants cannot go to most job interviews naked.) Still another policy reason for some property exemptions is that certain items of personal property, such as clothes, have little monetary value for the creditor but are crucial to the debtor. Although the line between the two can be fuzzy, the law attempts to distinguish between seizing property to satisfy a debt and seizing property solely to inflict pain.

Recall that "exempt" property under state law means exempt from seizure by writ through the formal collections law. When the debtor waives that exemption, by granting a voluntary security interest with a home mortgage or car lien, the exemption protection falls by the wayside. This results in a neat divide among creditor groups: secured lenders like home mortgage companies, car lenders, and pawnbrokers care little about the scope of an exemption law, while credit card issuers, health care providers, tort victims, and others who cannot get a security agreement in advance feel the statute's teeth.

In bankruptcy, all property not listed as exempt is denominated non-exempt and will be sold by the trustee so that the proceeds can be distributed to the creditors. This may be the general unsecured creditor's last chance to get paid. Having said that, it is important to remember that most consumer debtors have so little unencumbered property it is not worthwhile for a trustee or creditor to bother objecting to their exemption claims.

B. FEDERALISM IN EXEMPTION LAWS

Every state has exemption laws, although the amount of protection varies widely. Once a debtor files for bankruptcy, federal law preempts state collection efforts with the automatic stay, but the question about which property is exempt becomes even sharper. After all, the deal in chapter 7 is that the debtor will give up all non-exempt property to get a debt discharge. The federal bankruptcy process must have rules about what the debtor must give up.

The 1898 Bankruptcy Act deferred to the states on the exemption issue. This meant, for example, that a Texas debtor in bankruptcy could protect whatever a Texas debtor outside bankruptcy could protect, while a Wyoming debtor in or out of bankruptcy could protect whatever property Wyoming exempted. The fact that Texas and Wyoming protected very different items or values was irrelevant, even though bankruptcy law is federal.

When the bankruptcy laws were modernized in 1978, many experts believed that it was time to develop uniform national exemptions. That proposal drew fire from two opposing camps: those in Congress who represented states with much smaller exemptions who thought the uniform proposals were too generous and (you guessed it) those in Congress who represented states with far more generous exemptions who thought the federal exemptions were too stingy. A compromise that only lawyers could love was born: the Code would establish uniform federal exemptions, *but* states would be permitted to "opt out" of those exemptions, forbidding their own citizens the ability to claim them upon bankruptcy. 11 U.S.C. §522(b)(2). That's a pretty big "but"—and we cannot lie—of which thirty-five states have availed themselves. The constitutionality of opting-out has been challenged, upheld, and has ceased to be widely disputed. See, e.g., In re Lauch, 16 B.R. 162 (Bankr. M.D. Fla. 1981).

1. State Exemptions

We reproduce illustrative excerpts from two states' exemption laws. The first is from Texas, and the second is from Wyoming. (Several specific exemptions from each state are omitted.)

─────── **TEXAS EXEMPTION STATUTES** ───────
Texas Property Code Annotated (Vernon 2009)

§41.001. INTERESTS IN LAND EXEMPT FROM SEIZURE

(a) A homestead and one or more lots used for a place of burial of the dead are exempt from seizure for the claims of creditors except for encumbrances properly fixed on homestead property.

(b) Encumbrances may be properly fixed on homestead property for
    (1) purchase money;
    (2) taxes on the property;
    (3) work and material used in constructing improvements on the property if contracted for in writing. . . .

(c) The homestead claimant's proceeds of a sale of a homestead are not subject to seizure for a creditor's claim for six months after the date of sale.

§41.002. DEFINITION OF HOMESTEAD

(a) If used for the purposes of an urban home or as both an urban home and a place to exercise a calling or business, the homestead of a family or a single, adult person, not otherwise entitled to a homestead, shall consist of not more than 10 acres of land which may be in one or more contiguous lots, together with any improvements thereon.

(b) If used for the purposes of a rural home, the homestead shall consist of
    (1) for a family, not more than 200 acres, which may be in one or more parcels, with the improvements thereon; or
    (2) for a single, adult person, not otherwise entitled to a homestead, not more than 100 acres, which may be in one or more parcels, with the improvements thereon.

(c) A homestead is considered to be urban if, at the time the designation is made, the property is
    (1) located within the limits of a municipality or its extraterritorial jurisdiction or a platted subdivision; and
    (2) served by police protection, paid or volunteer fire protection, and at least three of the following services provided by a municipality or under contract to a municipality
      (A) electric;
      (B) natural gas;
      (C) sewer;

(D) storm sewer; and

(E) water.

(c) The definition of a homestead as provided in this section applies to all homesteads in this state whenever created.

§41.003. Temporary Renting of a Homestead

Temporary renting of a homestead does not change its homestead character if the homestead claimant has not acquired another homestead.

§42.001. Personal Property Exemption

(a) Personal property, as described in Section 42.002, is exempt from garnishment, attachment, execution, or other seizure if

   (1) the property is provided for a family and has an aggregate fair market value of not more than $60,000, exclusive of the amount of any liens, security interests, or other charges encumbering the property; or

   (2) the property is owned by a single adult, who is not a member of a family, and has an aggregate fair market value of not more than $30,000, exclusive of the amount of any liens, security interests, or other charges encumbering the property.

(b) The following personal property is exempt from seizure and is not included in the aggregate limitations prescribed by Subsection (a)

   (1) current wages for personal services, except for the enforcement of court-ordered child support payments;

   (2) professionally prescribed health aids of a debtor or a dependent of a debtor; and

   (3) alimony, support, or separate maintenance received or to be received by the debtor for the support of the debtor or a dependent of the debtor.

(c) This section does not prevent seizure by a secured creditor with a contractual landlord's lien or other security in the property to be seized.

(d) Unpaid commissions for personal services not to exceed 25 percent of the aggregate limitations prescribed by Subsection (a) are exempt from seizure and are included in the aggregate.

§42.002. Personal Property

(a) The following personal property is exempt under Section 42.001(a)

   (1) home furnishings, including family heirlooms;

(2) provisions for consumption;

(3) farming or ranching vehicles and implements;

(4) tools, equipment, books, and apparatus, including boats and motor vehicles used in a trade or profession;

(5) wearing apparel;

(6) jewelry not to exceed 25 percent of the aggregate limitations prescribed by Section 42.001(a);

(7) two firearms;

(8) athletic and sporting equipment, including bicycles;

(9) a two-wheeled, three-wheeled, or four-wheeled motor vehicle for each member of a family or single adult who holds a driver's license or who does not hold a driver's license but who relies on another person to operate the vehicle for the benefit of the nonlicensed person;

(10) the following animals and forage on hand for their consumption

(A) two horses, mules, or donkeys and a saddle, blanket, and bridle for each;

(B) 12 head of cattle;

(C) 60 head of other types of livestock; and

(D) 120 fowl; and

(11) household pets.

(b) Personal property, unless precluded from being encumbered by other law, may be encumbered by a security interest under Section 9.203, Business & Commerce Code, or Subchapter F, Chapter 501, Transportation Code, or by a lien fixed by other law, and the security interest or lien may not be avoided on the ground that the property is exempt under this chapter.

§42.005. CHILD SUPPORT LIENS

Sections 42.001, 42.002, and 42.0021 of this code do not apply to a child support lien established under Subchapter G, Chapter 157, Family Code.

§42.0021. ADDITIONAL EXEMPTION FOR CERTAIN SAVINGS PLANS

(a) In addition to the exemption prescribed by Section 42.001, a person's right to the assets held in or to receive payments, whether vested or not, under any stock bonus, pension, profit-sharing, or similar plan, including a retirement plan for self-employed individuals, and under any annuity or similar contract purchased with assets distributed from that type of plan, and under any retirement annuity or account described by Section 403(b) or 408A of the Internal Revenue Code of 1986, and under any individual retirement account or any individual retirement annuity, including a simplified employee pension plan, and under any health savings account described by Section 223 of the Internal Revenue Code of 1986, is exempt from attachment, execution, and seizure for the satisfaction of debts unless the plan, contract, or account does not qualify under the applicable provisions of the Internal Revenue Code of 1986. . . .

TEX. INS. CODE §885.316

§1108.051. EXEMPTIONS FOR CERTAIN INSURANCE AND ANNUITY BENEFITS

(a) Except as provided by Section 1108.053, this section applies to any benefits, including the cash value and proceeds of an insurance policy, to be provided to an insured or beneficiary under:
  (1) an insurance policy or annuity contract issued by a life, health, or accident insurance company, including a mutual company or fraternal benefit society; or
  (2) an annuity or benefit plan used by an employer or individual.

(b) Notwithstanding any other provision of this code, insurance or annuity benefits described by Subsection (a):
  (1) inure exclusively to the benefit of the person for whose use and benefit the insurance or annuity is designated in the policy or contract; and
  (2) are fully exempt from:
    (A) garnishment, attachment, execution, or other seizure;
    (B) seizure, appropriation, or application by any legal or equitable process or by operation of law to pay a debt or other liability of an insured or of a beneficiary, either before or after the benefits are provided; and
    (C) a demand in a bankruptcy proceeding of the insured or beneficiary.

§1108.053. EXCEPTIONS TO EXEMPTIONS

The exemptions provided by Section 1108.051 do not apply to:

(1) a premium payment made in fraud of a creditor, subject to the applicable statute of limitations for recovering the payment;

(2) a debt of the insured or beneficiary secured by a pledge of the insurance policy or the proceeds of the policy; or

(3) a child support lien or levy under Chapter 157, Family Code.

WYOMING EXEMPTION STATUTES

WYO. CONST., ART. 19 §9. EXEMPTION OF HOMESTEAD

A homestead as provided by law shall be exempt from forced sale under any process of law, and shall not be alienated without the joint consent of husband and wife, when that relation exists; but no property shall be exempt from sale for taxes, or for the payment of obligations contracted for the purchase of said premises, or for the erection of improvements thereon.

WYO. STAT. §1-15-511 (2008)
§1-15-511. LIMITATION ON CONTINUING GARNISHMENT

(a) The maximum portion of the aggregate disposable earnings of a judgment debtor which are subject to continuing garnishment under this article is the lesser of:

   (i) Twenty-five percent (25%) of the judgment debtor's disposable earnings for that week; or

   (ii) The amount by which the judgment debtor's aggregate disposable earnings computed for that week exceeds thirty (30) times the federal minimum hourly wage prescribed by the Fair Labor Standards Act of 1938, 29 U.S.C. 206(a)(1), in effect at the time the earnings are payable, or, in case of earnings for any pay period other than a week, any equivalent multiple thereof prescribed by the administrator of the Wyoming Uniform Consumer Credit Code in the manner provided by W.S. 40-14-505(b)(iii).

§1-20-101. HOMESTEAD EXEMPTION; RIGHT AND AMOUNT

Every resident of the state is entitled to a homestead not exceeding twenty thousand dollars ($20,000.00) in value, exempt from execution and attachment arising from any debt, contract or civil obligation entered into or incurred.

§1-20-102. HOMESTEAD EXEMPTION; WHEN OPERATIVE

(a) The homestead is only exempt as provided in W.S. 1-20-101 while occupied as such by the owner or the person entitled thereto, or his or her family.

(b) When two (2) or more persons jointly own and occupy the same residence, each shall be entitled to the homestead exemption.

§1-20-104. HOMESTEAD EXEMPTION; COMPOSITION

The homestead may consist of a house on a lot or lots or other lands of any number of acres, or a house trailer or other movable home on a lot or lots, whether or not the house trailer or other movable home is equipped with wheels or resting upon immovable support.

§1-20-105. WEARING APPAREL

The necessary wearing apparel of every person not exceeding two thousand dollars ($2,000.00) in value, determined in the manner provided in W.S. 1-20-106 is exempt from levy or sale upon execution, writ of attachment or any process issuing out of any court in this state. Necessary wearing apparel shall not include jewelry of any type other than wedding rings.

§1-20-106. EXEMPTION OF OTHER PERSONAL PROPERTY; PERSONALTY USED IN LIVELIHOOD; APPRAISEMENT

(a) The following property, when owned by any person, is exempt from levy or sale upon execution, writ of attachment or any process issuing out of any court in this state and shall continue to be exempt while the person or the family of the person is moving from one (1) place of residence to another in this state:
(i) The family bible, pictures and school books;
(ii) A lot in any cemetery or burial ground;
(iii) Furniture, bedding, provisions and other household articles of any kind or character as the debtor may select, not exceeding in all the value of four thousand dollars ($4,000.00). When two (2) or more persons occupy the same residence, each shall be entitled to a separate exemption;
(iv) A motor vehicle not exceeding in value five thousand dollars ($5,000.00).

(b) The tools, team, implements or stock in trade of any person, used and kept for the purpose of carrying on his trade or business, not exceeding in value four thousand dollars ($4,000.00), or the library, instruments and implements of any professional person, not exceeding in value four thousand dollars ($4,000.00), are exempt from levy or sale upon execution, writ of attachment or any process out of any court in this state.

§1-20-108. EXCEPTION; RESIDENCY REQUIRED

(a) No property claimed as exempt under W.S. 1-20-101 through 1-20-106 is exempt from attachment or sale upon execution for the purchase money of the property.

(b) Any person claiming these exemptions shall be a bona fide resident of this state.

§1-20-110. EXEMPTION FOR RETIREMENT FUNDS AND ACCOUNTS

(a) The following are exempt from execution, attachment, garnishment or any other process issued by any court:

(i) Any person's interest in a retirement plan, pension or annuity, whether by way of a gratuity or otherwise, granted, paid or payable;

    (A) By any private corporation or employer to an employee or a retired employee under a plan or contract which provides that the pension or annuity shall not be assignable; or

    (B) To any city, town or county employee or retired employee who is not covered by the state retirement system, under a plan or contract which provides that the pension or annuity shall not be assignable.

(ii) Any retirement or annuity fund of any person, to the extent of payments made to the fund while solvent, but not exceeding the amount actually excluded or deducted as retirement funding for federal income tax purposes, and the appreciation thereon, the income therefrom and the benefits or annuity payable thereunder;

(iii) Any retirement or annuity fund of any person, including individual retirement accounts (IRAs) Roth individual retirement accounts (Roth IRAs) and simplified employee pension individual retirement accounts (SEP IRAs), to the extent payments are made to the fund while solvent, provided the earnings on the fund are protected from federal income tax or subject to deferral of federal income tax, or are not subject to federal income tax upon withdrawal, and the appreciation thereon, the income therefrom and the benefits or annuity payable thereunder; and

(iv) All property in this state of the judgment debtor where the judgment is in favor of any state or any political subdivision of any state for failure to pay that state's or political subdivision's income tax on benefits received from a pension or other retirement plan. This paragraph shall apply only to judgments obtained after the judgment debtor has established residency in Wyoming and has been domiciled in Wyoming for at least one hundred eighty (180) days.

§26-15-129. EXEMPTION OF PROCEEDS; LIFE INSURANCE

(a) If a policy of insurance is executed by any person on his own life or on another life, in favor of a person other than himself, or except in cases of transfer with intent to defraud creditors, if a policy of life insurance is assigned or in any way made payable to that person, the lawful beneficiary or assignee thereof, other than the insured or the person executing insurance or executors or administrators of such insured or the person executing the insurance, are entitled to its proceeds, including death benefits, cash surrender and loan values, premiums waived and dividends, whether used in reduction of premiums or otherwise, excepting only where the debtor, subsequent to issuance of the policy, has actually elected to receive the dividends in cash, against the creditors and representatives of the insured and of the person executing the policy, and are not liable to be applied by any legal or equitable process to pay any debt or liability of the insured individual or his beneficiary or of any other person having a right under the policy, whether or not:

(i) The right to change the beneficiary is reserved or permitted; and

(ii) The policy is made payable to the person whose life is insured if the beneficiary or assignee predeceases that person, and the proceeds are exempt from all liability for any debt of the beneficiary existing at the time the policy is made available for his use.

(b) However, subject to the statute of limitations, the amount of any premiums paid for insurance with intent to defraud creditors, with interest thereon shall inure to their benefit from the policy proceeds. . . .

§26-15-132. SAME; ANNUITY CONTRACTS; ASSIGNABILITY OF RIGHTS

(a) The benefits, rights, privileges and options which under any annuity contract issued are due or prospectively due the annuitant, are not subject to execution nor is the annuitant compelled to exercise any such rights, powers or options. Creditors are not allowed to interfere with or terminate the contract, except:

(i) As to amounts paid for or as premium on the annuity with intent to defraud creditors with interest thereon, and of which the creditor gives the insurer written notice at its home office prior to the making of the payment to the annuitant out of which the creditor seeks to recover, which notice shall specify:

(A) The amount claimed or facts to enable the ascertainment of the amount; and

(B) Facts to enable the insurer to ascertain the annuity contract, the annuitant and the payment sought to be avoided on the ground of fraud.

(ii) The total exemption of benefits presently due and payable to any annuitant periodically or at stated times under all annuity contracts under which he is an annuitant shall not at any time exceed three hundred fifty dollars ($350.00) per month for the length of time represented by the installments, and any periodic payments in excess of three hundred fifty dollars ($350.00) per month are subject to garnishee execution to the same extent as are wages and salaries;

(iii) If the total benefits presently due and payable to any annuitant under any annuity contracts at any time exceed three hundred fifty dollars ($350.00) per month, the court may order the annuitant to pay to a judgment creditor or apply on the judgment, in installments, that portion of the excess benefits as to the court appear just and proper, after regard for the reasonable requirements of the judgment debtor and his family, if dependent upon him, as well as any payments required to be made by the annuitant to other creditors under prior court order.

(b) If the contract provides, the benefits, rights, privileges or options accruing under that contract to a beneficiary or assignee are not transferable nor subject to commutation, and if the benefits are payable periodically or at stated times, the same exemptions and exceptions contained in this section for the annuitant, apply to the beneficiary or assignee.

The opt-out provision offers yet another place for irony. Texas, with its generous exemptions, did not opt out, leaving a Texan free to choose between an unlimited homestead and $30,000 in value in other property or a federal homestead exemption of $22,975 and about $20,000 or so in other property under the Code. §522(d). While Texas lets its citizens choose between federal and state exemptions, Wyoming says no. Wyoming opted out.

A number of states have bifurcated their exemptions by giving debtors struggling in the state court system one set of exemptions but by having another set of exemptions for those who have filed bankruptcy. Among the states enacting these various "bankruptcy-specific" exemptions are Delaware, Georgia, Indiana, Iowa, Kentucky, Michigan, New York, Ohio, and West Virginia. In some of these states, the bankrupt debtor will be limited to smaller exemptions than the generally applicable state exemptions, and in some cases a bankruptcy filing will entitle the debtor to greater values of property or more kinds of property.

Changing exemptions when a debtor files bankruptcy might mean that the state has impermissibly encroached on the federal bankruptcy power, on the theory that the Code allows for opt-out *vel non*. The contrary position is the greater federal power conferring the opt-out decision to the states surely includes the lesser power of "limited opt-out," which is what a bankruptcy-specific exemption really is. There is a sharp split among the federal courts on this question. See, e.g., In re Schafer, 455 B.R. 590 (BAP 6th Cir. 2011) (reviewing split in holding Michigan provision unconstitutional under the Bankruptcy Clause), *rev'd* 689 F.3d 601 (2012) (upholding statute but implying as one basis the fact that the bankruptcy-specific exemptions were more generous than the general state ones).

All states (and the federal government) must wrestle with the same set of issues about what a debtor can keep and what a creditor can demand that the debtor give up to satisfy unpaid debts. It is unsurprising that exemption amounts may range from non-existent to unlimited. The policy questions can be sliced razor-thin. For example, some states have age-contingent exemptions that allow senior debtors to exempt more than others; others have proposed treating debtors with certain causes of financial distress (e.g., medical problems) more generously. See John A.E. Pottow, The Rise in Elder Bankruptcy Filings and the Failure of U.S. Bankruptcy Law, 19 Elder L. J. 119, 155 (2011) (canvassing existent laws and proposals).

Nowhere are these disparities more evident (or hotly debated) than with homesteads. The Texas statute cited above limits a homestead in terms of acreage. So long as the home is on less than ten acres in a city or 200 acres in the country, the debtor is entitled to exempt that property from attachment, regardless of its dollar value. Near the other end of the spectrum is Wyoming, which limits the homestead exemption to $40,000 for a married couple and only $20,000 for a single person.

Homestead exemptions are the sorts of laws likely to be important only for the subset of debtors who (a) own homes, and (b) have enough equity in their homes to have exemptible amounts. But the flipside is they are likely to be *very* important to those debtors; homestead equity is precisely what gets wiped out (more accurately, transferred from the debtor to the creditor) in foreclosure sale where the winning bid is the foreclosing creditor's exact mortgage amount and not a cent more. Other exemption types carry a similarly disproportionate punch. An office worker with no tools of the trade couldn't care less about that exemption category, but a plumber trying to make a living depends on it—and the cap may look very low. Can laws be updated rapidly enough to reflect changing market conditions? A casual stroll through exemption laws reveals more protections for church pews than for smart phones.

2. *Federal Exemptions*

The federal exemptions range from crime reparation payments to unmatured life insurance policies. To the extent that exemptions are limited to specific dollar amounts, such as the $3,675 exemption in a car, those amounts are adjusted every three years for inflation. §104(b). In its most recent amendments, Congress expanded the federal exemption for retirement funds and flexed a bit of Supremacy Clause might (perhaps in response to the rise of bankruptcy-specific state exemptions), protecting retirement funds *regardless* whether the debtor lives in an opt-out state. §522(b)(3)(C), (d)(12). In fact, it took most retirement funds out of the estate altogether, adding a belt to the suspenders, §541(b)(7), or possibly even another set of pants to the belt and suspenders given that many pension plans are already structured as trusts. §541(c). Phew for the generous pension plan enjoyed by members of Congress, we suppose, but little comfort to the median (and modal) debtor in our empirical studies, whose pension assets upon filing are *zero*.

As generous as they are, the Texas exemptions add no special protection for renters to match the protection available to homeowners. By comparison, section 522(d) gives a special boost to renters. Anyone who does not claim a homestead exemption under (d)(1) is permitted to claim about half the value of the unclaimed homestead exemption in any property at all under (d)(5). Why half? It looks like another atheoretical but pragmatic compromise—halfway between those who believe only homes should be protected and those who believe renters should have the same chance to protect value, whether it is in a home or checking account.

Recall that both Texas and Wyoming, like most states, make the exemption laws unavailable to debtors being pursued for various domestic support obligations and liens. There are other "exceptions from exemptions" (try saying that phrase five times quickly). The big, federal elephant in the room—a stampeding, angry elephant—is the IRS. Nothing precludes Congress from preempting state exemption laws (subject to the Due Process Clause), and it has done so with federal tax collection statutes. If you don't pay your federal taxes in Texas, the IRS comes after your home, and nothing in Texas law can stop it—all the more reason to secede.

C. CLASSIFICATION OF PROPERTY

Because exemption statutes are often written to exempt only listed types of property, disputes between debtors and creditors frequently center on classification issues. Debtors argue that the property they intend to keep fits within the statutory classifications, and judgment creditors argue the reverse. Ironically, federal bankruptcy judges are thus often called upon to determine the meaning of state exemption laws more frequently than state judges themselves.

———— **In re JOHNSON** ————

14 B.R. 14 (Bankr. W.D. Ky. 1981)

DEITZ, Bankruptcy Judge.

Is a bus a bus, or is it a car? Reluctantly we conclude that it is a car. Bankruptcy petitioner, Theodore Roosevelt Johnson, Sr., has claimed as exempt his 1969 Dodge bus. The bus has a seating capacity of 60 passengers. Upon it are occasionally transported members of Johnson's church congregation.

The trustee vehemently objects. He points to the state exemption statute, KRS 427.010, which in pertinent part permits the exemption of "one motor vehicle and its necessary accessories, including one spare tire, not exceeding $2,500 in value. . . ."

The trustee patiently explains that the legislature intended the term "motor vehicle" to be synonymous with "automobile."

Enacted in 1980, the statute excluded earlier statutory limits upon the *uses* to which a motor vehicle might be put, so we must cast altogether aside the trustee's concern with the voluminous seating capacity of the behemoth. The record is silent on the size of the petitioner's family and their transportation needs.

Is a Moped a motor vehicle? What would the licensing arm of the state Department of Transportation say to the contention that a bus is not a motor vehicle? What would Gertrude Stein have to say about what a motor vehicle is?

Such rhetorical questions having been considered, we are bold to say that a bus is a motor vehicle.

In our dialectic, during this era of motorized evolution, we are inclined to regard the "bus" and the "automobile" as species of the genus, "motor vehicle."

This Bankruptcy Court is answerable to an appellate forum of literal bent. That is good, for it gives us guidance and certainty in ascribing to the legislature the ability to express its intent in clear, simple, precise English.

As this trustee will recall, District Judge Thomas Ballantine, in reviewing a decision of this court, recently held that a statutory 15-day limitation upon the recording of chattel mortgages imposed a recording limitation *not* of indeterminate length, as was contended, but a limitation of 15 days.

Guided by that clarity of perception, we find with conviction that a motor vehicle is a motor vehicle, and not necessarily an automobile. We expressly reserve, until it is properly presented, any consideration of the reverse proposition that an automobile is neither a bus nor a motor vehicle.

Abundantly confident that this opinion will find its way alongside Marbury v. Madison and McCulloch v. Maryland in the lasting library of legal logic, it is hereby ordered that Theodore Roosevelt Johnson, Sr., is entitled to the claimed exemption, and the trustee shall comport his activities accordingly in administration of the estate.

===================

The only near competitor to *Johnson* as our favorite classification case is In re Hall, 169 B.R. 732 (Bankr. N.D. Okla. 1994), in which the court rejected the debtor's claim that a tractor-lawnmower is "household furniture" in Oklahoma. One of us was surprised.

The fun in this area is ample; disputes such as the one below show the active controversy over exemptions.

———————— **In re WILKINSON, [M.D.]** ————————
402 B.R. 756 (Bankr. W.D. Texas 2009)

CLARK, Bankruptcy Judge. The debtors claimed an exemption in firearms. The Trustee objected. This decision explains why the court sustains the objection to exemption.

Factual and Procedural Background

On August 26, 2008, the debtors filed amended schedules in which they claimed state law exemptions in the following items:

- MP .45 rifle, .380 pistol, two .22 caliber pistols, .30–.30 rifle and a .45 caliber pistol (collectively, the "Firearms") under Texas Property Code §§42.001(a), 42.002(a)(8) (sporting goods and equipment).

- 17 antique handguns and 1 dummy gun (the "Collection") under Texas Property Code §§42.001(a), 42.002(a)(1) (home furnishings, including heirlooms).

On November 5, 2008, the chapter 7 trustee (the "Trustee") filed an objection to the debtors' claim of exemption to the Firearms and the Collection [Docket No. 184]. The Trustee argues that, pursuant to Texas Property Code §42.002(7), "[t]he Debtors must select only two firearms eligible for exemption." . . .

After the Objection was filed, on November 14, 2008, the debtors amended Schedule C [Docket No. 196], so that they now claim as exempt the following firearms:

- a Sharps cavalry carbine circa 1863; a Sharps new model rifle, .52 caliber C. 1860; a Spencer repeating rifle, .52 caliber C. 1860; an English Blunderbuss saddle gun, silver, c. 1845; a Burnside cavalry carbine, c. 1863; an English blunderbuss, flintlock, with bayonet; and an English blunderbuss, flintlock, c. 1750.

. . .

The debtors assert that those Guns that are not replicas saw action in wars that took place prior to 1898 and are each "affixed to a wooden plaque bearing a brass plate which describes the weapon . . . [and] adorn the walls of the Debtors' rural home." Response, ¶ 15 at 4. Due to the age of the Guns, the debtors argue, they are no longer considered firearms under the Texas Property Code. Although the debtors cannot point to any specific provision of the Texas Property Code to support this contention (since none exists), the debtors rely by analogy on §46.01 of the Texas Penal Code, which criminalizes possession of a firearm by certain persons (felons). That statute excludes from its definition of "firearm" any gun that is "(A) an antique or curio firearm manufactured before 1899." . . . [T] the debtors argue that the court should overrule the Trustee's objection to the debtors' exemption claim with respect to the Guns and allow the debtors to claim them as exempt home furnishings under §42.002(a)(1) of the Texas Property Code.

. . .

In the context of both statutes' use of the term "firearm," the Texas Property Code and the Texas Penal Code do not have a similar object or purpose. One governs the relationship between debtors and creditors, limiting the latters' rights in order to assure debtors are permitted to keep a certain modicum of property regardless of how much they owe their creditors. Firearms happen to be one of a number of specifically described items or categories of property deemed to be appropriate for debtors in this state to have, free of the demands of their creditors. The Penal Code, meanwhile criminalizes ownership of certain types of firearms by certain kinds of individuals in Texas, to wit, convicted felons, in the interests of protecting the peace and safety of the rest of the citizenry of Texas. One statute focuses on what all Texans should be allowed to keep (at least relative to the claims of their creditors),[1] while the other statute focuses on what certain Texans (convicted felons) are not allowed to keep, for reasons having nothing to do with their creditors. One statute regulates commercial activity. One is a health and safety regulation.

---

1. Here is how this court described the function and purpose of Texas' exemption law in an earlier opinion:
   [E]xemptions represent a statement of public policy regarding what the citizens of this state believe all persons are entitled to retain, no matter how much they might owe to their creditors. Some exemptions are preserved primarily because they truly are necessary to the very survival of the family as an independent economic unit not on the public dole. Others, such as jewelry, are allowed not so much to assure mere survival as to assure survival with a modicum of dignity. . . . The purpose underlying exemption legislation is securing to the unfortunate debtor the means to support himself and his family, the protection of the family being the main consideration.

. . .

Thus, whether a convicted felon may carry an antique firearm—apparently deemed by the legislature not to be a threat to public safety due to its age—does not have much to do at all with whether a creditor may reach that same antique gun for purposes of getting repaid. It is certainly not a threat to public safety for a debtor to repay his debts by the sale of an antique gun.

. . .

The Texas Property Code

Up to a cap of $60,000 per family, or $30,000 per single person, the current iteration of the Texas Property Code allows a debtor to exempt certain categories of personal property from the reach of creditors, including two firearms. Another permitted category of personal property available for exemption is "home furnishings, including family heirlooms." Because the Texas Property Code does not define "firearm," the court must look to other interpretive aids, the first of which is to consult the term's ordinary meaning.

Black's Law Dictionary says that a firearm is "[a] weapon that expels a projectile (such as a bullet or pellets) by the combustion of gunpowder or other explosive." BLACK'S LAW DICTIONARY 666 (8th Ed.2004). . . .

One way to test a word's meaning is to examine how it is ordinarily used. In that regard, common usage gives a word meaning when it can be said that one person using a given word will be easily understood to mean the same thing as the user intended the word to convey. See Ludwig Wittgenstein, Philosophical Investigations, at 43 (G.E.M. Anscombe, transl.) (Oxford Press 1953) ("[T]he meaning of a word is its use in the language."). In ordinary usage, the fact that a firearm or gun is antique would not preclude one from referring to it as a firearm. One visiting the Wilkinsons' home could well comment, "[T]hat's a very nice firearm you have mounted up there on the wall," and no one would wonder what he or she was talking about. By the same token, one would be surprised if, in response to the query, "[W]hat's that firearm[?]" Wilkinson were to reply, "[T]hat's not a firearm, that's a home furnishing."

. . .

Even if the term were thought to be ambiguous, however, the court would still arrive at the same conclusion regarding its intended scope in the Texas Property Code. Although Texas, as early as 1866, listed specific items of personal property as qualified for exemption, guns or firearms did not specifically show up on the list until the Act of 1870, at which point "one gun" was, for the first time, explicitly protected from forced sale for debts. Acts 1870, 12th Leg., p.127,

Ch. LXXVI, §2 reprinted in TEX.REV.CIV. STAT. ANN., art. 2335 (repealed) (1879). It is no stretch to believe that guns were vital to a Texan's survival in 1870, perhaps explaining their being included on the list of property qualified for exemption. The court was unable to locate either legislative reports or testimony to glean the legislature's intent in exempting a gun in 1870, but a Texas Supreme Court case from 1857 perhaps sheds some light on what might have been on the Legislature's mind just over a decade later. In *Choate v. Redding*, 18 Tex. 579 (1857), the Texas Supreme Court rather reluctantly denied a debtor's request that his rifle gun be exempt from his creditor's reach. . . . The court lamented that it was "extraordinary" that there was not a Texas statute exempting the gun from execution. The court colorfully explained its frustration thusly:

> It has been comparatively but a few years since the first settlements of Americans were made in Texas. The whole country was then infested by savages. Subsequently there were hostilities with Mexicans, and the frontiers are still exposed to the incursions of Indians. The country has been settled, and still is settling, by, in a great measure, force of arms. The people of Texas are now, and ever have been, emphatically an armed population.

Id. at 581. [The more we change, the more we stay the same? —Eds.] The court added that the right to bear arms was protected in both the Constitutions of the United States and Texas for the purpose of securing a free state through a well-armed militia. (Indeed, the court dryly observed that, if militia laws were enforced, were a man to show up to the "muster ground" without his gun, he could be fined). Said the court—with evident chagrin—although "the right to keep and bear arms cannot be infringed by legislation, yet, strange as it may be, it must succumb to the power of a creditor." *Id.* Based upon the court's analysis, it would not be a stretch to infer that the Texas Legislature, in adding "one gun" to the list of personal property eligible for exemption . . . to provide Texans with the ability to defend their home[s] and provide for their family, and perhaps to be able, regardless their financial circumstances, to answer the call to arms should the militia be called up.[2]

. . .

Obviously, by 1973, Texas was no longer the frontier it had been when the Texas Supreme Court discussed the vital role guns played in everyday life in 1857. . . . However, "the [gun] exemption survived . . . [as] a witness to the Texas ethos that still cherishes the frontier spirit, and celebrates it every hunting

---

2. This early authority also suggests that the only firearms that it made sense for a debtor to even claim as exempt were working firearms—creditors could have the firearms that didn't work, as they would be of no use against "savages" or in the Texas Militia.

season." In re Schwarzbach, 1989 WL 360742, at *4. In fact, because in 1973 the statute required that personal property be reasonably necessary to the debtor, the specific allowance of two guns could be read as a nod to "[t]he typical hunter serious about his or her sport [since he or she] will have a shotgun for birds and a rifle for other game." *Id.* As it turned out, the debtor in *Schwarzbach*, an avid hunter, was not allowed to exempt more than two of his guns, on the theory that the additional guns could qualify as athletic and sporting equipment.

. . .

As this court stated in In re Mitchell, 103 B.R. 819, 823 (Bankr. W.D. Tex. 1989), the Texas Property Code, subject to the cap in §42.001(a), provides Texans with an explicit, approved list of items that the legislature has decided debtors should be allowed to keep regardless of what they owe their creditors. "Exemptions are in fact a limit on a creditor's right to satisfaction of its claim out of the debtor's assets. The limitations are imposed for reasons of public policy. There is no public policy served in preserving the lifestyles of the rich and bankrupt." *Id.* at n.7 (emphasis original).

═══════════════

Doctor Wilkinson might be a stereotypical "rich and bankrupt" debtor given his valuable collection of antiques (most other debtors' older property would carry less flattering labels), but he had a colorable argument based on the statute that his collection fit within the exemption. This raises the serious question of the importance of classifying property. Is fighting over whether a Texan's thirteenth cow is a pet (or heirloom, or provision for consumption, or [future] wearing apparel) the absurd but inescapable consequence of laws based on categories? If so, should the approach be jettisoned? And if not, how flexibly should courts read these statutes that are likely designed with a "typical" family in mind? If there is ambiguity, do lenity concerns suggest ties should go to the debtor? See A. Mechele Dickerson, Race Matters in Bankruptcy Reform, 71 Mo. L. Rev. 919 (2006).

D. VALUATION OF EXEMPT PROPERTY

In addition to determining whether property claimed as exempt fits within the allowed categories, it is often necessary to determine whether the property has a value below any statutory cap as well.

─────── **In re SUMERELL** ───────
194 B.R. 818 (Bankr. E.D. Tenn. 1996)

PARSONS, Bankruptcy Judge.

This case is presently before the court upon the objection filed by Wachovia Bank of South Carolina ("Wachovia") to the debtors' claim of exemptions in certain personal property owned by them. Wachovia alleges that the exemptions should be denied because the debtors have substantially undervalued their property. . . . For the reasons set forth below, the court will sustain the objection with respect to the majority of the exemptions claimed by the debtor, the court having concluded that the debtors have incorrectly valued their household property at liquidation value.

This joint chapter 7 case was filed by the debtors, husband and wife, on May 18, 1995. Along with the filing of the petition, the debtors filed their required schedules and statements, including Schedule B, the List of Personal Property and Schedule C, the List of Property Claimed As Exempt. Schedule B indicated that as of May 18, 1995, the debtors had an interest in the following personal property:

TYPE OF PROPERTY	CURRENT MARKET VALUE OF DEBTORS' INTEREST
Cash on hand	$60.00
Checking accounts	$427.94
Various household goods and furnishings [this listing was itemized]	$2,135.00
Clothing	$200.00
Jewelry [with separate appraisal list]	$2,165.00
Mink stole, fox full length mink, and 8 place settings of silverware	$1,700.00
Three firearms	$50.00
Office equipment (desk, three chairs and table)	$50.00
Air conditioning unit (Fully secured)	$15,000.00
IBM AT personal computer, typewriter, P51 computer with printer, non-running riding mower, washer and dryer, VCR, wicker sofa, three chairs, coffee table and aluminum patio furniture	$435.00
TOTAL	$21,841.00

All of the items of [unencumbered] personal property set forth on Schedule B were restated and claimed as exempt on Schedule C pursuant to the $4,000.00 personal property exemption for individuals, the exemption for reasonable and necessary wearing apparel, or the $750.00 exemption for tools of the trade. The debtors subsequently amended both Schedules B and C to add an additional checking account with a balance of $381.94, golf clubs valued at $125.00 and two dolls valued together at $35.00.

. . .

The court will first address Wachovia's assertion that the debtors have substantially undervalued their assets. Specifically, Wachovia alleges that the household goods and furnishings listed in Schedules B and C as having a collective value of $2,135.00, actually have a fair market value of $27,405.00 based on the appraisal conducted by Wachovia's expert. The wide disparity between the two amounts is attributable in part to the fact that different valuation methods were applied by the parties. The values set forth in the schedules were based on the debtors' opinion of the furnishings' "liquidation value," while the value asserted by Wachovia is said to be based on "fair market value," as that term is generally understood.

Testifying at trial as to value was Wachovia's expert, Kimball Sterling, a Johnson City appraiser and auctioneer, the debtors' expert, Rex Davis, and debtor Amy Sumerell. Mr. Sterling stated that he was in the business of evaluating and selling used furniture, antiques, and entire contents of homes and had done so for numerous years. He testified that he frequently testifies as an expert appraiser and has handled numerous estate auctions including that of the late Alex Haley, the noted Pulitzer Prize winner. Based on his examination of the debtors' household furnishings, Mr. Sterling concluded that the collective fair market value of the furnishings, within ten percent, was $27,405.00. Mr. Sterling testified that he based this amount on what he thought he could sell the items for at an auction with three weeks advertising, and was so confident that he could obtain this price at auction that he was willing to immediately purchase all of the items included in the appraisal for $19,700.00.

Rex Davis, the debtors' expert, testified that he was in the retail furniture business, having worked for retail furniture stores for the past 32 years, with primary responsibility as vice-president and general manager for the stores' purchases. In this capacity, Mr. Davis had also bought, sold and traded used furniture and within the past week, had been involved in attempts to sell bankruptcy estate furniture. Mr. Davis testified that he had inspected the debtors' household furnishings, that the majority of the furniture was in the medium price range and that the total value of the furniture from a retail or a manufacturers' suggested retail standpoint was $19,850.00. He opined that if the furniture were liquidated over a quick period of time, "you'd be lucky to get 20¢ on the dollar which would be approximately $3,900.00," and when asked if he thought this was a "fair market value" for used furniture, responded that it was "for used furniture and being able to dispose of it pretty quick. I really can't say that you could expect much more than that." On cross-examination when asked his opinion as to the "true value" of the furniture, Mr. Davis testified that he thought the furniture would be worth around 20¢ on the dollar on a quick sale.

. . .

[T]he debtors concede that fair market value is the appropriate standard, appropriately noting that the Sixth Circuit Court of Appeals, albeit in dicta, has endorsed the fair market value standard. The debtors note, however, that §522 does not further define the phrase "fair market value" and gives no guidance as to how it should be determined. The debtors assert that there is a split of authority between the different jurisdictions as to the definition of fair market value and maintain that the phrase should be interpreted in a liquidation context, citing *In re Walsh*, 5 B.R. 239 (Bankr. D.C. 1980).

. . .

. . . *Walsh* was urging that the applicable market when one speaks of fair market value is the market available to a bankruptcy trustee and that the values generated in that market will reflect the sales circumstances by being somewhat depressed. [In joining the majority of courts in rejecting this stance, one explained:]

> There are a number of difficulties with this position, however. The argument is essentially circular and turns the generally accepted definition of fair market value on its ear. An essential component of fair market valuation is a reasonable holding period, the antithesis of Walsh's "liquidation" market. . . .
>
> There should simply be no such thing as a "bankruptcy market" when it comes to fair market value, especially insofar as the holding period is concerned. The directive to find fair market value compels the fact finder to act as though there were no bankruptcy. . . . [F]air market value must, by definition, be computed as if there were no proceedings to eliminate that market.

This court is persuaded by the reasoning and the analysis of [the majority cases] and specifically rejects *Walsh*.

. . .

The debtors make the further argument that in determining fair market value, there must be a reduction for hypothetical costs of sale. Mr. Sterling testified that if he were to auction the debtors' household goods and furnishings, his costs would run anywhere from 14% to 35% depending on the size and location of the sale and the requirements of the seller, with his average cost about 25% of the gross sales. The debtors argue that any fair market value determined by this court should be reduced not only by such costs of sale, but also sales tax and a trustee's statutory commission, asserting that the estate would not realize these sums if the subject property were liquidated.

Again, the debtors are inappropriately applying liquidation considerations to a non-liquidation valuation. As stated above, the amount the estate would receive in a hypothetical liquidation is not the appropriate standard for determining fair market value for exemption purposes. By definition, in claiming property as exempt, a debtor is proposing that he or she be allowed to retain the property rather than have the property liquidated.

. . .

The court found Mr. Sterling extremely knowledgeable and credible regarding the current market for antique reproductions, used furniture, antiques and collectibles such as that owned by the debtors. Mr. Sterling's confidence as to his valuation of the debtors' goods was exemplified by his offer to immediately purchase the appraised items for $19,700.00. This testimony was extremely persuasive as to value, as it is obvious that someone in Mr. Sterling's line of work would not make such an offer without the expectation that the items can be resold at a significant profit. Accordingly, with the exceptions discussed below, this court concludes that the fair market value of the items appraised by Mr. Sterling are the values listed by him in his appraisal wherein he sets forth with detail each item appraised by him and its value.

. . .

In conclusion, the debtors are directed to file a new Schedule C setting forth their exemption claims in accordance with the rulings of the court set forth in this memorandum.

The court was surely engaged in understatement when it said that Sterling's offer to purchase the property was "extremely persuasive" of value: isn't in fact the *definition* of "value" what an arm's-length party is willing to pay?

Oftentimes there is no Sterling offer, and so courts have to decide these questions based on whose expert is more persuasive, which may be a poor, second-best methodology, although it's still the second-best. This case also suggests that liquidation is not a good measure of the value of property claimed as exempt because anticipating what creditors would get from sale of the property is not the point of value limitations in exemptions. If not, what is the point?

E. PROCEEDS AND TRACING

Exemptions are typically by category of property—wages, tools of the trade, motor vehicles, etc.—but property is not static in nature. Wages may be deposited in checking accounts, and checking accounts may be withdrawn as cash on hand. Property may be sold, and contract obligations may be satisfied. Whenever the form of property changes, issues arise about *proceeds*—that is, whether the property's "former" or "current" state is relevant for exemption purposes. For example, states that do not exempt bank accounts differ as to the status of a bank account that consists of a debtor's exempt wages, with some saying the account retains the exemption of the wages while others do not. Although social security payments are exempt under federal nonbankruptcy law, courts have divided as to their exempt status after deposit in a bank account. The split has been resolved by a federal regulation that protects recently deposited social security payments. 31 CFR 212.

All these rules raise the possibility of "exemption planning" by the clever, discussed in the next assignment, but there are equally pitfalls for the less clever. For example, in a feat of financial planning that may give some clue as to why he ended up in bankruptcy, Kenneth Dasher cashed out every last nickel in his exempt retirement account to buy a non-exempt pick-up truck. In re Dasher, 2002 U.S. Dist. Lexis 10563 (Neb. 2002). His schedules claimed his new pick-up as exempt, pointing out that it was just his retirement account invested in a tangible portfolio. The court said no, carefully distinguishing "retirement account" from "pick-up truck." If Mr. Dasher had just waited to cash in his retirement account until after his bankruptcy case was closed a few weeks later, presumably he would have discharged his debts and owned the pick-up outright instead of losing it to the trustee. But sometimes a man can't wait.

F. PARTIALLY EXEMPT PROPERTY

If there is a dollar limit on an exempt category, does property of a greater value cease to be exempt? Yes and no. We call this property "partially exempt," and in most cases the property can be levied on and sold. The exemption does attach, up to its dollar limit, but to the net proceeds after sheriff sale, rather than the property itself. If there are extra proceeds after the debtor's exemption has been paid off, they go to the seizing judgment creditor (at state law) or the trustee (in bankruptcy). A few examples help illustrate. A debtor in a state with a $1,000 automobile exemption who owns a car, free and clear of any liens, worth $800 will be able to protect that car from creditor attachment, period. Another debtor who owns a car worth $2,800 free and clear in the same state will be subject to having the car sold for the benefit of creditors. If a creditor is owed $3,000, the car brings its full $2,800 at sale, and there are $100 in sales costs, the proceeds will go as follows: Sale costs, $100; Debtor, $1,000; Creditor, $1,700. Once again, the importance of valuation is apparent, and here most strikingly; it makes or breaks the difference between the debtor keeping the exempt property on the one hand and having it involuntarily sold on the other (with the consolation prize of a portion of the proceeds equaling the exemption amount). Thus property may have a "retention value" for the debtor beyond its market value or the exemption amount.

G. SECURITY INTERESTS IN EXEMPT PROPERTY

When exempt property is encumbered by a valid security interest, the secured party moves ahead of both the debtor and the levying creditor (at state law) and the trustee (in bankruptcy). If the car mentioned above were worth $1,000, but the secured creditor's debt was for $2,000, the secured party would take the car, and the state's $1,000 exemption would be irrelevant. The debtor would have no equity in the car to claim as exempt. In bankruptcy, the car is thus useless to the trustee, although as Nissan learned the hard way in the case reproduced in Assignment 3, the car is still property of the estate until the trustee abandons it. §554.

If the car were worth $3,000, however, then the car would be sold, sale expenses paid, and the secured party would take the first $2,000 of the net proceeds (the full amount of its debt); the debtor would receive the remaining money under the exemption. Only when the value of the car is so great that it exceeds the sum of the sales costs, the secured creditor's debt, and the debtor's exemption would the trustee in bankruptcy (or levying creditor at state law) get any money. Many otherwise exemptible consumer items subject to liens, especially PMSIs, are abandoned by bankruptcy trustees for this very reason. Their bankruptcy sale value is dwarfed either by liens or by the costs of sale. Sometimes debtors move to compel abandonment to clarify that property will not be sold by a trustee; other times trustees are eager to abandon property.

H. AVOIDING JUDICIAL LIENS AND NON-PMSI LIENS

In addition to exemptions, Congress fashioned another protection to improve the economic position of debtors after bankruptcy. Section 522(f)(1) permits the avoidance of certain kinds of liens on certain categories of exempt property. Two kinds of liens are made avoidable: *judicial* liens, which are liens imposed by a court after a judgment has been rendered, property has been levied, and a defendant has not paid, section (f)(1)(A), and "*nonpossessory, nonpurchase-money*" consensual security interests in certain consumer goods, section (f)(1)(B). This cumbersome second category refers to non-PMSI liens, i.e., loans made on the debtor's existing consumer goods. It also excludes pawnbrokers, whose security interests, while non-PMSI, are still possessory (they hold physical possession of the collateral). A nonpossessory, nonpurchase-money loan would be when a debtor pledges a car as collateral for a title loan. Section (f)(1)(B) only covers low-ticket exemptions, like household furniture and clothes. The statute contains some very specific restrictions, which was drafted at a time when VCRs were of interest as collateral. §522(f)(4)(vi).

Lien avoidance on the denominated exempt property allows the debtor to "reclaim" an exemption by bumping the lienholder back into the general unsecured creditor pile to the extent the lien impedes the exemption. With judicial liens, this is not a big deal; federal law can invalidate or trump judicial liens under the Supremacy Clause and Bankruptcy Clause. The lien avoidance power of consensually granted security interests is more controversial. After all, the liens at issue are security interests, in which the debtor fully and freely waived exemptions. So why the freebie in bankruptcy on this property? Congress reviewed several studies documenting creditors' practices of taking security interests in all of a debtor's clothing, in children's toys, in family photographs, etc. Critics pointed out that these security interests were not taken to provide alternative resources to satisfy the loan if the debtor should become unable to pay. (Do you buy used underwear from the sheriff? *But cf.* Bernie Madoff Auction (£120 for 14 pairs of boxers).) Instead, the security interests were taken for their "hostage value" the likelihood that threatened repossession would cause the debtor to make any sacrifice to find a way to pay and keep the property. Section (f)(1)(B) was adopted in 1978 to defeat these practices. The FTC soon followed suit by imposing similar restraints on creditors outside bankruptcy, making it an unfair practice for a company to take a nonpossessory, nonpurchase-money security interest in certain listed goods. FTC Trade Regulation Rule on Credit Practices, 16 C.F.R. §444.1 (1985). The rule was adopted in part to limit consumers from needing to file bankruptcy solely to guard against these non-possessory, non-PMSI security interests in household goods and the like.

Can Congress just rub consensual liens off property? Isn't that an unconstitutional taking? Six justices of the Supreme Court opined in dictum yes, while three believed no, but the majority used the avoidance doctrine to duck the question by interpreting §522(f) to apply prospectively—only to security interests created after its enactment, which everyone agreed was fine. United States v. Security Indus. Bank, 459 U.S. 70 (1982). The larger point—to what extent can Congress use the bankruptcy power to affect established property rights—has arisen many times. For example, it is said that Congress has considerable power to displace otherwise enforceable "contract rights," but not to deprive persons of "property" under the Fifth Amendment. That can be a very tenuous distinction to maintain. In many contexts, such as enforcement of security agreements in accounts receivable under Article 9 of the UCC, "contract rights" are treated as property. See generally Frank I. Michelman, Property,

Utility and Fairness: Comments on the Ethical Foundations of "Just Compensation" Law, 80 Harv. L. Rev. 1165 (1967).

Perhaps in response to the *Security Bank* opinion, or a concern that §522(f)(1)(B) was frustrating the expectations of the "high-yield" lending market, Congress passed §522(f)(3). It seems to say that if the debtor takes the state-law exemptions in an opt-out state (or one that allows the debtor to waive the federal exemptions, a power we think is likely either redundant or unconstitutional) *and* those exemptions are *either* really generous (unlimited in amount) *or* really strict (cannot be invalidated under state law), then for a *limited subset* of otherwise lien-erasable property, the debtor may not strip off *at least part* of the lien under (f)(1)(B). For fun, see if you can figure it out. If you can, please tell us. (Perhaps this is the note topic you've been searching for!) In parsing the statute, do be sure to give full effect to the plain meaning, and if that doesn't help, just try to further the goal Congress was trying to achieve with the provision, which is, umm, let us get back to you.

Problem Set 4

4.1. Harv and Lois Hughes live in an apartment in Houston, Texas. They are unable to pay several of their debts and are worried about which of their assets may be vulnerable to creditor attachment. Their largest creditor is their credit union, to whom they owe about $5,000. They list their assets as follows:

Item	Value
Household furniture and appliances	$8,000
Clothing	$2,000
Lois's law books	$2,400
Lois's Moped	$800
Harv's 1970 convertible (left over from high school, now up on blocks)	$500
Cash value on Lois's insurance	$2,000
Lois's wedding ring	$1,000
Lois's computer	$1,200
100 shares Disney Co. (Lois's dad knew Walt)	$5,000
Joint checking account	$400
Harv's customized computer set-up	$7,500
1804 French one-pounder cannon	$6,000
Harv's motorized wheelchair	$18,000
Fluffy (Persian cat, nasty temper but very beautiful)	$200

Soccer ball	$2
Anticipated tax refund (estimated to arrive in three weeks)	$1,000

Harv, who is a computer programmer, was injured last year when his car was struck by a train. He has been rated at a 40 percent disability as a result. His lawyer says he can likely settle with the railroad for about $250,000. (There were some serious contributory negligence issues.) Both are very reluctant to file for bankruptcy. Absent bankruptcy, what can Harv and Lois protect as the creditors begin to move in? What if they filed a chapter 7? What could they protect if they lived in Cheyenne, Wyoming?

4.2. Harv's cousin, Suzan Hughes Berttus, ran away from home at seventeen, married the partner of the Dusty R Bar in Running Springs, Wyoming at eighteen, and is now a widow at 21. Her financial affairs are a mess, plagued by high credit card bills, delinquent car loans, and her debts as a co-signer for her husband's business loans. The bank has repossessed the bar, and she is ready to walk away from the old double-wide trailer and start her life again. Suzan's grief is lessened a little bit by the fact that Mr. B had a $1 million dollar insurance policy. If Suzan decides to declare bankruptcy, what can she keep? If Suzan and Mr. B had been living in Odessa, Texas, would the outcome be the same?

4.3. Lynh Tran bought her home in 2005. She paid $15,000 down and signed a mortgage obligation for $135,000, which she has now paid down to $130,000. (Like all standard mortgages, it provides automatic default if a creditor levies on the house.) Similar houses are now selling for about $180,000 when they are put on the retail market for two or three months and listed with a real estate broker, who charges a 6% commission. A similar house sold in a sheriff's auction last month for $135,352. It was bought by the creditor for whom the sale was being held for exactly the amount of the debt owed the creditor. The creditor was the only one who showed up at the sale. The sheriff charged his standard $1,000 fee to conduct a sale of real property.

Lynh owes a judgment creditor $25,000. The state where she lives permits an individual debtor to exempt $30,000 in a homestead. If she voluntarily sold her property, how much would the judgment creditor receive? In a judicial sale, how much would the creditor receive? If the state court is not bound by any precedential decisions, should the judge order a sale upon the judgment creditor's levy? If she files for bankruptcy, do the options available to the court change? See §522(a)(2); cf. UCC §9-611(c)(3)(B), §9-601(f).

4.4. Charley Wilson has worked for twelve years on construction sites, most recently as a crane operator. When the local construction industry crashed, Charley took decided to go into business by himself. His new business has not been very successful, and Charley filed for bankruptcy two months after opening, although he was still trying to make a go of the business. Charley filed bankruptcy because a creditor from the business got a default judgment for

$6,500 and got the sheriff to seize the truck, which is worth $8,000 and owned free and clear by Charley. Charley has taken the federal exemptions, using his full home exemption and "wildcard" for other property.

A. Can he keep the truck? What if he backed his truck into a tree at a construction site and now the truck is worth only $4,000 (or maybe even $2,000)? See §522(f).

B. What if his new business was called "Charley's Trash Hauling and Light Deliveries" and he had used his pickup as collateral for a secured loan from Jingle Finance, a company specializing in high-interest loans for people with cars, to get $6,500 in debt (instead of the judgment creditor)? See §§522(d) and (f).

Assignment 5.

Exemption Planning: Homesteads, Trusts, and Moves

You have learned the basics about exemptions as they affect most debtors. Because the great majority of debtors have few assets of any value, apart from a heavily mortgaged home, exemptions are important to them only at the "barrel" level—that is, enough protection to cover their clothes, basic household goods, unfancy vehicles to get to work, and the like. For just that reason, exemptions beyond a very basic floor don't matter to most bankruptcy debtors. The process of disclosing assets and trying to fit everything into a category protected by an exemption adds expense and complexity to the process, but most debtors only dream of having such problems.

Exemptions do matter, however, to a small minority of more affluent debtors. These people need sophisticated legal advice if they are going to hang onto their assets. Exemptions that are capped serve as a check on affluent debtors who might exploit laws that are too forgiving. The fear of bankruptcy abuse drives a rigorous and ongoing debate about unlimited exemptions, which many states have for homesteads. Part of that debate—as with any debate—is likely driven by high-salience public events: well publicized instances of famous people escaping their debts by manipulating luxury property, while their creditors, including sometimes fraud victims or worse, get left in the cold. Thus, the debate about bankruptcy exemptions has a curious skew. The barrel-level exemptions affect the vast majority of debtors, and in a significant way, but not even the most heartless churl begrudges them (okay, maybe there is some economist out there that has an argument but we aren't persuaded). The policy action is over that sliver of the debtor population for whom exemptions are important to retain assets of high value and who have the capacity to maximize legal protections.

This assignment addresses the issues surrounding that small minority. It is not limited to exemption laws because they are only part of the available tools. The other way more affluent debtors protect assets from creditors is by excluding certain assets from their estates altogether. Exclusions may be built directly into the Bankruptcy Code (e.g., section 541's exclusion of most retirement funds requires little planning on the debtor's part other than sound pension investments). Other property requires a little more work and requires the debtor to structure holdings in specifically advantageous ways (e.g., holding marital property in the entirety). The most significant of these "structured exclusions" is holding property in trusts, which you will recall are excluded under section 541(c)(2). Either route—exemptions or exclusion—parks the debtor's assets beyond the reach of unpaid creditors.

A. HOMESTEAD EXEMPTIONS

The struggle over what property debtors may or may not keep has deep social and economic implications. Nowhere do they come into greater collision than in the protection afforded homeowners.

The most important type of exempt property for many debtors is their homestead, which is typically the real property they occupy as a residence. Financially, homes are the most significant assets owned by most Americans. Even after several years of a sorry homeownership market, primary residences accounted for 29.5% of total family assets in 2010 (Federal Reserve Board, 2010 Survey of Consumer Finance). Homeownership is a cumulative phenomenon, with about 68% of the total population owning their own homes, and even higher ownership rates among couples and older Americans. Homeownership is particularly popular among wealthier families; over 90% of the top quartile of households by income own the homes they live in. For many families, a home represents not only a valuable asset but is also a visible marker of middle-class status (or beyond). Empirical research has shown that more than half of debtors own their homes and that many of them file bankruptcy specifically to attempt to save their homes.

The homestead exemption as we know it developed largely in the nineteenth century. In his article, Protection of the Family Home from Seizure by Creditors: The Sources and Evolution of a Legal Principle, 86 S.W. Hist. L.Q. 364 (1983), Professor Joseph McKnight examined the sources of the modern homestead exemption laws:

> In popular as well as legal parlance, homestead means not only family home but property that is accorded particular protection because it is the family home. From one American state to another, and elsewhere as well, the most significant protection of the home is that which is accorded it against seizure by the owner's creditors for payment of general, private debts. The term homestead was also once used to refer to a sovereign grant of western lands where the frontiersman and his family made their home. But it is in the sense of a home protected from creditors that the concept of homestead is one of the most significant later contributions to family jurisprudence. Legal tradition has long

acknowledged that this notion of homestead emerged on the Mexican-Texan frontier.

Id. at 369.

Professor McKnight bases his analysis on dual themes of the Anglo-American and Hispanic legal traditions of the time, and of the continuing political concerns of the independent government of Coahuila y Texas to protect resident debtors (and attract new settlers). He explains one interaction between debtor-creditor laws and migration:

> Moving West was a frequent early nineteenth-century response to the series of economic crises in the new American nation. A move to Texas where land was cheap was particularly attractive to venturous spirits in the southern United States. The Texas colonists were by no means generally insolvent, but there were some who came to Texas with the hope of leaving debts permanently behind them, and those debts were sometimes large. By the mid-1820s Texas had achieved the reputation as a haven for debtors. First in 1826 and again in 1828 the United States Congress directed questions to the president concerning the obvious irritant to American creditors whose debtors had removed themselves to Mexican territory. The perception of Texas as a refuge for debtors was a consequence of several factors: Texas's primitive judicial system, the difficulty of finding debtors there, and, most particularly, the reluctance of local judges to enforce foreign debts against fellow colonists.

> The American financial crisis of 1837, which precipitated the movement of so many distressed debtors into Texas, was a likely catalyst to the 1839 Texas enactment.

Id. at 375, 393.

The Texas enactment in 1839 was the predecessor of generous homestead and family property exemptions that followed. The homestead exemption, born of a blending of two legal cultures, soon expanded to other states:

> The Hispanic and Anglo-American traditions of exempt property thus interacted to produce the lasting concept of protecting the family home and certain movables from the claims of creditors. These ideas came to full flower in the formulation of the homestead and chattel-exemption provision of the Texas Constitution of 1845. Forceful minds, well versed in the Hispanic concepts of exempt property and their further development in the decree of 1829, composed and passed the constitutional provision that would publish the expanded concept of exempt property in louder tones to the rest of the United States. The idea had already spread, on the apparent inspiration of the 1839 act, to Mississippi, Georgia, and Florida; within a few years more, similar provisions were enacted in a number of other states and were added to some state constitutions. Well

before the end of the century the family home had been extended protection from creditors in almost every American state.

Id. at 396.

Homestead exemptions are now available in a large number of jurisdictions. Even so, not every homeowner is protected. Typically, a homestead is exempt only up to a given dollar amount. Fifteen states protect less than $20,000 equity in a homestead, at least for some debtors. But seven states and the District of Columbia now offer homestead protection based on area or some other test. For example, Iowa protects homesteads up to a half-acre in a city and 40 acres in the country. Iowa Code §561.2. Some states offer differing exemptions based on debtor attributes; California, for instance, has a greater exemption for low-income homeowners who are over age 55, and for older residents who are disabled. Cal. Civ. Proc. Code §704.950. These specialty exemptions statutes are often well intentioned, but every act of legislative kindness adds complexity and creates transactional incentives.

Some states, such as Pennsylvania, only offer homestead protection through a property doctrine known as "tenancy by the entirety" rather than by a separate homestead provision. The rule prohibits a creditor of only one spouse from foreclosing on a homestead held by the entirety—that is, jointly owned by the married couple. See, e.g., Patterson v. Hopkins, 371 A.2d 1378 (Penn. 1977). This effectively stops a general unsecured creditor from forcing a sale of a home to satisfy a debt if the creditor is owed an obligation by only one spouse, regardless of the value of the home. It does not, of course, have any restraining effect if the creditor was careful to have both husband and wife sign for the debt, as you can bet most Pennsylvanian mortgage lenders do. Nor does it help the single debtor, an outcome we find romantically regressive.

Recall the Code allows debtors picking the federal exemptions to claim a homestead of $22,975. §522(d)(1). It can be doubled by a couple filing a joint bankruptcy petition, allowing for the protection of what might strike law students on their way to be first-time homebuyers as a lot of equity. But most bankruptcy debtors are well into their middle age, and even after years of plummeting (or at best, stagnant) home prices, the typical American family has a home valued at $209,500 (Federal Reserve Board, 2010 Survey of Consumer Finance). If that family made a 20% down payment at purchase, it would be nip-tuck to protect all its equity, which tees up a valuation battle with the trustee and adds a lot of risk to a bankruptcy filing. Then again, perhaps the lesson of the last decade is that few families put down 20%, or if they did, cash-out refinancing eliminated all or most of their equity.

At the legislative level, policy debates continue over how generous exemptions should be and what classes of debtor should find favor. One loud debate is in Florida, where a homestead of unlimited value can be protected, a circumstance that is said to have attracted several noteworthy personages, including O.J. Simpson and former baseball commissioner Bowie Kuhn (who moved to Florida and bought extensive homes notwithstanding owing even more substantial amounts to creditors). The other states with unlimited homestead exemptions evidently have not been so attractive to those fleeing their creditors. The explanation in some states, such as Iowa, is that the homestead exemption only halts creditors trying to recover on debts that became owed after the debtor purchased the homestead. Iowa Code §561.21. Or it could be the metereologic handicap most unlimited homestead states, such as South Dakota, suffer compared to the Sunshine State.

B. EXEMPTION PLANNING: REALLOCATING ASSETS

1. Homesteads

In states like Florida and Texas with unlimited homestead exemptions, the debtor has the opportunity to do some careful planning.

————— **In re REED** —————
12 B.R. 41 (Bankr. N.D. Tex. 1981)

BRISTER, Bankruptcy Judge.

The debtors filed petition for order for relief under Chapter 7 of Title 11, United States Code, on December 21, 1979. During the two week period preceding the filing of the petition the debtors, obviously engaging in prebankruptcy planning, sold nonexempt personal property for approximately 50% of the value which they had assigned to those properties and applied the proceeds of $34,500.00 towards liquidation of liens against their residence homestead. The trustee filed a complaint challenging entitlement to the exemptions. The following summary constitutes the findings of fact contemplated by Rule 752 after nonjury trial.

Since his childhood Hugh D. Reed had collected approximately 35 guns, some of them commemorative guns or otherwise having collector's value. On a financial statement dated April 1, 1979, he had valued the gun collection at $20,000.00. On December 11, 1979, ten days prior to filing the petition in bankruptcy, he sold the entire gun collection to a friend, Steve Gallagher, for $5,000.00 cash.

Reed had been an antique collector, also. On the April 1, 1979, financial statement he had valued his antiques at $3,000.00. Three months later, in August, 1979, he purchased additional antiques from an estate for $11,000.00. In late November, 1979, he sold three items from the antique collection to an acquaintance, Charles Tharpe, for $3,500.00, applying the proceeds to payment of a note to Bank of the West. On December 11, 1979, he sold the remaining antiques to the friend, Steve Gallagher, for $5,000.00 cash.

In November 1979, approximately one month prior to the commencement of the bankruptcy proceedings, he purchased for $15,000.00 an interest in a corporation with the intriguing name of Triple BS Corporation. He sold that interest to the friend, Steve Gallagher, on December 11, 1979, for $5,000.00 cash.

In three separate transactions between October 5, 1979, and November 13, 1979, Reed had purchased gold coins—Krugerrands and Mexican Pesos—for the total sum of $22,115.00. On or about December 10, 1979, he sold those coins for $19,500.00 cash.

Thus, ten days prior to bankruptcy debtors sold nonexempt assets with aggregate value of $68,500.00 (according to their financial statements or based upon the amount actually paid by them on recent purchases), receiving as proceeds the sum of $34,500.00. They received market value for the gold and when that transaction is not considered they received less than 20% of the apparent value of the guns, the antiques and the interest in Triple BS Corporation.

In October 1978, the debtors had executed a note and mechanic's lien to a lending institution in the sum of $20,000.00 to pay for improvements to their residence, consisting of a sun-deck room, swimming pool and pool facilities. On December 11, 1979, $19,892.00 from the proceeds of sale of nonexempt assets were applied to pay off that improvement loan. The balance of $15,000.00 was applied by the debtors towards the vendor's lien note against the residence, reducing the balance of that note to approximately $28,000.00.

The scope of this memorandum is narrow. The trustee insists that the homestead exemption on the residence should be avoided, because of the flagrant prebankruptcy planning in which they engaged. As evidence of fraudulent intent, the trustee contends that the debtors received less than a reasonably equivalent value for the nonexempt assets.[7] Mr. Reed very candidly testified that had he received more money for the nonexempt assets he would have applied those additional monies to the homestead liens.

The issue as to whether the homestead exemptions may be set aside under those facts is clearly drawn.

The debtor, in support of his contention that he could properly pay the liens with proceeds of nonexempt property, and thus engage in obvious exemption planning, cites a comment in the legislative history following §522(b):

> As under current law, the debtor will be permitted to convert nonexempted property into exempt property before filing a bankruptcy petition. See Hearings,

---

7. [As we will study in a later assignment, transfers of the debtor's property for less than "reasonably equivalent value"—a standard Reed likely flunked on his transactions with his willing friend, Steve Gallagher—are voidable in bankruptcy, which allows the trustee to claw that property back into the estate. §548.—Eds.]

pt. 3, at 1355-58. The practice is not fraudulent as to creditors, and permits the debtor to make full use of the exemptions to which he is entitled under the law.

While that language may express the law in some jurisdictions, it is not universally true. Certainly it is not an accurate expression of Texas law because Texas law specifically prohibits the retention of an exemption in personal property so acquired with proceeds of nonexempt property where there was intent to defraud, delay or hinder a creditor or other interested persons.

In this case, however, there was no proof that the debtors had applied the proceeds to acquisition of exempt personal property. All of the evidence indicates that the entire proceeds of $34,500.00 were applied on the real estate liens. The Texas legislature, at the time it adopted V.A.T.S. Article 3836(b), [predecessor to §42.004, *supra*—Eds.] had the opportunity to include the same language in V.A.T.S. Article 3833, [predecessor to §41.002, *supra*—Eds.] which provides the homestead exemption in real estate. It failed to do so, and had it included that type of language it is doubtful that it would have passed constitutional muster. Historically Texas law has jealously protected the homestead from forced sale except under very limited conditions. Article 16, §50 of the Texas Constitution prohibits forced sale for any purpose except for purchase money liens, improvement liens, or taxes.

That provision in the Texas constitution prohibits the granting of the relief sought by the trustee in this case and the challenge to the homestead exemption in the residence is denied.

———

But Mr. Reed was not, dare we say, "home" free. His trip to bankruptcy court was to discharge all his debt but keep his (dramatically deleveraged) exempt property, a strategy on which the bankruptcy court had something to say. On appeal, the Fifth Circuit took a hard look at Mr. Reed and the Triple BS Corporation and was not amused.

In re REED
700 F.2d 986 (5th Cir. 1983)

RUBIN, Circuit Judge.

We hold that a debtor who converts nonexempt assets to an exempt homestead immediately before bankruptcy, with intent to defraud his creditors, must be denied a discharge in bankruptcy because of the provisions of Section 727 of the Bankruptcy Code, 11 U.S.C.A. §727 (West 1979), and, therefore, we affirm the decision of the district court.

I

Hugh D. Reed, as sole proprietor, opened a shop using the trade name, Reed's Men's Wear, in Lubbock, Texas. He financed the venture in part by obtaining from the Texas Bank & Trust Company a $150,000 loan which was guaranteed by the Small Business Administration (SBA). Three months later, the bank gave Reed a $50,000 line of credit, and the SBA agreed that the original loan would be subordinated to the line of credit. The store showed a profit for the first nine months of operation in 1977, but began to lose money in 1978.

By February 1979, Reed knew that his business was insolvent. After meeting with the bank, the SBA, and his major trade creditors, he signed an agreement to turn over management of the store to a consulting firm for the year 1979. In turn, Reed's trade creditors agreed to postpone collection efforts and Reed promised to resume payments in January 1980. Despite management by the consultant, the business continued to fail, and on December 15, 1979, Reed and his wife, Sharon Marcus Reed, signed a foreclosure agreement surrendering the store to the bank. Six days later, the Reeds filed voluntary petitions for bankruptcy.

. . .

Reed had catholic interests and much energy. He found time to collect antiques, gold coins, and guns, and to make other investments. In a financial statement provided to the bank and to the SBA on April 1, 1979, Reed valued his gun collection at $20,000 and his antiques collection at $3,000. In the four months prior to bankruptcy, Reed augmented each of his collections. He caused Reyata [Corporation, which Reed owned] to borrow $11,000, which he used to purchase more antiques. In three separate transactions during October and November, Reed accumulated, at a cost of $22,115, a collection of Krugerrands and Mexican fifty-peso pieces. One month before filing for bankruptcy, Reed purchased, for $15,000, a one-third interest in a business known as Triple BS Corporation.[1]

Two months before bankruptcy, Reed opened an account at the Bank of the West without the knowledge of his creditors. From that time until the store closed in mid-December, he deposited the daily receipts from Reed's Men's Wear in this separate account. From this account, in late November Reed repaid the loan Reyata made to purchase the antiques.

Reed began selling his personal assets in late November. He first sold three items from his antiques collection to an acquaintance, Charles Tharpe, for $3,500. He sold the remainder of his antiques on December 11 to a friend, Steve Gallagher, for $5,000. Whether this represented their fair market value was not established, but the total realized on the antiques was $8,500, while the original

---

1. The significance of the initials is not elucidated in the record.

value plus the cost of recent purchases was $14,000. On December 10, he sold his gold coins through a broker for $19,500 cash, their approximate market value. The next day, on December 11, Reed sold to Gallagher for $5,000 each both his gun collection and his Triple BS stock. Whether or not Gallagher paid fair market value for the items was not established, but the stock had been purchased only one month earlier for $15,000.

Reed applied all of the proceeds to reduce the mortgages on his family residence, which was exempt from creditor's claims under Texas law, with the objective, the bankruptcy court found, of reducing the value of his nonexempt assets and increasing the value of his homestead exemption prior to bankruptcy. Thus he raised about $35,000, applying about $30,000 [should read "$20,000"— Eds.] to wipe out a second mortgage home improvement loan and applying the balance of approximately $15,000 to reduce the first mortgage on his home to about $28,000.

Reed cavalierly justified his sale of assets for what appeared to be less than their fair market value. This was of no concern to his creditors, he testified, because, if he had received more for the assets, he would have simply applied the additional sum to reduce the mortgage on his homestead. No matter how much he got, there would be nothing for his creditors.

Reed also failed to account for the disposition of $19,586.83 in cash during the year preceding filing. Reed attempted to explain the "unaccounted for" cash by testifying that he habitually carried huge sums of money in cash on his person and frequently made purchases and payments in cash without obtaining receipts. He argued that the amount of "unaccounted for" cash represents only a small percentage of the amount of money which went through his hands in 1979.

The bankruptcy judge found that Reed had effected transfers designed to convert nonexempt property into exempt property less than two weeks before bankruptcy with the intent to hinder, delay, or defraud creditors. 11 U.S.C.A. §727(a)(2) (West 1979). He found that, regardless of the amount of money that might have passed through Reed's accounts, $19,586.83 is a significant sum, and that Reed had failed satisfactorily to explain its loss. This constituted an additional basis for denying discharge. 11 U.S.C.A. §727(a)(5) (West 1979).

The district court affirmed the judgment.

II

The Bankruptcy Code provides that a debtor may be denied discharge if he has transferred property "with intent to hinder, delay, or defraud a creditor," 11 U.S.C.A. §727(a)(2) (West 1979), or has "failed to explain satisfactorily…any loss of assets.…" 11 U.S.C.A. §727(a)(5) (West 1979), Reed was denied discharge on both bases. Though either would suffice, we review the grounds seriatim.

In considering the effect of Reed's transfers of assets, we distinguish, as did the careful opinion of the bankruptcy court, the debtor's entitlement to the exemption of property from the claims of his creditors and his right to a discharge from his debts. The Bankruptcy Code allows a debtor to retain property exempt either (1) under the provisions of the Bankruptcy Code, if not forbidden by state law, 11 U.S.C.A. §522(b) and (d) (West 1979), or (2) under the provisions of state law and federal law other than the minimum allowances in the Bankruptcy Code, 11 U.S.C.A. §522(b)(2) (West 1979).

Under the Bankruptcy Act of 1898, most courts, applying state exemption laws, had held property that would otherwise have been exempt to be deprived of its immunity if there was evidence other than the simple act of conversion showing that the debtor had acquired it with the intention of defrauding his creditors. If intent to defraud was not proved, however, and it was shown only that granting the exemption would defeat the creditor's claim, the exemption was granted. As stated in 3 Collier on Bankruptcy, ¶522.08[4] (15th ed. 1982): "Under the Act, the mere conversion of nonexempt property into exempt property on the eve of bankruptcy was not of itself such fraud as will [sic] deprive the bankrupt *of his right to exemptions.* " (Emphasis supplied.)

Before the Bankruptcy Code was adopted in 1978, it had been urged that property obtained in such last-minute conversions be ineligible for exemption. *Id.* The Code, however, adopts the position that the conversion of nonexempt to exempt property, without more, will not deprive the debtor of the exemption to which he would otherwise be entitled. 3 Collier, supra, ¶522.08[4]. Thus, both the House and Senate Reports state:

> As under current law, the debtor will be permitted to convert nonexempt property into exempt property before filing a bankruptcy petition. The practice is not fraudulent as to creditors, and permits the debtor to make full use of the exemptions to which he is entitled under the law.

H.R. Rep. No. 595, 95th Cong., 1st Sess. 361 (1977), reprinted in 1978 U.S. Code Cong. & Ad. News 5963, 6317; S. Rep. No. 989, 95th Cong., 2d Sess. 76, reprinted in 1978 U.S. Code Cong. & Ad. News 5787, 5862. The rationale behind this congressional decision is summed up at 3 Collier, *supra*, ¶522.08[4]: "The result which would obtain if debtors were not allowed to convert property into allowable exempt property would be extremely harsh, especially in those jurisdictions where the exemption allowance is minimal." Nonetheless, the phrase, "[a]s under current law," qualifies the apparently blanket approval of conversion, since as noted above, courts denied exemptions under the Act if there was extrinsic evidence of actual intent to defraud (and if the state law permitted disallowance of the exemption for fraud).

Reed elected to claim his exemptions under state law. The bankruptcy judge, therefore, referred to Texas law to determine both what property was exempt and whether the exemption was defeated by the eleventh-hour conversion. Texas constitutional and statutory protection of the homestead is absolute, and the bankruptcy judge interpreted Texas law to allow the exemption in full regardless of Reed's intent.

While the Code requires that, when the debtor claims a state-created exemption, the scope of the claim is determined by state law, it sets separate standards for determining whether the debtor shall be denied a discharge. The debtor's entitlement to a discharge must, therefore, be determined by federal, not state, law. In this respect, 11 U.S.C. §727(a)(2) is absolute: the discharge shall be denied a debtor who has transferred property with intent to defraud his creditors. The legislative history of the exemption section, as noted above, does not mean that conversion is never fraudulent as to creditors, but simply that, as under prior law, mere conversion is not to be considered fraudulent unless other evidence proves actual intent to defraud creditors. While pre-bankruptcy conversion of nonexempt into exempt assets is frequently motivated by the intent to put those assets beyond the reach of creditors, which is, after all, the function of an exemption, evidence of actual intent to defraud creditors is required to support a finding sufficient to deny a discharge. For example, evidence that the debtor, on the eve of bankruptcy, borrowed money that was then converted into exempt assets would suffice to support a finding of actual intent to defraud. Only if such a finding is made may a discharge be denied.

The evidence amply supports the bankruptcy court's finding that Reed had an actual intent to defraud. Reed's whole pattern of conduct evinces that intent. *Cf.* Farmers Co-op. Assn. v. Strunk, 671 F.2d 391, 395 (10th Cir. 1982) ("Fraudulent intent of course may be established by circumstantial evidence, or by inferences drawn from a course of conduct"). His rapid conversion of nonexempt assets to extinguish one home mortgage and to reduce another four months before bankruptcy, after arranging with his creditors to be free of payment obligations until the following year, speaks for itself as a transfer of property in fraud of creditors. His diversion of the daily receipts of Reed's Men's Wear into an account unknown to his creditors and management consultant and his subsequent use of the receipts to repay a loan that had been a vehicle for this conversion confirm his fraudulent motivation. . . .

The fact findings of the bankruptcy judge, affirmed by the district court, are to be credited by us unless clearly erroneous. . . . [T]he finding of actual intent to defraud, based on evidence other than the fact of the conversion, patently was not permeated with error. The denial of a discharge on this ground alone was appropriate. It would constitute a perversion of the purposes of the Bankruptcy Code to permit a debtor earning $180,000 a year to convert every one of his major nonexempt assets into sheltered property on the eve of bankruptcy with actual intent to defraud his creditors and then emerge washed clean of future obligation by carefully concocted immersion in bankruptcy waters.

Reed asserts that denial of a discharge makes the exemption meaningless. This is but fulmination. Reed may retain his home, mortgages substantially reduced, free of claims by his creditors. In light of the ample evidence, aside from the conversion itself, that Reed had an actual intent to defraud his creditors, he simply is not entitled to a discharge despite the fact that a generous state law may protect his exemption.

The argument that we should reject the other ground for denying discharge gets but the short shrift it deserves. . . .

III

The district court found that Sharon Marcus Reed benefited from the "prohibited activities" and possibly had knowledge of them but that she did not participate in them. Accordingly, he granted her discharge. The evidence showed that Sharon Reed made out the daily reports of the sales receipts of Reed's Men's Wear during the time that Reed was surreptitiously diverting those receipts to a bank account unknown to his creditors and management consultant. From this, it would have been possible to infer that Sharon Reed shared her husband's fraudulent intent, but the bankruptcy judge's findings to the contrary are not clearly erroneous. . . .

The double *Reed* opinions show how the courts have tried to negotiate a line that provides protection for debtors and yet does not permit them to take undue advantage. It also illustrates how courts may see themselves bound by the legislature that created exemptions, or how they can read extremely open-ended language to craft what they believe is a more sensible solution, albeit one that defies precise definition.

Mr. Reed elicits many reactions, few of them sympathetic. But surely many debtors with much more innocent intent convert assets from non-exempt to exempt before bankruptcy (think of paying your monthly car loan out of your non-exempt checking account). Somewhere in the more complex middle is a debtor who asks a bankruptcy attorney if it's better to use the remainder of a Christmas bonus in that account to pay down a car loan early or save it up for a condo down payment. When does active exemption planning and maximizing statutory entitlements lose the virtue of prudence and acquire the tinge of intent to defraud? When does tax planning become tax avoidance? It is said bankruptcy courts are courts of equity, and so perhaps precise definition in some instances is neither possible nor desirable.

2. *Beyond Homesteads*

The sound and fury over homestead exemptions overshadows unlimited exemptions in personal property, but those exemptions raise the same concerns of justice and fairness as homestead exemptions.

One example came out of Minnesota. Dr. Tveten, a physician who dabbled in more than the healing arts, managed to amass $19 million in debts in a real estate partnership that went south. He consulted his attorney, who had two pieces of advice: Convert your assets to protect as much as you can and then file for bankruptcy. The good doctor took the advice, using 17 transfers to sell off his land and liquidate his non-exempt life insurance and retirement accounts. All the transactions were for fair value. Dr. T put the money into about $700,000 of life insurance and annuity contracts with the Lutheran Brotherhood, a fraternal benefit association. Under Minnesota law, creditors could not attach these contracts. Best of all, the exemption has no dollar limit.

Dr. T conceded that the purpose of these transfers was to shield his assets from creditors. He wasn't trying to cheat anyone, he said. He was just trying to meet the legal requirements of how he should best hold his assets. When Dr. T came up for a discharge in bankruptcy court, the bank that had financed the real estate deal and obtained his unsecured guarantee objected to his discharge. Norwest Bank Nebraska, N.A. v. Tveten, 848 F.2d 871 (8th Cir. 1988). The bankruptcy judge, following the analysis of the Fifth Circuit in *Reed,* denied the discharge and both was affirmed on district and circuit appeal.

But there was a stinging dissent by Judge Richard Arnold:

> The Court reaches a result that appeals to one's general sense of righteousness. I believe, however, that it is contrary to clearly established law, and I therefore respectfully dissent.
>
> Dr. Tveten has never made any bones about what he is doing, or trying to do, in this case. He deliberately set out to convert as much property as possible into a form exempt from attachment by creditors under Minnesota law. Such a design necessarily involves an attempt to delay or hinder creditors, in the ordinary, non-legal sense of those words, but, under long-standing principles embodied both in judicial decisions and in statute, such a purpose is not unlawful. The governing authority in this Court is Forsberg v. Security State Bank, 15 F.2d 499 (8th Cir. 1926). There we said:
>
> > It is well settled that it is not a fraudulent act by an individual who knows he is insolvent to convert a part of his property which is not exempt into property which is exempt, for the purpose of claiming his exemptions therein, and of thereby placing it out of the reach of his creditors.

Id. at 501. Thus, under the controlling law of this Circuit, someone who is insolvent may convert property into exempt form for the very purpose of placing that property beyond the reach of his creditors. . . . The same principle was confirmed by Congress when it enacted the Bankruptcy Code of 1978. The report of the House Judiciary Committee states as follows:

> As under current law, the debtor will be permitted to convert nonexempt property into exempt property before filing a bankruptcy petition. See Hearings, Pt. Ill, at 1355-58. The practice is not fraudulent as to creditors, and permits the debtor to make full use of the exemptions to which he is entitled under the law.

In re Tveten, 848 F.2d at 877.

What made the *Tveten* case particularly noteworthy was that on the very day that it was announced the same court also announced the unanimous opinion in Hanson v. First Natl. Bank in Brookings, 848 F.2d 866 (8th Cir. 1988). The Hansons were South Dakota farmers who, on similar advice of counsel, sold all their non-exempt property, two vans, a car, a motor home, and all their household goods to family members. On agreement with the purchasers, the Hansons retained possession of many of the goods. They received the market value of the goods, $27,115, which they promptly used to pay down their mortgage and to buy exempt life insurance policies. Their lender bank objected to the Hansons' exemptions, wanting to reach the assets they had secreted away. The court explored the same questions about whether the debtors had engaged in fraudulent conduct. The bankruptcy judge said the Hansons got their discharge and kept their newly exempt property. Both the district court and the Eighth Circuit affirmed.

Judge Arnold sided with the majority in the *Hanson*, but he used that decision to sharpen his outrage about the result in *Tveten:*

> The Court is entirely correct in holding that there is no extrinsic fraud [in *Hanson*]. The money placed into exempt property was not borrowed, the cash received from the sales was accounted for, and the property was sold for fair market value. The fact that the sale was to family members, "standing on its own, does not establish extrinsic evidence of fraud." Ante, at 869.
>
> With all of this I agree completely, but exactly the same statements can be made, just as accurately, with respect to Dr. Tveten's case. So far as I can tell, there are only three differences between Dr. Tveten and the Hansons, and all of them are legally irrelevant: (1) Dr. Tveten is a physician, and the Hansons are farmers; (2) Dr. Tveten attempted to claim exempt status for about $700,000 worth of property, while the Hansons are claiming it for about $31,000 worth of property; and (3) the Minnesota exemption statute whose shelter Dr. Tveten sought had no dollar limit, while the South Dakota statute exempting the

proceeds of life-insurance policies, is limited to $20,000. The first of these three differences—the occupation of the parties—is plainly immaterial, and no one contends otherwise. The second—the amounts of money involved—is also irrelevant, in my view, because the relevant statute contains no dollar limit, and for judges to set one involves essentially a legislative decision not suitable for the judicial branch. The relevant statute for present purposes is 11 U.S.C. §522(b)(2)(A), which authorizes debtors to claim exemptions available under "State or local law," and says nothing about any dollar limitations, by contrast to 11 U.S.C. §522(d), the federal schedule of exemptions, which contains a number of dollar limitations. The third difference—that between the Minnesota and South Dakota statutes—is also legally immaterial, and for a closely related reason. The federal exemption statute, just referred to, simply incorporates state and local exemption laws without regard to whether those laws contain dollar limitations of their own. . . . If there ought to be a dollar limit, and I am inclined to think that there should be, and if practices such as those engaged in by the debtor here can become abusive, and I admit that they can, the problem is simply not one susceptible of a judicial solution according to manageable objective standard.

Hanson, 848 F.2d at 870-71 (Arnold, J., concurring).

This pair of cases is notable for another feature that does not play a prominent part in the opinion: both states let people squirrel away cash—that most precious of resource for the financially troubled debtor—in a Fraternal Benefit Association fund. Fraternal Benefit Associations? They sound so, um, *pokey*, but some lawyers have seen real potential in the idea of using them to hide a client's assets so that they cannot be reached by creditors—whether the debtor eventually files for bankruptcy or not. According to the Collier bankruptcy treatise, 42 states, the District of Columbia, and Puerto Rico all permit such unlimited exemptions in beneficiary associations—even as they slap hard caps on cars and homesteads.

Homesteads had a rich legal and cultural history. What's going on with insurance accounts—is this a lobbying story? Has the whole game quietly changed while no one was looking? And who will take advantage of these provisions? We've come a long way from the skinny guy's barrel.

3. Exemption Planning Reform

In the debates leading up to the 2005 bankruptcy reforms, Congress engaged in heated debates about the existing approach to exemptions. To respond to repeated complaints about millionaires protecting too much money in a homestead, Senator Herb Kohl, D-WI, proposed an amendment to cap permissible homestead exemptions at $250,000 in bankruptcy. States could continue to provide unlimited homestead exemptions to govern all state law collection suits, but anyone who wanted a federal discharge in bankruptcy would have to give up anything beyond $250,000 in home equity. The amendment had widespread support, but the Texas contingent threatened to block any bankruptcy bill with such a cap. The amendment failed.

Congress did add some restrictions on the value a debtor can protect in a homestead. The Code now includes a provision that reduces the dollar value of the homestead protection by any amount that is attributable to otherwise non-exempt "property that the debtor disposed of . . . with intent to hinder, delay or defraud a creditor." §522(o). To catch even long-time planners, the provision has a ten-year reach-back period. So now debtors will have to come up with better plans than Mr. Reed and Triple BS—or start their planning a lot further in advance. If a court finds "intent to hinder, delay, or defraud" in the ten years before bankruptcy, the debtor's homestead exemption would be reduced by the amount transferred.

Another provision addresses a specific kind of actor who might try to use unlimited homestead protections. In the wake of Enron and other the mega-fraud chapter 11 cases in the early 2000s, some newspapers ran pictures of luxurious homes of executives who decided it was time to build sumptuous residences in upscale Houston neighborhoods; of course, such homes are exempt under Texas law. In response, Congress added an absolute cap on the homestead for people who were convicted of securities law violations, fraud in a fiduciary capacity, and a handful of other related bad acts. §522(q). Some call it the "Enron Amendment." If necessary, the discharge can be delayed to see if the debtor is subject to a proceeding that might give rise to a limitation of the homestead exemption. §§727(a)(12); 1121(d)(5)(C); 1328(h). (Congress also added an absolute cap on new-home buyers and interstate movers, which we address in the next section of this assignment). Notwithstanding these changes, the real joker in the deck remains that not all debtors will be as forthcoming as Mr. Reed, especially after they (or their lawyers) read about the outcome of *In re Reed*. Recall that even though the Fifth Circuit nabbed Mr. Reed with intent to defraud, not even Mr. Reed's bankruptcy trustee who took the appeal to the Fifth Circuit, claimed that he could prove *actual* intent to hinder, delay, or defraud the creditors—and Mr. Reed was a man who named his corporation "Triple BS."

C. EXEMPTION PLANNING: MOVING TO BETTER EXEMPTIONS

While it has refused to cap the homestead exemption overall, Congress in BAPCPA further restricted the ability of debtors to engage in pre-bankruptcy planning by limiting their ability to move to take advantage of better exemptions. The thrust of the law is to make sure that generous state exemptions are not available when a person crosses state lines to flee creditors. For a time after relocation, a debtor's exemptions are determined by the earlier place of residence.

According to section 522(b)(3), the applicable exemptions are those of the state where the debtor resided for 730 days (two years in the parlance of ordinary speakers of English) before the bankruptcy filing. In other words, it takes a full two years of residence to take advantage of your new home state's exemptions. Surely that is long enough for an angry creditor to find the debtor and begin the collection process.

What if the debtor did not have only one home state during the two-year period before bankruptcy, say because they moved before? Then go back and look at where the debtor resided during the 180 days that preceded the 730 days to see where the debtor resided for the majority of the time *then*. People who move a lot might find themselves in bankruptcy governed by exemption laws several states ago.

Few state exemption laws were written anticipating these new twists and turns of federal bankruptcy law. Many laws protect only a homestead "in the jurisdiction." Consider Edward and Cecilia Tate. They left Texas for Oregon, bought a home, and by the time of their bankruptcy, had $60,000 in equity. Because they had not lived in Oregon for the requisite 730 days, the court determined that Texas exemptions applied. Unfortunately for the Tates (and fortunately for their creditors), the bankruptcy court decided that Texas homestead law did not cover an "extra-territorial" home in Oregon. In re Tate, 2007 Bankr. Lexis 98 (Bankr. D. Or. 2007). Trying to fix this, the Code says that if the debtors are not eligible for any state exemption they can take the federal exemptions, even in their state has opted-out. §522(b)(3); the Tates did so.

The consequences of section 522(b)(3) keep everyone on their toes, as the players in an otherwise ordinary consumer bankruptcy case filed in the Middle District of Tennessee must suddenly learn to interpret the state exemption laws for Alaska merely because the debtor moved to Nashville from Anchorage a year and a half ago. Better-off debtors are more likely to get attorneys who are thinking about exemption planning and they are more likely to have the resources to wait out the various time period restrictions in the Code's exemption laws.

Given its concern with homesteads in particular, Congress passed an additional BAPCPA rule dissuading debtor flight. The "mansion loophole" amendment imposes a hard cap of about $155,675 for anyone moving across state lines within the 1,215 days preceding bankruptcy. §522(p). (We don't know where they come up with these numbers and what important policy interest underlies the distinction between 1,215 days and 730 days; these numbers sound like the compromise of sausage-making.) The statute also seeks to nab people who stay put in their home states during the lookback period, but plow money into their homes—like good old Mr. Reed. The statute says the debtor "may not exempt any amount of interest [in property] that was acquired by the debtor during the 1,215-day period preceding the filing of the petition that exceeds in the aggregate $155,675 in value in real or personal property that the debtor . . . uses as a residence." §522(p)(1)(A). The million-dollar homestead is available only for those who bought a fancy place at least 3.33 years ago. The newly rich need to find somewhere else to protect their wealth besides their home—and moving to another "where" doesn't help.

That outcome may seem fair enough to some, but what does it mean to "acquire" an interest in property? Buying a home, sure. How about paying down its mortgage, a la Reed? Compare In re Anderson, 374 B.R. 848, 858 (Bankr. Kan. 2007) (not acquiring an interest, but could try to show actual intent under §522(o)), with In re Rasmussen, 349 B.R. 747 (Bankr. M.D. Fla. 2006) (yes, in dicta, that it is acquiring an interest, but passive appreciation due to inflation/housing market is not an acquisition covered by §522). If you believe legislative history is important and Congress was battling exemption *arbitrageurs*, should it matter whether the payment is a monthly mortgage payment (with some principal amortization) due in the ordinary course or a lump-sum paydown? Mr. Anderson plonked down $240,000 in Kansas (unlimited homestead exemption), but the court held fast, saying that acquiring an interest in property is not the same as getting more equity in the property. In a later hearing on actual intent to defraud under section 522(o), the court concluded "that the debtor here did nothing more than take advantage of an exemption to which he is entitled." In re Anderson, 386 B.R. 315, 331 (Bankr. Kan. 2008).

Although *Anderson* was decided long after *Reed*, and the Code now includes far more restrictions on homesteads, it all came down to the judgment of a judge.

D. BEYOND EXEMPTIONS: ASSET TRUSTS AND EXCLUSIONS

1. Domestic Asset Protection Trusts

The fancier way to hide assets (and the one most heavily advertised in certain circles) is called an asset protection trust. The operation is fairly simple. For example, Ryan Spear transfers a big batch of his property to The Ryan Spear Trust, names himself both trustee and beneficiary, then sits back and smiles. Ryan keeps right on using the property—driving the car, sailing the boat, dropping in on the winter place in Aspen and the summer place in Maine. If Ryan runs over someone with his Hummer or lets his attention wander and commits malpractice during open-heart surgery or does some other thing that gets him sued, the victim can take a judgment, but when she tries to seize the cars/boats/condos, Ryan smiles and says, "Sorry, but those aren't mine. They are the property of the Ryan Spear Trust. The trustee lets me use them sometimes."

The idea of a self-settled trust (self-settled because Ryan gave assets to a trust for which Ryan was the beneficiary) was anathema to trust law. Anything like this looked like a plain old fraud on the creditors. And that remains the law in most places. Most. A few years back, Alaska made self-settled asset protection trusts legal. Never one to pass up something that might generate legal fees, Delaware immediately jumped in and made them legal as well. The race was afoot. Competition for legal business in the emerging field of "asset protection" has heated up. With a newcomer every year or two joining the club, there are now at least thirteen states that permit asset protection trusts, including Alaska, Delaware, Hawaii, Missouri, Nevada, New Hampshire, Oklahoma, Rhode Island, South Dakota, Tennessee, Utah, Virginia, and Wyoming. Best of all, many of these states make the trusts available to out-of-state residents. Unlike the Texas or Florida homesteads, the asset protection trusts are available without ever leaving home. Are those guys moving to Florida shrewd operators or are they suffering humidity in July because they are using yesterday's solution?

As an internet ad proclaims,

ARE YOU BEING SUED?
Buy our book to learn how to
create a solid, secure and
flexible asset protection plan.
Learn what your lawyer does
not want you to know.
It's not too late.

2. Offshore Asset Protection Trusts

Domestic asset protection trusts reflect the willingness of elected representatives to make sure wealthy people can dodge creditors, at least if the debtors plan in advance. But they may not be attracting many users; proponents complain loudly that these domestic asset protection trusts are poor cousins to their offshore relatives.

Basking in Islands of Legalisms
Floyd Norris, *New York Times*, pB10 (Jan. 22, 2010)

The Cook Islands have a smaller population — about 20,000 — than one apartment complex in Manhattan, and an economy with little to offer except tourism and pearl exports. The country contracts out its national defense to New Zealand, which is four hours away by plane.

But sand and sun are not the attractions for some Americans who have sent their money to the Cook Islands. Under Cook Islands law, foreign court orders are generally disregarded, which is helpful for someone trying to keep assets away from creditors.

In fact, getting an American court order can make it harder to get money out of the Cook Islands. If someone who stashed funds in a Cook Islands trust asks for the money back because a court ordered him to do so, Cook Islands law says that person is acting under duress, and the local trustee can refuse to return the money.

Over the years, a number of less-than-upstanding Americans have found the islands attractive for that reason. . . .

The latest to use that tactic is the wife of Jamie L. Solow, a former broker in Florida who evidently has a silver tongue and certainly has a lot of angry former customers. In one year, he earned more than $3 million in commissions selling a form of collateralized debt obligations known as "inverse floaters". . . .

The investments proved to be disastrous, and the Securities and Exchange Commission persuaded a jury in West Palm Beach, Fla., that he had committed securities fraud. Now a federal judge has ordered Mr. Solow to go to prison on Monday for civil contempt for failing to come up with a large part of the $6 million he was ordered to pay in disgorgement, interest and penalties.

Mr. Solow claimed he had virtually no assets, since his wife owned everything in the family and had put most of it in a Cook Islands trust. . . .

Mr. Solow did sell all the assets he acknowledged owning — an old pickup truck and some office furniture — and sent $2,639 to the court. The family Rolls Royce was also sold, for $205,000, but the Solows say it was actually owned by Mrs. Solow, even though her husband had put up the money to buy it and signed the sale documents.

This week, Mr. Solow asked that his incarceration be delayed, on the grounds that he and his wife were now willing to ask the Cook Islands trustee to return the money. They have not actually made that request, and in the past, Cook Islands trustees have refused to honor such requests. In ordering Mr. Solow to prison, Judge Donald M. Middlebrooks, of the United States District Court for the Southern District of Florida, said his inability to pay was self-created, and thus no excuse.. . . .

In setting up the trust, Mr. Solow's wife, Gina, followed a blueprint laid out in a 2005 article in an accounting publication, written by Howard D. Rosen, a lawyer in Florida whom she hired a few days after the jury verdict in early 2008.

The Solows own a waterfront home in Hillsboro Beach, Fla., which they view as their permanent residence even though they have not lived in it for several years because of hurricane damage. . . .

The house was already encumbered by $2.4 million in mortgages, but a Cook Islands bank lent $5.2 million more secured by the house. The money from that was immediately placed in a Cook Islands trust to benefit only Mrs. Solow.

The judge noted that the mortgage could not have been taken out without Mr. Solow's consent.

The house is now listed for sale for $6.1 million, far less than the combined mortgages, but the bank in the Cook Islands was taking no real risk. The proceeds from the mortgage were deposited in the Cook Islands, and the interest earned is used to pay the interest on the mortgage.

. . .

In a telephone interview, Mr. Rosen, who had testified in the case on behalf of Mr. Solow, told me that Judge Middlebrooks "simply does not understand the laws of the United States" and voiced confidence that an appeals court would overturn the ruling.

In an e-mail message, he compared the use of an offshore trust to a company's decision to incorporate in Delaware rather than some other state. "Establishing a trust in the Cook Islands or other suitable asset protection jurisdiction in order to gain a protective advantage is no different," he wrote. "It is a choice-of-law matter."

How much value is tucked away in these accounts? In fact, how many of them are there? Hard numbers are hard to come by. A few years ago, the marketing was clearly to a select demographic. There were glossy brochures to take cruises and learn about asset protection trusts (presumably the cruise ships were well stocked with fast talkers ready to take your money to set up a trust on the spot). Now anyone can click on Nexis and search for "asset protection trusts" and turn up more than 2.5 million hits, including one like the following:

Call Today for a <u>Free</u> 20 Minute <u>Consultation!</u> 1-800-800-xxxx
We specialize in protecting Personal and Business and Professional assets from claims and creditors. We help you preserve your wealth from credators, liitigation, divorce and estate taxation.

Asset protection maybe, spelling no.

What happens to asset protection trusts in bankruptcy? If they are structured correctly, including a spendthrift provision and an automatic appointment of a third party as trustee if the trustee-debtor is sued, they are excluded from the estate outright. §541(c)(2). The reference in the statute to state law seems to give the trusts full protection, at least in 13 states if the trust is a domestic one. Of course, in the same way that the funds placed with fraternal orders are exempt in most states, the states intent on sheltering asset protection trusts can also make the property in such trusts exempt from any creditor attachment. Such laws would be recognized in bankruptcy through section 522(b). In other words, excluding property from the estate and exempting property from creditor attachment are devices that are separated more by paper forms and large attorneys' fees than by any effect in reality (in either instance, creditors aren't getting paid, although exclusion might be more hidden from a court's gaze (or shall we say "glare")).

As far as we can tell, asset protection plans seems to work well from the debtor's perspective. The Asset Protection Society, a tradegroup, boasts that "simply put, to date there has **never** been a situation where an offshore asset protection trust has been broken and where the money in such a trust has been forced to return to the U.S. and returned to a creditor." Ryan Spears, keep smiling and counting your cash (sorry, *the trust's* cash).

The lynchpin, of course, is a cadre of professionals willing to do the good work of keeping the world safe from creditors. Note the reassuring themes in the advertisement below to attract clients to a device that basically involves giving a stranger control over all your wealth.

The Harris Organisation
About the Founder

Marc M. Harris graduated from North Carolina Wesleyan College with a 4.0 average at the age of 18. Shortly thereafter, while still only 18, he passed his Certified Public Accountant (CPA) examination and is believed to be the youngest person in the United States to accomplish this. He went on to Columbia University for his MBA with a concentration in Investment Finance. . . .

After substantial changes in the American tax law in 1986, Mr. Harris refocussed the firm's strategy in favor of international tax planning and legitimate methods for Americans to take advantage of offshore tax havens. In order to better service his growing international clientele, he relocated the center of operations to Panama. Today, with over 150 employees, The Firm of Marc M. Harris, Inc. has become the largest independent provider of . . . financial services in Latin America and the Caribbean.

Mr. Harris . . . has personally received many awards which include the key to the city of Miami Beach and Most Distinguished Alumni at North Carolina Wesleyan College. He has established a personal foundation that contributes to Panamanian society by funding nutritional project. . . . [He] has assisted in drafting new financial services legislation for several Latin American countries and is a contributor to various financial journals and newsletters on a regular basis.

. . .

The Marc M. Harris Advantage

The Firm of Marc M. Harris, Inc. is run by Americans, for Americans, specializing in American needs. All work is done by The Firm's experienced in-house accountants, attorneys, investment advisors, investment bankers, brokers and administrators. Panama is a jurisdiction that imposes severe civil and criminal penalties for disclosure of confidential information. . . . The timing in asset protection and financial planning is everything. You can't purchase fire insurance while the building is on fire. An attack on your assets can come from any direction at any time, i.e., law suits, tax increases, currency crashes, etc. . . . We will only advise and complete transactions that are completely legal. . . .

You may contact us by e-mail at globalinvesting@marc-harris.com. Initial contact by telephone is not recommended. . . .

Is Marc Harris just a guy making a buck within the law or a bottom-feeder (top-feeder?) who should be ashamed of himself?

Can creditors do anything about debtors who opt their assets out of bankruptcy? Asset protection trusts and their fraternal order cousins in exemption law can always be set aside by the approach taken in *In re Reed* by the Fifth Circuit: even if the trust works at state law, the debtor will be denied the protection of a discharge in bankruptcy. And BAPCPA's section 522(o) is supposed to help, but as *Anderson* reveals, that's a high hurdle to clear. As the *Reed-Anderson* dichotomy demonstrates, one man's hindering is another man's prudence; there is a lot of room for debtors to litigate over intent. As a result, some people have suggested that the law needs to be clarified to prohibit asset protection trusts. Of course, others are exhorting their states to enact a domestic asset protection law.

3. Reform of Asset Trust Exclusions

An amendment to BAPCPA that proposed all assets in asset protection trusts be brought into the bankruptcy estate, and that the exempt portion be limited to a $125,000 cap, failed. Section 548(e) did get in, with a ten-year lookback for trusts created with actual intent to hinder, delay or defraud creditors. We suspect section 548(e) will have as much success as section 522(o); that is to say, limited success. The enduring problem is how to determine intent. Indeed, a court's reach may be even more circumscribed than before the amendment because of the language in section 548(e)(2) that describes such transfers as including those made "in anticipation of any money judgment" or to escape "judgments in connection with securities fraud" (but not "murdering your ex-spouse while wearing ill-fitting gloves"). Does the inclusion of specific examples mean that transfers for other reasons would otherwise *not* indicate a fraudulent intent?

So far as we know, the change in the bankruptcy laws has not slowed down traffic in asset protection trusts, and, just for good measure, the various state fraternal benefit associations remain open for business.

E.   WHO CARES ABOUT EXEMPTIONS?

We began our study of exemptions with the guy in the barrel, thinking about why he might get to keep his clothes. We end the section with a Congress not willing to prevent multimillionaires from protecting unlimited assets, if they can negotiate a carefully laid out chicane. The policy grounds for this result remain elusive.

In light of the difficulty of designing exemptions, what is at stake in setting the exemption level too low or too high? What is the real world effect of a given set of exemption laws? The studies are sparse and inconclusive. Michelle White, Professor of Economics at the University of California at San Diego, studied state exemptions and entrepreneurial start-ups. She concluded that the likelihood of a homeowner owning a business was 35% higher in states with unlimited homestead exemptions. Michelle White, Bankruptcy and Small Business, Regulation (Summer 2001, p.18). She concluded that changing bankruptcy laws and narrowing exemptions would "discourage many entrepreneurs from going into business and some of the discouraged businesses would inevitably involve innovative new ideas that would have generated jobs and economic growth."

What about the unsecured creditors who, at least in theory, recover less in high-exemption states? Should those creditors charge Texans higher interest than they charge folks in Wyoming? Do they? A group of economists claimed to answer the empirical question with a yes, but they compared the rates on secured car loans that aren't likely to be much affected by exemption levels. See Reint Gropp, John Karl Scholz, and Michelle J. White, Personal Bankruptcy and Credit Supply and Demand, 112 Quarterly Journal of Economics 217-51 (February 1997). Sure, we understand that there could be some spillover effects on secured creditors from the exemptions (they might have less opportunity to collect deficiency judgments). But that takes attenuated analysis and stylized factual assumptions (that deficiencies occur with regularity, that car lenders in turn go after them, and that the payoff has an upfront pricing effect in lending). Besides, if car lenders were worried about deficiencies, wouldn't credit card companies, who are unsecured, be far more affected? Yet they show no sensitivity in either the terms of their loans or the amount of credit they offer. Indeed, shouldn't secured lenders like *higher* exemptions, which protect debtors from unsecured creditors, leaving more breathing room to pay the secureds? We confess that the Gropp et al. study based on secured car loans leaves us scratching our heads.

In his dissertation at MIT, economist Fredrick Link examined the cost and availability of general unsecured credit (the debt that should have been affected by exemption levels) in states with high exemptions and those with low exemptions. He determined that the differences among the states were statistically indistinguishable. Fredrick Link, The Economics of Personal Bankruptcy (MIT June 2004). He also found that homestead exemptions were negatively correlated with homeownership, suggesting that state protection seems to yield fewer, not more, homeowners. Link's findings should caution against making easy assumptions on the effect exemptions have on credit.

There has been a great deal of press about unlimited homestead exemptions and the unsavory characters who seem to be attracted to expensive homes. Interestingly, the stingy homestead exemptions that will cost people their homes in low- or no-exemption states have drawn little press attention. During the debates over BAPCPA, Senator Russell Feingold, D-WI, proposed a floor on homestead protection for older Americans: anyone 65 or older could protect equity in a homestead up to $125,000 in value, regardless of state exemption laws or state opt-outs. The amendment was defeated. Cook Islands 1, AARP 0.

Problem Set 5

5.1. Kevin LoVecchio is battling a host of angry former partners in a real estate business scheme, who last week won a $10 million judgment against him in contract.

Kevin, a law school grad who never wanted to settle down and practice law ("too boring"), owns a gorgeous penthouse condo in Chicago and not much else ("temporary slump"). He has lived in the condo for five years, except for about two-and-a-half years ago when he rented an apartment in Florida for 91 days ("moved there for business, but I couldn't take the heat") and a period last year when he moved to Wisconsin for a couple of months ("thought I could commute to Chicago, but it was too far"). In both Florida and Wisconsin he applied for a drivers' license, registered to vote, and changed the address for his Financial Times subscription. Kevin came to see you yesterday to ask that you file his chapter 7 petition. Can he keep his condo? (Illinois is an opt-out state that permits a debtor to protect a $15,000 homestead.) Does he face any other obvious problems? §522(b)(3)(A).

5.2. Woody Woodward ran a stock scam that was so tangled that it took years for his investors to figure out. The SEC still can't explain it well enough to get an indictment, but a civil jury just awarded some of the victims $25 million. Woody and his fourth wife, Ingrid, just bought a home in Pennsylvania Dutch Country, a beautiful estate on 16 acres, for $10 million cash. Woody and Ingrid are current on all their bills, and Woody is ready to file for bankruptcy to deal with the big judgment. He tells you with cool confidence, "We plan to keep the house." Can he do that? §522(b)(3)(B).

5.3.A. On their wedding day, Emily and Ryan Morrissey closed on what they describe as a "nice normal house" in Texas. They paid $1,000,000 cash for the purchase price and have spent the last several years filling up the six bedrooms with children. About three years ago, they purchased the adjoining five-acre empty lot and added bedrooms to their house to accommodate the nanny, the tutor, and the housekeeper, all of whom help care for their brace of children. These home improvements cost another million, including a second pool and a backyard guest house for Grandma when she visits. Famous neighbors, mostly retired Texas Rangers, have moved nearby, adding to their home's worth; they estimate it at $4 million.

The Morrisseys are in serious financial trouble because of medical bills relating to their new children, triplets who were born prematurely. Despite both being licensed physicians, the Morrisseys had no medical insurance, figuring they didn't need it because they could care for each other. The medical creditors—including the hospital where they work—hound them about the unpaid bills, and they are at their breaking point with the stress. They know bankruptcy will let them discharge their medical debts but they want to make sure they can protect the house too. What do you tell them? See §§522(b)(3) and (p)(1).

5.3.B. The Morriseys' less affluent cousins, Frank and Leslie Shankly, have their own problems. Mr. Shankly, now 62, was transferred by his employer just over two years ago from Las Vegas to Providence. Although the couple's whole life was in Nevada, including their four grown children, they decided they couldn't afford retirement for another six years, so they took the transfer rather than looking for work in a rough market. When they sold their home, which they had paid off in full 26 years after its purchase, they netted $350,000. In Rhode Island they downsized to a three-bedroom condo that cost $200,000. The other $150,000 from the sale of the Nevada home went into their retirement account, accelerating their retirement plans by two years. The bad news is Frank co-signed his brother Jim's $500,000 business loan, which has been reduced to judgment after default. (Jim was last seen in the presence of a cocktail waitress named Ali in Northern Canada.) The worse news is Leslie just passed away. Frankly, Mr. Shankly is a sickening wreck and wants the psychic anguish of a pending judgment to be behind him. Nevada has a $550,000 homestead exemption; Rhode Island's is $300,000. Retirement accounts are exempt under Rhode Island law. How will the Shankly assets fare in bankruptcy? Assuming the condo and retirement accounts are the only major assets, what should Mr. Shankly do?

5.4. Your long-time tennis partner, Dr. Panoply, is an ob-gyn who is known and beloved throughout your community as a fine doctor and a community leader who always has time for charities. He knows you are a tort litigator and has always joked that he's always been proud that he's never needed your services for malpractice defense. He came to your office last week, *sans blancs*, and said, "I've heard so many frightening things, and the malpractice premiums have become so extraordinary, I think I should try an asset-protection plan, like the kind my friends have." He wants to set up a trust to hold all his investments safe from juries "who apparently don't understand that medicine is an art, not a science." What sort of state remedies should he fear, and how will your advice help? Are there collection remedies that might threaten him regardless of advice?

After you discuss things with him awhile, he says, "I have to admit, it's not just the malpractice thing. I have been in this terrible dispute with Stock, Lock, and Barrel, the well-known brokerage firm, and it's in arbitration, and I am afraid they may win, to the tune of a million dollars." Does this fact change your advice? Or your interest in representing him?

5.5. You are the new legislative aide to Virginia Bethania Herring, the ranking member of the Judiciary Committee. Two proposals for amending the Bankruptcy Code have just been dropped in the hopper, and she asks you to give her a preliminary assessment on each.

• Drop the categories in section 522(d) and simply put in a dollar amount. Debtors can protect any value up to that amount, regardless of how the type of asset.

• Remove the ability of states to opt-out so that all bankruptcy debtors have only federal exemptions available.

What do you tell her? Be prepared to begin your discussion with a clear position on whether she should defend the existing system or adopt one of the two alternatives above.

Assignment 6.

Claims and Distributions

Once it is clear what property belongs in the debtor's estate and what property the debtor may properly exempt, the trustee begins to assemble any non-exempt property for sale. In order to give each creditor the appropriate share of those sale proceeds, the trustee's attention turns from the debtor to the creditors. We thus now examine the process of asserting, calculating, and disputing creditors' claims, as well as to look at some insights into the modern consumer debt market that that process accords.

A. FILING CLAIMS

Ordinarily a creditor will receive and complete a straightforward *proof of claim* form (Official Form No. 10) with the notice of the bankruptcy. Its completion and filing are governed by Rules 3001-3008. In chapter 7 and chapter 13 cases, a proof of claim must be filed within 90 days after the 341 hearing, with certain exceptions. Bankr. R. 3002. In chapter 11 cases, the court fixes a *bar date* before which claims must be filed. Bankr. R. 3003. In chapter 7 or 13 cases, a creditor must file a claim in order to receive a dividend, even if the creditor was listed on the debtor's schedules; in chapter 11, a creditor who is scheduled is not so required. Bankr. R. 3002, 3003.

Practitioners report that some creditors simply fail to file claims in consumer cases. In chapter 7 cases, the habit of non-filing might be understandable since few cases involve non-exempt assets available for distribution. A U.S. Trustee report from 2002 pegs around 96% of chapter 7 cases as no-asset, a percentage that has not varied much in decades. In chapter 13 cases, in which there is typically some payout for all creditors, the failure to file a proof of claim is more surprising. Perhaps most unsecured creditors just do not bother to distinguish between chapter 7 and chapter 13 cases in their collection practices, and there are more than twice as many chapter 7s as 13s. Still, identifying the debts that will produce payment in bankruptcy can be a lucrative business. Before its demise, investment bank Bear Stearns owned a debt buyer devoted to purchasing consumer bankruptcy debts at a steep discount. It *did* file proofs of claim and got checks from trustees that aggregated to millions each year. Irony.

Unless a party objects, a claim is deemed "allowed." §502(a). Contrast how efficient and rapid this process is to the cumbersome obtaining and enforcing of judgments at state law that was introduced back in Assignment 2. Most claims are so resolved without objection and paid a pro rata dividend of the bankruptcy estate's proceeds. It is worth a moment's reflection to note this remarkable occurrence: claims are satisfied, through a court, without any state or federal adjudication that the money is owed. The parties simply agree on claims, and the trustee, representing the interests of all the creditors, ratifies them. This speed illustrates the efforts taken in bankruptcy to spend the available money on distribution to the creditors rather than on litigation about which creditors are entitled to collect.

We don't want to suggest, however, that the claims process is a free pass. There are *some* rules. One notable requirement is that a claim based on a writing must have a copy of the writing attached. Bankr. R. 3001. In the case that follows, there was shoddy documentation—not enough to kill the claim, but enough to enrage the judge sufficiently to resolve ambiguities adversely.

In re LANZA
51 B.R. 125 (Bankr. E.D. Pa. 1985)

GOLDHABER, Bankruptcy Judge:

The pivotal inquiry . . . is whether the evidence supports a bank's entitlement to the . . . claim[] at issue, notwithstanding its apparent gross deviations from standard banking practice. After carefully weighing the evidence, we will reduce the amount of the . . . first claim. . . . First Peoples National Bank ("the Bank") filed three proofs of claim. In support of the first proof of claim (No. 15) it appears that the debtors conveyed a mortgage on a parcel of real estate to the Bank in exchange for a construction loan with which to improve the subject property. This mortgage was executed for a denominated indebtedness of $200,000.00, although only $125,000.00 was advanced at settlement. The Bank later advanced $170,000.00 to the debtors through a series of unsecured loans, none of which, the Bank concedes, were charged against the original mortgage. Apparently, after some criticism of these advances from its auditors, the Bank convinced the debtors to grant another mortgage for $350,000.00 using the now improved property as collateral and allocating $125,000.00 of the proceeds to satisfy the original mortgage and $177,520.00 to discharge the unsecured indebtedness and interest. The mortgage was then properly filed and recorded. At the hearing the Bank presented conflicting testimony on the outstanding balance remaining on the mortgage and, weighing this discrepancy against the bank, we adopt the lowest figure presented by the Bank—namely, $300,000.00.

. . .

. . . The examples of so-called bookkeeping for a public financial institution that were presented to us as evidence could easily warrant for a half-dozen or so loan officers an other-worldly judgment [3] of perdition, forever condemning them to scramble about the floor of Pandemonium, each looking for the missing beads of his shattered abacus.

. . .

On the . . . claim, the debtors argued that the lack of supporting documents and mismanagement of the file should invalidate the Bank's claim. However, as stated above, the burden of proof is not on the Bank to substantiate its claim with extensive documentation, the onus is on the debtor to overcome the presumption of validity. . . . However, because of conflicting statements by the Bank's own employees on the balance of the indebtedness, we adopt the Bank's lowest figure of $300,000.00. The Bank should rightfully bear the burden of the ambiguity in light of its abysmal bookkeeping.

═══════════════

Ironically, the rise of technology has been making matters worse. E-commerce has facilitated a debt-trading market, and loans now change hands faster than you can say, "housing market collapse." (Recall the Bear Stearns consumer-debt buying subsidiary.) As a result:

> Th[e] growth of the [multibillion-dollar] debt buying industry has transformed the bankruptcy claims process. Driven by the economics of the assignment process, debt buyers in particular have given short shrift to the Bankruptcy Rules. Rather than attaching card member agreements, promissory notes and account statements to proofs of claim, and providing itemized statements of interest and additional charges, debt buyers have been attaching to the claim form a one-page "Accounting Summary" that provides the debtor's name and account number and merely restates the balance owed listed in paragraph 4 on Official Form 10. Proofs of claim are filed in this manner without any actual review of loan documents or account statements because the supporting documents required by Rule 3001 are not provided to debt buyers.

John Rao, Debt Buyers Rewriting of Rule 3001: Taking the "Proof" out of the Claims Process, 23-6 ABI J. 16 (July/August 2004) (footnotes omitted). In 2011,

---

3. We of the bankruptcy court could enter no such final judgment, the subject matter not being a core proceeding since that power is justifiably reserved to a higher "judicial" authority.

the Bankruptcy Rules were amended to address concerns about the accuracy of consumer claims. Some changes are arguably just clarifications, but the amendments allow sanctions if a proof of claim fails to meet the requirements. A court can preclude the offending creditor from presenting as evidence any information that should have been included that was not and/or award other relief, including reasonable attorney's fees for the additional proceedings required due to noncompliance.

B. CALCULATING CLAIMS

1. *Unsecured Claims*

a. The Claim

While section 501 lays out the procedure for filing a claim, section 502 explains the mechanics of calculating it. All claims, whether secured or unsecured, begin with a section 502 calculation. This section is the beginning point for claims against the debtor.

Let's work through an example. Sarina has a charge account with Sears. The terms are cash in full within 30 days or interest thereafter at an annual rate of 12% (unrealistic, but it keeps the calculations easy). Sears is also entitled under the agreement to attorney's fees and costs of collection equal to 20% of the debt if it has to take legal action to collect (a standard clause in credit agreements). At the date of bankruptcy Sarina had made one charge for $1,000, was three months late in paying, and Sears had begun collection efforts. Under these facts, Sears would file a proof of claim for $1,000, plus $30 interest for three months before bankruptcy (simple interest, not compounded, which is also unrealistic, but again it keeps the calculations easy). For clarity, this $30 is called "prepetition" interest because it accrued before Sarina filed her bankruptcy petition. Sears would also claim the $200 it spent on prepetition collection costs, for a total of $1,230. Under section 502, Sears is entitled to assert the full amount as an *allowed claim* because all of the amounts are treated as having accrued before bankruptcy and are therefore permissible prepetition claims. Because Sears has no security, it has an *unsecured claim*.

After the non-exempt assets have been sold, if the proceeds equal ten percent of the total value of all allowed unsecured claims, the trustee will send Sears a check for $123, i.e., "ten cents on the dollar," as its pro rata share. The shortfall between what Sears will be allowed as its unsecured claim—the same amount as it would in a nonbankruptcy lawsuit—and what it will receive as its dividend from the trustee upon liquidating Sarina's estate is "lost" to Sears; at the conclusion of the case, this amount is *discharged* (a subject to which we turn in Assignment 8). In this example, Sears only got $123 on its allowed unsecured claim of $1,230, and so $1,107 was discharged.

b. Interest on the Claim

It will probably take some time for Sarina's estate to be liquidated and Sears to get paid. If five months elapse between the bankruptcy filing and the distribution, does Sears get another $50 in *postpetition* interest? If Sears is an unsecured creditor, the answer is no. Assuming someone objects, Sears will be denied the opportunity to collect interest on its unsecured claim after the filing while the bankruptcy is pending. §502(b)(2). In the terms of the statute, this interest, while contractually obligated, is "unmatured" on the filing date. Admittedly, "unmatured interest" is like "unfallen rain"—a concept only a lawyer could love. It refers to interest in which the right to payment has not yet vested. Does that just mean not yet due? No. Interest can be vested but not yet due. Consider a loan that provides for a lump-sum payment of interest all at the end rather than interest calculated and payable over time in installments. Even though none of the interest is yet due if a filing occurs midway through its term, a bankruptcy court would reanalyze which portion of the interest was "matured," and hence could be added to the claim, and which was not.

There is no doubt that the delay in distribution is costly to Sears. It loses the time value of money, and yet it can make no claim for this interest after the bankruptcy is filed. That may seem unfair, but think of it from the perspective of Sarina's other creditors. The prohibition on unmatured interest is an extension of the pro rata distribution among unsecured creditors in bankruptcy: everyone rides in the same boat and shares together in proportion to allowed claims. Because the amount available for distribution doesn't increase, any postpetition interest tacked onto Sears claim—unless the same interest rate is applied to every other creditor's claim—will increase Sears' relative recovery, giving it a larger slice of the pie than other creditors.

There are only three ways to deal with postpetition interest soundly: (1) no unsecured creditors collect interest, period; (2) every unsecured creditor collects interest, at the same rate (perhaps a statutory one), or (3) every unsecured creditor collects interest, at whatever rate, if any, its contract, if any, allows. The Code takes approach (1). It rejects option (2) presumably on the theory that to add interest to claims of an already bankrupt debtor will not increase the collective recovery; on the contrary, it'll just add more debt to be discharged. It rejects option (3) for the reasons of equity discussed above. Some creditors will have high interest rates by contract and others will have low or no interest running. The Code should not incentivize the higher-interest creditors to languish and the lower ones to rush in to bankruptcy. Remember, many creditors may not have negotiated for an interest rate at all (think tort victim). By treating all unsecured creditors the same—that is, for all to collect a pro rata share of whatever is available for distribution, without postpetition interest—bankruptcy reinforces the goal of equality among these unsecured creditors. (For those who feel bad, consider never-employed section 726(a)(5).)

c. Complications with the Claim: Acceleration

Unmatured interest is not allowed, but what about unmatured principal? Because bankruptcy means all of the debtor's obligations are about to be resolved in a single forum, once and forever, there exists a need to accelerate all prepetition debts whether they have matured or not. Otherwise, long-term creditors whose loans were not in default (and therefore would have no immediate claim) could not recover from the estates of debtors about to discharge all their debts. A *statutory acceleration* of claims (to be differentiated from a *contractual acceleration* clause that makes the entire balance of a loan fall due upon default) derives from the broad definition of "claim," §101(5)(A), which you will note includes "unmatured" rights to payment. It has few parallels outside bankruptcy law. As a result, sometimes the claims process can involve difficult esoteric questions. A debtor who has guaranteed a loan before the bankruptcy filing, for example, has an undisputed prepetition obligation. But the debtor may never have to pay anything on the guaranty, and any amount that might have to be paid will change depending on how many payments the primary obligor makes before defaulting. Figuring out how to value such a guaranty claim can be hard. Or perhaps the debtor has polluted, and both the pollution and its effects remain unknown. Or perhaps the debtor has engaged in conduct alleged to be in restraint of trade, for which it is not sure whether it is liable (and if so, what damages it might face). These valuation questions all end up in the lap of the bankruptcy judge to be sorted out. We flag the issue now but will address it in more detail in a later assignment.

d. Postpetition Claims

We can anticipate a distinction that will be important in the next section. Suppose the trustee decided to repaint some of Sarina's non-exempt furniture before selling it (in order to get a better price) and the paint was coincidentally purchased at Sears on credit. Sears would have another claim to be paid by the estate, but it would be a *postpetition* claim and therefore made under section 503—"expenses of administration"—not section 502. Ordinarily Sears would be paid in full on its section 503 claim; administrative claims are usually paid first before all other unsecured claims. §507(a)(1)-(2). (Do you see why? That furniture's not going to paint itself.) We will explore priority claims in the next assignment when we discuss distribution.

2. Secured Claims

a. The Claim

If Sears has a secured claim, the first part of the calculation remains the same. Sears shows what it is owed pre-bankruptcy through the calculation of a section 502 claim. But as creditors line up for payment from the trustee, bankruptcy newbies rapidly find that the oft-repeated maxim "equity is equality" takes on unexpected meanings. The largest differentiation among creditors is the distinction between the treatment afforded creditors with valid security interests and that given to their unsecured counterparts. Section 502(b) governs the permissible nature and extent of an allowed prepetition claim, but section 506 adds special postpetition and collection rights of secured creditors.

Section 506(a) grants a secured creditor an *allowed secured claim* up to the value of its collateral. If the total claim is less than or equal to the value of that collateral, then the entire claim is secured, or in the parlance of the trade, "fully secured." If the claim is greater than the value of the collateral, then the claim is only "partially secured." (You may have heard the more colloquial term "underwater," which we guess means by analogy a fully secured creditor could be considered "overwater."). For partially secured claims, the portion that exceeds the value of the collateral is still allowed, but only as an unsecured claim against the estate.

The typical treatment of a secured creditor is illustrated by another Sarina purchase from Sears. Let's assume she bought a top-of-the-line riding lawnmower that Sears took a security interest in and consider two scenarios. First, say Sarina made substantial payments so at the time of filing Sears still owed $5,000 but the lawnmower is worth $6,500. This gives Sears an allowed secured claim of $5,000 against the estate under section 506(a). If the trustee sells the lawnmower, the costs of sale come of first from the proceeds, §506(c), and then Sears will get paid in full on its claim. The remaining proceeds go to the trustee for distribution to the unsecured creditors.

If, however, in a second scenario, the lawnmower had been ridden hard and poorly maintained, it might be worth $3,500 and an unsecured claim for $1,500 (the difference between the section 502 claim and the allowed secured claim under section 506). Sears will get all proceeds from the sale (after sales costs, §506(c)) with nothing left for the trustee. If the costs of sale were, say $500, Sears would get $3,000 from the sale and have to add another $500 to its allowed unsecured claim (bringing it to $2,000). If we continue the assumption from earlier this is a "ten cents on the dollar" case, Sears will get another $200 for its allowed unsecured claim, resulting in a grand total recovery of $3,200. In effect an *undersecured* creditor gets a bifurcated claim under section 506: a secured claim equal to the value of the collateral and an unsecured claim for the deficiency. This isn't nearly as good as if Sears had been fully secured and collected the full $5,000, but it isn't nearly as bad as if the whole claim were unsecured and Sears had collected only $500 (the ten cents on the dollar all other unsecured claims got).

b. Interest on the Claim

Another important difference between secured and unsecured creditors is in their entitlement to interest for the period following the filing of the bankruptcy petition. As we saw, both secured and unsecured creditors are entitled to prepetition interest, assuming that their agreements with the debtor so provide, but an unsecured creditor cannot claim any interest for the period following bankruptcy. Not so with secured creditors. The rich get richer, and some secured creditors can receive postpetition interest under section 506(b), whose explicit grant of postpetition interest trumps the general ban on unmatured interest in 502(b)(2). Specifically, if the secured creditor is *oversecured*, i.e., if the value of its collateral exceeds the full pre-bankruptcy debt (including pre-bankruptcy interest), then it can receive post-bankruptcy interest, generally at its contract rate, until the value of the collateral is exhausted.

In the scenarios above, Sears could have collected interest in the first but not in the second. In the first, where the net value of the lawnmower ($6,000) exceeded the allowed claim ($5,000), Sears would have had an allowed secured claim for $5,000 and it would have collected postpetition interest on that amount during the pending bankruptcy (sometimes called *pendency* interest). As the bankruptcy wore on, Sears could have its allowed interest grow and augment its secured claim until it reached a total claim amount that matched the collateral's net value. In our example, Sears could get up to another $1,000 in postpetition interest. If the bankruptcy dragged on after that point, it would then be in the same interest-deprived boat as unsecured creditors. In the second scenario, in which the claim exceeded the value of the collateral, Sears could not have collected any postpetition interest. This point emphasizes that being a secured creditor is not so much an abstract status as it is an entitlement to a priority claim on the value of a certain asset.

c. Complications with the Claim: Attorney's Fees

Not only do the rich get richer under section 506, they get positively spoiled. Attorney's fees incurred prior to the bankruptcy filing are treated the same as prepetition interest: if a creditor, secured or unsecured, is entitled to prepetition attorney's fees by contract or state law at the moment of bankruptcy, then the fees are part of the creditor's allowed (secured or unsecured) claim. Secured creditors who are oversecured, however, are also entitled to *postpetition* attorney's fees, similar to postpetition interest, until the total claim exceeds the remaining value of the collateral. §506(b). Even so, those fees must still be authorized and appropriate.

────── **JONES v. WELLS FARGO BANK, N.A. (In re JONES)** ──────
366 B.R. 584 (Bankr. E.D. La. 2007)

MAGNER, Bankruptcy Judge.

. . .

4. *Assessment of Postpetition Fees and Charges . . .*
b. Post-Confirmation Fees and Charges

Therefore, a creditor's right to assess postpetition attorney's fees and charges is prescribed by state law and the terms of its contract with Debtor. Unless allowed under state law and Wells Fargo's documents, no fee or charge may be assessed. The postpetition . . . charges and fees assessed by Wells Fargo are itemized as: 1) attorney's fees, 2) statutory expenses, and 3) inspection charges. Under the terms of the Wells Fargo Note and mortgage, Wells Fargo was entitled to charge Debtor's account for attorney's fees and inspection charges incurred in connection with the loan. Beyond the actual right to charge the amounts requested, the Wells Fargo documents also require that the assessments be reasonable. *See,* Exh. 2, Mortgage of Wells Fargo, page 8, ¶ 7 (Lender or its agent may make reasonable inspections of the property), page 8, ¶ 9 (if borrower fails to perform or if there is a significant proceeding that may affect lender's rights such as bankruptcy, lender may do *whatever is reasonable* to protect its interests in the property and borrower will be obligated to reimburse lender for said expenses, including reasonable attorney's fees); Wells Fargo Note, ¶ 9 (borrower commits to reimburse lender for costs of collection including *reasonable* attorney's fees) (emphasis supplied).

Under Louisiana law, the creditor bears the burden of establishing its debt. Additionally, the fees and charges must be reasonable. The right to seek reimbursement for a charge is not the equivalent of an unfettered right to assess the charge against the loan. For example, Louisiana law provides that attorney's fees and charges may be contractually authorized, but even if contractually allowed, their assessment must be reasonable. Thus, both under the terms of the Wells Fargo Note and mortgage and Louisiana law, this Court reviews the charges and fees assessed for reasonableness.

At trial, Wells Fargo offered no evidence as to the nature of the attorney's fees imposed post confirmation or their reasonableness. It neglected to produce invoices identifying the counsel who performed the services or any description regarding the services performed, time spent, or amounts charged. As a result, the Court cannot determine the reasonableness of the fees incurred because the Court was given no evidence as to what services were performed, much less why they were necessary. Wells Fargo simply failed to meet its burden of proof on this issue. Therefore, the attorney's fees . . . are denied.

At trial, Wells Fargo offered no explanation or evidence to support its "statutory charge" of $106.58. Therefore, it is also disallowed.

Following the institution of this case, Wells Fargo ordered sixteen (16) inspections against Debtor's property during the twenty-nine (29) months the case was pending and Wells Fargo's debt remained outstanding. Wells Fargo testified that, upon default, the employee in charge of administering the loan had discretion to order an inspection as often as he or she deemed advisable. Wells Fargo also testified that once a bankruptcy is filed, the loan is considered to be in default whether or not any amounts are actually past due. It also admitted that inspections are not performed on all property subject to bankruptcy administration. No other criteria or parameters for requiring an inspection were delineated. Following the filing of the bankruptcy petition, Wells Fargo performed monthly inspections beginning in October 2003 and continuing until September 2004. Reports delivered as a result of these inspections, were admitted into evidence. Throughout this period, the reports reflect that the property was generally in good condition. In fact, there is little to no change in the property's condition from month to month reflected in the reporting. Under questioning by Debtor's counsel, Wells Fargo's representative could not list a single reason why an inspection would have been ordered postpetition, nor could she detail any reason why continuous monthly monitoring of the property was necessary or reasonable. Wells Fargo appears to have no policy guidelines regarding the taking of inspections, and its representative could offer nothing approximating a justification. . . . Wells Fargo bears the burden of establishing that the charges it seeks to impose against Debtor's loan are reasonable. [T]his Court concludes that Wells Fargo has failed to meet its burden. Wells Fargo did not show that Debtor's property was improperly maintained, nor did it show that Debtor had a history of failure to maintain his property. The inspection reports change little from month to month, and nothing in them gives cause for concern. Thus, nothing in the reports justified continued monitoring. Given Wells Fargo's failure to explain the necessity of the services or their reasonableness, the charges may not be assessed against Debtor's account. Exhibit "C" to this Opinion reflects the post-filing loan history for this debt after taking into account the above findings. All postpetition charges not previously approved by the Court and denied as set forth in this Opinion have been removed from the history.

———————

The entitlement of *undersecured* creditors to postpetition attorney's fees is less clear. In our view, which is widely but by no means universally shared, undersecured creditors (like unsecured creditors) cannot claim postpetition attorney's fees. The reason is that postpetition claims are governed by section 503 of the Code, which only allows attorney's fees under specific circumstances. (Recall section 502 deals with the calculation of regular, prepetition claims against the estate.) Our conclusion is supported by section 506(b), which explicitly grants postpetition attorney's fees to oversecured creditors, thus showing that Congress knows how to grant postpetition fees when it so desires. There is no analogue to section 506(b) for undersecured (or unsecured) creditors. Notwithstanding what we believe to be a fairly clear statement in the Code, the case law is somewhat confused. Cases holding to the contrary hang on the specific disallowance of unmatured (e.g., postpetition) interest in section 502(b)(2). These cases observe that there is no proscription of unmatured attorneys' fees in section 502(b)'s disallowance list.

Unfortunately, this situation became more muddled after the Supreme Court's decision in Travelers Casualty & Ins. Co. v. Pacific Gas & Electric Co., 549 U.S. 443 (2007). The Court upheld postpetition attorney's fees in an unsecured claim, but in a bizarre procedural posture, in which it admitted it did not address section 506(b)'s textual relevance (whoops!), but explained somewhat defensively it was only because the parties forgot to plead it in time. (Civ Pro 1, Bankruptcy 0.) For a careful analysis, see Mark S. Scarberry, Interpreting Bankruptcy Code Sections 502 and 506: Post-Petition Attorneys' Fees in a Post-Travelers World, 15 Am. Bankr. Inst. L. Rev. 611 (2007). Incredibly, two circuits have tried to "follow" *Travelers* and cheerfully held postpetition fees are recoverable by unsecured creditors. See Ogle v. Fidelity & Deposit Company Of Maryland, 586 F.3d 143 (2d Cir. 2009) (postpetition attorney's fees allowed to unsecured creditor because "deemed" to arise prepetition); In re SNTL Corp., 571 F.3d 826 (9th Cir. 2009) (permissibility of postpetition fees depends on *state* law). Sigh.

d. Postpetition Claims

Can the trustee grant liens to secure debts postpetition, thus creating a *postpetition* secured claim (i.e., can the trustee buy that paint at Sears and grant a security interest in it)? The answer is yes, but under very constrained circumstances (and complex enough to warrant their own assignment, which we provide later on in the business section).

C. DISPUTING CLAIMS

The most frequent challenge by a debtor or trustee is that there was no valid debt under state law or that the amount of the debt was lower than claimed, either through calculation error or setoff (e.g., the lawnmower Sears sold was defective). But challenges are rare. In a study of mortgage claims in chapter 13 cases filed by homeowners—where high stakes would suggest closer scrutiny—

one of us found only four percent of claims drew objections, despite facial defects in paperwork and other failures in rule compliance. Katherine Porter, Misbehavior and Mistake in Bankruptcy Mortgage Claims, 87 Tex. L. Rev. 168 (2008) (*Misbehavior*). The rareness of objections is likely because lawyers aren't free. Similarly, once a debtor has filed for bankruptcy, if the claim is to be discharged anyway, the debtor may have little incentive to spend money fighting rather than settling a claim. Of course, the debtor's loss of interest in whether he is going to discharge $2,859 or $2,589 in unsecured credit card debt—he's too busy doing a little discharge dance—is precisely why the trustee must review the claims; accepting the larger amount means a bigger piece of the pie for the claiming creditor but a smaller piece for the others, and the trustee keeps things fair.

In the rare case of objection, the dispute is resolved as a "contested matter" by motion under Rule 9014, unless the objection involves the sort of demand that bumps it up to the more formalized "adversary proceeding" under Rule 7001, which requires service of a complaint, etc. In the event of a dispute, fact-finding and dispute resolution is quick. Courts usually consider the papers filed by the parties and schedule an hour or two to hear evidence.

As mentioned above, claims disputes are actually increasing in the brave new world of debt trading. We believe this has been especially fueled by *securitization*, especially in the residential mortgage market. What's securitization? Simply: selling stakes in loans. More complexly: it starts with a lender making a loan to a homeowner for a home mortgage. The thought of that lender keeping that loan while the debtor repays for decades is now, in many circles, charmingly quaint. Instead, the lender packages up its loans and sells them, just as a manufacturer boxes up radios from an assembly line for sale. The buyers are entities, who in turn sell shares of the bundle of loans they bought. Technically, the loan bundles are often put into a trust, which then sells ownership interests—securities—to investors.

The investors don't bear equal risk of nonpayment. Rather, the trust is sliced into tranches, with the lowest-risk (and most expensive) securities taking the first set of mortgage payments that come in for the month, and the riskiest (and cheapest) taking the last payments (or no payments if the riskiest debtors default). These securitization trusts work the same way investors in corporations with different risk appetites might buy bonds, preferred, or common stock. When the underlying loans in the trust are secured debts, the securities issued by the trust are *asset-backed securities*, of which *mortgage-backed securities* are a specific type. For more detail on securitization, see generally Steven Schwarcz, Bruce Markell, and Lisa Broome, Securitization, Structured Finance and Capital Markets (2001).

One problem that might arise is that if unprecedented defaults occur in the loans, failure might start creeping up the risk ladder, wiping out not just junior investors but senior investors, such as pension funds that think they are safely invested. That in turn could have a feedback effect on drying up credit for the underlying consumers, making it harder to make their payments. But that would never happen.

Securitization is so complicated, the trusts even need specialists whose sole job is to keep track of all the underlying debtors and process their monthly payments, making sure they go to the right place. These *servicers* are the ones who interact with the homeowner on the phone and by mail, but they as servicers actually have no ownership of the underlying mortgages and so have limited investment in the fate of the debtor. This a *simplified* version of a securitization chart.

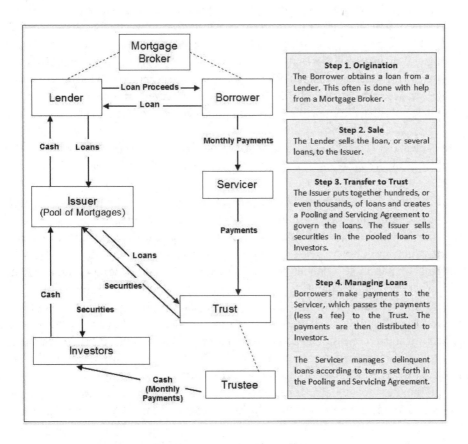

As one court candidly observes:

> The securitization of home mortgage loans has divorced the lending community from borrowers. Not only are the new holders of the mortgage notes nontraditional lenders, but a mortgage service provider is a buffer in the relationship between lender and borrower. The holders of notes do not see themselves as lenders, but investors in an asset. They have little interest in the

relationship between lender and borrower except as it might affect their return on investment.

Mortgage service providers administer notes for a fee. The terms of their agreements with investors, as well as the guidelines the investors set for administration of the loan, have ramifications for the borrower. Most servicing agreements allow the service provider to charge a flat fee, usually stated as a percentage of the portfolio under administration. All principal and interest payments collected are paid to the note holder. Usually, fees are additional income to the service provider while costs are simply a pass through, or reimbursable items. In addition, servicers invest the "float," or funds held on deposit, and retain earnings on that investment. Therefore, amounts held in escrow or in debtor suspense are an additional source of revenue for the servicer. While a mortgage service provider and note holder's interests are closely aligned, they are not perfectly aligned. It is in a mortgage service provider's interest to collect fees and hold funds, both of which generate additional income for its account. Conversely, a note holder or investor is interested in the collection and application of payments to principal and interest.

In re Stewart, 391 B.R. 327, 335-36 (Bankr. E.D. La. 2008), 2009 WL 2448054 (E.D. La. Aug. 7, 2009), *vacated in part, appeal dismissed in part*, 647 F.3d 553 (5th Cir. 2011).

Servicers are thus more likely to drive homeowners into foreclosure given their divergent incentives than the actual loan owners. Fees, delay, and miscommunication create problems. This is because the sheer complexity of the securitization process provides both increased risk of genuine error (lots of changing of hands so chances to mistype numbers, likely compounded by the need to rely on rote automation) as well as an incentive to cut corners or even to defraud (lots of paperwork to hide behind in byzantine file systems). This in turn means more disputes in bankruptcy that will come to a head in the claims process. In the recent mortgage crisis, for example, it is not surprising some of the first problems became exposed in the bankruptcy courts, which play an important watchguard role for consumer protection.

In the next case, Mr. Jones (previously discussed), midway through his chapter 13 plan, sought to refinance his mortgage. The payoff statement that Wells Fargo sent to close out the prior loan stated a balance he thought was suspiciously high. When Jones called Wells Fargo, it stalled and gave answers that he found to be evasive. He brought an action in bankruptcy court to obtain a correct accounting. Even that proved near-impenetrable, which the court said "resulted in such a tangled mess that neither Debtor, who is a certified public accountant, nor Wells Fargo's own representative could fully understand or explain the accounting offered."

In re JONES (con't)

. . .

I. FACTUAL FINDINGS

Debtor filed a voluntary petition for relief under Chapter 13 of the Bankruptcy Code on August 26, 2003. At the time of his filing, Debtor was obligated to Wells Fargo on a debt secured by his residence. Prior to the institution of this case, Wells Fargo had filed a foreclosure action against Debtor in State Court. . . . It also filed a proof of claim setting forth the amounts owed by Debtor as of the petition date. The proof of claim contained a schedule reflecting the following prepetition amounts as due:

1. Eight (8) mortgage payments totaling $18,796.19
2. Accrued late charges $823.04
3. Foreclosure fees $750.00
4. Court costs $1,283.87
5. Inspection fees $60.00
6. Escrow shortage $111.59
7. Broker's price opinion charges $435.00
             Total $22,259.69.

Attached to the proof of claim was a copy of an adjustable rate note dated April 4, 2001, evidencing the Wells Fargo debt ("Wells Fargo Note").

Debtor's plan of reorganization provided for payments to the Chapter 13 Trustee ("Trustee") of $2,105.35 per month for thirty-six months followed by a final payment of $625.97. From these payments, Wells Fargo was to be repaid on the prepetition arrearage represented by Wells Fargo's proof of claim. . . . [The debtor was also paying his ongoing regular monthly mortgage payments in addition to the payments on arrearages—Eds.]

II. LAW AND ANALYSIS

A. *Calculation of Amounts Due Under the Wells Fargo Note*

The indebtedness due to Wells Fargo is represented by an adjustable rate note dated April 4, 2001. The interest rate on the Wells Fargo Note is based on a published financial index plus 8.25%. The initial interest rate was 12.375%, but the Wells Fargo Note was subject to adjustment beginning on April 1, 2003, and every six months thereafter. However, under the Wells Fargo Note the interest rate was in no event to be greater than 15.375% nor less than 12.375%. If the rate were to change, Wells Fargo was required to notify Debtor in writing.

Despite the terms of the Wells Fargo Note, the interest rate charged from April 1, 2003, through April 1, 2005, was lower than the contractual floor rate. During a review of Debtor's loan records, Wells Fargo discovered this error and in a letter dated November 30, 2005, agreed to waive any claim for additional interest. . . .

1. *Prepetition Debt Calculation*

A review of Wells Fargo's accounting from the date of the loan's inception until the petition date reveals several accounting errors. These errors can be generally described as: 1) simple mathematical errors and 2) mistakes in the amount Wells Fargo reported were incurred. There do not appear to be any errors caused by an improper calculation of interest as the loan's effective interest rate was constant through the date the last prepetition payment was received in December of 2002. The first mistake in the calculation of the prepetition arrearage involved Wells Fargo's representations as to the amount of foreclosure costs it incurred. . . . [The court made several adjustments due to errors in the way the claim calculated the amount owed for escrow, which are payments made for taxes, insurance and the like, as well as foreclosure costs and other prepetition charges] . . . The end result is that as of January 4, 2006, Wells Fargo was owed a prepetition past due balance of $2,251.21.

2. *Assessment of Additional Prepetition Charges*

Wells Fargo has also added to its prepetition arrearage, without amendment to its proof of claim or disclosure to the Trustee or Court, additional prepetition charges. As previously stated, Wells Fargo's prepetition arrearage was calculated based on its proof of claim and included in Debtor's confirmed plan. Nevertheless, when Wells Fargo learned of the refinancing and a payoff quote was requested, it added additional Sheriff's commissions to its debt based on the amounts it anticipated receiving. . . . [Wells Fargo was later embarrassed by the sheriff's testimony that those commissions would not have been charged had Well Fargo told him that Jones was in bankruptcy, per longstanding and well known protocol—Eds.]

3. *Calculation of Postpetition Debt*

Starting on August 26, 2003, Debtor's loan was current. From that date forward, Debtor's past due account was "zeroed out" because the arrearage was payable through the plan. Therefore, Debtor's postpetition balance consisted of only principal, or $213,949.06, and Debtor's next installment was due for September 1, 2003.

Initially, Debtor's case did not go well. Because Debtor suffered a heart attack in November 2003, he immediately fell behind in his direct payments to Wells Fargo. These payments were aggregated into the Consent Order Sum, once again bringing Debtor's account current by agreement.

Wells Fargo's subsequent actions, however, caused Debtor to pay almost $13,000.00 in additional interest charges over the life of the plan. Throughout the succeeding years, Debtor made his payments in the amounts directed by Wells Fargo. However, rather than apply the amounts received to the postpetition installments for which they were intended, Wells Fargo applied them to prepetition installments, prepetition costs or fees, and postpetition charges not authorized or disclosed to Debtor, the Court, or the Trustee. . . .

The result was the addition of significant interest charges not really due and a loan balance out of sync with the actual amounts owed.

4. Assessment of Postpetition Fees and Charges

Postpetition, Preconfirmation Fees

Postpetition charges incurred prior to confirmation may be included in the debts necessary to cure a default under a plan. Therefore, they must be disclosed and are subject to review by the bankruptcy court for reasonableness. . . . [Several were not disclosed.] [See prior case excerpt for a discussion of reasonableness—Eds.]

Violations of the Stay

Wells Fargo charged Debtor's account with unreasonable fees and costs; failed to notify Debtor that any of these postpetition charges were being added to his account; failed to seek Court approval for same; and paid itself out of estate funds delivered to it for the payment of other debt. All of this was accomplished without notifying anyone, Debtor, the Trustee, or the Court, that Wells Fargo was assessing postpetition charges and diverting estate funds for their satisfaction. . . .

IV. CONCLUSION

For the above stated reasons, this Court determines that the amount owed by Debtor on the loan as of January 4, 2006, was $207,013.32 and that the collection of $231,463.97 from Debtor at the closing of his refinancing was substantially in excess of the sums due. As a result, Wells Fargo owed Debtor the full sum of $24,450.65 as of January 4, 2006. Since $7,598.64 was returned on April 20, 2006, a remaining balance of $16,852.01 is still outstanding and due to Debtor. For the reasons set forth above, Wells Fargo will be ordered to return the sum of $16,852.01 in accordance with this Opinion. The amounts due will bear interest at the legal rate from date of judicial demand until paid in full.

Debtor's request for damages incurred as a loss of personal time are denied because he did not prove at trial that he suffered any monetary loss as a result of the time he spent working. Although Debtor testified that he spent nights and weekends working on this matter, there was no testimony that he missed work or incurred a loss of income due to the time he spent. [A hearing on sanctions for violation of the automatic stay was held, and the judge entered an order compelling Wells Fargo to clean up its accounting procedures in lieu of sanctions—Eds.]

═══════════

It took a diligent court quite some time to untangle a mess that Wells Fargo itself could not explain. Had the debtor not been a CPA refinancing his home—and represented by counsel—would he have even known to challenge a payoff statement in the first place that was off by tens of thousands of dollars? Perhaps this is isolated madness: do we have systemic dysfunction, or is Wells Fargo just the one bad apple? One of us reports:

> Using original data from 1,700 recent Chapter 13 bankruptcy cases, I conclude that mortgage companies frequently do not comply with bankruptcy law. A majority of mortgage claims are missing one or more of the required pieces of documentation for a bankruptcy claim. Furthermore, fees and charges on claims often are poorly identified, making it impossible to verify if such fees are legally permissible or accurate. In nearly all cases, debtors and mortgage companies disagree on the amount of outstanding mortgage debt.

Porter, *Misbehavior*, at 121.

D. THE INSTITUTIONAL FUNCTION OF THE CLAIMS PROCESS

This Assignment began with an analysis of the claims filing and calculation process. It may appear to be a dry and technical area of bankruptcy law, crawling with numbers and percent signs, but that should not mask an important socio-legal truth: Bankruptcy is a public proceeding (sometimes a spectacle) in a court of law. While many debtors are mortified to see the details of their financial lives splashed across the pages of the bankruptcy reporters, lenders too find themselves coming under open scrutiny. Wells Fargo's curious "statutory charge"—we would guess charged on the account of any homeowner who files bankruptcy—and unnecessary sheriff's commissions left the *Jones* court nonplussed; its hidden charges on the postpetition workout plan—incurred seemingly out of thin air and with no notice to the debtor, trustee, or court—made the court irate. And this is the tip of the iceberg. Some of what has come to light in bankruptcy courts and in state courts processing mortgage foreclosure suits has been shocking to even the most jaded observers of commercial law. More from the good people at Wells Fargo, who were doubtless delighted to face Judge Magner once again.

———— **In re STEWART** ————
391 B.R. 327 (Bankr. E.D. La. 2008)

MAGNER, Bankruptcy Judge.

LAW AND ANALYSIS

Damages and Sanctions
Accounting and Administrative Abuses

. . .

The reconciliation of Debtor's account took Wells Fargo four months to research and three hearings before this Court to explain. An account history was not produced until two months after the filing of the Objection. An additional two months were spent obtaining the necessary information to explain or establish the substantial charges, costs, and fees reflected on the account.

In the end, Wells Fargo charged nine (9) BPOs [Broker Price Opinions—Eds.] to Debtor's account but could only produce two corresponding reports. At least three sets of BPOs were duplicative of each other; two BPOs were probably never performed due to the closure of Jefferson parish following Hurricane Katrina; and all contained hidden fees for Wells Fargo disguised as costs. Only two BPOs were ultimately accepted as validly performed.

Wells Fargo charged Debtor with forty-four (44) inspections; the Court allowed one (1). Wells Fargo also charged Debtor forty-nine (49) late charges; only ten (10) of which were approved. Almost every disallowed inspection and late fee was imposed while Debtor was making regular monthly payments [in the bankruptcy], was assessed under circumstances contrary to Wells Fargo's stated policies or the Note's terms, and was unreasonable under the circumstances. Substantial legal fees were also claimed without over $1,800.00 in credits being posted.

The calculation of Debtor's monthly escrow was almost incomprehensible and virtually incorrect in every instance. This caused Wells Fargo to demand substantially erroneous and increased payments from Debtor. But one of the most troubling problems with the accounting delivered by Wells Fargo was the preference for the payment of fees and charges over escrow, principal, and interest payments in contravention of the Note and Mortgage's clear terms. . . .

Improper Conduct in Connection with Bankruptcy Filings

Although Wells Fargo was specifically asked to reconcile the amounts reflected on its prior proofs of claim with the amounts claimed on its account history, it did not. A review by the Court revealed why: the proofs of claim filed in the 2004 and 2007 Bankruptcies were so significantly erroneous that a reconciliation was not possible. Charges for NSF [non-sufficient funds—Eds.] fees, tax searches, property preservation fees, and unapproved bankruptcy fees appeared on the proofs of claim filed in this and previous cases without explanation or substantiation. Further, these charges never appeared as entries on the account history. . . .

. . .

The Court finds that Wells Fargo was negligent in its practices and took insufficient remedial action following this Court's rulings in *Jones v. Wells Fargo* to remedy problems with its accounting. . . . In order to rectify this problem in the future, the Court orders Wells Fargo to audit every proof of claim it has filed in this District in any case pending on or filed after April 13, 2007, and to provide a complete loan history on every account. For every debtor with a case still pending in the District, the loan histories shall be filed into the claims register and Wells Fargo is ordered to amend, where necessary, the proofs of claim already on file to comply with the principles established in this case and *Jones*. For closed cases, Wells Fargo is ordered to deliver to Debtor, Debtor's counsel and Trustee a copy of the accounting.

The Court will enter an administrative order for the review of these accountings and proofs of claim. The Court reserves the right, if warranted after an initial review of the accountings, proofs of claim and any amended claims filed of record, to appoint experts, at Wells Fargo's expense, to review each accounting and submit recommendations to the Court for further adjustments based on the principles set forth in this Memorandum Opinion and *Jones*.

━━━━━━━━━━

Wells Fargo seemed to have dodged a bullet, with a clearly exasperated judge (once again) only ordering an accounting slap on the wrist in lieu of sanctions. Incredibly, *it appealed*—to protest the indignity of having a mere (Article I) bankruptcy judge issue such creative relief. The Fifth Circuit ultimately agreed and vacated the order. This meant the *Jones* decision, still pending on appeal with its similar injunction, was vacated too. Thus, thanks to a like-minded Court of Appeals panel and a tireless litigation strategy, Wells Fargo got just what it asked for.

JONES v. WELLS FARGO HOME MTG. INC. (In re JONES)
2012 WL 1155715 (Bankr. E.D. La., April 5, 2012)

MAGNER, Bankruptcy Judge.

This matter is on remand from the United States Court of Appeals for the Fifth Circuit ("Fifth Circuit"). . . . The mandate required reconsideration of monetary sanctions in light of *In re Stewart.*

. . .

II. PROCEDURAL BACKGROUND
. . .

This Court previously found that Wells Fargo willfully violated the automatic stay imposed by 11 U.S.C. §362. That ruling is not at issue. The only issue before the Court is the appropriate relief available. In light of the Fifth Circuit's ruling in *Stewart,* the application of the Accounting Procedures to all debtors in the district would be an improper exercise of authority beyond the bounds of this case. Because this relief was ordered *in lieu* of punitive sanctions, the mandate on remand directs that monetary relief be considered. . . .

A. Degree of Reprehensibility
. . .

The net effect of Wells Fargo's actions was an overcharge in excess of $24,000.00. When Jones questioned the amounts owed, Wells Fargo refused to explain its calculations or provide an amortization schedule. When Jones sued Wells Fargo, it again failed to properly account for its calculations. After judgment was awarded, Wells Fargo fought the compensatory portion of the award despite never challenging the calculations of the overpayment. In fact, Wells Fargo's initial legal position both before this Court and in its first appeal denied any responsibility to refund payments demanded in error! The cost to Jones was hundreds of thousands of dollars in legal fees and five (5) years of litigation. . . .

Wells Fargo has taken the position that every debtor in the district should be made to challenge, by separate suit, the proofs of claim or motions for relief from the automatic stay it files. It has steadfastly refused to audit its pleadings or proofs of claim for errors and has refused to voluntarily correct any errors that come to light except through threat of litigation. Although its own representatives have admitted that it routinely misapplied payments on loans and improperly charged fees, they have refused to correct past errors. They stubbornly insist on limiting any change in their conduct prospectively, even as they seek to collect on loans in other cases for amounts owed in error.

Wells Fargo's conduct is clandestine. Rather than provide Jones with a complete history of his debt on an ongoing basis, Wells Fargo simply stopped communicating with Jones once it deemed him in default. At that point in time, fees and costs were assessed against his account and satisfied with postpetition payments intended for other debt without notice. Only through litigation was this practice discovered. Wells Fargo admitted to the same practices for all other loans in bankruptcy or default. As a result, it is unlikely that most debtors will be able to discern problems with their accounts without extensive discovery.

Unfortunately, the threat of future litigation is a poor motivator for honesty in practice. Because litigation with Wells Fargo has already cost this and other plaintiffs considerable time and expense, the Court can only assume that others who challenge Wells Fargo's claims will meet a similar fate.

Over eighty percent (80%) of the chapter 13 debtors in this district have incomes of less than $40,000.00 per year. The burden of extensive discovery and delay is particularly overwhelming. In this Court's experience, it takes four (4) to six (6) months for Wells Fargo to produce a simple accounting of a loan's history and over four (4) court hearings. Most debtors simply do not have the personal resources to demand the production of a simple accounting for their loans, much less verify its accuracy, through a litigation process.

Wells Fargo has taken advantage of borrowers who rely on it to accurately apply payments and calculate the amounts owed. But perhaps more disturbing is Wells Fargo's refusal to voluntarily correct its errors. It prefers to rely on the ignorance of borrowers or their inability to fund a challenge to its demands, rather than voluntarily relinquish gains obtained through improper accounting methods. Wells Fargo's conduct was a breach of its contractual obligations to its borrowers. More importantly, when exposed, it revealed its true corporate character by denying any obligation to correct its past transgressions and mounting a legal assault ensure it never had to. . . .

. . .

VI. CONCLUSION

Wells Fargo's actions were not only highly reprehensible, but its subsequent reaction on their exposure has been less than satisfactory. . . . [T]he Court finds that a punitive damage award of $3,171,154.00 is warranted to deter

Wells Fargo from similar conduct in the future. This Court hopes that the relief granted will finally motivate Wells Fargo to rectify its practices and comply with the terms of court orders, plans and the automatic stay.

═══════════

Drinks on Jones and Stewart! Incidentally, how expensive would it have been to reprogram the "proprietary software" that Wells Fargo pointed to in explaining its procedures in bankruptcy cases? If less than $3 million, Wells Fargo goofed. Apparently not a company to change strategies lightly, Wells Fargo appealed the sanction award. The decision was upheld. 2013 U.S. Dist. LEXIS 37810.

For all its problems, Wells Fargo is only one mortgage servicer. But the problems with de-linked lending and mass processing of debts have extended across much of the industry and many of its practices. Another illustration of these problems lies in the apparently simple process of transferring the consumer's note from each originating bank to the securitization trust. That process creates a chain of title showing who actually owns what interest in each note. Because an actual human being has to execute those transfer documents, curious developments have arisen. To wit, some banks hired minimum-wage "robo-signers" to sign the name of purported corporate officers hundreds of times per hour in soulless monotony. One company, DOCX, specialized in the logistics of these mortgage transfers (and foreclosure affidavits, which require a sworn signature), had the absurdity of its forgeries exposed when it was discovered that someone named "Linda Green" had apparently executed a considerable percentage of all mortgage transfer documents in the entire United States. For an excellent report, see the expose at *60 Minutes: The Next Housing Shock* (CBS television broadcast Aug. 7, 2011), available at http://www.cbsnews.com/video/watch/?id=7375936n&tag=contentMain;content Body, which includes tracking down the actual Ms. Linda Green, a mail room clerk, whose name was apparently chosen for its brevity and ease in remembering by robo-signers.

When the mortgage default rate skyrocketed in the Great Recession and homeowners found themselves in state court foreclosure and federal bankruptcy proceedings, these brazen legal violations were finally discovered. (Warren Buffett says that it is only when the tide goes out that we discover who was swimming nude.) We end by letting these pictures speak a thousand words for themselves about the high-volume world of consumer collection that the bankruptcy claims process helps reveal.

Problem Set 6

6.1. Corinne Zeppo lost her job last month and filed a chapter 7 bankruptcy last week. One creditor, Miller Plumbing Co., claimed $3,000, plus (a) $200 in past-due interest accrued prior to bankruptcy; and (b) another $100 in interest accrued since the bankruptcy began. Interest was calculated for the pre-bankruptcy period according to the contract between Zeppo and Miller Plumbing and according to the state law judgment rate for the post-bankruptcy period. Miller Plumbing, however, has no security interest in any of Corinne's property. What is the amount of Miller's allowed unsecured claim in bankruptcy? See §502(a), (b).

6.2. Corinne had only two non-exempt assets: her car, worth $10,000, and 1,000 shares of MacroSoft stock, worth $15,000. At the time of filing, she owed her bank $8,000 on the car, and the bank had a valid and enforceable security interest in the car to secure its loan. In addition to the $8,000 principal, the bank claimed (a) past-due interest that accrued prior to bankruptcy of $500; (b) interest since the bankruptcy was filed of $400, and (c) attorney's fees of $1,000 expended in trying to collect. The bank was entitled to collect all these amounts under its loan and security agreement and under state law. What is the amount of the bank's allowed secured claim in bankruptcy? See §§502(b); 506(a), (b).

6.3. If, contrary to the pre-sale estimates, the car had brought only $5,000 when it was sold, how would the bank stand? See §§502(b); 506 (a), (b).

6.4. Ten other creditors of Corinne are owed a total of $20,000, but none of them is claiming any interest. If you were appointed trustee and collected $5,000 for the car and $15,000 for the stock, how should you distribute the money (ignoring costs, including your own fee as trustee)?

6.5. Josh Clark has missed four months of mortgage payments and received default notices from Four Clothes Bank, which services the mortgage. The house was bought a few years ago for $150,000 and Josh's balance is now down to

$140,000. But the property values in the area have fallen on average by a third since when Josh purchased the home.

You are in charge of the Default Department at Four Clothes, and upon reviewing Josh's file, your interest is piqued by several things: that a Default Relationship Manager made several calls to Josh around 10:00 p.m. to encourage him to make a payment, that the debtor has recently sent in several amounts constituting partial payments that are sitting in a suspense account rather than having been applied to the loan balance, and that inspections have been ordered weekly, pursuant to standard operating procedure. The mortgage agreement allows Josh to be billed "reasonable fees" should Josh's mortgage ever go into default, and the servicing agreement allows the servicer to agree to "reasonable" financial workouts and to bill the investors for its "reasonable" time in doing so. It gets a fixed fee (generally higher) if it has to initiate a foreclosure. State law forbids deficiency judgments against homeowners after foreclosure sales.

Josh's lawyer, Garth Ceia, just called to say that Josh has gotten a better job. He proposes a repayment plan: all penalty charges and interest will be waived, and Josh can complete "catch-up" payments over twelve months in addition to resumption of his regular monthly payments. He needs to know by the day after tomorrow, though, because Josh will file for bankruptcy if he can't get his mortgage situation worked out, as he also faces the threat of an overdue credit card lender garnishing his wages unless he starts making payments on the judgment immediately—something he can't do without a reduced mortgage payment. What do you think? What if it will take you a week to order Josh's original mortgage loan documents from archives?

Assignment 7.

Priority Among Unsecured Creditors

Although secured creditors have priority only in their collateral, their security interests often swallow virtually all the value in an estate, making secured credit the highest priority of them all. If there is value remaining, however, the trustee distributes that value to the unsecured creditors. The secured creditors who were undersecured because the sale of their collateral did not satisfy their allowed secured claims also receive distributions in this process.

Because unsecured creditors have not received priority by contract as the secured creditors have, Congress in section 507 determines the appropriate order and amount of the payout to them. The creditors again find that "equity is equality" is not strictly the rule. Some unsecured creditors are, by congressional preference, paid ahead of other unsecured creditors. In creating this priority scheme, does Congress (a) simply solve a collective action problem among private parties who cannot contract for priority among themselves; (b) serve various broader public interests; (c) simply respond to various political pressures; or (d) some of each? Consider these possible justifications as you read the priority rules in section 507.

In the great majority of liquidation cases, only priority creditors—and sometimes not all of them—will actually receive a distribution or "dividend" from the estate under section 726. In the minority of cases in which there is enough value left, creditors may be willing to litigate if necessary to get paid in the order and amount to which they believe the law entitles them. Note too that this priority scheme applies indirectly in large chapter 11 cases, where there is plenty to fight over.

Problem Set 7

Harold Smith declared chapter 7 bankruptcy on April 7, 2013. His non-exempt assets consisted of his vacation condo in Kitty Hawk, which the trustee sold for $400,000 but which was subject to a $360,000 mortgage, and miscellaneous personal property that sold for $25,000 after expenses of sale. All his other property was exempt. The claims filed in bankruptcy court were the following:

1. John Nelson, a private duty nurse whom Harold hired while his father was seriously ill: $14,000.

2. Social Security Administration, Social Security deducted from John's earlier paychecks: $1,260.

3. City of Eden, property taxes: $3,000 per year for the last three years, plus $500 penalties per each-year-unpaid for the three years—the standard fee for any delay in paying.

4. George Nartowski, down payment against a tractor lawnmower Harold had agreed to sell to George but had not yet given him: $300.

5. State Department of Revenue and IRS, income taxes: state $4,000, federal $14,000.

6. Telephone, utility, and other regular bills following bankruptcy: $3,000.

7. Sara Fleet, Harold's attorney: $1,750 in fees ($500 for a will; $1,250 for preparing this bankruptcy filing).

8. Sue Smith, Harold's ex-wife, negotiable note: $25,000.

9. First Bank of Seminole, deficiency on Harold's car loan after the car was sold prior to bankruptcy: $2,200.

10. Trustee's fee for administering estate and performing legal work for it: $4,000.

11. Insurance premiums for insurance on the non-exempt personal property prior to its sale by the trustee: $750.

12. Costs of sale of Harold's non-exempt real estate, including advertising: $2,800.

13. Harold missed a stop sign, but didn't miss the pedestrian crossing the street. The jury verdict against him was $10,000.

14. Other unsecured claims: $7,000.

Who will get what under sections 507 and 726(a)(4), (b)?

Assignment 8.
Discharge

A. THE POST-DISCHARGE INJUNCTION

After the debtor's non-exempt assets are liquidated by the trustee and the creditors receive their dividends (if any), the debtor finally gets a discharge. The discharge enjoins most, but not all, creditor conduct after bankruptcy, the same way as the automatic stay enjoins creditor conduct during bankruptcy. Technically, the judge grants the debtor the discharge to trigger the section 524 injunction after a discharge hearing. §727; cf.§§944, 1141, 1228, 1328 (parallel provisions).

The post-discharge injunction is not simply "Automatic Stay, the Sequel," however, as the case below explains.

In re HENRY
266 B.R. 457 (Bankr. C.D. Cal. 2001)

BUFFORD, Bankruptcy Judge.

. . .

B. Discharge Injunction Violations— §524(a)(2)

The automatic stay in a bankruptcy case does not last indefinitely. In a chapter 7 case for an individual, the automatic stay terminates when a discharge is granted or denied. In this case the discharge was granted on March 9, 1998. Upon the grant of a discharge, the automatic stay is replaced with the discharge injunction provided by §524(a).

The discharge injunction provision relevant to this case is §524(a)(2), which provides that a bankruptcy discharge "operates as an injunction against an act, to collect, recover or offset any such debt as a personal liability of the debtor, whether or not discharge of such debt is waived." See Molloy v. Primus Automotive Fin. Servs., 247 B.R. 804, 815 (C.D. Cal. 2000).

The discharge injunction is permanent. It survives the bankruptcy case and applies forever with respect to every debt that is discharged. [T]he Senate Report explains the impact of the injunction:

> The injunction is to give complete effect to the discharge and to eliminate any doubt concerning the effect of the discharge as a total prohibition on debt collection efforts. This paragraph cover[s] any act to collect, such as dunning by telephone or letter, or indirectly through friends, relatives, or employers, harassment, threats of repossession and the like.

S. REP. No. 95–989, at 182–83 (1979). The permanency of the discharge injunction contrasts with the temporary character of the automatic stay.

At the same time, the discharge injunction is narrower than the automatic stay in a material way. . . . While the automatic stay prohibits essentially all creditor collection activities absent court order, the discharge injunction is more selective.

Although the discharge eliminates a debt as a personal liability, it does not affect a lien that provides security for the debt. See §522(c)(2). Indeed, the law has been settled since 1886 that a discharge in a liquidation bankruptcy case (a chapter 7 case under present law) does not discharge a lien against real or personal property: liens survive or pass through bankruptcy unaffected. See, e.g., Johnson v. Home State Bank, 501 U.S. 78, 83, (1991); Long v. Bullard, 117 U.S. 617, 620 (1886). The Supreme Court expressed the principle as follows in Johnson: "Notwithstanding the discharge, the [secured creditor]'s right to proceed against [the debtor] in rem survived the Chapter 7 liquidation." 501 U.S. at 80. . . .

Johnson dealt with the question of whether a debtor can reorganize a secured debt under chapter 13 after having discharged it in a chapter 7 case. As a prelude to answering this question, the Supreme Court described the nature of the security interest that survives a chapter 7 liquidation as follows:

> A mortgage is an interest in real property that secures a creditor's right to repayment. But unless the debtor and creditor have provided otherwise, the creditor ordinarily is not limited to foreclosure on the mortgaged property throughout the United States, Ch. 176, §20, 14 Stat. 517 (1867) (repealed 1878). While under Bankruptcy Code §101(5) a secured claim can now be made, the principle remains valid should the debtor default on his obligation; rather, the creditor may in addition sue to establish the debtor's in personam liability for any deficiency on the debt and may enforce any judgment against the debtor's assets generally. A defaulting debtor can protect himself from personal liability by

obtaining a discharge in a Chapter 7 liquidation. However, such a discharge extinguishes only the personal liability of the debtor. Codifying the rule of Long v. Bullard, the Code provides that a creditor's right to foreclose on the mortgage survives or passes through the bankruptcy.

Id. at 83 . . . (citations omitted). . . .

A chapter 7 discharge extinguishes only one mode of enforcing a claim, an action in personam against the debtor. It leaves intact the right to proceed in rem against the property. *Johnson*, 501 U.S. at 84, 111 S. Ct. 2150.

This difference is reflected in the statutory scope of the automatic stay and the discharge injunction. While the automatic stay prohibits any act to enforce a lien against property of the estate, there is no comparable provision in the discharge injunction. Thus the bankruptcy discharge eliminates the personal liability of the debtors on the debt, and converts the loan into a non-recourse loan. See id. at 86–87, 111 S. Ct. 2150. However, the lien on the property remains, and the creditor may proceed to enforce the lien, to the extent authorized by state law, once the automatic stay terminates (whether by operation of law or by order of the court).

Once again the differential treatment of unsecured and secured creditors is stark. Chapter 7 enjoins all further action by unsecured creditors, but secured creditors can spring back to action with respect to collateral because the lien is typically unaffected by the bankruptcy. This means that chapter 7 is more of a respite than an escape from debt for debtors wanting to avoid repossession of property that is collateral.

Procedurally, the discharge in chapter 7 is usually efficient. In those courts that still require the debtor to attend, the debtor appears at a hearing before a judge, who will review the bankruptcy file, sign the papers declaring the debtor discharged from all listed debts, and close the case. Such hearings are usually mass affairs, with the judge making a few remarks to dozens of debtors gathered for the occasion. Nearly all courts now dispense with the hearing, instead mailing the discharge papers to the debtor on the theory that requiring a struggling debtor to lose a day's pay to attend a discharge ceremony is wasteful.

B. EXCEPTIONS TO DISCHARGE

Discharge is not a right but a privilege. That said, the overall discharge will be granted unless it is challenged. The trustee or creditors may object to the debtor's discharge of particular debts under section 523 or of all debts under section 727. It is important to see the distinction between a section 523 denial of discharge and one made under section 727. The former renders only one debt nondischargeable (a "rifle shot"), while a denial of discharge under section 727 renders all of the debts nondischargeable (a "shotgun"). Global denial of discharge under section 727 leaves a debtor who has turned assets over to the trustee for sale and distribution with no relief from debt other than the actual payments made. Even a rifle shot denial leaves the debtor without complete relief; if the excepted debt was substantial, it may leave the debtor in almost as bad shape as before.

For a creditor, of course, prevention of a discharge is usually the creditor's last remaining hope to receive any payment on the debt. As a result, when the grounds for denial of discharge arise, they are often more hotly disputed than other points of potential conflict in consumer bankruptcies.

The list of nondischargeable debts or the events for which a debtor can be denied any discharge at all continues to grow. In some cases the growth has come in response to unanticipated abuses that Congress wants to stop. In other cases, special interest groups have lobbied for an exception to the bankruptcy discharge. The categories of specific nondischargeable debts in section 523 presently number 19, a panoply that now includes debts obtained by lying on a credit application, debts for luxury goods worth more than $650 obtained within 90 days of bankruptcy, fraud by a fiduciary, alimony and child support, and judgments resulting from drunk driving (or drunk boating) accidents. The grounds for total denial of a discharge now number twelve, starting with the declaration that corporations do not receive discharges in chapter 7 and continuing with denials of any discharge for debtors who have lied or filed false documents in connection with the bankruptcy case or failed to complete a personal finance course. Reading them all is worthwhile. They are stern reminders of the edges of forgiveness in the bankruptcy system.

The following cases reflect a sampling of the grounds for denial of discharge and a flavor of the courts' analyses. First, a case involving a global challenge to the discharge.

———— In re McNAMARA ————
310 B.R. 664 (Bankr. D. Conn. 2004)

SHIFF, Bankruptcy Judge.

...

BACKGROUND

The debtor was the only witness at the trial. He testified that he had $150,000 in a briefcase as a result of numerous withdrawals from bank accounts during the summer of 1998 and that immediately after he was ordered to deposit the money in an escrow account, he gambled $130,000 in a winner-take-all stud poker game at a private residence in Brooklyn, New York. He was not able to provide any further details about the poker game except that someone, who no longer lives in the country, drove him there. In an effort to explain his failure to remember details, the debtor claimed that he was under the influence of alcohol and medication for severe depression. He further stated that he had just lost his job and had been taken to a hospital in New York with what he initially thought was a second heart attack. He did not, however, produce any evidence to corroborate that claim, such as medical or hospital records or the testimony of anyone who witnessed his condition. The debtor testified that he reserved enough money to pay for a Caribbean vacation, which was supported by receipts from that trip. He denied that he deposited any money into offshore bank accounts.

Apart from his difficulty to recall the details of the poker game, the debtor's credibility was also challenged by an unlikely difficulty recalling the details of significant bank account deposits and withdrawals prior to and concurrent with the alleged gambling losses. For example, he was unable to remember the source of an October 14, 1998 deposit of $44,247.87. He speculated that it was either from life insurance policies, despite testimony that other deposits were from those policies, or from his salary, even though it was a single large deposit, and he claims to have lost his job more than a month earlier. The debtor was also unable to credibly testify how he spent over $200,000 between June 1998 [and] February 1999. For example, he claimed that he spent a part of that money on renovations to his former marital residence, but the trustee reminded him that the property was sold in May 1998.

The evidence justified the trustee's suspicion that the debtor's claimed gambling loss in a fictional attempt to hide money that he considered to be his and not subject to his former wife's claims. He testified that he had an agreement with her that they would separate for five years rather than get divorced, so that he could maintain his health insurance through her employment. That issue was prompted by the debtor's claim that he was told he would require a heart transplant in the future. In return for her agreement, he claims to have agreed to give her custody of the children and repair the marital residence. The debtor testified that after she repudiated the agreement, he believed he was entitled to the $150,000:

I told her that if that was the case, that if she would not change her mind and go along with the agreement, that I would be forced to sell the house, take the $150,000 that I felt was mine. . . .

. . .

I told her that I would take my monies—if she would not go along [with his plan to set up a trust]..., that I would be forced to sell the home, take the $150,000 that I felt . . . was my part. . . .

(Tr. of 11/8/00 at 56).

I had taken my 150 that I thought was mine.

(Tr. of 11/8/00 at 60).

DISCUSSION
11 U.S.C. §727(a)(5)

11 U.S.C. §727(a)(5) provides that the debtor shall be granted a discharge unless "the debtor has failed to explain satisfactorily, before determination of denial of discharge under this paragraph, any loss of assets or deficiency of assets to meet the debtor's liabilities."

The plaintiff has the burden of introducing evidence of the disappearance of assets or of unusual transactions. The burden then shifts to the defendant to satisfactorily explain the loss or deficiency of assets. The test under this subsection relates to the credibility of the proffered explanation, not the propriety of the disposition. An explanation is not satisfactory if it is not offered in good faith or if it is vague, indefinite and uncorroborated. In re Maletta, 159 B.R. 108, 116 (Bankr. D. Conn. 1993) (citations omitted).

The standard of proof is a preponderance of the evidence. Id. at 111.

The trustee satisfied her burden by her effective cross-examination of the debtor, which demonstrated that he could not recall any details to support his claim that he lost $130,000 in a winner-take-all stud poker game. A person who loses $130,000 in a poker game would be expected to have some recollection of the details of the event which could be corroborated, or at least a credible explanation for why he did not.

For the same reasons that the trustee has satisfied her burden of proof, the debtor has not. Although the debtor attempted to excuse his inability to recall any details on the claim that he was suffering from depression, he did not provide a scintilla of evidence to support that claim, such as a medical report or a witness testifying that he was in poor health. Apparently, his alleged condition did not interfere with his decision to reserve at least $11,000 for a Caribbean vacation, which supports the trustee's suspicion that he deposited money in offshore banks. The fact that the debtor withdrew the money over a period of months further supports the conclusion that he was formulating a plan to hide it from his wife.

...

The debtor's schedules listed his former wife as a creditor, with a debt that is nearly all of his total liabilities. The parties agree that the alleged gambling occurred within one year of the bankruptcy filing.

[T]he debtor's testimony demonstrated he was angered by his former wife for breaking an alleged agreement not to divorce him, and he believed he was entitled to the $150,000. So, he took money he had been ordered to turn over to a state court escrow fund...and lost it in a poker game. In the best light, it was his intention to take a chance on either increasing the money, which would enable him to satisfy the court order and still keep the original amount, or lose it all. He cavalierly explained that his plan "didn't work out":

> [A friend] told me about this gambling situation. I went to try to double the money so that I would have money for my medical and pay them off [his former wife and/or the court ordered escrow] before the 25th. It didn't work out. I lost. I then went on that vacation for ten grand or whatever it was.

(Tr. of 11/8/00 at 78). The debtor's testimony demonstrated he did not care that he lost the money because he believed it was his to lose and that his wife had no right to it.

Bankruptcy is a privilege, not a right.

...

For the foregoing reasons, IT IS ORDERED that the debtor's discharge is denied under 11 U.S.C. §727(a)(2)(A) & (5).

As with the cases discussed earlier in the homestead section of the previous assignment, these discharge cases involve a great deal of judgment and discretion. In a case in Texas involving an elderly couple, the court in a thoughtful opinion accepted their explanation for the disappearance of large amounts of cash on the basis that South Texas ranchers often carry around a lot of cash to hire day laborers for work on the land. The fact that the debtors had disclosed everything was a major factor in the decision. In re Lee, 309 B.R. 468 (Bankr. W.D. Tex. 2004). In the opinion the court quoted a famous test to be applied to the phrase "explain satisfactorily" in section 727(a)(5):

> The word "satisfactorily" . . . may mean reasonable, or it may mean that the court, after having heard the excuse, the explanation, has that mental attitude which finds contentment in saying that he believes the explanation—he believes

what the bankrupts say with reference to the disappearance or shortage. He is satisfied. He no longer wonders. He is contented.

In re Shapiro & Ornish, 37 F.2d 403, 406 (N.D. Tex. 1929).

Very different from a global denial is denial of discharge of just one debt. For certain kinds of rifle-shot denials under section 523(a), the creditor must object to discharge in bankruptcy court or the debt will be discharged automatically. §523(c).

—————— **In re SHARPE** ——————
351 B.R. 409 (Bankr. N.D. Tex. 2006)

JERNIGAN, Bankruptcy Judge.

I.

. . .

The matter before the court is essentially a dispute between two parties, former friends, regarding various loans in the aggregate sum of $150,000 made by Ms. Baker to Mr. Sharpe in 2005. It was the undisputed testimony of the parties that Ms. Baker and Mr. Sharpe met sometime in December of 2004, shortly after Ms. Baker's divorce had become final, and that they became fast friends. Both parties, in fact, agreed that at one point their relationship could be fairly characterized as that of "best friends." During the period of their friendship, Ms. Baker and Mr. Sharpe spent a large amount of time together and spoke to each other most every day on the telephone.

In 2005, Mr. Sharpe and Ms. Baker were both involved in a business known as UltimateMatch.com. . . . During the first part of 2005, Ms. Baker made two loans to Mr. Sharpe evidenced by promissory notes, and made several other loans not so documented. All of such loans, the parties agree, aggregate to $150,000. The loans were made starting late 2004 through August or September of 2005. Mr. Sharpe does not dispute that he took such loans and, in fact, scheduled Ms. Baker as an unsecured creditor in the amount of $175,000 describing the nature of her debt as a "personal loan." . . .

There was . . . testimony that Mr. Sharpe had, for some months, been preparing to file for bankruptcy protection. Mr. Sharpe's former office assistant, Eileen Wolkowitz, testified that Mr. Sharpe maintained a file into which bills were placed, which at her deposition she had referred to as a "bankruptcy file."

The parties agree that Mr. Sharpe dressed expensively at the time the loans were made, wearing custom-made suits and designer label clothes and accessories, and that he continues to so clothe himself today. Mr. Sharpe characterized his manner of dress as "dressing for success." Ms. Baker testified that Mr. Sharpe's manner of dress led her to believe that he was a wealthy man. She also testified that based upon his demeanor and appearance she thought he had money. Ms. Wolkowitz also testified that Mr. Sharpe led a lifestyle that led her to believe that he was a successful, wealthy person and that she believed Mr. Sharpe intended to lead people to believe that he was a wealthy person. There was testimony that Mr. Sharpe utilized an American Express card, which had his name on it, but was to an account belonging to a Johnny Vaughn, a friend of Mr. Sharpe, to make many extravagant purchases. Mr. Sharpe stipulated to the fact that high-dollar charges reflected on an American Express bill, Plaintiff's Exhibit 7, were his charges.

Next, Ms. Wolkowitz testified that, over the 11 years that she has known Mr. Sharpe, she has known him to make a lot of money and to have lost a lot of money. She also testified that his disposition is such that he often attempts and genuinely desires to do more than he is financially capable of doing. And, indeed, what is remarkable about Mr. Sharpe's testimony throughout the trial, though convoluted and often confused, is the sense of a desperate, "pie-in-the-sky" optimism on his part that maybe, someday things will work out his way and he will be as rich as he aspires to be.

The parties also agree that, in addition to dressing extravagantly, Mr. Sharpe lived extravagantly, flying on a business associate's Lear jet, dining in expensive restaurants (often with Ms. Baker in tow), drinking expensive wines, and shopping in designer boutiques and expensive stores, such as Cartier. . . . Finally, there was also undisputed testimony that Mr. Sharpe described himself on MySpace.com, at some point during 2006, as "Funny guy with killer body and money to burn seeks classy woman who doesn't believe everything she reads!" Ms. Baker emphasizes the phrase "money to burn;" Mr. Sharpe emphasizes the phrase "doesn't believe everything she reads!"

Ms. Baker also recounted, as evidence of Mr. Sharpe's extravagant bent, a particular evening out with Mr. Sharpe and other friends or associates at one of the Dallas/Fort Worth area's finer steakhouses, Del Frisco's Double Eagle Steak House (Del Frisco's). Ms. Baker testified that she became familiar with Mr. Sharpe's spending habits by watching him spend money and that she knew that he would spend hundreds and hundreds of dollars on his frequent trips to Del Frisco's. Indeed, during the evening in question, Ms. Baker testified that Mr. Sharpe had ordered the most expensive bottle of wine the restaurant offered, a bottle priced at $15,000, and that Ms. Baker took it upon herself to approach the owner or manager of the restaurant to request that a less expensive bottle of wine be served instead. Upon Ms. Baker's request, a $5,000 bottle of wine was delivered for the evening's consumption. . . .

Further to the allegations of false representations on the part of Mr. Sharpe is Ms. Baker's testimony that Mr. Sharpe had represented to her at the time the loans were made that he was able to repay the loans because he was essentially hiding assets from his second wife, Jennifer Sharpe, in order to prevent her from obtaining her share of those assets as part of the then-pending divorce settlement. . . . Mr. Sharpe absolutely disputes Ms. Baker's assertion. . . .

The court finds Ms. Baker's testimony concerning the proposed plan to repay the loans to be the most credible. The court finds it difficult to fathom that repayment of Ms. Baker's loans would be out of income from UltimateMatch.com to which Ms. Baker would be legally entitled in any event. Moreover, Mr. Sharpe's alternative testimony that Ms. Baker made the loans based upon his own future earning potential was directly contradicted by Ms. Baker and the court finds her to be a more credible witness, if for no other reason but that she has but one, consistent story regarding why the loans were made and how they were to be repaid. . . .

III. CONCLUSIONS OF LAW

A. Do the trappings of wealth, demeanor and an extravagant lifestyle, together with an oral representation by the Debtor that he has sufficient funds to repay a debt, rise to the level of false pretenses, false representation or actual fraud such that the debt is nondischargeable pursuant to 11 U.S.C. §523(a)(2)(A)?

"A discharge under section 727 . . . of this title does not discharge an individual debtor from any debt for money, property, services, or an extension, renewal, or refinancing of credit, to the extent obtained by false pretenses, a false representation, or actual fraud, other than a statement respecting the debtor's or an insider's financial condition." 11 U.S.C. §523(a)(2)(A). Ms. Baker is hamstrung by the last clause of this provision, which—when read in conjunction with section 523(a)(2)(B)—requires that a statement respecting the debtor's financial condition be in writing in order to result in nondischargeability. Ms. Baker, by her own admission, relied upon Mr. Sharpe's *oral* representations that he had hidden away funds which were sufficient to repay Ms. Baker upon his divorce from Jennifer Sharpe. Ms. Baker, therefore, could not move under section 523(a)(2)(B) to seek nondischargeability of her debt. . . .

B. Mr. Sharpe made oral verbal and nonverbal misrepresentations concerning his financial condition to Ms. Baker.

This court finds that, during 2005, Mr. Sharpe lived a lifestyle and put forth a demeanor that suggested wealth. The expensive clothes, the expensive dinners, the extravagant spending, and all the rest were calculated by Mr. Sharpe to portray himself as a successful man of means. Mr. Sharpe characterizes this as "dressing for success"—and the court, having spent many years in private legal practice, certainly understands this maxim well. Ms. Baker sees a more sinister motive, one designed to dupe her (and, one presumes, others like her) into giving him large sums of money. The court also finds that Mr. Sharpe's concealment of his dire financial condition during 2005, and his, at least, vague intention to file bankruptcy—as reflected by the so-called "bankruptcy file"—are also misrepresentations of his financial wherewithal to repay the loans to Ms. Baker. But there is a problem with Ms. Baker's argument: the clothes, food, spending habits, *et cetera* are all false representations concerning Mr. Sharpe's financial condition. Patently, these do not fall within the ambit of section 523(a)(2)(A), which specifically excludes from it statements concerning a debtor's financial condition.[1]

These representations pale, however, in comparison to the admitted linchpin representation to Ms. Baker: in obtaining from Ms. Baker, at least, the two large loans aggregating $95,000 in principal, Mr. Sharpe represented to her that he had the funds available to repay her hidden away pending his divorce from Jennifer Sharpe.... Ms. Baker's unequivocal testimony is that the key inducement to her making the loans was Mr. Sharpe's oral representations to her that he had the funds to repay her and that he would repay her from such funds.

Every representation made by Mr. Sharpe to Ms. Baker in inducement of the loans was either explicitly or implicitly a representation concerning his financial condition. As such, they cannot form the basis of a cause of action under section 523(a)(2)(A). Section 523(a)(2)(A) excepts from it the broad category of "statements respecting the debtor's...financial condition," and does not require that such statements be formalized financial statements. The Tenth Circuit has set forth succinctly the policy behind requiring that statements concerning a debtor's financial condition be in writing:

> [G]iving a statement of financial condition is a solemn part of significant credit transactions; therefore, it is only natural that solemnity be sanctified by a document which the debtor either prepares or sees and adopts. . . .
>
> A creditor who forsakes that protection, abandoning caution and sound business practices in the name of convenience, may find itself without protection.

Bellco First Federal Credit Union v. Kaspar (In re Kaspar), 125 F.3d 1358, 1361 (10th Cir. 1997).

For these reasons, the court concludes that it cannot provide relief to Ms. Baker under section 523(a)(2)(A). Mr. Sharpe's representations, though false, all concerned his financial condition, which fall under section 523(a)(2)(B), and which requires a writing to accord relief....

---

1. Indeed, Ms. Baker—or at least her attorney—knew there was this very large flaw in her argument, for in the Plaintiff's Brief in Support of Non-Dischargeability of Indebtedness Under 11 U.S.C. §523(a)(2)(A) and (a)(6) filed with this court in advance of trial, the Plaintiff quoted section 523(a)(2)(A), but left out, with the convenient use of an ellipsis, the critical phrase "other than a statement respecting the debtor's or an insider's financial condition." Thankfully, the court has several copies of the Bankruptcy Code handy so it could consult the entire statutory provision in addressing this question.

IV. CONCLUSION

For the foregoing reasons, Plaintiff's $150,000 debt is found to be dischargeable....

━━━━━━━━

The next case involves a popular form of loan in the pre-crash housing industry: the "stated income" loan, so called because the applicant's statement of income did not have to be verified by pay stubs, income tax returns, or the like. They were widely available, often over the Internet. Because of the lack of the usual verification, in some quarters they were called "liar loans." With a nickname like that, satisfying the formal requirements for a financial statement may not be enough.

─────── **In re HILL** ───────

2008 WL 2227359 (Bankr. N.D. Cal. 2008)

TCHAIKOVSKY, Bankruptcy Judge.

In this adversary proceeding, plaintiff National City Bank (the "Bank"), a foreclosed out former junior deed of trust holder, seeks to except its approximately $250,000 claim from the above-captioned debtors' (the "Debtors") chapter 7 discharge pursuant to 11 U.S.C. §523(a)(2)(B). For the reasons stated below, the Court will enter judgment in favor of the Debtors.

SUMMARY OF FACTS

This adversary proceeding is a poster child for some of the practices that have led to the current crisis in our housing market.

The Debtors bought their home in El Sobrante, California (the "House") nearly 20 years ago for $220,000. They filed for chapter 7 bankruptcy in April 2007. After purchasing the House, as the value of the House increased, the Debtors refinanced the original first deed of trust to obtain additional cash. They also obtained a junior deed of trust, which they refinanced several times. At the time they filed their bankruptcy petition, the Debtors scheduled the debt secured by the House as totaling approximately $683,000.

The Debtors' income was modest. Mr. Hill was a parts manager at Auto Wholesaling, earning an annual salary of up to $39,000, depending on overtime. Mrs. Hill was self-employed, using a dba of C Ann H Distributing, distributing free periodicals for various companies. Her income also fluctuated, depending on how many companies were employing her for this purpose. According to the Debtors' Statement of Financial Affairs, filed in their bankruptcy case, in 2006, Mrs. Hill's annual gross income was between $25,000 and $26,000. It appears doubtful that the Debtors' combined annual gross income was ever greater than $65,000.

In April 2006, Mrs. Hill contacted a mortgage broker, Winston Ellerback ("Ellerback"), seeking to refinance the Debtors' existing second deed of trust debt. Ellerback, who testified at trial, stated that he had acted as the Debtors' loan broker on five prior occasions. At that time, the second deed of trust was held by someone other than the Bank. The debt secured by the second deed of trust had a balance of approximately $100,000. The Debtors sought and obtained from Bank an equity line of credit for $200,000, thereby obtaining approximately $60,000 in cash after paying the cost of the refinance and other consumer obligations. They used the cash to pay off their consumer debt and to "fix up" the House.

In the loan application submitted to obtain this loan (the "April Loan Application"), Mr. Hill's monthly income was listed as $8,176 (i.e., $98,112 on an annual basis) and Mrs. Hill's [monthly] income was listed as $3,967 (i.e., $47,604 on an annual basis) for a combined [monthly] income of approximately $12,143 (i.e., $145,716 on an annual basis). Ellerback stated that he obtained this income information from Mrs. Hill over the phone, inputted it into the application form, and sent the application to the Debtors for their signature.[1]

In October 2006, the Debtors were in need of more cash. The Bank permitted them to increase their equity line of credit to $250,000. This time, instead of contacting Ellerback to handle the transaction, Mrs. Hill dealt with the Bank directly. . . .

[A bank manager] noted that both this loan and the loan obtained by the Debtors in April 2006 were "stated income" loans which did not require verification of income. Eubanks testified that the loans were generated for the purposes of sale and that certain guidelines (the "Guidelines") had to be followed to render them acceptable for that purpose. . . .

According to the Guidelines, for a borrower who was self-employed, the Bank could choose one of three types of verification: (1) a copy of the borrower's business license, (2) a copy of the most recent month's bank statement reflecting liquidity at least equal to one-tenth of the borrower's annual income, or (3) a CPA letter verifying the existence and ownership of the business. . . . A copy of a letter verifying the existence and ownership of Mrs. Hill's business was introduced into evidence. The letter was written on the letterhead of a CPA, but was signed by someone other than the CPA whose name was on the letterhead . . . .

---

1. Mrs. Hill denied having told Ellerback that her and her husband's incomes were in the amounts set forth on the loan application. She and her husband both testified that they had not read the loan application before signing it and that moreover they had never read a loan application in their lives. The Bank presented evidence that called into question the credibility of this testimony. In April 2006, together with the loan application, Ellerback sent the Debtors an estimated closing statement for their signatures. He had inadvertently checked a box on the second page of the document in a section dealing with pre-payment penalties. Mrs. Hill called Ellerback and told him about the error. He told her to cross it out and initial the change. She did so.

In April 2006, the House had been appraised at $785,000. In October 2006, the House was appraised at $856,000. Shortly after the Debtors filed for bankruptcy in April 2007, the first deed of trust holder purchased the House at its foreclosure sale pursuant to a credit bid based on a secured debt of approximately $450,000, no one having submitted an overbid.

DISCUSSION

A. Applicable Law

A creditor seeking to establish a debt as nondischargeable under §523(a)(2)(B) must demonstrate that: (1) The debtor made a written representation . . . respecting the debtor's financial condition; (2) the representation was material; (3) the debtor knew at the time the representation was made that it was false; (4) the representation was made with the intent to deceive the creditor; (5) the creditor relied on the representation; (6) the reliance was reasonable; and (7) the damage suffered by the creditor proximately resulted from the representation. . . .

B. Decision

As set forth above, the Ninth Circuit has identified seven elements to a claim under §523(a)(2)(B). The creditor seeking to except its debt from the debtor's discharge must prove each of these elements by a preponderance of the evidence.

The first two elements of the Bank's claim were not in dispute: i.e., that the Debtors made a false representation to the Bank in writing concerning their financial condition and that the misrepresentation was material. The Debtors admitted that they submitted the October Loan Application and that the figures listed for their incomes were significantly overstated. Those representations concerned their financial condition and were false. Thus, the first element of the Bank's claim is established. If their true incomes had been disclosed, the Debtors would not have qualified for the loan. Their debt to income ratio would have exceeded the maximum permitted by the Guidelines. Thus, the false representation was material, thereby establishing the second element of the Bank's claim.

The Court concludes that the Bank met its burden of proof with respect to the second and third elements of its claim: i.e., that the Debtors knew that the representation was false at the time it was made and that they made the representation with the intent to deceive the Bank. The Debtors testified that they did not supply the false figures regarding their income and did not read the October Loan Application before they signed it. As a result, they contended, the Bank failed to establish either their knowledge or the falsity of the representation or their intent to deceive the Bank. The Court did not find their testimony credible.

In large part, this conclusion is drawn from the evidence presented with respect to the April 2006 loan....

Ellerback testified that Mrs. Hill provided him with the income information. He also testified that, before signing and submitting the April Loan Application, Mrs. Hill caught a mistake he had made in one of the loan documents and called it to his attention. The Court found Ellerback to be a more credible witness than Mrs. Hill. The Debtors' lack of credibility concerning the April 2006 loan transaction undermines the credibility of their testimony concerning the October 2006 loan transaction.[5]

Moreover, the Hills, while not highly educated, were not unsophisticated. They had obtained numerous home and car loans and were familiar with the loan application process. . . .

However, the Bank's suit fails due to its failure to prove the sixth element of its claim: i.e., the reasonableness of its reliance. As stated above, the reasonableness of a creditor's reliance is judged by an objective standard. In general, a lender's reliance is reasonable if it followed its normal business practices. However, this may not be enough if those practices deviate from industry standards or if the creditor ignored a "red flag." Here, it is highly questionable whether the industry standards—as those standards are reflected by the Guidelines—were objectively reasonable. However, even if they were, the Bank clearly deviated to some extent from those standards. In addition, the Bank ignored a "red flag" that should have called for more investigation concerning the accuracy of the income figures.

As noted above, the Guidelines required an evaluation of the reasonableness of the salary listed by an employed borrower based on job type and geographical area, among other things. No evidence was provided by the Bank that this evaluation was done. Additionally, with respect to a self-employed individual, the Guidelines required a letter from a CPA verifying the existence and ownership of the business. While the letter relied upon by the Bank verifying the existence and ownership of Mrs. Hill's business was on the letterhead of a CPA, whose existence was itself independently verified by the Bank, the letter was not signed by the CPA. The person signing the letter did not identify himself as a CPA and may not even have been an employee of the CPA on whose letterhead the letter was written.

More important, the Bank ignored the "red flag" established by the variation in the incomes set forth on the April Loan Application as compared to the incomes set forth on the October Loan Application. The Bank employee handling the loan transaction in October 2006 knew that the Bank had made a loan to the

5. The Court also found it likely that Mrs. Hill avoided using Ellerback to obtain the October 2006 loan for fear that he would have questioned her concerning the changes in their income figures as compared to six months earlier.

Debtors just six months earlier and that they were now attempting to increase the amount of the loan. The employee necessarily had at her disposal the file with respect to the earlier loan. Not only were the total income figures on the October 2006 Loan Application substantially higher than the figures on the [April] 2006 Loan Application, the income figures for the spouses were switched. The total annual income listed for the Debtors on the April 2006 Loan Application was $145,716. On the October Loan Application, it was $190,000. On the April Loan Application, Mr. Hill's annual income was listed as $98,112 and Mrs. Hill's as $47,604. On the October Loan Application, Mr. Hill's annual income was listed as $67,200 and Mrs. Hill's as $123,600.

Based on the foregoing, the Court concludes that either the Bank did not rely on the Debtors' representations concerning their income or that its reliance was not reasonable based on an objective standard. In fact, the minimal verification required by an "income stated" loan, as established by the Guidelines, suggests that this type of loan is essentially an "asset based" loan. In other words, the Court surmises that the Bank made the loan principally in reliance on the value of the collateral: i.e., the House. If so, the Bank obtained the appraisal upon which it principally relied in making the loan. Subsequent events strongly suggest that the appraisal was inflated. However, under these circumstances, the Debtors cannot be blamed for the Bank's loss, and the Bank's claim should be discharged.

CONCLUSION

While the Court finds and concludes that the Debtors made a material false representation concerning their financial condition to the Bank in October 2006, with knowledge of its falsity and the intent to deceive the Bank, the Court finds and concludes that the Bank's nondischargeability claim under §523(a)(2)(B) must fail. The Bank failed to prove that it reasonably relied on the Debtors' false representation concerning their income, as set forth in the October Loan Application. As a result, the Bank's claim has been discharged.

One particular debt that has been singled out for special protection against discharge in bankruptcy is the student loan. While some people may fear soon-to-be-rich doctors and lawyers waltzing into bankruptcy to discharge huge loans incurred in college and grad school, many people are struggling with student loans used to acquire skills that do not pay nearly so well, a topic gaining greater significance as scrutiny of for-profit schools intensifies. Andrew Delbanco, College: What It Was, Is, and Should Be (Princeton University Press, 2012). In 2007, one-quarter of consumer bankruptcy debtors owed student loans. Among this group, 30% had dropped out of their educational program, adding further fuel to a heated debate about student loans in bankruptcy. Katherine Porter, *Broke*, 85, 93.

Given the high stakes of nondischargeability and the considerable discretion accorded bankruptcy judges, disagreement is inevitable, even within the same case.

―――― **EDUCATIONAL CREDIT MGMT. CORP. v. JESPERSON** ――――
571 F.3d 775 (8th Cir. 2009)

LOKEN, Chief Judge.

Mark Allen Jesperson, a recently licensed Minnesota attorney, petitioned for Chapter 7 bankruptcy relief in October 2005 and commenced this core proceeding against his student loan creditors, seeking an undue hardship discharge of substantial student loan debts, which would otherwise be non-dischargeable under 11 U.S.C. §523(a)(8). The bankruptcy court concluded that Jesperson's student loan debts "constitute an undue hardship . . . and are accordingly discharged." . . . The district court affirmed. Creditor Educational Credit Management Corporation (ECMC) appeals this final judgment. The issue, as we perceive it, is whether a recent law school graduate who is reasonably likely to be able to make significant debt repayments in the foreseeable future, and who qualifies for the Department of Education's twenty-five year Income Contingent Repayment Plan, is entitled to an undue hardship discharge because, as the bankruptcy court put it, it is unlikely that his "shockingly immense" student loan debts will be totally repaid and therefore, "without the relief of discharge now, the debtor would, in effect, be sentenced to 25 years in a debtors' prison without walls." Reviewing the determination of undue hardship *de novo*, we reverse. . . .

I.

Section 523(a)(8) of the Bankruptcy Code provides that debts for educational loans . . . may not be discharged unless "excepting such debt from discharge . . . would impose an undue hardship on the debtor and the debtor's dependents." Federal government student loan programs began in 1958. In 1973, to curb perceived abuses, the Commission on the Bankruptcy Laws of the United States recommended that "educational loans be nondischargeable unless the first payment falls due more than five years prior to the petition." H.R. Doc. No. 93-137 (1973), reprinted in B App. Collier on Bankruptcy, pt. 4(c), at 4-432 (15th rev. ed. 2008). Congress enacted this recommendation in the Bankruptcy Reform Act of 1978. Pub. L. No. 95-598, §523(a)(8), 92 Stat. 2549, 2591 (1978), codified at 11 U.S.C. §523(a)(8). In 1990, Congress lengthened from five to seven years the period beyond which government-assisted student loans became automatically dischargeable. Pub. L. No. 101-647, §3621, 104 Stat. 4789, 4964-65 (1990), amending 11 U.S.C. §523(a)(8)(A). Then, in the Higher Education

Amendments of 1998, Congress eliminated this time limitation, making "undue hardship" the only exception to non-dischargeability. Pub. L. No. 105-244, §971(a), 112 Stat. 1581, 1837 (1998).

We apply a totality-of-the-circumstances test in determining undue hardship under §523(a)(8). Reviewing courts must consider the debtor's past, present, and reasonably reliable future financial resources, the debtor's reasonable and necessary living expenses, and "any other relevant facts and circumstances." Long, 322 F.3d at 554. The debtor has the burden of proving undue hardship by a preponderance of the evidence. The burden is rigorous. "Simply put, if the debtor's reasonable future financial resources will sufficiently cover payment of the student loan debt – while still allowing for a minimal standard of living – then the debt should not be discharged." Id. at 554-55. Undue hardship "is a question of law, which we review de novo. Subsidiary findings of fact on which the legal conclusion is based are reviewed for clear error." In re Reynolds, 425 F.3d 526, 531 (8th Cir. 2005).

II.

When this case was tried in February 2007, Jesperson was forty-three years old, in good health, and unmarried, with two sons from different relationships living with their mothers. He began college in 1983, attended three schools over the next eleven years, and graduated from the University of Minnesota-Duluth in 1994. He began law school in 1996, changed schools in 1997, completed his legal education in 2000, and passed the bar on his first attempt in February 2002. At the time of trial, he owed ECMC $304,463.62 in principal, interest, and collection costs on eighteen student loans, and he owed Arrow Financial Services $58,755.26 on seven other student loans. He has never repaid any part of any loan.

The bankruptcy court found that Jesperson's "record of work experience is besmirched by a patent lack of ambition, cooperation and commitment." . . . After passing the bar, Jesperson was hired as a judicial clerk on the island of Saipan, then as an attorney with Alaska Legal Services, and then as a legal temporary with Kelly Services, Inc. He quit each job for a variety of personal reasons. Several months after leaving Kelly, he began work for another placement agency, Spherion Professional Services. At the time of trial, he was working on a project that paid $25 an hour. He was one of only ten lawyers Spherion retained out of a pool of sixty. He testified[:]

> Q It's true, Mr. Jesperson, that you think this debt should just go away, isn't that true?
> A Yes.
> Q And even if you had, Mr. Jesperson, an extra $500 per month, you don't think you should have to put that towards your student loans, do you?
> A No.

Based on gross monthly income of $4,000, Jesperson stipulated that he was likely in the 33% combined federal and state income tax bracket. Using this inflated tax rate, the bankruptcy court found that his current after-tax income was $2,680 per month. Use of the inflated tax rate was clear error. Arguably, Jesperson's failure to make a good faith estimate of his applicable tax rate means that he failed to prove undue hardship. Alternatively, a reasonable estimate of the combined rate for gross income of $48,000 would be 17.5%, producing after-tax net income of $3,300 per month rather than $2,680 per month. The bankruptcy court estimated Jesperson's "basic necessary monthly expenses" as $2857 – $1,000 for housing, $1,000 for child support, $325 for food, $142 for auto maintenance and insurance, $250 for gasoline, and $140 for parking. [The bankruptcy court also questioned, but ultimately allowed, $125 in expenses toward cigarettes.–Eds.] However, Jesperson testified at trial that he lived rent free with his brother, expected to pay his brother $500 per month, and was looking for an apartment. Estimating his basic necessary monthly housing expense at $1,000 per month, rather than $500, was clear error. A debtor making a good faith effort to repay loans would continue to live with his brother to save money. While Jesperson is under a court order to pay $500 per month to support his elder son, he testified he has never made a full monthly payment. He does not owe child support for the younger son, but occasionally pays $200-$400 to the mother of this son, and feels an obligation to pay $500 to support each child.

Based on these estimates, the bankruptcy court concluded that "Jesperson's current surplus is at best a trifle and more likely a fiction." This was clear error. A court may not engage in speculation when determining net income and reasonable and necessary living expenses. . . . To be reasonable and necessary, an expense must be "modest and commensurate with the debtor's resources." In re DeBrower, 387 B.R. 587, 590 (Bankr. N.D. Iowa 2008). On this record, it is apparent that the court underestimated Jesperson's monthly net income and overestimated his reasonable and necessary living expenses. . . . A reasonable estimate would be a surplus of approximately $900 per month.

III.

Jesperson's young age, good health, number of degrees, marketable skills, and lack of substantial obligations to dependents or mental or physical impairments weigh in favor of *not* granting an undue hardship discharge. . . . Thus, on this record, the only reason he has even a colorable claim of undue hardship is the sheer magnitude of his student loan debts. While the size of student loan debts relative to the debtor's financial condition is relevant, this should rarely be a determining factor:

It would be perverse to allow the debtor to benefit from [his] own inaction, delay and recalcitrance by automatically granting discharge simply because the debt is a sizeable one. This, of course, would benefit those who delay and obstruct the longest and could encourage other students to follow the [same] course.

United States v. Kephart, 170 B.R. 787, 792 (W.D.N.Y. 1994).

When the size of the debts is the principal basis for a claim of undue hardship, the generous repayment plans Congress authorized the Secretary of Education to design and offer under the William D. Ford Federal Direct Student Loan Program become more relevant to a totality-of-the-circumstances undue hardship analysis. See Student Loan Reform Act of 1993, Pub. L. No. 103-66, tit. IV, §4021, 107 Stat. 312, 341, codified at 20 U.S.C. §1087e(d); 34 C.F.R. §685.208. The most generous plan is the Income Contingent Repayment Plan ("ICRP"), which permits an eligible borrower to make "varying annual repayment amounts based on the income of the borrower, paid over an extended period of time prescribed by the Secretary, not to exceed 25 years." §1087e(d)(1)(D); see 34 C.F.R. §685.209. Though the House and Senate bills initially provided that loans issued under the Direct Student Loan Program would not be dischargeable, the House Conference Report explained why this provision was deleted from the final bill:

> The conferees believe that current provisions of the Bankruptcy Code are sufficient to protect against unnecessary discharge of direct student loans in bankruptcy. Section 523(a)(8) of the Bankruptcy Code operates to prevent the discharge of federally guaranteed education loans except in cases . . . where failure to allow the discharge would impose an undue hardship. . . . It is the intent of the conferees that loans made pursuant to the Federal Direct Student Loan Program would be subject to these same limitations on discharge.

H.R. Conf. Rep. No. 103-213, at 448-49 (1993), reprinted in 1993 U.S.C.C.A.N. 1088, 1137-38. Thus, undue hardship under §523(a)(8) continues to require separate analysis under which, in this circuit, the ICRP is "a factor" to consider in evaluating the totality of the debtor's circumstances. In re Lee, 352 B.R. 91, 95 (B.A.P. 8th Cir. 2006). However, a student loan should not be discharged when the debtor has "the ability to earn sufficient income to make student loan payments under the various special opportunities made available through the Student Loan Program." In re VerMaas, 302 B.R. 650, 660 (Bankr. D. Neb. 2003).

Under the ICRP, an eligible debtor's annual loan payment is equal to twenty percent of the difference between his adjusted gross income and the poverty level for his family size, regardless of the amount of unpaid student loan debt. 34 C.F.R. §685.209(a)(2)-(3). Repayments are made monthly. §685.208(k). The Secretary recalculates the annual payment amount each year based on changes in the borrower's adjusted gross income and the HHS Poverty Guidelines and may adjust the obligation based upon special circumstances such as a loss of employment. §§685.209(a)(5), (c)(3). If the borrower has not repaid the loan at the end of twenty five years, "the Secretary cancels the unpaid portion of the loan." §685.209(c)(4)(iv). The Secretary may require a borrower who has defaulted to repay the student loan pursuant to an ICRP, 20 U.S.C. §1087e(d)(5)(B), confirming that the ICRP is an appropriate way for borrowers to avoid undue hardship while repaying their loans.

The bankruptcy court and the district court rejected reliance on the ICRP because "it does not offer a fresh start" and "might even be viewed as inimical to the goals of the fresh start because the ICRP allows for negative amortization of the student loan debt and a potentially significant tax bill if the student loan is ultimately forgiven after 25 years." 366 B.R. at 915, quoting Lee, 352 B.R. at 97. We disagree. In §523(a)(8), Congress carved an exception to the "fresh start" permitted by discharge for unpaid, federally subsidized student loans. If the debtor with the help of an ICRP program can make student loan repayments while still maintaining a minimal standard of living, the absence of a fresh start is not undue hardship. The bankruptcy court and the district court also relied on a flawed analysis of the ICRP. To demonstrate "negative amortization," the bankruptcy court presented a chart showing Jesperson's student loan debt to ECMC growing to $1,746,256 over the twenty-five-year ICRP repayment period on account of the capitalization of unpaid interest if he made $514 monthly ICRP payments. But the chart ignored the ICRP's explicit ten percent limit on the capitalization of unpaid interest. 34 C.F.R. §685.209(c)(5). Likewise, the court's reference to "a potentially significant tax bill" when any unpaid balance is cancelled after twenty-five years ignored the fact that cancellation results in taxable income only if the borrower has assets exceeding the amount of debt being cancelled. See 26 U.S.C. §108(a)(1)(B).

Jesperson is a paradigmatic example of a student loan debtor for whom ICRP eligibility combined with his other circumstances require a conclusion of no undue hardship. Near the start of his legal career, he seeks bankruptcy discharge of multiple student loan debts he never tried to repay. Recent employment is evidence that, if motivated, he will enjoy sustained legal employment in future years, profiting from his many years of loan-subsidized higher education. Based on Jesperson's "history of employment retention difficulty," the bankruptcy court thought it unlikely he would increase or even maintain his current rate of pay in the future. But this pessimistic speculation is unwarranted and inappropriate. A debtor is not entitled to an undue hardship discharge of student loan debts when his current income is the result of self-imposed limitations, rather than lack of job skills, and he has not made payments on his student loan debt despite the ability to do so. In re Loftus, 371 B.R. 402, 410-11 (Bankr. N.D. Iowa 2007). "With the receipt of a government-guaranteed education, the student assumes an obligation to make a good faith effort to repay those loans, as measured by his or her efforts to obtain employment, maximize income, and minimize expenses." In re Roberson, 999 F.2d 1132, 1136 (7th Cir. 1993). . . .

On this record, we conclude that, with the aid of an income contingent repayment plan, Mark Allen Jesperson can presently make student loan payments without compromising a minimal standard of living, and he has the potential of repaying at least a substantial portion of his student loan debts during the ICRP repayment period. When a debtor is eligible for the ICRP, the court in determining undue hardship should be less concerned that future income may decline. The ICRP formula adjusts for such declines, without regard to the unpaid student loan balance, which in most cases will avoid undue hardship. Therefore, however unattractive or unfair Jesperson may find this situation, he is not entitled to an undue hardship discharge under §523(a)(8). The judgment of the district court is reversed, and the case is remanded with directions to enter an order declaring that Jesperson's student loan debts to ECMC are not discharged.

SMITH, Circuit Judge, Concurring.

I concur in the court's judgment that, applying de novo review, Jesperson is ineligible for an undue hardship discharge of his student loan debt under 11 U.S.C. §523(a)(8). I write separately to emphasize that whether the debtor enrolled in the Income Contingent Repayment Plan (ICRP) remains merely "a factor" to consider when applying the totality-of-the-circumstances test. . . .

[F]airness and equity require each undue hardship case to be examined on the unique facts and circumstances that surround the particular bankruptcy. . . .

Because the totality-of-the-circumstances test is "very broad," "courts in the Eighth Circuit have looked to a number of facts and circumstances to assist them in making this determination." *McLaughlin v. U.S. Funds (In re McLaughlin)*, 359 B.R. 746, 750 (Bankr. W.D. Mo. 2007). Such factors include:

> (1) total present and future incapacity to pay debts for reasons not within the control of the debtor; (2) whether the debtor has made a good faith effort to negotiate a deferment or forbearance of payment; (3) whether the hardship will be long-term; (4) whether the debtor has made payments on the student loan; (5) whether there is permanent or long-term disability of the debtor; (6) the ability of the debtor to obtain gainful employment in the area of the study; (7) whether the debtor has made a good faith effort to maximize income and minimize expenses; (8) whether the dominant purpose of the bankruptcy petition was to discharge the student loan; and (9) the ratio of student loan debt to total indebtedness.

Id. . . .

In the present case, considering the totality of the circumstances, one of which is participation in the ICRP, Jesperson exemplifies the type of debtor who *is not e*ligible for a discharge of his student loan debt under §523(a)(8). Jesperson (1) is well educated, (2) is skilled in a specific profession (the law), (3) is young, (4) is in good health, (5) suffers from no physical or mental impairments at the present time, (6) is unmarried, (7) has the capacity to work, and (8) has made no payments toward his student loan debt, indicating a lack of interest in repaying his debt via the ICRP or otherwise. Jesperson's current situation seems to be the result of his own self-imposed limitations, evidenced by his routinely quitting jobs after a short period of time. Such a "patent lack of ambition, cooperation and commitment," does not support a finding of dischargeability under §523(a)(8).

[A massive string cite follows, including the following: *U.S. Dep't of Educ. v. Gerhardt (In re Gerhardt)*, 348 F.3d 89, 93 (5th Cir. 2003) (holding that "nothing in the Bankruptcy Code suggests that a debtor may choose to work only in the field in which he was trained, obtain a low-paying job, and then claim that it would be an undue hardship to repay his student loans"); *Goulet v. Educ. Credit Mgmt. Corp.*, 284 F.3d 773, 779 (7th Cir. 2002) ("As the bankruptcy court noted, Goulet is an intelligent man. The record does not reveal that he lacks usable job skills or that he is hindered by a limited education. In fact, because of the loans, he received an excellent education. The natural conclusion, when considering his exemplary educational record and nearly-completed graduate work, is that Goulet can apply himself when he desires to do so. The record does not demonstrate that he lacks the capacity to work, only that he does not seem anxious to do so."); *Loftus v. Sallie Mae Servicing (In re Loftus)*, 371 B.R. 402, 410-11 (Bankr. N.D. Iowa 2007) ("Timothy's decision to live in a small town in northwest Iowa has been a self-imposed geographical limitation on his employment options.").— Eds.]

Accordingly, based on the totality of the circumstances, I concur in the court's reversal. . . .

BYE, Circuit Judge, joining, in part, Judge Smith's concurring opinion, and dissenting.

The court holds the bankruptcy court erred in discharging Mark Jesperson's student loans under 11 U.S.C. §523(a)(8)'s undue hardship provision. I write separately to emphasize that, in accordance with the overwhelming majority of courts, a debtor is not ineligible for a hardship discharge if capable of making payments under the William D. Ford Federal Direct Student Loan Program's Income Contingent Repayment Plan (ICRP). 20 U.S.C. §1087e(d)(1)(D); 34 C.F.R. §685.208; see also 20 U.S.C. §1087e(d) (authorizing the Secretary of Education to implement alternative plans for repayment of student loans). Additionally, I dissent from the majority's opinion denying Jesperson a hardship discharge, and its rejection of the bankruptcy court's findings of fact and application of those facts to its §523(a)(8) analysis. . . .

Since 1976, Congress has demonstrated its willingness to restrict the ability to discharge student load debt, but has refused to abrogate §523(a)(8)'s undue hardship provision. It expressly declined to do so when the ICRP was established, even though it offers a less onerous means by which student loan debt may be managed. Based on this legislative history, I conclude Congress' express refusal to further circumscribe or eliminate §523(a)(8) demonstrates its continued viability—even when the ICRP is an available option. . . . [O]veremphasizing the impact of the ICRP would be antithetical to the exercise of judicial discretion mandated by §523(a)(8) and reflected in our totality-of-the-circumstances analysis. Accordingly, I concur in Judge Smith's conclusion that the ICRP is merely a factor to consider under our court's totality-of-the-circumstances test.

Applying these principles, I dissent from majority's rejection of the bankruptcy court's findings of fact and application of those facts to its §523(a)(8) analysis. . . .

For a finding to be clearly erroneous, it "must strike the reviewing court as more than just maybe or probably wrong; it must strike the court as wrong with the force of a five-week-old, unrefrigerated dead fish." *In re Papio Keno Club,* 262 F.3d 725, 728 (8th Cir. 2001) (quoting *Parts & Elec. Motors, Inc. v. Sterling Elec., Inc.,* 866 F.2d 228, 233 (7th Cir.1988)). Findings necessary to a determination of undue hardship include, "a special consideration of the debtor's present employment and financial situation—including assets, expenses, and earnings—along with the prospect of future changes—positive or adverse—in the debtor's financial position." *In re Long,* 322 F.3d at 554–55.

The bankruptcy court found Jesperson had reasonable monthly expenses of $2,857. This amount included $1,000 for rent, $1,000 in child support for two children, $325 for food, and $431.66 for vehicle maintenance, gas, and parking.

. . .

Jesperson has previously paid $700 per month for rent, and, although at the time of trial he was living in a relative's basement and anticipated spending only $500, the court concluded his future rent expenses would increase, and in the relevant urban housing market, $1,000 was reasonable. Further, Jesperson was court ordered to pay $500 in monthly child support for one child, and, though no order was in place as to the second child, when financially able, he voluntarily paid child support for the second. As for the vehicle expenses, Jesperson owned a 1988 truck with over 200,000 miles on the odometer. He used the vehicle to drive to work, for visiting his children (one in Duluth), and to regularly attend AA meetings several times per week. These undisputed findings are not clearly erroneous and demonstrate the reasonable nature of Jesperson's claimed expenses. I reject the majority's assertion that Jesperson failed to demonstrate good faith because he aspired to live somewhere other than his brother's basement. I also reject the majority's implicit conclusion that in the absence of a court order, Jesperson's contributions toward the support of his second child cannot be credited. Furthermore, the court noted Jesperson's projected monthly budget failed to account for medical or dental expenses, savings or retirement, and he owned no assets with more than nominal value. Thus, I conclude it was not clearly erroneous to find Jesperson proved reasonable monthly expenses of at least $2,750. Indeed, the bankruptcy court's belief that the expenses were understated is almost certainly true.

The district court also considered Jesperson's past, current, and future earning capacity. At the time of trial Jesperson was enjoying an unprecedented period of prosperity. For approximately four months, he had been earning the annual equivalent of $48,000, working in a temporary legal position. Prior to that, Jesperson took and abandoned two full-time legal jobs [one of which, according to the bankruptcy judge, was because a supervisor allegedly drank at work—Eds.], as well as a third through a temp agency, and proved a failure at starting his own law practice [he had only two clients in one year, one of which was a relative—Eds.]. His adjusted gross income for the years leading up to his bankruptcy petition included: $13,207 in 2003; $14,828 in 2004; $21,584 in 2005; and $13,692 in 2006. The bankruptcy court found "his employment history does not openly demonstrate substantive ineptitude, [but] his record of work experience is besmirched by a patent lack of ambition, cooperation and commitment." These facts are undisputed, and based thereon, it was not unreasonable for the court to conclude "the expectation that Jesperson maintain or increase his current rate of pay is one part rational to two parts imagination."

The bankruptcy court next factored the availability of the ICRP into its totality-of-the-circumstances analysis. Assuming Jesperson maintained his current level of earnings—an assumption bordering on fanciful—his ICRP payment for a family of three (himself and two minor dependents) would be $514. The bankruptcy court, however, found, based on Jesperson's after-tax adjusted gross income and reasonable monthly expenses, his approximate monthly surplus was only $55. Thus, he was financially unable to make the ICRP payment. Moreover, even assuming Jesperson made a nominal monthly ICRP payment, i.e., $5 or even $0, the court concluded he would 1) never reduce the principal, 2) be unable to cover unexpected expenses, e.g., unfunded medical, dental, or vehicle replacement costs, and 3) never contribute to a savings or retirement plan. Instead, Jesperson would remain saddled with the debt, "only to look forward to a quarter century of negative amortization, the burden of poor credit and a cash-only lifestyle."

Once again, the bankruptcy courts findings are adequately supported by the record. . . . [T]he facts, and the court's analysis thereof, demonstrate that continuing to carry the undischarged student loan debt will relegate Jesperson and his two minor children to a life punctuated by constant financial crisis and impoverishment.

The court characterizes Jesperson as the "paradigmatic example of a student loan debtor for whom ICRP eligibility requires a conclusion of no hardship." . . . I understand the court's frustration—Jesperson is not a sympathetic figure. After availing himself of the federal student loan program and amassing a large debt, he has failed to achieve any demonstrable success in his chosen profession, and has ignored his promise to repay the debt. Nonetheless, bankruptcy law does not only provide relief to the well-intentioned or to hapless victims of circumstance. Even malfeasants may seek a fresh start. Today's decision punishes Jesperson for his financial mismanagement and is the paradigmatic example of bad facts leading to bad law.

Do the diverging outcomes of the judges in the case above reflect different legal philosophies on textualism, legislative intent, and the harmonization of overlapping laws (ICRP and Bankruptcy Code)? Or are they nothing more than differing assessments whether Mark Jesperson is the Frank Galvin or Barry Zuckerkorn of the Minnesota bar? Do you share their consensus on the one thing on which all three judges agreed: a 45-year-old student loan obligor was "young"? On the broader question why student loans are nondischargeable in the first place, one of us has subjected various proffered rationales to scrutiny and found them theoretically wanting. See John Pottow, The Nondischargeability of Student Loans in Personal Bankruptcy Proceedings: The Search for a Theory, 44 Can. Bus. L. J. 245 (2006).

C. TAX PRIORITIES AND DISCHARGE

The protected position for tax obligations raises important policy questions for both the debtor and the other creditors.

The kinds of taxes specified in section 507(a)(8)(A)-(G) are not only given priority in payment, but any unpaid portion of those taxes is exempted from discharge by section 523(a)(1)(A). If the estate generates any money, the tax payment will receive a priority distribution, and the debtor remains personally liable for any unpaid portion post-discharge.

Prepetition interest on section 507(a)(8) priority claims shares the priority of the claims themselves and enjoys their nondischargeable status. Collier on Bankruptcy §523.07[7] (16th ed. 2009). Postpetition interest does not accrue on unsecured tax claims against the trustee and the property of the estate, §502(b), but postpetition interest does accrue against the debtor as to any unpaid, undischarged tax debts that survive discharge. Id. In other words, the part the debtor will have to pay after bankruptcy is growing larger by the day, even during the course of the bankruptcy. The Taxman Cometh.

Penalties on nondischargeable taxes are also nondischargeable, §523(a)(7), regardless whether entitled to priority by virtue of their relation to pecuniary loss, §507(a)(8)(G).

It gets worse for the debtor. Not only are these tax debts nondischargeable, but the Internal Revenue Service has the right to satisfy them by seizing property that is otherwise exempt under state law. See United States v. Rodgers, 461 U.S. 677 (1983). State Exemptions 0, Supremacy Clause 1. Strapped debtors are frequently advised by counsel to pay their tax debts above all else.

D. WORSE THAN NO DISCHARGE—BANKRUPTCY CRIMES

In the basic course on bankruptcy there is insufficient time to deal with bankruptcy crimes. Nonetheless, it is important to note that the acts that trigger denial of discharge may also put the debtor in jeopardy for criminal prosecution. Concealment of assets, false oaths, false claims, fee fixing, and a number of other bankruptcy specific actions are made federal crimes in 18 U.S.C. §§151-155.

This case is a tale of a mendacious lawyer who discovers poetic justice.

———— UNITED STATES v. CLUCK ————
143 F.3d 174 (5th Cir. 1998)

JOLLY, Circuit Judge:

Elwood "Jack" Cluck appeals his conviction and sentence for committing bankruptcy fraud in violation of 18 U.S.C. §152(1) & (3). Finding no merit in any of Cluck's multitudinous and niggling points of error, we affirm. . . .

A.

Before the events in this case, Cluck was an attorney who specialized, by his own admission, in the legal avoidance of income, estate, and gift taxes.[1] His practice was, by all accounts, quite successful, allowing Cluck to enjoy many of the finer things in life. In his case, the finer things ranged from an assortment of properties located throughout the state of Texas, to his own Beechcraft Bonanza airplane, to a collection of classic Jaguar automobiles.

Smooth travel sometimes comes to an abrupt halt, however, and so it was in the case of Cluck. In October 1989, the road ahead worsened considerably when a state court rendered judgment against him in the staggering amount of $2.9 million.[2] Although Cluck had high hopes that an appellate detour would shortly

---

1. An undoubtedly satisfying profession that we do not disparage. See Estate of McLendon v. Commissioner of Internal Revenue, 135 F.3d 1017, 1025 n.16 (5th Cir. 1998).

2. The suit was based on alleged fraudulent conduct by Cluck in his handling of the estate of Booney M. Moore, one of his tax planning clients. It was brought pursuant to Texas's Deceptive Trade Practices Act, whose punitive damage provisions gave rise to the large award.

return him to his golden highway,[3] he soon found that the detour itself would require a steep toll of 10 percent in the form of the supersedeas bond necessary to forestall execution. Short of funds and in need of a cul de sac in which to safely park his troubled vehicle for a while, Cluck turned to the refuge of the bankruptcy court, as many a similarly threatened sojourner had done before him.

Unlike these other voyagers, however, Cluck apparently concluded that his resources would need more protection than the bankruptcy court could provide until his appellate travels had reached their final destination. Thus, before invoking the power of Title 11, he perceived that it might be useful to keep some Jaguars in reserve, some money within easy access, and, maybe, just for good measure, a few of his favorite things beyond the reach of his creditors and the bankruptcy court. To this end, on March 26, 1990, Cluck returned a note for $50,000 to its grantor, Perfect Union Lodge. Perfect Union was one of Cluck's clients, and the note had been originally tendered in payment of certain legal services. Three days later, on March 29, Cluck pawned three Jaguars, a 1983 Chevrolet truck, his airplane, a Lone Star boat, and a Winnebago camper shell ("the Jaguars, etc.") to a used car dealer for $32,000,[4] retaining for himself and his designee a right to reacquire at a set price[5] within thirty to ninety days of the sale.

B.

His affairs now in preliminary order, on March 30, Cluck filed his petition for Chapter 7 liquidation in the United States Bankruptcy Court for the Western District of Texas. As part of the standard Chapter 7 procedure, Cluck was required to file a Schedule of Assets and a Statement of Financial Affairs. These documents required, among other things, disclosure of all accounts receivable, rights of acquisition, and asset transfers during the prior year. On his forms, Cluck made no mention of the assets recently pawned to the used car dealer or of his right to reacquire. He also did not disclose his return of the $50,000 note or the corresponding account receivable from Perfect Union Lodge. In addition, Cluck failed to list a transfer of 351 acres of land in McMullen County, Texas, that he had made on June 21, 1989. Finally, and significantly for this appeal, Cluck also neglected to include a further $150,000 in pre-petition accounts receivable from another of his clients, the O. D. Dooley Estate.

On July 31, Cluck's bankruptcy came to its first purported close, and the bankruptcy court entered an order discharging him from all dischargeable debts. Thinking his plan to have succeeded, on November 9, Cluck collected $48,000 from the O. D. Dooley Estate in partial payment of that client's aforementioned pre-petition account receivable. On November 16, the remaining $102,000

3. As well he should have. The judgment entered on the jury's verdict was reversed....
4. A price that was, needless to say, significantly below the assets' fair market value.
5. About $38,000.

followed. About seven months later, on June 28, 1991, Cluck collected $35,000 from Perfect Union in settlement of its still-outstanding $50,000 account receivable. Of these funds, a portion was deposited into the account of First Capitol Mortgage, a Nevada corporation owned by Cluck's wife, Kristine. By this time, First Capitol had also reacquired all of the assets that had been pawned to the used car dealer. As might be suspected, neither the receipt of the money nor the reacquisition of the assets was revealed to the bankruptcy trustee....

II.

The bankruptcy court's finding of intentional concealment apparently aroused the interest of the U.S. Attorney, and on March 27, 1995, Cluck was charged with eight counts of bankruptcy fraud in violation of 18 U.S.C. §152(1) & (3). The counts were essentially as follows:

[False statements and fraudulent concealment.]

On January 16, 1997, a jury found Cluck guilty on counts one, three, four, five, six, seven, and eight, and not guilty on count two. On May 22, 1997, Cluck was sentenced to concurrent terms of twenty-four months imprisonment on each count, and ordered to pay restitution in the amount of $185,000. Cluck appeals his conviction, sentence, and restitution order on multiple grounds. . . .

C.

Cluck next attempts to persuade us that the evidence was insufficient on all the counts of his indictment with respect to intent. Under §152(1) & (3), the prosecution must show that the concealment or false statement was made "knowingly and fraudulently." Cluck argues, essentially, that the evidence showed only that he was careless in providing information to his bankruptcy attorney, not that he committed intentional fraud. . . .

. . . It is well established that "'[c]ircumstances altogether inconclusive, if separately considered, may, by their number and joint operation, especially when corroborated by moral coincidences, be sufficient to constitute conclusive proof.'" United States v. Ayala, 887 F.2d 62, 67 (5th Cir. 1989) (quoting The Slavers (Reindeer), 69 U.S. (2 Wall.) 383, 401, 17 L. Ed. 911 (1864)).

In this case, it is manifestly clear that Cluck's repeated omissions and history of coincidental and questionable transfers formed just the sort of "circumstances" that the Supreme Court had in mind in the *Reindeer* case. Based on our review of the record, we are convinced that a rational jury could have inferred the existence of an intentional plan to defraud from the bare facts of Cluck's systematic concealment and false statements. We therefore find no merit to his argument that the evidence was insufficient on this point. . . .

Having found no merit in any of Cluck's numerous points of error, for the foregoing reasons, the judgment of the district court is AFFIRMED.

Denial of discharge is one form of discipline, and prison is another. While our consumer bankruptcy laws may fairly be characterized as generous to troubled debtors, it is important that the debtors be fair with the system. The threat of jail is useful in keeping the system in balance, and many other countries' bankruptcy systems are far more punitive on debtors. Unfortunately, not many U.S. attorneys are prepared to invest resources in this kind of prosecution. In the *Cluck* case, it may be that the spectacle of a fellow lawyer behaving as he did was enough to produce action.

Problem Set 8

8.1. Wallace Laymon has held a variety of jobs during the past ten years. He is restless and has some difficulty getting along with co-workers. He sometimes walks off jobs, gets fired, abruptly moves, or just "gets tired." Laymon's financial records are a complete disaster. He has no checking statements, no bill receipts, and no clear record of any of his financial dealings except a handful of bills and dunning notices that have arrived in the past two months. Nor is he even remotely computer literate. Does Laymon face any difficulties in bankruptcy? Should he? Was he required by any law to keep better financial records? See §727.

8.2. Gordon Gram was in serious financial difficulty for several months before he sought your advice. During this time he gave a financial statement to his principal creditor, Dina Chapman, to persuade her to hold off on enforcing the judgment she had gotten against him. The statement falsely stated that he owned 1,000 shares of AT&T stock, which he promised he would deliver to Dina as security for the debt. In the meantime, he also fraudulently conveyed his only significant asset, a ski chalet, to his daughter. When the stock was not forthcoming, Dina started searching for property to grab. She found out about the chalet scam, she initiated execution on the judgment and a levy but before she could collect, Gram filed for chapter 7. Ignoring the question whether her judgment lien survives in bankruptcy, and assuming respectful compliance with the automatic stay, will Dina be able to continue her quest after Gram's bankruptcy? See §§523, 727. If Dina has an option, under which provision should she file her objection?

8.3. Chickie Narduchi makes his living through "creative debt collection services." Chickie has been very successful, but recently he has encountered a series of financial reversals that have forced him into bankruptcy. Among Chickie's creditors is a tort claimant who had owed money to one of Chickie's clients. The claimant has an $800,000 judgment against Chickie for breaking four of his fingers, a favorite kneecap, and his big toe. Will the judgment creditor be discharged in bankruptcy? (Keep in mind that you might later discover that

Chickie secretly owns 5% of the Forbidden Pleasures Casino, so he is not without assets worth pursuing.) See §523(a).

8.4. Shortly after Reynaldo and Maria Lujan were married, having watched a lot of HGTV, they purchased a rambling old home advertised as a "handyman's special." While they had visions of creating a quaint and charming nest, the home sucked up virtually all their cash. During the next three years, they worked constantly on the house and added such decorator touches as replacing the septic tank and rewiring the entire second floor. During that time, they carried maximum amounts on their credit cards, using the cards to support purchases for their house and to meet as many personal needs as they could finance through extended credit. Four months ago Maria was laid off and Reynaldo's income could not support the house and all the credit cards. Unfortunately, during that time their reliance on credit cards increased rather than decreased, so that their cards now represent $16,000 in unsecured debt.

Reynaldo and Maria have filed for chapter 7 bankruptcy and sold the house, which brought just enough to pay off all the mortgages and home improvement loans and leave them with a small amount of exempt cash. As their attorney, you have looked over their credit card charges, and you see purchases of wallpaper ($450), plane tickets ($1,200), and clothes from a nice men's store ($400) within the three months preceding the filing. The card issuers have filed exceptions to discharge. What will you do at the hearing? See §523(a).

8.5. Craig O'Connor is a struggling young law student who has coped with inadequate parking facilities near his law school by parking wherever he wanted to, thereby collecting 122 parking tickets over three years. If O'Connor declares bankruptcy, will the parking tickets be discharged? See §523(a).

8.6. You are a young but up-and-coming consumer bankruptcy practitioner in Topeka, Kansas. You've acquired a reputation for honesty with clients and level-headed decision making. You chalk up much of your success to the bankruptcy text your class used in law school and your keeping up to date on the latest research. This morning you read a study that found that student loans are discharged in bankruptcy about 40% of the time. This was contrary to what all your mentors had taught you but surely the numbers don't lie. Later that day, 32-year old Jamarah Harris came to see you about her financial problems, primary of which is $23,700 in defaulted student loans from six years ago when she attended an accredited, online graphic design school. She has never worked as a graphic designer and has struggled with lupus, diagnosed while she was in school. She is a single mother to four young children and would have to scrape hard to pay your fee for a chapter 7 case. She asks you, point blank, what are my odds of discharging these student loans? What do you tell her? Do you have any thoughts on what you can do to improve those odds?

Assignment 9.
The Debtor's Position after Bankruptcy

You learned in the previous assignment that the discharge injunction forbids any attempt to collect a dischargeable debt. Like the automatic stay, it has potentially unlimited penalties and is enforced summarily by contempt. While discharge is the capstone of a bankruptcy case, it often is merely the beginning of an elaborate end game in which disappointed creditors may retaliate and shrewd ones may maneuver. This means that despite the language of financial rebirth and fresh start so pervasive in bankruptcy literature, postbankruptcy debtors are not like new babies unstained by past events. Instead, families exit bankruptcy with many of the same underlying problems—illness, job problems, or low incomes—that led them to seek relief in the first place. Also, in some instances, the same debt that sank these families the first time around can remain a burden, even after discharge. We turn to this post-discharge world.

A. SECURED DEBTS: KEEPING COLLATERAL

Many debtors file bankruptcy in an effort to hang onto their homes, cars, and other property. Chapter 13 bankruptcy, covered in the upcoming two assignments, has some special tools to help families keep property. What happens to chapter 7 debtors' property? As we have already said, exempt property is kept and non-exempt property lost. But what about exempt property that is collateral for a secured creditor's lien? The Code suggests a pretty list of three options; the reality is a messy scramble of strategic choices.

While unsecured debt is mostly discharged, secured debt plays a huge role in the postbankruptcy financial lives of debtors. The 2007 Consumer Bankruptcy Project found that 74% of the debtors had loans secured by their cars, their furniture, their appliances, and other personal property. These debtors owed secured debts that were, on average, equal to nearly 85% of their total assets. Secured debt, and the collateral that backs it, is important in the lives of bankruptcy debtors.

As we noted in the prior assignment, a lien remains attached to its collateral and can be enforced against that property after bankruptcy even though the debtor cannot be sued for any deficiency. §506(d). The discharge injunction forbids only an attempt to collect a debt "as a personal liability" of the discharged debtor. §524(a). Collection by seizure of collateral is not only permissible but often anticipated.

Individuals who file chapter 7 are thus required to file a "Statement of Intention" (Official Bankruptcy Form 8) with respect to collateral. This form must be filed within 30 days of the first date set for the section 341 meeting (described in Assignment 3). This duty applies to *all* debts secured by property: consumer or nonconsumer, real or personal property, etc. The debtor only faces these choices if the collateral is exempt property or has been abandoned by the trustee. See §§521(a)(2), 554. After all, non-exempt property is none of the debtor's business in chapter 7; the trustee gets to sell it and distribute its value to the estate, with the secured creditor's lien attaching to the proceeds. Occasionally, a debtor will pay the trustee the value the estate would receive at liquidation to keep that collateral. "Occasionally" is probably too generous a term given the typical financial position of a bankrupt debtor, but sometimes a relative will help out, particularly when the property has sentimental value that exceeds its market value.

The Statement of Intention lists three choices for exempt or abandoned collateral encumbered by a security interest: (1) *surrender* it to the creditor; (2) *redeem* it under section 722; or (3) negotiate a *reaffirmation* agreement with the creditor under section 524(c). Case law has created a fourth option, which is usually called *ride-through*, or sometimes known as *retention*. It appears nowhere on the Statement of Intention form (or in the Code for that matter), which should be the first tip-off to its controversial status and uncertain permissibility.

The first alternative, surrender, sounds simple. Debtors let creditors know they do not want to keep the collateral, and creditors go get it. In most instances, it works just like that. The down real-estate market of the last several years, however, has created an interesting twist: creditors who decline this gracious invitation to reclaim the collateral promptly—and debtors who try to force them to. One example arises because of a curious twist in section 523(a)(16) of the Code. One court described the problem: "In the case of a chapter 7 debtor who has surrendered her home in bankruptcy and been relieved of any personal liability on the mortgage, she cannot truly be given a fresh start because HOA [Home Owners Association] fees are still accumulating until a lender chooses to foreclose. If the lender never forecloses, that homeowner's liability for the HOA fees continues in perpetuity. . . [which] deprives the debtor of a fresh start, and thwarts the goals of the entire Bankruptcy Code." In re Pigg, 453 B.R. 728, 733 (Bankr. M.D. Tenn. 2011). Similar problems can occur with taxes, tort liability, or blight violations if a lender does not foreclose after a debtor surrenders the property; these problems are quite a reversal of the stories about debtor's strategically filing bankruptcy merely to stall foreclosure.

The debtor's calculation on whether to surrender property or to try to use what we call bankruptcy's "3Rs" (Redemption, Reaffirmation, or Ridethrough) depends both on the applicable law and on the economics of the situation. Say Jane Debtor owns a car worth $5,000 and the loan is $7,500. If it is a spare vehicle, surrender is the easy answer. Bankruptcy discharges the remaining $2,500 on the loan, and she reduces her carbon footprint. But Jane may want to— or need to—keep the car. The reasons are myriad, ranging from the unassailable (only way to get to work) to the sentimental (vintage model she lovingly restored). The considerations Jane would think about include whether she can afford the monthly payments on the loan (easily or with difficulty or not at all), whether she believes she would have trouble getting credit to buy a new car after bankruptcy, and whether the property is replaceable. Each of the 3R choices requires Jane to meet certain conditions—and pay a certain price—to keep the car. We examine each in turn.

1. Redemption

Redemption allows the debtor to keep certain types of collateral by paying the creditor the full loan or the full value of the collateral in cash, whichever is less. §722. This option is a big benefit of bankruptcy over state law. Under Article 9 of the UCC, a debtor is allowed to redeem collateral after default by paying the full amount owed, including late charges and other costs. UCC §9-623. The leverage created by permitting the creditor to demand more than the value of the collateral ($7,500 for a car worth $5,000, for example) was too much for Congress to sanction in consumer bankruptcy cases, so bankruptcy redemption allows the debtor to keep the collateral by paying the amount of the allowed secured claim, i.e., the value of the collateral. In the previous example, Jane Debtor could redeem the $5,000 car by paying $5,000 in cash, with the remaining amount owed on the loan being treated as an unsecured and dischargeable claim. This outcome may seem to disadvantage creditors unfairly in bankruptcy but note that it leaves the creditor in the same economic position it would have been in had Jane surrendered the car and the lender repossessed and sold it postbankruptcy. Any benefit to the debtor from redemption is coming from the discharge of unsecured obligations. Creditors should theoretically be indifferent between surrender and redemption, but we suspect, assuming the collateral is fairly valued, that most prefer having hard cash in hand to a car that has to be tracked down and sold, while carry costs are mounting.

The rub in the real world is that the debtor does not have $5,000 cash to realize this marked-to-market buyout. For most debtors, section 722 might as well base redemption on the debtor successfully running a three-minute mile. Perhaps the most practical possibility for a few debtors is a loan from a friend or relative, in which case the debtor emerges from bankruptcy still greatly encumbered by debt. A business aptly named 722 Redemption has popped up in some states, offering to lend money to debtors (at high interest rates) so that they can redeem their cars. The math is simple. Any debtor who is better off with the terms offered by 722 Redemption now has an alternative to reaffirming with the original creditor: refinancing the loan on 722 Redemption's terms and electing to redeem under the statute. Even 722 Redemption has underwriting standards, however—we asked—and most debtors have financial problems serious enough that even a bankruptcy specialist will be selective.

2. *Reaffirmation*

The Code provides the alternative of reaffirmation for debtors who want to negotiate to keep their collateral. The consequence of reaffirmation of a secured debt is that debtors sign a legally binding agreement to waive the discharge on a given debt, subjecting themselves once again to losing the collateral *and* being sued for a deficiency claim if the debt is not paid off according to the terms of the reaffirmation.

Reaffirmation requires a creditor willing to agree to let the debtor keep the collateral in return for a promise to repay that will survive the bankruptcy. The reaffirmation process illustrates a negotiating tension between the debtor and the creditor—what each wants with respect to the collateral—and the procedural hurdles both must clear to create an enforceable agreement. In many instances, the creditor will insist the debtor agree that certain amounts be included in the reaffirmation agreements that were never in the original contract. For example, the creditor in the case below required as a condition of reaffirmation that the debtors pay $250 in attorney's fees to cover the costs of negotiating and preparing the reaffirmation agreement. The debtors objected, but the court explained the leverage in these situations:

> Debtors fail to recognize that the reaffirmation process involves negotiation. Even if debtors were correct in their assertions respecting the lack of a clause providing for attorney's fees in their original contracts, Leader Federal is nonetheless not prohibited from negotiating a provision for the payment of attorney's fees in its reaffirmation agreements. Likewise, the debtors are not prohibited from endeavoring to negotiate reaffirmation agreements with terms differing from those contained in their original contracts.

> Clearly, as in any negotiation process, give and take will be required. It appears to the court that, under circumstances involving reaffirmation, a debtor has considerable bargaining power. In the first place, the creditor must recognize that in the absence of reaffirmation its debt will be discharged leaving recourse against its collateral as its sole remedy. Secondly, the creditor must consider reaffirmation in terms of expenses associated with repossession and foreclosure. It must also consider the resale value of its collateral. Merchants and secured lenders are in business to make a profit. They recognize the impact of

bankruptcy and realize the advantage of negotiating a reaffirmation agreement which maintains an existing security interest, retains personal liability on the debtor and continues an uninterrupted stream of payments. Foreclosing a security interest in property whose value is generally speculative would, in this court's opinion, be a creditor's least desirable option.

In re Pendlebury, 94 B.R. 120 (Bankr. E.D. Pa. 1988).

As this excerpt underscores, reaffirmation is not a right but a free-market activity. While the statute requires certain disclosures and affidavits, the price is up for grabs.

Does something worry you about reaffirmation's "undischarge"? Should the Code protect these debtors from improvidence? Before the 1978 Code, the statute did not address the enforceability of a promise to pay a debt discharged in bankruptcy. This bounced the question back to the common law of contracts, which remains quite clear: such debts would be enforced. See Restatement of Contracts (Second), §83 (1981); Zavelo v. Reeves, 227 U.S. 625, 629 (1913) ("It is settled, however, that a discharge, while releasing the bankrupt from legal liability to pay a debt that was provable in the bankruptcy, leaves him under a moral obligation that is sufficient to support a new promise to pay the debt."). The 1970s era of consumer protection deemed this result unacceptable, and the 1973 Report of the Bankruptcy Commission recommended a complete ban on reaffirmations. The credit industry objected, and the result in the 1978 Code was a requirement that the court make an independent inquiry into whether a reaffirmation was in the "debtor's best interests" before approving the agreement.

Unsurprisingly, this cut the number of reaffirmations dramatically. The credit industry didn't like this, so came back in 1984 with a Code amendment that substituted the debtor's lawyer for the courts as the signing-off entity (with courts as back up for pro se debtors). As the authors of an important empirical study of reaffirmation noted, "The new reaffirmation routine placed debtors' attorneys in a difficult position. They were to be decision-makers for, rather than advisors to, their clients." Marianne B. Culhane and Michaela M. White, Debt after Discharge: An Empirical Study of Reaffirmation, 73 Am. Bankr. Inst. L. Rev. 709, 716 (1999). Lawyers remain in this trick box after the 2005 amendments but have developed some counter-tricks to protect themselves that are discussed below.

Today, the reaffirmation process is subject to numerous procedures, set forth in sections 524(c) and (k). An agreement now must contain aggressive disclosures about the interest and fees associated with the reaffirmed debt, as well as a brief description of the credit agreement—a task that can be surprisingly difficult in light of the complexity of many consumer loans. The disclosures run to seven pages or more, making it quite a task for debtors to certify to the court that they are "fully informed" of their "rights and responsibilities" with regard to reaffirmations. See §524(c)(3)(A).

The Code requires the debtor to work through a mini-budget to show that the debtor has adequate income (after necessary expenses) to pay the reaffirmed debt and provide an explanation if the numbers in the debtor's proposed reaffirmation budget differ from those on the schedules I and J (monthly income and expenses). §524(k)(6) This last requirement takes aim at concerns that debtors dream up rosy budgets at reaffirmation time to convince the court they can make the payments to keep the property. The Code clearly commands that if the debtor cannot manage the loan then the court must refuse the reaffirmation. §524(m).

While courts review only the cases in which the debtor is not represented by counsel, lawyers are taking themselves out of the reaffirmation business. The first maneuver was simply trying to divorce reaffirmation from the routine job of bankruptcy counsel. Courts were hostile to this, noting that "the decision to reaffirm an otherwise dischargeable debt plays a critical role in the bankruptcy process—so critical, that assistance with the decision must be counted among the necessary services that make up competent representation of a Chapter 7 debtor." In re Minardi, 399 B.R. 841, 848 (Bankr. N.D. Okla. 2009). The court also refused to relieve counsel of responsibility for addressing a client's desire to reaffirm a debt because the Code itself put such a responsibility "at the feet of debtor's counsel." Id. Lawyers faced a tough choice in the wake of this case law—get out of the bankruptcy business entirely or get into the details of reaffirmations. Some lawyers, particularly nonspecialists, took the former route.

Lawyers who kept filing bankruptcies remained uncomfortable with the reaffirmation obligations, particularly the certification that in the attorney's opinion the debtor can make the payments. §524(k)(5). Continuing legal education programs were filled with lamentations by attorneys that they were not certified financial planners or accredited credit counselors—or generally their client's keepers. Yet lawyers often give business advice to their commercial clients, so were they protesting too much? While the consumer lawyer is not a financial counselor, the lawyer may have more experience that bears on these decisions than anyone otherwise available to a consumer debtor.

Nonetheless, the fundamental point for many lawyers is that they traditionally are their clients' advocates, not the arbiters of their decisions. No question could cut closer to the lawyerly bone than a debtor who has been refused the lawyer's signature on a reaffirmation agreement and asks "Whose side are you on, anyway?"

The National Consumer Law Center sums up the recommended position in response to these 2005 amendments and case law interpreting them.

> Attorneys should be extremely cautious in negotiating and validating reaffirmation agreements. There are serious problems of possible malpractice liability if such an agreement later causes harm to the debtor, for example through the debtor's loss of property if the debtor does not later pay the

reaffirmed debt. . . . Thus, it is usually better practice to avoid reaffirmations if at all possible.

Consumer Bankruptcy Law and Practice, §15.5.3.

As a future lawyer, you should like the sound of avoiding malpractice liability, but wonder exactly how to "avoid" reaffirmations. Many lawyers, while unable to carve out reaffirmations from their representation, do have a blanket policy of refusing to approve them, particularly when the debtor lacks equity in the property. Returning to the example of Jane Debtor and her car loan, many lawyers would say it is not in Jane's interest to sign a reaffirmation if her car is worth $5,000 and the outstanding loan is $7,500, and the creditor is demanding she pay more than $5,000. As one firm explains in its website, the result of no reaffirmation in such a situation is that "Certainly you will have to find another vehicle. This takes some effort but it can be done." We wonder if the retention agreement for these attorneys now includes in its package of service the cost of an attorney negotiating a new car loan for the debtor at a buy-here, pay-here car dealer. Ken Bensinger, "A Vicious Cycle in the Used-Car Business," Los Angeles Times (Oct. 30, 2011).

Because reaffirmation isn't complicated enough with all the above, there are special rules for credit unions. This impressive bit of political maneuvering resulted from credit card companies trying to keep the credit unions on board with BAPCPA. Now a credit union can get a reaffirmation agreement, even if the numbers show that the debtor cannot pay for it and the debtor is not represented by counsel. §524(m)(2). It might seem an odd position for the consumer-friendly credit unions to take, pressing for special rights to squeeze their members for demonstrably unpayable debts, but credit unions have taken the position that making people stick to their promises is a good lesson in financial literacy and "responsibility." Does that mean the fresh start of the bankruptcy discharge promotes illiteracy and irresponsibility?

One last note on reaffirmation. Nothing in the Code differentiates secured debt from unsecured debt. That means a debtor could, if inclined, reaffirm a wholly unsecured and thus completely dischargeable debt that can't imperil any of the debtor's property. We explore this later in the Assignment, but note here that the concerns about protecting debtors from improvident decisions and the discomfort of lawyers are even sharper in the context of unsecured debts.

3. Ride-through

The third of the 3Rs for keeping property is ride-through or retention. You will search the Code in vain for mention of this option because it results from case law, not statute. The basic idea is simple—the debtor just keeps on keepin' on, making the contractual payments without signing any new agreements and the creditor cashes those payments while letting the collateral stay put with the debtor. Keeping the collateral by continuing to make the pre-bankruptcy payments, without redeeming or reaffirming—but discharging any personal liability on the debt—sounds great for the debtor compared to the alternatives. If the collateral is damaged or destroyed, the debtor can simply walk away from it, bearing no responsibility for any deficiency. But the creditor might make out better too. If the debtor keeps paying, the creditor will be repaid *in full* notwithstanding the debtor's bankruptcy, a much greater return than if the debtor cashed out the creditor with a redemption, paying only the market value of the collateral and taking a pass on the rest of the loan amount. Crucially, to ride through the debtor must not be in default at the time of bankruptcy (otherwise there would be a default likely authorizing repossession after bankruptcy).

Because the Code made no specific reference to ride-through, the issue of whether a debtor could even make such a move reached the courts of appeals, with a number of decisions each way. Congress appears to have tried to eliminate ride-through in BAPCPA. The majority of courts have concluded that ride-through is indeed eliminated for personal property, at least in some situations. In re Dumont, 383 B.R. 481 (9th Cir. BAP 2007).

The twists and turns of the law on ride-through are now incredibly complex, making what used to be one of the simplest ideas in bankruptcy—I keep paying you and you let me keep the collateral—into a real puzzler. At the heart of the confusion are multiple Code provisions added by BAPCPA that provide room for inconsistent readings. For example, section 521(a)(2) commands debtors to state an intention to do one of three things and then to do them: surrender the property, reaffirm the contract with the secured party, or redeem pursuant to section 722. Nowhere on that Statement of Intention (Form 8) is ride-through, although some debtors apparently write that option onto the form.

Creditors have two separate Code sections that seem to mandate performance of the stated intention. §§362(h); 521(a)(2), (6). The former section is the stronger of the two. It simply removes the collateral from the estate and lifts the stay unless the debtor takes action. It might help to think of this as the Lift Stay Penalty. There is an exception if the debtor tries to reaffirm on the loan's original terms and the creditor refuses to agree (a small shake of the congressional finger at the *Pendlebury* court?). Section 521(a)(6) is similar, forbidding the debtor from "retain[ing] possession" without reaffirming or redeeming.

Notwithstanding these changes to the law, ride-through is alive and well in practice, at least in certain circumstances. These forms of "backdoor" ride-through require a series of clever maneuvers, including timely filing the Statement of Intention and indicating one of the three choices, but then not performing. The following case provides a good review of how the statutes fit together.

———————— **In re SCHWASS** ————————
378 B.R. 859 (Bankr. S.D. Cal. 2007)

BOWIE, Chief Judge.

. . .

On July 2, 2007, Mary Catherine Schwass (Debtor) filed a petition commencing this chapter 7 case. Prior to the filing Debtor had borrowed money from Pacific Capital Bancorp dba Santa Barbara Bank & Trust (Movant) to purchase a 2001 Ford Explorer (Vehicle). Debtor granted Movant a security interest in the Vehicle to secured repayment of the loan.

With her petition Debtor filed a Statement of Intention which indicated that she intended to reaffirm her obligation to Movant. Counsel for Movant wrote to Debtor's counsel requesting that he prepare the reaffirmation agreement. Debtor's counsel replied that Debtor had no obligation to prepare the agreement, but that he would do so for a fee payable by Movant. Movant replied that it was Debtor's responsibility, thus completing the stalemate. Thirty days elapsed from the date set for the first meeting of creditors with no reaffirmation agreement having been filed. Thereafter, Movant moved for relief from stay on the ground that Debtor did not timely follow through with her intention to reaffirm. A hearing was held and the Court took the matter under submission.

DISCUSSION

Movant seeks relief from stay under 11 U.S.C. §362(h)(1)(B) which provides in relevant part:

(h)(1) In a case in which the debtor is an individual, the stay provided by subsection (a) is terminated with respect to personal property of the estate or of the debtor securing in whole or in part a claim ... if the debtor fails within the applicable time set by section 521(a)(2)—

(A) to file timely any statement of intention required under section 521(a)(2) with respect to such personal property or to indicate in such statement that the debtor will either surrender such personal property or retain it and, if retaining such personal property, either redeem such personal property pursuant to section 722, enter into an agreement of the kind specified in section 524(c) applicable to the debt secured by such personal property ...; and

(B) to take timely the action specified in such statement ... unless such statement specifies the debtor's intention to reaffirm such debt on the original contract terms and the creditor refuses to agree to the reaffirmation on such terms.

Section 521(a)(2)(A) requires that the statement of intention be filed within 30 days of the petition. As noted, Debtor included with her petition a statement of intention to reaffirm her debt to Movant, thus complying with subsection (A).

Section 521(a)(2)(B) provides that a debtor must perform her stated intention within 30 days after the first date set for the §341(a) meeting of creditors. In this case the meeting was set for August 9, 2007. Thus, under §521(a)(2)(B) Debtor was required to "perform" on her statement of intention to reaffirm on or before September 8, 2007. It is undisputed that no reaffirmation agreement has been filed in this case. Thus, the issue is whether performance under §521(b)(2)(B) requires a debtor to prepare and file the reaffirmation agreement, or whether it is sufficient that a debtor state her intent to reaffirm and stand by ready to execute a reaffirmation agreement prepared by the secured creditor—in this case Movant.

Reaffirmation of debts and the agreements and disclosures required therefor is governed by 11 U.S.C. §524(c) and (k). The Court is aware of no express provision or court decision dictating that one party or the other shall prepare the reaffirmation agreement. However, it appears clear to the Court from a review of the requirements of §524(c) and (k) that the responsibility for preparing the agreement falls on the secured creditor.

Section 524(c)(2) provides that a reaffirmed debt is excepted from discharge only if "the debtor received the disclosures described in subsection (k) at or before the time at which the debtor signed the agreement ..." If the debtor is to receive the disclosures under subsection (k), it makes sense that the disclosures come from the secured party—it would be nonsensical to have a debtor receive the disclosures from herself. It is of course possible for a debtor to receive the disclosures from her own counsel. However, debtors acting pro se are also able to reaffirm debts. See subsection 524(k)(5)(A) ("Certification of Debtor's Attorney (If Any) . . . ").

Subsection (k) is even more convincing. First, the disclosure statement required under subsection (c) must contain the total amount of the debt to be reaffirmed including fees and costs incurred as of the date of the disclosure statement. See subsection 524(k)(3)(C). Obviously, this is information most readily supplied by the secured creditor. Second, the disclosure statement is replete with phrases such as "may obligate you," "you have agreed," "your loan," "if you have questions," and "if you want to reaffirm." This is clearly language directed to the debtor. It would make no sense for a debtor to prepare such a disclosure statement with such disclosures to herself. Finally, the reaffirmation agreement as described in subsection (4) begins with the required phrase "I (we) agree to reaffirm" which clearly refers to the debtor(s). There is also a requirement for certification by debtor's attorney. Again, these are apparent indications that the reaffirmation agreement, along with the disclosure statement, are designed to be directed to, as opposed to prepared by, the debtor. Since the only other party to the agreement is the secured creditor whose debt is to reaffirmed, it follows that the responsibility to prepare the documents falls on such secured creditor.

The Court is comfortable with this arrangement, since it is the secured creditor who stands to benefit from the reaffirmation of the debt. Further, under §524(c) the reaffirmation agreement is enforceable only if, among other things, the debtor receives the prescribed disclosures on or before the time the debtor signs the agreement.

Thus, the Court holds that the statutory scheme and requirements for reaffirmation place upon the secured party whose debt is to be reaffirmed the obligation to prepare the reaffirmation agreement and the accompanying disclosure statement. The Court also holds that where, as in the case at hand, a debtor has timely filed a statement of intention to reaffirm, she complies with the requirement to "perform" such intention under subsection 521(a)(2)(B) by standing ready and willing to execute the reaffirmation agreement prepared by the secured creditor. Accordingly, the Court holds that in the case at hand relief from the automatic stay under §362(h) is not warranted because Debtor has not failed to reaffirm. The same result may be reached by finding that Movant, by failing to provide a reaffirmation agreement for Debtor's signature, has refused to agree to reaffirmation on the original terms and thus relief is not warranted under §362(h)(B).

CONCLUSION

For the reasons set forth above the Court denies . . . relief from stay. IT IS SO ORDERED.

The key point of *Schwass* is that the debtor had performed to the extent required; it is the creditor's problem to figure out how to proceed from there. That insight has given debtors some other options. One is to have counsel prepare a reaffirmation agreement that he or she then refuses to sign. In such situations, some courts have held that the Lift Stay Penalty doesn't trigger and so presumably ride-through can occur. Another situation occurs when the court is presented with a reaffirmation agreement but declines to approve it, finding it would impose an undue hardship. In such circumstances, some courts have said that ride-through remains an option because the debtor did all the Code required. In re Moustafi, 371 B.R. 434 (Bankr. D. Ariz. 2007). Others have disagreed. Given the multiple steps required for reaffirmation—from making a timely indication of intent to having a court approve the reaffirmation agreement—the law is in flux and plays out along dozens of different factual scenarios.

After discharge or the lifting of the stay under section 362(h), state law governs to determine whether a creditor can repossess collateral if the debtor is current on payments under the contract. The language of §521(d) reverses the Code's usual invalidation of *ipso facto* clauses, which are standard contractual language that make the act of filing bankruptcy itself a default. §365(e)(1). Again, however, some creditors have found that state law bars them from repossession when the debtor is current on the loan payments. In particular, creditors may find themselves in a bind if they have accepted the debtor's payments after the bankruptcy filing as some courts construe this as a waiver of the *ipso facto* clause.

While the parties' legal rights are important, it is also important to understand how the system actually functions. Many attorneys tell us that most of the time creditors are happy to just keep taking the money, preferring an uncertain income stream to a forced sale that would be guaranteed in most instances to produce a more certain substantial loss.

B. UNSECURED DEBTS: FUTURE OBLIGATIONS

While courts may question the wisdom of reaffirmations, debtors continue to file such agreements at a steady clip. The Administrative Office of the U.S. Courts reports that there was at least one reaffirmation agreement filed in 23% of chapter 7 cases closed in 2011. Unfortunately, no reliable data exist on how many of these agreements pertain to secured versus unsecured debts, let alone the approval rate by courts or attorneys.

Of course, a debtor can always repay a creditor voluntarily after bankruptcy. §524(f). A properly obtained reaffirmation agreement, however, goes much further than voluntary repayment; its effect is to revive the debt and make it fully enforceable in a court of law. The concerns about the potential drag that reaffirmations can place on the debtor's financial recovery after bankruptcy are even more acute for unsecured debts, when the debtor cannot offer the justification of reaffirming to keep collateral that applies to secured debt. Unsecured debt reaffirmations are viewed as eroding the core public policy of the fresh start.

Creditors do have leverage to persuade debtors to reaffirm unsecured debts. For example, a creditor may be willing to drop or eschew filing an objection to discharge if a debtor reaffirms an obligation. Or a debtor might reaffirm to prevent a creditor from pursuing a co-signer on the debt, especially when the co-signer is a family member. In re Paglia, 302 B.R. 162 (Bankr. W.D. Pa. 2003). The case below explores a creditor's other major leverage point: the opportunity to engage in future borrowing.

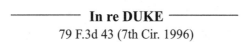

In re DUKE
79 F.3d 43 (7th Cir. 1996)

WOOD, Circuit Judge.

Although bankruptcy is normally viewed as a process through which a debtor obtains relief from pre-petition obligations and gets a fresh start in life (financially, at least), things are not always that simple. This case presents a wrinkle that occurs when, during the bankruptcy proceeding, a creditor makes an offer to a debtor to reaffirm a pre-petition debt, in exchange for certain benefits. The debtor's lawyer here believes that the creditor was too heavy-handed in its tactics, and thus ran afoul of the automatic stay rule of 11 U.S.C. §362(a). The district court disagreed and ruled that the creditor had played by the rules. We affirm.

On September 23, 1994, William Duke filed a Chapter 7 bankruptcy petition in which he listed Sears, Roebuck & Co. (Sears) as one of his creditors. Duke's filing triggered the automatic stay provision of the Bankruptcy Code, 11 U.S.C. §362(a)(6), which prohibits a creditor from engaging in "any act to collect, assess, or recover a claim against the debtor that arose before commencement of the case under this title." After it received notice of the automatic stay, Sears sent the following letter to Duke's attorney, with a copy to Duke himself "for information purposes":

> Dear Robert L. Adams:
>
> We have been notified that you are representing our customer in Chapter 7 bankruptcy proceedings.
>
> There is a balance of $317.10 on this account.
>
> Should your client elect to reaffirm the Sears account upon liquidation of the outstanding balance in accordance with the Reaffirmation Agreement, charge privileges will be reinstated with a line of credit in the amount of $500.00.
>
> Enclosed are copies of the proposed Reaffirmation Agreement. Your courtesy and cooperation in this matter are greatly appreciated. Please let me know if we may be of further assistance.
>
> Very truly yours,
> K. Jaggers
> Bankruptcy Representative

cc: Debtor (For information purposes only)

First before the bankruptcy court, then in the district court, and now here, Duke claimed that this letter amounted to an impermissible attempt to "collect, assess, or recover a claim" in violation of §362(a)(6).

In essence, this case presents a question about the relation between the automatic stay of §362(a)(6) and reaffirmation agreements, which are authorized and regulated by 11 U.S.C. §524. A reaffirmation agreement is one in which the debtor agrees to repay all or part of a dischargeable debt after a bankruptcy petition has been filed. As one bankruptcy court explained it, "a reaffirmation agreement has the effect of reaffirming a debtor's preexisting in personam liability on the underlying obligations giving rise to the debt." *In re Walker,* 180 B.R. 834, 846 (Bankr. W.D .La. 1995). See also *In re Grabinski,* 150 B.R. 427, 430 (Bankr. N.D. Ill. 1993). The debtor choice to reaffirm creates a voluntary exception to the "fresh start" that bankruptcy otherwise confers. For that reason, the Bankruptcy Code contains various safeguards designed to assure that reaffirmations are genuine and that they are not the product of abusive creditor practices. See 11 U.S.C. §524(d); . . . [s]ee also *In re Edwards,* 901 F.2d 1383, 1386 (7th Cir. 1990) (reaffirmation is a fully voluntary negotiation on both sides).

The automatic stay provision of §362, as noted above, generally prohibits the creditor from taking "any act" to collect pre-petition debts. Its purpose, as this Court explained in *Matthews v. Rosene,* 739 F.2d 249, 251 (7th Cir. 1984), is "to benefit a debtor by preventing harassment and frustration of rehabilitation efforts through pursuit by creditors in individual actions." Taken to its logical extreme, §362 could be construed to prohibit all contact between creditors and debtors after a petition has been filed, with respect to dischargeable debts. The courts have not pushed it that far, however, not least because to do so would create significant tension with the right to reaffirm. Instead, they have focussed on the anti-harassment purpose of §362. . . .

This Court has not yet had the occasion to decide whether a creditor violates §362(a)(6) when it sends a letter to a debtor offering to reaffirm a pre-petition debt. A majority of the bankruptcy courts have found that these actions do not violate §362(a)(6) as long as the letter is nonthreatening and non-coercive. See, e.g., *In re Hazzard,* 1995 WL 110588 (Bankr. N.D. Ill.1995); *In re Jefferson,* 144 B.R. 620, 623 (Bankr. D. R.I. 1992) (citing additional cases); see also *In re Epperson,* 189 B.R. 195, 198 (E.D.Mo.1995). Duke can prevail here only if we accept one of two propositions: (1) that all creditor-initiated offers to reaffirm debts violate §362(a)(6); or (2) that offers to reaffirm in general are permissible if they are not threatening or coercive, but this one falls within the prohibited group.

As we note above, other courts have rejected the extreme reading of §362(a)(6) that the first of these propositions would require, and we think rightly so. The option of reaffirming would be empty if creditors were forbidden to engage in any communication whatsoever with debtors who have pre-petition obligations. If that were the rule, it is also hard to see what purpose the detailed rules governing enforceability of reaffirmation agreements contained in §524(c) would serve. By requiring a right to rescind, filing with the court, and an attorney's affidavit attesting that the debtor was fully informed, acted voluntarily, and that the agreement does not impose an undue hardship on the debtor, §524(c) addresses the fairness of a completed reaffirmation agreement. The assumption behind these provisions is that debtors will be agreeing to enter into some reaffirmation agreements, and that it is important to have in place certain institutional protections to guard against creditor overreaching. See Collier on Bankruptcy, para. 524.04 & n.2 (15th ed. 1995).

There is no reason to believe that reaffirmation agreements inevitably disadvantage debtors, and thus that the automatic stay should be used to protect debtors against this type of creditor effort to collect a pre-petition debt. Debtors might find the idea of a new credit relationship attractive, since this too can be part of a fresh financial start after bankruptcy. A line of credit can be a convenience for larger purchases, as the habits of millions of Americans so richly attest. See generally *Consumer Debt Grew by 9.3 percent Annual Rate in the Latest Month,* Wall St. J., Feb. 8, 1996, at A2 (as of Feb. 1996 consumer installment debt totaled almost $1,049 billion); Glen B. Canne, et al., *Payment of Household Debts,* Fed. Reserve Bull. 218 (1991) (debt-to-income ratio for consumer installment debt rose from fourteen percent in mid-1980 to nineteen percent in late 1989). Creditors, obviously, like the idea that bankruptcy may not result in a complete write-off of amounts due to them. Under both the rule that ensures that creditor offers to reaffirm are not coercive or threatening and the statutory protections of §524(c), both parties can enjoy the legitimate benefits of reaffirmations, and the debtor is protected from abuse of the system. . . .

Duke does not argue that this particular letter was threatening or coercive in its contents. It is true that the letter extends the "carrot" of the $500 line of credit for Duke if he decides to reaffirm the $317.10 debt and he pays it off. It is also true that the line between withholding of a benefit and imposition of a penalty can be elusive at times. Nevertheless, this letter is as bare-bones and straightforward as one can get. There is not a hint of unfavorable action that would be taken against Duke if he does not reaffirm. It does not even say that his chances of re-establishing credit with Sears would be prejudiced if he chooses not to reaffirm and then later seeks new credit after his discharge in bankruptcy. Under the circumstances, Duke was wise not to rely on this line of argument.

That leaves the possibility that it is inherently coercive to send a copy of a letter to an attorney directly to the debtor-client, for information purposes only (as the letter stated). The record is not clear as to whether "K. Jaggers, Bankruptcy Representative," was acting as an attorney for Sears or as an employee of the Sears collection department. If K. Jaggers was acting as an attorney or under the direction of an attorney, the Sears practice of "cc'ing" represented consumer debtors raises questions under the rules of professional conduct for attorneys. Illinois Rule of Professional Conduct 4.2 states generally that a lawyer should not communicate or cause another to communicate with a represented person unless the first lawyer obtains the prior consent of the second lawyer, "or as may otherwise be authorized by law." If K. Jaggers was acting purely as a debt collector, the practice Sears has adopted raises questions under the Fair Debt Collection Practices Act. 15 U.S.C. §§1692 et seq. Under §1692c(a)(2), a debt collector may not communicate with a consumer, without the consumer's permission, "if the debt collector knows the consumer is represented by an attorney with respect to such debt and has knowledge of, or can readily ascertain such attorney's name and address." In either case, there is no dispute that Sears knew that Duke was represented, and it knew the name and address of Duke's attorney. Duke, however, did not raise these points either in the lower courts or before this Court, and they are therefore not before us.

We conclude that the letter Sears sent to Duke did not violate the automatic stay provisions of §362, nor does the Bankruptcy Code require as a matter of law that the creditor refrain from copying the debtor on correspondence to the debtor's attorney. We therefore AFFIRM the judgment of the district court.

Note the economics of the deal presented to Mr. Duke. Sears offered him $500.00 in credit in return for committing to repay $317.10. This is not the same as offering him a "net" $182.90 in new credit, however, because he has to pay interest on the full outstanding balance. In essence, Duke has to draw 63% of his new credit line upfront and start the interest clock ticking if he wants to keep a Sears account. Ouch.

One year after the *Duke* decision, another court took a hard look at Sears' reaffirmation process and came to a very different conclusion. Judge Carol Kenner held hearings in which a number of abuses came to light, revealing that Sears signed debtors up for reaffirmation agreements that failed to meet the statutory standards and did not, as is required, file those agreements with the court. Barnaby J. Feder, The Harder Side of Sears, N.Y. Times (July 20, 1997). Sears proceeded to collect from the postbankruptcy debtors in direct violation of the discharge injunction. In re Lantanowich, 207 B.R. 326 (Bankr. D. Mass. 1997). Judge Kenner also called in many of the lawyers for debtors who had been involved in these deficient reaffirmations and discovered that they routinely signed reaffirmation agreements for debtors that simply did not have enough income after essential expenses to make the payments on the reaffirmed debt. They said they did so because their clients really wanted the future credit, even at its inflated price.

The fallout from the reaffirmation scandal was extensive. These revelations were followed by civil and criminal investigations and class-action lawsuits. Sears' final bill for its expedited reaffirmation process (unfettered by such speed bumps as legal compliance) was between $300 and $500 million dollars, plus an incalculable amount of bad press. Why would a major corporation take such a risk? Professors Culhane and White, who have called the Sears-type procedures "rogue reaffirmations," suggest the answer. With some important caveats, they estimate from their data that reaffirmations may represent $2.75 billion per year in potential recovery for creditors. Although Sears is only one creditor, because of its enormous size in the consumer market, Culhane and White estimated that Sears is involved in one-third of all the consumer bankruptcies filed in the United States each year. So it had a lot to gain from breaking the rules. Each consumer bankruptcy is a small event, except for the family involved, but consumer bankruptcy is a major component of the consumer credit economy.

Some research suggests that all the debate and lawmaking about reaffirmations may be missing the larger problem that hinders financial recovery: some people simply do not earn enough to pay their ongoing bills, even with a discharge of past debt. Consider this finding. One year after receiving a discharge, one-third of chapter 7 debtors reported to researchers that their financial situation was the same or worse than when they filed bankruptcy. See Katherine Porter & Deborah Thorne, The Failure of the Fresh Start, 92 Cornell L. Rev. 67, 87 (2006). Reaffirmations did not seem to be a factor. Id. at 98-99. Instead, ongoing income problems from things like weak employment situations or chronic illness that prevented full-time work held families back from recovering their financial footing. Id. at 94. The fact that chapter 7 does nothing in and of itself to give a family enough income to buy food, pay rent, and keep the lights on seemed to get lost in some remarks from members of Congress who derided chapter 7 as a ticket to "easy street," during the debate that preceded the 2005 amendments.

Recent empirical research has opened a window into how bankruptcy affects access to credit. One of us found that not only was it possible for debtors to borrow after bankruptcy but that creditors aggressively market to those they lament to Congress as "deadbeats." Katherine Porter, Bankrupt Profits: The Credit Industry's Business Model for Postbankruptcy Lending, 93 Iowa L. Rev. 1369 (2008) (reporting that 87% of households said they had received credit offers specifically mentioning their bankruptcies); see also Song Han & Geng Li, Household Borrowing After Personal Bankruptcy, 43 J. of Money, Credit & Banking 491 (2011). Freed from old debts, these families are attractive borrowers because the postbankruptcy creditor will not have to compete with dozens of other lenders for repayment. People who have filed bankruptcy do pay higher rates than non-bankrupts for credit, even secured credit, notwithstanding the hungry lenders.

Despite this widespread credit availability, many debtors eschew borrowing or sharply curb prior habits, particularly with respect to credit cards. Katherine Porter, Life After Debt: Understanding the Credit Restraint of Postbankruptcy Debtors, 18 Am. Bank. L. Rev. 1, 9 (2010) (finding that 75% of debtors who filed chapter 7 in 2001 had not accepted new credit in first year after bankruptcy). Families who reported improved circumstances three years after bankruptcy were more likely to have accepted credit, which may just as much be evidence that families who return to credit after bankruptcy are stabilizing and rebuilding financially, as it is proof that they are being sucked back into a learned reliance on borrowing. Id. at 35-36.

The law gives chapter 7 debtors a powerful incentive to steer clear of debt in the years after a discharge. Section 727(a)(8) prohibits a chapter 7 discharge for any debtor who was given a chapter 7 discharge in a prior case in the eight years preceding the filing of the debtor's current case. A debtor given a chapter 13 discharge in the prior six years is similarly prohibited from getting a chapter 7 discharge. Repeat filing is not uncommon but it is hardly a contagion. In the 2007 Consumer Bankruptcy Project sample, fewer than 15% of filers had ever filed bankruptcy previously (in any year).

C. NONDISCRIMINATION AND CREDIT SCORING

In addition to worrying about creditors that try to avoid the effects of the discharge, debtors seeking a fresh start also face the risk that employers or government agencies will look askance at someone who has been bankrupt and will refuse a job, a license, or a permit crucial to the debtor's livelihood or well-being. Conscious of that risk, Congress included section 525 in the Code, which forbids that sort of discrimination. On the whole, however, the reported cases find the courts interpreting these provisions narrowly. It appears more debtors have lost than won.

The Fair Credit Reporting Act permits a bankruptcy filing to remain on a person's credit record for ten years. 15 U.S.C. §1681c(a)(1). The major credit bureaus have policies of removing bankruptcies after seven years, which suggests that analytical models may show this to be a crucial break point for debtors becoming a decent credit risk. While they may be similar in terms of repayment risk, other research suggests that people who file bankruptcy continue to lag behind their non-bankrupt peers for fifteen to thirty years in accumulation of home equity, net worth, and cash savings. Jay L. Zagorsky & Lois R. Lupica, A Study of Consumers' Post-Discharge Finances: Struggle, Stasis of Fresh-Start, 16 Am. Bankr. Inst. L. Rev. 1 (2010).

People who file bankruptcy may find their fresh start in life encumbered by the double dings to their credit score: the late payments and defaults that typically preceded the bankruptcy, and the act of filing for bankruptcy relief itself. Low credit scores now negatively influence everything from car insurance premiums to apartment rental applications to hiring. Deborah Thorne, Personal Bankruptcy and the Credit Report: Conflicting Mechanisms of Social Mobility, 11 J. of Poverty 4 (2007). Dr. Thorne notes the ironic confluence of policies that make bankruptcy available so that families can have a fresh start at the same time that credit reports will raise costs and reduce opportunities for these families for years to come.

Problem Set 9

9.1. The Muscle Mart is the only complete bodybuilding gym in Missoula, Montana. It charges a monthly membership and adds assessments for use of the sauna and items ordered at the juice bar. MM has a firm policy (would they have flabby policies?): if two months of dues or sauna fees are left unpaid, the membership is revoked, and the former member is not permitted to use any of the equipment until the unpaid balance is paid in full.

Peter Lanier has just filed for a chapter 7 bankruptcy, discharging among his other debts two months' worth of MM dues. MM has revoked Peter's membership, and Peter is frantic to get back to his workouts. He has offered to pay a month in advance, but MM refuses. What would you advise Peter? See §524(a).

9.2. Two months ago, you handled a routine chapter 7 bankruptcy for Kevin James. Kevin is a gentle soul, and the bankruptcy has been bothering him. Last week, he was in a local hardware store when the owner (a former creditor) made a remark about "stiffing your friends." Kevin said he felt terrible and offered to repay the debt. The owner, an enterprising fellow, got this promise in writing. Now Kevin fears this was not very smart. He is struggling with his current obligations and is not sure he can pay the hardware store. He calls you to ask if that written agreement is enforceable. What do you tell him? See §524(c).

9.3. Bob "Bull" Horne supports his wife and five children at a marginal level with his job as a janitor at a local bar. Bull lives for weekends in the mountains at his home-away-from-home, "Carnage Cabin." Bull hunts from dawn to dusk and often invites friends to join him. He uses much of the meat, including venison, to feed his family, but you got the impression from his wife that she would rather have him helping with the kids. The cabin is subject to a $10,000 mortgage, with $500 monthly payments. Bull says the cabin is "priceless," pointing out he built it with his own hands, but you suspect its market value is close to $5,000. Bull has a few exempt assets, including a retirement account worth $25,000, but his family lives pretty much hand-to-mouth on its budget. The creditor on the cabin loan is a national bank; you've called counsel several times with no response yet and you aren't waiting by the phone for it to ring. Bull has forcefully told you that he wants to keep the cabin and that he thinks it's your job to make that happen. Consider all options for Bull in chapter 7 bankruptcy. See §§524(c), 722.

9.4. Christine Johnson is a single mother of two children who until recently has managed to keep the family in reasonable shape after her husband's death in a car-train accident. Her skills as a die etcher in the local microchip plant produced a decent income until a year ago, when the plant headed for somewhere in Asia. She held out for a technical job for quite a while, running up substantial bills, but she has been waiting tables and working a night-shift cleaning job the last four months to keep food on the table. Her big worry is holding on to her house and her car. The credit union has the mortgage. You've dealt with them before and know their policy: They'll happily agree to a reaff on the mortgage, but only if Christine also reaffirms in full all her other debts to the credit union, which include three loans. One is a credit card, one is a personal loan (unsecured), and the third is a car loan. The car is a four-year-old Honda the couple bought used almost three years ago. She owes $7,300 on it, although its bluebook value is $5,900. She is desperate to keep it, because it works pretty well (her husband was a mechanic and knew cars). If she had to buy a new one, "they could sell me trash and I wouldn't know it." Without a car, she couldn't get to either job. The house was their dream home and Christine says she'd work three jobs to keep it. What do you advise her? What are you able and willing to do for her in this situation? §524(c), (m).

9.5. Your firm represents Peoples State Bank, which does a substantial amount of consumer lending. With the rising number of consumer bankruptcies, PSB has decided it needs help in determining what to do when it holds a security interest in an automobile and the debtor declares bankruptcy. Because your firm has taken care of PSB's legal work for years, you know that PSB has a very protective lending agreement that includes a provision that the debtor's declaration of bankruptcy is an automatic default under the contract.

PSB brings its first case to you: The debtor, Jason Jansen, has gone into bankruptcy owing PSB $7,899. The loan is at slightly better than average market rates. The loan is secured by a valid PMSI on a car worth $6,000. It would cost PSB about $500 to repossess and resell the car. Assuming average depreciation of the car and maintenance of the current payment schedule, if payments are continued the loan balance would decrease faster than the value of the car will decline. Jansen is not in default on the payments. He has a good job and says he plans to continue to pay on schedule.

PSB has three questions, two specific and one general: (1) can it get the car back in this situation, if it wants to; (2) if Jansen keeps the car, what portion of the amount owed will be repaid; and (3) what is your overall advice about how to handle this sort of problem? Keep in mind as you deal with PSB that they want you to develop some generalized principles that they can give to a loan officer so the loan officer can deal with bankrupt debtors without having to call you for expensive individualized analyses each time.

9.6. A new client, Edwin Peraza contacted you for advice about an employment matter. Edwin interviewed with Buster Accounting, an industry leader, for a position as a mid-level accountant. Linda Townsend, the supervisor who interviewed Edwin, called him immediately after the interview. She told him he was the most impressive applicant and offered him the job. Linda said the offer was contingent upon Edwin's successful completion of the firm's hiring process, which includes a review of the applicant's credit report and a background check. Edwin accepted and completed the hiring paperwork. A week later, Linda called Edwin to inform him that the firm was rescinding its offer of employment. Edwin tells you that he believes the firm refused to hire him due to his chapter 7 bankruptcy case, which was a routine matter with a discharge entered a few months after filing. Will Edwin succeed in an action against Buster Accounting? He also asks you for any tips you have on his job search in light of Buster Accounting's actions. What would you advise? 11 U.S.C. §525.

Section 3:
Chapter 13 Repayment

In the next two assignments we look at the special rules in chapter 13, focusing in the first on secured creditors and then in the second on unsecured creditors.

Assignment 10.

Secured Creditors in Chapter 13

A. ELEMENTS OF AN ACCEPTABLE PLAN

1. Overview of Chapter 13

In the preceding assignments, we have taken a consumer debtor through the steps of a chapter 7 bankruptcy. The Bankruptcy Code provides an alternative for consumer debtors in financial trouble called a chapter 13 adjustment of debts or "wage earner's plan," as it was once known, to which we now turn. This section of the book has two main purposes. The first is to provide an overview of the chapter 13 process and the key elements of a chapter 13 plan. The second is to discuss creditor entitlements in chapter 13, with a specific emphasis on what goes by the term "cramdown," another piece of bankruptcy jargon that everyone uses but that is nowhere in the Code. "Cramdown" is the minimum amount a debtor can pay to a creditor and still have the repayment plan confirmed over creditor objection—evocatively, the plan is crammed down such creditors' throats. As with much of the Code, this requirement is different for secured and unsecured creditors, and so the next two assignments proceed accordingly.

Although chapters 7 and 13 have much in common, including the creation of an estate consisting of all the debtor's property and an automatic stay that freezes collection efforts, the chapter 13 repayment option differs significantly from chapter 7 liquidation. In chapter 7, debtors effectively freeze their assets and debts at the moment they file for bankruptcy. Their non-exempt *assets* (if any) are the source of paying claims. In return, the debtor is relieved of any future obligations to pay dischargeable, prepetition debts, and all the debtor's subsequent earnings are free from the reach of these former creditors.

By contrast, chapter 13 focuses on using *future earnings*, rather than accumulated assets, to pay creditors. This means chapter 13 lets the debtor keep all assets—even if not exempt—in exchange for an agreement to tithe future income for the benefit of creditors for a minimum of three years. Secured creditors must receive certain minimum payments for the debtor to retain collateral, while unsecured creditors must be paid all of the debtors' disposable income. The trustee takes a percentage of the debtor's income for each pay period, deducts a part to cover administrative expenses, and then distributes the remainder to the creditors according to a court-approved plan. When the debtor has completed the agreed payout, the debtor's remaining obligations are discharged. If the debtor fails to complete the repayment plan, the case is dismissed, and the debtor gets no discharge (although the debtor may be able to convert to chapter 7 or refile bankruptcy).

As a result, every debtor who is eligible for both chapters 7 and 13 must make a fundamental choice: seek an immediate discharge in chapter 7 but lose non-exempt assets, or try to pay some or all debts in installments under a chapter 13 plan and get to keep assets. The debtor who chooses chapter 13 must prepare a plan detailing the amounts to be repaid and the terms of repayment in accord with certain statutory requirements. As we will see in a later assignment, there are a number of provisions in chapter 7, including section 707(b), that may bar a debtor from that chapter, leaving a "choice" for some debtors between chapter 13 and no bankruptcy relief at all.

From a creditor's standpoint, the difference between chapters 7 and 13 is the prospect of payment obtained by selling the debtor's assets versus payment from the debtor's future income. In light of most debtors' circumstances, this usually boils down to no payment (chapter 7) versus waiting for some payment— or at least the prospect of some payment (chapter 13). From the debtor's viewpoint, chapter 13 is a much more involved, long-term process than chapter 7. Court supervision lasts from the day of filing until plan payments are completed, a period of three to five years. No discharge from debt will be granted until the debtor makes the very last payment on the plan. This is a marked contrast to the chapter 7 debtor who is usually discharged within six months of filing. The timing of the chapter 13 discharge also differs from a discharge in chapter 11, under which the court approval of a plan generates an immediate discharge even before the payments begin. For debtors, chapter 13 means a long wait until discharge, although the debtor is protected during the course of the case.

The chapter 13 trustee has a different role from that of the chapter 7 trustee. The debtor, not the trustee, retains control of property of the estate in chapter 13 cases, §1303, and that estate is broader than in chapter 7, specifically including the post-petition wages, which makes sense given those wages fund plan payments, §1306. Thus the chapter 13 trustee does not have the function of collecting, preserving, and selling the property of the estate as in chapter 7. §1302(b)(1). The debtor retains property and proposes the repayment plan.

The chapter 13 trustee does have several important responsibilities. The trustee makes a recommendation to the court on plan confirmation. §1302(b)(2)(B). Ordinarily, the plan provides that debtors will make a lump-sum monthly payment to the trustee for distribution, although some secured creditors may be paid directly (a procedure known as payment "outside the plan"). Trustees often use wage attachment orders to collect payments; these divert a portion of the debtor's wages directly to the trustee for plan payments. Because the attachment is made pursuant to federal bankruptcy law, state restrictions on wage garnishment are inapplicable. If the debtor's payments fall behind, it is usually the trustee who files to dismiss the debtor's case for nonpayment. The trustee is responsible for ensuring that the debtor gives up the required amount of income. The trustee also asserts any objections to the debtor's discharge. The trustee also is charged with objecting to improper creditor claims, and making distributions to creditors. §1326. At the same time the trustee has a duty to assist the debtor in the performance of the debtor's duties. §§1302(b)(1), (4). In short, the trustee scrutinizes everyone connected with the case—debtor and creditors—to make sure that they are following the Code.

Chapter 13 administration is complex. Many districts have a "standing" chapter 13 trustee perform this task for all cases, rather than an individual from a panel appointed anew in each case. §1302(a); 28 U.S.C. §586(b). In those districts, especially populous urban ones, the position of standing trustee is not just a full-time job but an active business relying on a highly sophisticated, computerized system of receipts and disbursements. Fees are fixed by the court and statute. Id. at §586(e). Billions of debtor dollars flow through this processing system each year.

Chapter 13 collection also means Big Business for speculators. Collection of sixteen cents on the dollar on debt for which one paid the original creditor eight cents produces a 100% profit. Making this a multimillion-dollar venture, of course, means investing major money. Enter Wall Street. An article in Forbes Magazine written prior to BAPCPA was headlined "Uncle Sam Is My Collection Agent." It explained that the investment bankers at Bear Stearns were making big bucks from "the growing multibillion dollar trade in personal debt" by buying chapter 13 debt at steep discount and then collecting the trustee's monthly disbursements, enjoying the subsidized public collection system the standing trustee provides. These bankers also anxiously awaited what would become BAPCPA, knowing then new law would increase their collections (and thus profits) still more. We pass in silence the irony of the subsequent collapse of Bear Stearns for reasons apparently unrelated to their successful collections business.

The financial and policy questions surrounding chapter 13 deserve attention, but first we will focus on how it works, starting with the required elements of a plan. The Code provisions that tell us what may or must be in a chapter 13 plan seem to be arbitrarily distributed between sections 1322 and 1325. Section 1322(a)(2) gives the debtor the power to use a plan to modify the rights of creditors, both secured and unsecured. This power includes, for example, paying a reduced amount of the obligation and stretching out the period of time over which payment can be made. Other provisions in the two sections then substantially constrain that broad power, especially with regard to secured creditors.

2. Payments to Secured Creditors

One of the most common reasons for choosing a chapter 13 bankruptcy is the debtor's desire to keep property that is subject to a security interest. When a significant asset, such as a car or furniture, is subject to a valid security interest, the chapter 13 plan is often built around satisfying the legal requirements for retaining that property and structuring a new payment schedule.

Just as secured creditors in chapter 7 enjoy enhanced status compared to unsecured creditors, so too the secured creditor in chapter 13 enjoys better protection. If a debtor proposes in a chapter 13 plan to retain collateral, the secured party will sometimes object, declaring the debtor in default and demanding the collateral. Whether the creditor can exercise its right to repossession and sale, realizing the value of the collateral and terminating its contract with the debtor, will depend on whether the debtor can comply with the provisions of chapter 13 that protect secured creditors. Because the collateral is property of the estate, albeit in the control of the debtor, the creditor still must ask the court for relief from the stay.

Courts must thus solve two separate but related issues when a secured creditor wants to repossess and sell the collateral. The first issue is *protection* of the secured party's interest in the collateral while the case is going on. Because the debtor proposes to keep the property, the secured party is naturally concerned about the risk that the collateral will lose its value during the three to five years of chapter 13 (think about whether you'd rather repossess a car now or after five more years of the debtor's driving). If the debtor defaults later on, the secured party could be left with collateral worth considerably less than when bankruptcy was originally filed. This problem is usually cast in terms of providing "adequate protection" for the secured party under section 362(d). The two principal types of risks that concern the secured creditor are a loss of the collateral (e.g., by fire, theft, or simple neglect) and a decline in its value (such as depreciation over time).

The second issue is adequate *payment* to the secured party if the debtor chooses to modify the debt (without a rule setting the payment terms, some debtors would surely modify the debt down to zero). There is a statutory formula, discussed below, that calculates the minimum amount the debtor must pay in order to keep collateral over the objection of the secured creditor. In the typical elegance of bankruptcy terminology, the process is called "cramdown."

In chapter 11 business cases the two issues are fairly distinct, with the first (adequate protection) focusing on immediate payments even while the plan negotiations are proceeding and the second (minimum payments) ensuring that the long-term payments will compensate the secured creditor on the obligation. Chapter 11 plans are often proposed months or years after filing, so that the protection issue must be dealt with quickly, while the payment issue can await the battle over plan confirmation. In a chapter 13, by contrast, the debtor's plan is frequently filed alongside the petition and confirmed within a month or two; the result of this condensed timeline is that the two issues often collapse into joint consideration. Because they are analytically distinct, however, we consider each in turn.

a. Adequate Protection

As we learned earlier, a creditor can move to lift the automatic stay by arguing under section 362(d) that its interest in the collateral is not adequately protected. In chapter 7, because an immediate liquidation is anticipated, adequate protection is rarely an issue. In chapter 13, by contrast, the debtor proposes to retain the collateral and make payments over a long period of time, often on quite different terms from the original loan. Creditors may argue that the debtor's proposed actions insufficiently protect their rights.

In the following case, creditor GMAC had already repossessed the debtor's car before the bankruptcy filing, and it wanted to retain and sell the car to pay off its outstanding loan balance. With the automatic stay in place, GMAC could not proceed with a sale, so it moved to lift the stay, arguing the application of both subsection 362(d)(1) and (2). Because GMAC had possession of the car, the debtor made two arguments in response: one against the lifting of the stay, to prevent GMAC from selling the car immediately, and the other for return of the car to the debtor, as custodian of estate property under chapter 13 and an avid fan of driving to work. (Note the second argument invoked the trustee's "turnover" power of section 542, which the chapter 13 debtor, *qua* trustee, gets to use, because the debtor retains control of property.)

────────── **In re RADDEN** ──────────

35 B.R. 821 (Bankr. E.D. Va. 1983)

SHELLEY, Bankruptcy Judge.

These matters involve the proper disposition of a 1979 Ford Mustang automobile (the "property"). The debtor, along with Priscilla Coe, purchased the property from Hechler Chevrolet, Inc. ("Hechler") on October 17, 1981. The property was titled in the debtor's name alone. Hechler financed this purchase by a retail installment sales contract secured by the vehicle. This installment sales agreement was assigned to GMAC pursuant to its agreement with Hechler entered July 3, 1980. . . .

The debtor failed to make the contractually required payments to GMAC for the month of June, 1983. This constituted the first default under the assigned installment sales contract. The debtor did not cure the default and also failed to make the required monthly payment in July, 1983. [Apparently GMAC lawfully repossessed the car prior to bankruptcy.—Eds.] GMAC notified the debtor and the cobuyer, Priscilla Coe, of their right to redeem the property and of a proposed sale of the property on August 12, 1983, if they did not redeem the property prior thereto.

On August 10, 1983, the debtor filed for relief under Chapter 13 of the Bankruptcy Code. In his Chapter 13 plan the debtor lists the value of the property as $2,700.00 and the balance due on the contract as $4,400.30. The Chapter 13 plan proposes to pay, through the standing Chapter 13 trustee, GMAC in full to the extent of the value of the collateral plus interest thereon at the rate of 5 percent per annum in deferred monthly cash payments of $89.68 over a period of 36 months. To the extent that the amount on the contract exceeds the value of the collateral, the obligation owing to GMAC is treated as an unsecured claim. Under the plan, unsecured claims are to receive seventy cents on the dollar.

The debtor lives about a mile and a half from his place of employment and about three blocks from a food store. He has been able to get groceries without difficulty since the time GMAC obtained possession of the property. He has gotten to and from work either by obtaining rides from friends, by using his mother's automobile, or by walking. The debtor testified that (1) he is presently working from 3:00 until 11:00 and that a friend with an automobile in the same apartment complex works the same shift; (2) that he has missed very little work in the past five years at Western Electric, except that on at least one occasion he was absent because of inability to get to work; (3) that when he must walk home he does so on a street that is busy with traffic, is not lighted, and does not have a sidewalk; (4) that he has not yet been required to walk home from work in cold weather; (5) that he seeks a turnover of the property to enable him to get to and from work; (6) that although the property is not presently insured by him for collision and liability, he would re-obtain insurance on the property; (7) that he has the present finances to procure such insurance; and (8) that he has presently a valid driver's license.

CONCLUSIONS OF LAW

GMAC here seeks relief based both on the lack of adequate protection, id. §362(d)(l), and on the grounds that the debtor does not have any equity in the property and that such property is not necessary for the debtor's effective reorganization. Id. §362(d)(2).

As to the latter basis for obtaining relief from the stay, this Court needs to find only that the property is necessary for an effective reorganization to deny GMAC relief pursuant to §362(d)(2). The debtor admits in his Chapter 13 plan and his memorandum in support of his adversary proceeding and in opposition to GMAC's adversary proceeding that he lacks equity in the property. Therefore, if the property questioned here is not necessary for the debtor's effective reorganization, the creditor is entitled to relief from stay.

The debtor bears the burden of proving that the property is necessary for his effective reorganization. §362(g). This Court is satisfied that an automobile is necessary for an individual's effective reorganization in today's society. As the debtor testified, he needs the property to get to and from his place of employment. Moreover, individuals need transportation to obtain medical as well as other necessary services. Having found that the property is necessary for an effective reorganization, this Court will not grant GMAC relief from the stay pursuant to §362(d)(2).

As an alternate basis for obtaining relief from the stay, GMAC alleges that it has an interest in property that is not adequately protected. Lack of adequate protection is sufficient "cause" pursuant to §362(d)(1) for a court to grant a creditor relief from the automatic stay. The resolution of GMAC's claim in this regard turns on the issue of what is GMAC's "interest in property. . . ."

The Court notes initially that the property in which GMAC has an interest is currently in GMAC's possession, therefore, GMAC is in the best position to protect its interest in the property from the likelihood of theft, vandalism, or destruction by natural cause.

Second, under the provisions of the debtor's plan, GMAC will retain their lien on the collateral and receive the amount of their allowed secured claim with interest and, therefore, its interest in property will be adequately protected if the plan is effectively consummated. GMAC has not demonstrated that the debtor's chances of rehabilitation are remote. To the contrary, the debtor has established that he has a stable employment record and that he is capable of meeting the payments to the standing trustee under the plan. The debtor has a reasonable likelihood of having his plan confirmed and consummated and, therefore, GMAC will likely receive the allowed amount of their secured claim through deferred cash payments. Recognizing this likelihood, GMAC's interest in property is adequately protected under the Chapter 13 plan and, therefore, GMAC requires no relief from the automatic stay to protect said interest. . . .

Finally, this Court now addresses the issue of the debtor's turnover complaint. The debtor seeks to recover the property that was returned voluntarily to GMAC prior to the filing of bankruptcy. The debtor seeks this turnover pursuant to §542. . . .

The debtor here has filed a petition pursuant to Chapter 13 of the Bankruptcy Code. Section 1303 provides the debtor with the rights and powers that a trustee would have under Chapter 7 or the debtor in possession would have under Chapter 11. Consequently the debtor is a proper party to seek turnover pursuant to §542(a) because the property that the debtor seeks to have turned over is property that he as debtor may use in the ordinary course of business. See §363.

Having found that the debtor is the proper party to bring a §542 turnover complaint, this Court notes the elements of §542 include (1) an entity has possession, custody, or control of property (2) that the debtor may use the property pursuant to §363 and (3) that the property has value or benefit to the estate. . . .

For the reasons discussed above, this Court should and will order that GMAC return possession of the property to the debtor. The Court will not, however, order such turnover without providing adequate protection to the creditor of his interest in the property. The debtor's "use of the vehicle pursuant to §363(b) will presumably cause the value of the vehicle to decline." In re Williams, 6 B.R. at 792. This Court is satisfied, however, that if the debtor (1) procures adequate insurance on the property at the time of recovering possession and (2) makes monthly payments under the contract with GMAC until the time that a plan is confirmed, GMAC's interest in the subject property will be adequately protected and, therefore, the requirements of §361 and [§362(d)] will be satisfied.

For Mr. Radden, chapter 13 became an extraordinarily powerful tool. He was able to restructure his loan payments and to reclaim a car from a creditor that had lawfully repossessed it after default. Once Radden filed for bankruptcy, GMAC could not sell the duly repossessed car and realize its value until the court granted its motion under section 362(d). With a lift-stay motion denied, GMAC was off down the path of the three- to five-year chapter 13 payout to recover on its debt.

Note that GMAC lost on both section 362(d) arguments. The court rejected application of section 362(d)(2). While conceding the debtor had no equity in the property, it concluded that the property was necessary for an effective reorganization. Did this strike you as a generous conclusion in light of the evidence that the debtor had little difficulty getting to work and nearby shopping? Concluding that an item of collateral is "necessary for an effective reorganization" can blur into a value judgment in the consumer context, but it usually has real bite in chapter 11 business cases, which use the exact same Code provisions on stay relief.

In its second argument, GMAC argued that the stay should be lifted because its interest in the car was not adequately protected as required in section 362(d)(1). The debtor would have possession of the car if the stay continued to restrain GMAC from selling the car due to the turnover action. Thus a real possibility existed that the car would decline in value or even be destroyed. The *Radden* court found that the debtor's payments and agreement to arrange for sufficient insurance addressed those risks such that GMAC was adequately protected.

b. Adequate Payment

For the secured creditor that does not succeed in a lift stay motion, which would effectively let it bypass chapter 13 and liquidate the collateral, the next battle is fighting for maximum payment under the chapter 13 plan. Unless the debtor and the secured creditor make a deal, a plan will be crammed down on the secured creditor if the debtor promises to pay a certain amount. A court must make two factual determinations to establish the minimum amount that a debtor must pay to a secured creditor to present a permissible chapter 13 plan:

1. The amount of the allowed secured claim under section 506(a); and
2. The present value of the allowed secured claim under section 1325(a)(5)(B)(ii).

The general rule about required payments to secured creditors is contained in section 1325(a)(5), which contains two requirements: a secured creditor must be paid its full allowed secured claim *and* it must be paid interest on that claim (i.e., the "value" of that claim, §1325(a)(5)(B)(ii)) because the debtor in chapter 13 spreads the payment over time. Of the minimum payment dividend, think of the first requirement as a principal component and the second as an interest component. To avoid a creditor derailing the chapter 13 case, the debtor's plan must satisfy both components.

i. *Value of the Claim*

We discussed previously the calculation of an allowed secured claim in Assignment 6 and saw that an undersecured debt is bifurcated by section 506(a) to yield two claims: a secured claim equal to the value of the collateral and an unsecured claim for the deficiency. Under the general rule of section 1325(a)(5), the cramdown section, the debtor promises to pay the allowed secured claim (i.e., the value of the collateral) in full, while treating the unsecured portion of the debt like any other unsecured claim under the plan, which often can be paid only in part.

The key factual question is therefore the value of the collateral; that figure will determine the amount of the allowed secured claim that must be paid in full. The Supreme Court addressed the issue in Associates Commercial Corp. v. Rash, 520 U.S. 952 (1997). The case was not about methods of valuation, which we will address in the business section, but rather about what definition of "value" should be used for chapter 13 cramdown: liquidation value or replacement value. That issue had split six circuits at least three ways, proving once again that this stuff is hard for everyone.

The Rashes were a couple that had purchased a truck for freight-hauling. They still owed $41,000, (about 60% of the purchase price) when they filed for chapter 13, but they alleged that the truck would bring only $28,500 in a liquidation sale. On that basis, their chapter 13 plan proposed to cram down the lender with a promise to pay $28,500 over 58 months of their plan. The creditor replied that it would cost the Rashes around $41,000 to buy a similar truck and that amount should be considered the value for purposes of determining if section 1325 is satisfied. Such a definition of value would have required the Rashes to pay the entire debt, $41,000, over the course of the plan if they wanted to keep the truck.

The Court's opinion turned on section 506(a), which the Fifth Circuit had noted refers to "the value of the creditor's interest in the estate's interest in [the collateral]." It reasoned that focus on the creditor's entitlement means that the creditor should get what it would get in a UCC (Uniform Commercial Code, Article 9) sale if it exercised its legal rights: liquidation value. Replacement value would give the creditor a bankruptcy windfall compared to its state-law entitlement. The Court, per Justice Ginsburg, disagreed in an 8-1 decision, pointing to section 506(a)'s next sentence, which directs that valuation be determined "in light of the proposed use of the property." Since the Rashes proposed to keep the truck, she concluded that what it would cost them to buy an equivalent truck was the proper measure of its value for the purposes of a chapter 13 plan. (The Court also specifically rejected a third approach, which split the difference between the replacement and liquidation values.) The Court's opinion had some qualifying footnotes too, including infamous footnote 6 that implies that deductions from replacement value could be made for marketing and other costs. While *Rash* clarified that at the very least, liquidation value was incorrect, its effort to define replacement value was pretty fuzzy. Many people read *Rash* to require the use of "modified replacement value," leaving fighting in the trenches about the modifications—and of course, the method of valuation used to come up with the replacement value.

BAPCPA both codified and revised *Rash* by adding a new paragraph (2) to section 506(a). Look carefully at its restrictions as to which sorts of property it applies. It generally adopts a replacement value approach but does not appear to allow the deductions from the *Rash* footnote. It also makes clear that replacement value means used value, not new. Yet disputes persist. The textual reference to "retail value" for some specific property implies to some that the proper measure for replacement for non-specified property might be wholesale value. As a practical matter, we think that many courts continue to split the difference between wholesale and retail prices as a rough-justice measure of value for cramdown purposes. In the context of cars, this is often the midpoint between the published retail and wholesale prices for any given used vehicle. This approach likely results from confusion on how to apply *Rash* and its footnotes and from the fact that the economics of consumer bankruptcy will not support an elaborate hearing, complete with experts, for each vehicle to be valued.

ii. Interest on the Claim

Once the allowed secured claim is determined, the court can establish a payment schedule that permits the creditor to recover the present value of the claim. The concept of "present value" (in statutory terms, "value, as of the effective date of the Plan," §1325(a)(5)(B)(ii)) reflects the elementary proposition that a dollar due to be paid a year from now is worth less than a dollar paid now. Absent bankruptcy, the secured creditor would be allowed to repossess and sell the collateral today, investing its proceeds; chapter 13 requires a three-to-five year wait. Because of this deferral, the Code gives the creditor the right to receive interest on its allowed secured claim. The total to be received by the creditor over time must equal the "present value" of the collateral at the time of plan confirmation.

For the math whizzes, a number of formulas can be used to calculate present value. One is given here:

$$PV_a = \left[\frac{1 - 1/(1+i)^n}{i} \right] \times (a)$$

where a = a dollar amount of installment payment
$\quad i$ = a current annual interest rate
$\quad n$ = the number of annual payments

(Computations for other than annual payments require corresponding adjustment of the i variable; e.g., monthly payments use $i/12$.) But perhaps that is a bit much. Before you conclude that present value is simple in theory but hopelessly complex to compute, be reassured that "there's an app for that," and for the Luddites, there are published tables to calculate present value.

Any formula requires the insertion of values, and in chapter 13, both value (as discussed in the prior section) and interest rate are up for grabs. Equally important to someone contemplating monthly payments for multiple years is the required interest rate. Chapter 13's requirement that the creditor receive the present value of its allowed secured claim depends on *current* interest rates, not the rate in the loan contract signed by the debtor possibly years ago, which may be higher or lower. This is another instance of a debtor modifying its loan contract via chapter 13. Not surprisingly, this maneuver tends to disappoint creditors when interest rates have gone down. To give certainty to the chapter 13 plan process, some courts held that when the debt is contractual and there was an interest rate specified for the loan, that rate should be rebuttably presumed to be the market rate a debtor must pay under the plan. The Supreme Court in a 4-1-4 opinion, said no. See Till v. SCS Credit Corporation, 541 U.S. 465 (2004). The interest rate for cramdown should be the current prime rate "adjusted" for the riskiness of the debt. It declined to tell the bankruptcy courts just how to make that adjustment, noting that it will vary from case to case, but did cite a collection of cases suggesting that it will usually be between 1-3% (empirical basis unspecified).

The cramdown power to mark-to-market a consumer loan to the current value of its collateral and to reset the interest rate is one of the processes by which a debtor can keep its collateral over creditor protest. Another, which we have already seen, is redemption under section 722. Chapter 13 has a great advantage over redemption, however, because it allows the debtor to make those collateral-preserving payments over a multiple-year plan. Chapter 13 can thus be thought of as a "redemption by installment" regime. Assignment 13 discusses the entire tool-kit that a debtor has available to keep collateral.

3. *Treatment of Liens Generally*

Recall in chapter 7 that after bankruptcy, a secured creditor's lien remains on collateral; once the stay is over, the creditor can go after that property in rem to redress default because the discharge is only of personal liability. But in chapter 13, the debtor's broad "modification" power of section 1322 includes the right to remove the lien altogether, at least after the plan is concluded. §§1325(a)(5)(B)(i)(I)(bb), 1327(c). This accords the debtor the power to "strip" a lien off encumbered property upon successful completion of a chapter 13 plan.

As an example, consider a couple who granted a security interest for a loan on their office equipment, then, two years later, filed for bankruptcy. At the time of filing, the loan was $10,000 but the collateral was worth only $4,000. Assuming they have promised to pay 50% of the amount of unsecured claims under the chapter 13 plan, they would pay the undersecured creditor $4,000 (secured claim for value of collateral, with interest to account for present value) and $3,000 (50% of the $6,000 unsecured claim). If the debtors complete the plan, they will discharge the remaining debt. For $7,000 total plus a little present-value interest, they keep the equipment during and after bankruptcy for less than the amount of the loan.

This treatment of an undersecured claim is often called "lienstripping." And because it can be imposed over the secured creditor's objection, it is a form of cramdown. (Contrast the power dynamic with reaffirming secured debt to keep collateral after chapter 7.) If the debtors fail to complete the plan, they will lose the benefits of lienstripping. The debt will not be discharged, and after bankruptcy the secured creditor will once again be able to enforce its security interest with regard to all the unpaid debt. §1325(a)(5)(B)(i). But if they complete the plan, the unpaid, unsecured amount of the debt is discharged and the lien is eliminated with complete payment on the secured claim. Chapter 13 therefore accords great leverage to debtors: they don't just keep, they *unencumber*, their collateral upon plan completion.

4. Special Rules for Purchase Money Liens and Mortgages

The lienstripping rules have never applied to mortgages on a debtor's principal residence. In 2005, BAPCPA added at the end of section 1325(a), provisions exempting certain purchase money liens on personal property. We discuss these new exceptions and then recent jurisprudence on the long-standing rule preventing debtors from lienstripping mortgages on their residences.

a. Purchase Money Liens

Because the new language exempting certain purchase money security interests was added as an unnumbered textual coda to pre-existing subsections, it is commonly referred to as the "hanging" paragraph; the best citation we've seen used is 11 U.S.C. §1325(a)(*). Although the language is inartful, to say the least, these additional exemptions seem to forbid lienstripping certain purchase money security interests on collateral acquired during specified periods before bankruptcy. If the secured creditor objects to the plan, a debtor who wants to keep the collateral must promise to pay the purchase-money debt in full. Ignoring nuance, the "allowed secured claim" *is* the full debt, regardless of the collateral's value.

The first purchase money security interest exempted from lienstripping is one granted within the year before bankruptcy, regardless of the nature of the collateral. Second, for one specially favored secured creditor—the holder of a purchase money security interest in a motor vehicle—the time period is rolled further back to exempt in a similar fashion the stripping of security interests granted within two and a half years (910 days) before the petition. This is a big change. For many people, keeping a car is critical, and many car loans are undersecured, for three typical reasons: because the debtor financed 100%, and the value of an automobile drops sharply upon leaving the dealer's lot; because the debtor overpaid in the first place; or because fees and penalties that were added when the debtor missed payments (along with high interest rates) have caused the debt to swell. One of the biggest attractions of chapter 13 used to be the ability to keep the car by paying only its replacement value (plus interest to present value the claim.) BAPCPA protects car dealers and their finance companies from the consequences of their undersecured loans to the annual tune of many millions of dollars.

Yet, as always in bankruptcy, things are not as simple as they seem. The courts have had to confront the Zen specter of "negative equity."

FORD MOTOR CREDIT CO. v. DALE
582 F.3d 568 (5th Cir. 2009)

HAYNES, Circuit Judge:

This appeal involves the proper construction of the "hanging paragraph" in 11 U.S.C. §1325(a), which was added to the Bankruptcy Code (Code) by the Bankruptcy Abuse Prevention and Consumer Protection Act of 2005 (BAPCPA). Under the Code, a lien creditor generally holds a secured claim only to the extent of the present value of the collateral that the lien encumbers. If the amount of the secured claim exceeds the present value of the collateral, the Code treats the excess amount as a separate, unsecured claim. This process is known as bifurcation or "stripping down" the secured claim to the value of the collateral. The hanging paragraph is an exception to this general rule, preventing bifurcation of a claim when the creditor has a "purchase-money security interest" (securing the claimed debt) in a motor vehicle acquired for the debtor's personal use within 910 days of the debtor's bankruptcy filing. The issue here is whether the purchase-money security interest exception contained in the hanging paragraph applies to those portions of a claim attributable to the pay-off of negative equity in a trade-in vehicle, gap insurance, and an extended warranty. The district court found that it does. We AFFIRM.

I. FACTS

The facts of this case are undisputed. Debtor Rebecca Ann Dale purchased a 2006 Ford F150 pick-up truck from Gullo Ford Mercury of Conroe, Texas. The vehicle was for her personal use and had a cash price of $38,291.42. Ford Motor Credit Company, LLC (Ford) financed the sale under a retail sales contract (Sales

Contract) and retained a security interest in the vehicle to secure the unpaid balance of the total sale price.

As part of the transaction, Dale traded in a 2003 Ford Expedition. That vehicle had a negative equity, with Dale owing $4,760 more on the vehicle than its then-market value. As required by Texas law, Ford paid off this negative equity before accepting Dale's trade-in and included the sum in the new vehicle's total sale price.[1] The total sale price also included a gap insurance premium of $576.84; taxes not included in the cash price totaling $1,450.03; fees totaling $162.73; and an extended warranty charge of $3,030. Dale financed this entire amount totaling $48,271.02 through Ford at 0% interest.

Dale filed for bankruptcy less than one year later and submitted a Chapter 13 reorganization plan. Of the $41,834.94 still owed under the Sales Contract, Dale's Chapter 13 plan proposed to pay Ford $23,900 over 37 months at 10.25% interest. Under Dale's proposal, the remaining amount owed to Ford would be paid pro-rata with other unsecured claims. Ford objected to this plan and filed a proof of claim in the amount of $41,834.94, secured by the 2006 F150. . . .The [bankruptcy] court ruled that Ford's purchase-money security interest did not extend to those portions of the vehicle loan attributable to the pay-off of negative equity, the gap insurance premium, and the extended warranty charge. The court deemed these portions of the loan unsecured.

[T]he district court reversed. The court held that Ford had a purchase-money security interest in the entire Sales Contract, including those portions attributable to negative equity, gap insurance, and the extended warranty. Dale challenges that conclusion in this appeal.

II. DISCUSSION

The proper scope of the hanging paragraph presents a legal question, which we review de novo. We must decide whether the Code's hanging paragraph applies to the portion of a secured claim attributable to the pay-off of a trade-in vehicle's negative equity, gap insurance, and an extended warranty.

While bankruptcy courts across the country have divided on this issue, see In re Graupner, 537 F.3d 1295, 1300 (11th Cir. 2008) (collecting cases), three circuit courts and a state's highest court on certified question have recently weighed in on the debate, uniformly holding that the hanging paragraph prevents

---

1. 13 Under Texas law, it is a felony for a dealer to accept a trade-in without discharging the existing lien on the vehicle. TEX. PENAL CODE §32.34.

bifurcation of vehicle loans, including those portions attributable to negative equity pay-off. . . .

We adopt this emerging majority position for the reasons explained below.

1. Statutory Scheme

The hanging paragraph was enacted as part of the BAPCPA. Prior to the enactment of the BAPCPA, the Code allowed a Chapter 13 debtor to modify the rights of a secured creditor with a purchase-money security interest in a vehicle by bifurcating the claim into secured and unsecured portions based on the vehicle's then-market value. 11 U.S.C. §§506(a)(1), 1325(a)(5).

Under this provision, a creditor with a $15,000 claim secured by a vehicle with a present market value of $10,000 would have a secured claim of $10,000 and an unsecured claim of $5,000. Under a Chapter 13 plan, the $10,000 secured claim would be paid in full with interest, while the $5,000 unsecured claim would be paid pro-rata with other unsecured claims. Use of §506 in this manner is known as "bifurcation and cramdown" because the secured claim is reduced to the present value of the collateral, while the remainder of the debt becomes unsecured, forcing the secured creditor to accept less than the full value of its claim. Before the enactment of the BAPCPA, this cramdown provision had a pernicious effect on car dealers: it forced them to sustain a deficiency loss on the unsecured portion of the claim, while also forcing them to wait for payout on a now-reduced loan balance, with all the attendant risks of default that accompanied the original loan.

In apparent response to the undesirable effects of this cramdown on car dealers, Congress enacted the hanging paragraph as part of the BAPCPA. That provision eliminates bifurcation and cramdown in value if the vehicle was purchased within 910 days of the filing of the bankruptcy petition, and "if the creditor has a purchase-money security interest securing the debt that is the subject of the claim." . . .

Under the hanging paragraph, a creditor with a $15,000 claim secured by a vehicle with a present market value of $10,000 would avoid bifurcation and cramdown under §506 and instead retain a secured claim in the entire purchase price of the vehicle.

2. Proper Scope of the Hanging Paragraph

In this case, it is undisputed that Dale incurred her debt within 910 days of filing for bankruptcy, that this debt was secured by a motor vehicle, and that Dale acquired this vehicle for her personal use. Thus, the sole issue is whether Ford has a "purchase-money security interest" securing that portion of the debt attributable to negative equity, gap insurance, and the extended warranty.

Ford urges, and the district court held, that the "plain and unambiguous" meaning of "purchase-money security interest" coupled with the hanging paragraph's pertinent legislative history is sufficient to resolve this issue. Statutory construction, of course, begins with the plain language of the statute. But the phrase "purchase-money security interest" does not have an ordinary or generally understood meaning; rather, it is a term of art. The phrase is used in only one other place in the Code, see 11 U.S.C. §522(f), and the Code itself does not provide a definition. In short, the plain text of the hanging paragraph is insufficient to resolve this appeal.

Because the Code does not define "purchase-money security interest" and that term does not have a common ordinary meaning, we agree with the great majority of courts to address this issue that state UCC law must be used to define the hanging paragraph's phrase "purchase-money security interest." It is common in the bankruptcy context to look to state law to define security interests created under state law. . . .

The parties agree that the relevant state law is that of Texas. In Texas, a "purchase-money security interest" in goods is defined as a security interest in goods that are "purchase-money collateral," and "purchase-money collateral" is in turn defined as goods that secure a "purchase-money obligation." TEX. BUS. & COM.CODE §9.103. Texas defines "purchase-money obligation" as "an obligation . . . incurred as all or part of the price of the collateral or for value given to enable the debtor to acquire rights in or the use of the collateral if the value is in fact so used." Id. The definition of "purchase-money obligation" thus contains two prongs: (i) the price of the collateral, and (ii) value given to enable the debtor to acquire rights in or use of the collateral. . . .

Official Comment 3 to the UCC elaborates on the scope of these prongs. That Comment provides:

> As used in subsection (a)(2), the definition of "purchase-money obligation," the "price" of collateral or the "value given to enable" includes obligations for expenses incurred in connection with acquiring rights in the collateral, sales taxes, duties, finance charges, interest, freight charges, costs of storage in transit, demurrage, administrative charges, expenses of collection and enforcement, attorney's fees, and other similar obligations.

TEX. BUS. & COM.CODE §9.103, Official Comment 3. As we have recognized, Official UCC Comments are "by far the most useful aids to interpretation and construction." Weathersby v. Gore, 556 F.2d 1247, 1256 (5th Cir. 1977).

Examining the language of the statute and the Comment, we conclude that "price" and "value given to enable" include certain expenses that might not otherwise come within the common understanding of "price," such as "freight charges," "demurrage," "administrative charges," "expenses of collection and enforcement," and "attorney's fees." Inclusion of these expenses dispels any notion that "price" and "value given" are limited to the price tag of the vehicle standing alone.

The Comment's language "and other similar obligations" demonstrates that the enumerated expenses are merely examples and do not constitute an exhaustive list of eligible expenses. . . .

Negative equity and related expenses fit perfectly within the "value given to enable" prong of §9.103. That prong states that a "purchase-money obligation" can consist of "value given to enable the debtor to acquire rights in or the use of the collateral if the value is in fact so used." . . .

Dale also argues that negative equity is antecedent debt, and thus cannot be considered value given to enable. This is not so. Ford extended new credit to pay off the negative equity on the trade-in vehicle, which enabled Dale to purchase the new F150. The discharge of the amount owed on the old vehicle was directly related to Dale's acquisition of the new car. The funds used to pay off Dale's negative equity are thus properly considered "value given to enable."

Based on this analysis, we conclude that negative equity, gap insurance, and extended warranties constitute "purchase-money obligations" under Texas law, meaning Ford has a "purchase-money security interest" in the debt associated with those items. As such, the Code's hanging paragraph operates to prevent bifurcation of this debt. . . .

═══════════

While most courts have agreed with *Dale,* there is a circuit split. In re Penrod, 611 F.3d 1158 (9th Cir. 2010) (holding that negative equity is not included in a purchase money security obligation.) Because the underlying issue is state law, there is also the possibility that any particular state's law could be held to differ from that examined in the opinions to date.

b. Home Mortgages

A home is the single biggest asset of more than half the debtors who file chapter 13. We mentioned earlier that one type of security interest has always been exempted from the lienstripping rule: the home mortgage. Yet chapter 13 can help debtors keep their homes, primarily by enabling them to catch up on the arrears in their mortgage payments. The typical homeowner in a chapter 13 case owes an arrearage to their mortgage company that is equal to six months in payments. Missed regular payments, as well as default fees, contribute to this arrearage. Katherine Porter, Arrears and Default Costs of Homeowners, 22 NACTT Quarterly 15 (2010). For such debtors, the automatic stay of chapter 13, combined with its tools to address secured debt may be the best way to save a home that is at risk of foreclosure.

As to the mortgage itself, the general rule is that a mortgage on the debtor's principal residence must be paid in full. The Supreme Court in Nobelman v. American Savings Bank, 508 U.S. 324 (1993) made it clear that this rule bars cramdown on home mortgages as long the loan is even partially covered by value in the house, leaving open whether the rule applies to second or third mortgages that might be entirely "out of the money," that is, when more senior mortgages swallow all the value in the home. The only relief in chapter 13 for first-lien home mortgages is to "cure and maintain," catching up on the past-due arrearages (cure) while making current payments on the mortgage as they come due (maintain). §1322(b)(5).

Because homes don't depreciate as fast as vehicles and homes are necessary for a family to reorganize, adequate protection fights are rare. Disputes in chapter 13 cases are more likely to involve two other problems: (1) in the short term, saving the home from foreclosure sale by defending a relief from stay motion, and (2) in the long term, proposing a plan to comply with the strict provisions of chapter 13 that protect the rights of mortgage lenders. In the following case, the debtors propose a chapter 13 plan to save their home from foreclosure and run into both issues.

———— **In re LITTON** ————
330 F.3d 636 (4th Cir. 2003)

KING, Circuit Judge:
This appeal arises from the third in a series of bankruptcy proceedings initiated in the Western District of Virginia by Mrs. Litton and her husband. The resolution of this appeal turns initially on our assessment of the intended meaning of a term used in an earlier court-approved settlement agreement that prohibited the Littons from seeking any modification of a debt they owed Wachovia. Because we conclude that the no-modification provision of the settlement agreement embodies the concepts contained in §1322 of the Bankruptcy Code, we must decide whether Mrs. Litton's proposed plan of reorganization seeks to "modify" the terms of that agreement or, alternatively, seeks to "cure" the Litton's default of their obligations to Wachovia. While a modification would indeed be prohibited by the provisions of 11 U.S.C. §1322(b)(2), a cure is expressly authorized under 11 U.S.C. §1322(b)(5). . . .

On May 16, 1988, the Littons granted a deed of trust on their Washington County farm (which is their principal residence) to Central Fidelity Bank. This deed of trust secured repayment of a promissory note in the sum of $193,764. The Littons granted an additional deed of trust to Central Fidelity Bank on September 21, 1990, for the purpose of providing additional security for the promissory note.

After encountering financial difficulties, Mr. Litton filed a petition in bankruptcy on March 23, 1992, seeking relief in the Western District of Virginia under Chapter 11 of the Bankruptcy Code (the "1992 Petition"). In order to dispose of the 1992 Petition, the bankruptcy court entered an agreed order of

November 14, 1994, the Non-Material Modification Order, which the Littons and Central Fidelity executed. At some point after the execution of the Non-Material Modification Order, Wachovia purchased the assets of Central Fidelity Bank, including the Littons' promissory note.

Faced with continuing financial difficulties, Mrs. Litton, on September 4, 1997, filed a Chapter 13 bankruptcy petition in the same court (the "1997 Petition"). Similar to their settlement of the 1992 Petition, the Littons, in March of 2000, entered into a settlement agreement with their creditors, including Wachovia. This settlement agreement disposed of the 1997 Petition and augmented the 1994 Non-Material Modification Order. The terms of this agreement were incorporated into an order entered by the bankruptcy court on March 3, 2000 (the "2000 Order").

Pursuant to the 2000 Order, the Littons were to pay $55,000 to Wachovia on or before June 30, 2000 (the "Initial Payment"). The 2000 Order further provided that, if the Littons made the Initial Payment in a timely manner, Wachovia would refinance the balance of its loan to the Littons. Conversely, if the Littons failed to make the Initial Payment in a timely manner, Wachovia could, under the terms of the 2000 Order, pursue its non-bankruptcy rights and remedies with respect to the deeds of trust on the Littons' real estate, i.e., by implementing foreclosure proceedings on the Littons' farm. Furthermore, the 2000 Order, mirroring the language of §1322(b)(2), prohibited the Littons from seeking any further modification of the "terms of the order" in any future bankruptcy proceeding.

The Littons failed to make the Initial Payment on time, and Wachovia promptly moved to foreclose on the Littons' farm. On November 21, 2000, Mrs. Litton filed this Chapter 13 petition in the Western District of Virginia (the "2000 Petition"), and the automatic stay arising under the Bankruptcy Code halted the foreclosure proceedings. At the time she filed the 2000 Petition, and in accordance with the provisions of §1321, Mrs. Litton proposed a plan of reorganization, seeking to reorganize her debts and emerge from bankruptcy (the "Plan"). The Plan proposed the reinstitution of the terms of the 2000 Order by obligating Mrs. Litton to resume her payments to Wachovia. In particular, the Plan provided: "[t]he term of this plan shall be three months. . . . Debtor proposes to catch up in arrearages in payments to Wachovia Bank ($55,000) . . . within 30 days, and to make regular payments as called for in the [2000 Order]. . . . The case will then be concluded."

Wachovia objected to confirmation of the Plan, and it also sought relief from the automatic stay. In a separate filing, the Chapter 13 trustee also objected to confirmation of the Plan, and she sought to have the 2000 Petition either dismissed or converted to a Chapter 7 liquidation proceeding. On February 9, 2001, the bankruptcy court entered an order dismissing the 2000 Petition, concluding that it constituted an improper use of Chapter 13. Mrs. Litton promptly sought reconsideration of the bankruptcy court's order, supporting her request with an affidavit that she jointly executed with her husband. The affidavit explained the extensive efforts that the Littons had made, and the various difficulties they had encountered, in seeking to comply with the 2000 Order.[2] On March 30, 2001, the bankruptcy court denied reconsideration.

Mrs. Litton appealed the bankruptcy court's rulings to the district court for the Western District of Virginia. The district court agreed that the 2000 Petition was an improper use of Chapter 13, and it affirmed the bankruptcy court's dismissal.

[Analysis]

A.

The resolution of this appeal turns, first of all, on whether the parties intended the term "modification," as used in the settlement agreement that was incorporated into the 2000 Order, to be interpreted in accordance with the narrow no-modification provision of §1322, or whether they instead intended the term to preclude all modifications, even those authorized by §1322. . . .

It is important – indeed, it is controlling – in this context, that the Littons and Wachovia agreed on the terms of the 2000 Order to settle a pending bankruptcy case (the 1997 Petition), and to augment the settlement terms of an earlier bankruptcy case (the 1992 Petition). Accordingly, we must conclude that the Littons and Wachovia intended the term "modification," as used in the 2000 Order, to be consistent with the meaning contemplated by §1322 of the Bankruptcy Code.[3] Therefore, we must assess the extent and breadth of the no-modification provision of §1322(b)(2).

B.

On appeal, Wachovia's primary contention in support of the bankruptcy court's dismissal of the 2000 Petition is that the Plan proposes a prohibited modification. By contrast, Mrs. Litton maintains that the Plan constitutes a permissible cure under §1322(b)(5), and that the 2000 Petition should not have been dismissed. In affirming the bankruptcy court's dismissal of the 2000 Petition, the district court concluded that, because the 2000 Order contained its

---

2. In their affidavit, the Littons stated that Mr. Litton had negotiated with six separate individuals seeking to sell timber, the proceeds of which were to be used to fund the Initial Payment to Wachovia. The affidavit further asserted that the Littons had lost over 70% of their tobacco crop in 2000, which represented a $15,000 loss of income.

3. Because the 2000 Order does not contain a provision expressly prohibiting the Littons from attempting to "cure" a default, we are not presented with, nor do we take any position on, the question of whether such a prohibition would be valid and enforceable. The parties, by their settlement agreement, merely prohibited "modification" of the 2000 Order, and we limit our inquiry to the interpretations accorded to the concepts of prohibited "modifications" and permissible "cures" under §1322.

no-modification provision, the Plan's proposed alterations of the 2000 Order would be impermissible.

Because the Littons' debt to Wachovia is secured by an interest in the Littons' primary residence, §1322 would ordinarily prohibit a modification of the 2000 Order. Nevertheless, a separate provision of the same statute, §1322(b)(5), provides that the Littons are entitled to cure any default of their obligations relating to the debt on their principal residence. We must therefore resolve whether the Plan seeks to "modify" the 2000 Order or, alternatively, whether it seeks to "cure" the Littons' default. In so doing, we must understand the interpretations accorded to the concepts of "modification" and "cure" in Chapter 13 jurisprudence.

1.

The bankruptcy courts have consistently interpreted the no-modification provision of §1322(b)(2) to prohibit any fundamental alteration in a debtor's obligations, e.g., lowering monthly payments, converting a variable interest rate to a fixed interest rate, or extending the repayment term of a note. *See, e.g., In re Schum*, 112 B.R. 159, 161-62 (Bankr. N.D. Tex. 1990) (concluding that plan was impermissible modification because it proposed to reduce monthly payments and secured valuation). In *In re Gwinn*, 34 B.R. 936, 944-45 (Bankr. S.D. Ohio 1983), the court approved a plan as a permissible cure under §1322(b)(5), because the plan did not propose to lower monthly payments, extend the repayment period, or make the obligation conditional. It instead sought only to reinstate the original contract with a minor delay in payment. *Id.; see also In re Cooper*, 98 B.R. 294 (Bankr. W.D.Mich.1989) (finding impermissible modification where plan proposed new payment schedule). Along similar lines, another bankruptcy court concluded that confirmation of a Chapter 13 plan would have constituted an impermissible modification because the plan proposed to alter fundamental aspects of the debtor's obligations, i.e., the nature and rate of interest, and the maturity features of the loan. *In re Coffey*, 52 B.R. 54, 55 (Bankr. D.N.H.1985). As these decisions have emphasized, §1322(b)(2) prohibits modifications that would alter at least one fundamental aspect of a claim.

2.

Conversely, a "cure" merely reinstates a debt to its pre-default position, or it returns the debtor and creditor to their respective positions before the default. In *Landmark Financial Services v. Hall*, 918 F.2d 1150 (4th Cir. 1990), we had occasion to assess the meaning of the term "cure," as it is used in §1322(b)(5). In that decision, Judge Hall determined that "a cure reinstates the original pre-bankruptcy agreement of the parties . . . [and] is not a modification of the [creditor's] rights. Cure by its very nature assumes a regime where debtors reinstate defaulted debt contracts in accordance with the conditions of their contracts." *Id.* at 1154 (emphasis added and internal citations omitted).

Our sister circuits have taken a similar view of the use of the term "cure" in bankruptcy proceedings. For example, the Second Circuit has observed that, "[c]uring a default commonly means taking care of the triggering event and returning to pre-default conditions." *DiPierro v. Taddeo*, 685 F.2d 24, 26-27 (2d Cir. 1982). The *DiPierro* court noted that "[w]e do not read 'curing defaults' under (b)(3) or 'curing defaults and maintaining payments' under (b)(5) to be modifications of claims." *Id.* at 27.

The Seventh Circuit has given a similar meaning to the term "cure," as it is used in the Bankruptcy Code. It observed that "[t]he terms 'modify' and 'cure' are nowhere defined in the Bankruptcy Code. However, it is clear that Congress intended 'cure' to mean something different from 'modify.' " *In [re] Clark*, 738 F.2d 869, 871-72 (7th Cir. 1984). Significantly, the *Clark* court also observed that, "[o]rdinarily, the means by which one cures a default is by paying all amounts due and owing. . . . Thus, the plain meaning of 'cure,' as used in §1322(b)(3) and (5), is to remedy or rectify the default and restore matters to the status quo ante." *Id.* at 872 (emphasis added); *see also In re Metz*, 820 F.2d 1495, 1497 (9th Cir. 1987) (interpreting "cure" provisions of Chapter 13 as permitting "the debtor to 'cure' (i.e., pay or bring current) arrearages on the debt and thereby reinstate the debt"). Given these definitions and interpretations of the terms "modify" and "cure," as they have been used in bankruptcy proceedings, we next examine whether the Plan would fundamentally alter the terms of the 2000 Order.

C.

The 2000 Petition was filed on November 21, 2000, when the Littons' only default, under the terms of the 2000 Order, was their failure to make the Initial Payment. By providing for terms of payment virtually identical to those required by the 2000 Order, the Plan simply sought to return the 2000 Order to its pre-default condition. *See Landmark*, 918 F.2d at 1154 (noting that cure reinstates defaulted debt contract to its original terms). It proposed that Mrs. Litton pay all arrearages and maintain all payments during the life of the Plan. It did not propose the reduction of any installment payments or of the amounts due to Wachovia under the 2000 Order; it did not propose an extension of the final maturity date on the Littons' debt to Wachovia; and it did not propose an alteration of any other terms of the 2000 Order. Under these circumstances, the Plan does not propose a "modification" of the 2000 Order. Rather, evaluated by its express terms, under the foregoing authorities, and by its proposed treatment of the 2000 Order, the Plan constitutes a "cure" under the Bankruptcy Code, in that it seeks to restore the "*status quo ante*." *Clark*, 738 F.2d at 872. . . .

Pursuant to the foregoing, we conclude that the bankruptcy court erred in dismissing the 2000 Petition. Accordingly, we vacate the district court's dismissal and direct that it remand Mrs. Litton's petition to the bankruptcy court for further proceedings.

===

Note that the Littons required three filings, and stays, to try to sort out their housing woes. Surely the facts in the footnote regarding the dire financial circumstances being faced by the family eliminate any suggestion of gamesmanship or bad faith. Consider, then, BAPCPA's addition of sections 362(c)(3) and (4) (and for renters, section 322(b)(22)). Limiting the applicability of the automatic stay is a different step than tightening eligibility requirements or restricting the scope of discharge. Like most recent amendments to the consumer bankruptcy law, however, they all create more hurdles to obtaining relief for families in financial trouble.

Problem Set 10

10.1. Fran Belinsky is a graphic artist with an income in excess of $52,000 per year. Last year she guaranteed a large business loan for her brother. Her brother skipped town, and now Fran is left to pay the loan. She has filed a chapter 13 and plans to make a substantial repayment in a five-year plan.

Fran's only asset of significant value is a one-year-old computer setup with high-end peripherals that is subject to a valid $4,600 purchase money security interest from InterNet CompFinance (IC). She testified at her 341 meeting that the setup is worth about $5,000. The IC people think that value is about right for now, but IC can predict that new technology will render the setup obsolete and almost valueless in three years. IC asks for your help in repossessing. What can you do? See §§361, 362(d).

10.2. George Grey has suffered a series of financial reversals. He was laid off for 17 months from his job as a steel worker, he has incurred medical bills for over $90,000 for his younger daughter, and his son just wrecked the car. But things may be looking up for George now. He has been rehired and is working nearly 20 hours per week overtime. Recognizing that he needs some protection from his creditors, he is prepared to file a chapter 13.

His chief concern at this point is his fishing cabin. Before he was laid off, he had bought the land from LeisureLand, Inc. for no money down and a $40,000 five-year note. During the time he was unemployed, he went out to the site almost every day. He cleared the land and built a one-room cabin with the materials he found on hand. It has no plumbing or electricity, but George cherishes the cabin. Now he is afraid he will lose it.

George made only four payments on the land; the principal balance owed is $39,980. In addition, LeisureLand claims $12,300 in past-due interest, penalties, and attorneys' fees provided for under the contract. They have begun foreclosure proceedings, and the land is scheduled for sale next week. The contract interest rate is now running at 14% on the principal balance and 21% on all accumulated past-due payments and penalties. Because the area where George lives is in a serious economic slump, even with George's improvements vacation land would not sell for more than $41,000. What can LeisureLand demand in a chapter 13? See §§506, 1322(b)(2), 1325(a)(5)(B)(ii).

10.3. Carlos Esposito had a successful dive shop in Key West, but it sank in a recent downturn. Although he has a lot of unsecured debt, he is mainly worried about his car, a 2010 Acura that he bought two years ago. His credit union has a lien on the Acura for the $9,000 balance of the purchase price and for some $15,000 of Visa charges that he owed when he bought the car. The credit union "loan facilitator" told him the Visa balance looked bad for his credit rating, but that the credit union would be glad to pay it off for him and add it to his car loan. Otherwise, the facilitator was unsure the loan committee would approve the loan. Carlos agreed. Now he is having trouble making the payments on the $25,000 balance and complains "the car has been banged up somewhat so can't be worth more than $15,000." He is ready to file for chapter 13. How much will he have to promise to pay under his plan in order to keep the car?

10.4. Jewel Snitz has filed a chapter 13 bankruptcy. She owns a Ford Explorer she bought about a year ago to haul around her real estate clients and to take to the beach on weekends. The outstanding loan balance, together with accumulated interest and penalty payments, is $30,000. During the period between filing the chapter 13 and the confirmation of the plan, another $250 in interest will accumulate. The local bankruptcy court has settled on 10% as a market interest rate for car loans in chapter 13.

The Dealer's Bluebook lists the retail value of the car as $32,100 and the wholesale value as $28,400. At a liquidation sale the car would probably bring $26,300. Through a private want ad it would likely sell for $33,300. How much will Jewel have to pay for her car in a chapter 13? If the car has some unusual scratches, chipped paint, and a funny little knock in the engine, who will want to point that out? See §§506(a), 1325(a).

10.5. Donnie Rhodes bought a house seven years ago and took out a 30-year mortgage to finance the purchase. The home is now valued at $55,000, and the outstanding mortgage is $62,000. Rhodes is required to make monthly payments of $250. Rhodes sells farm machinery and as the farming industry took a nosedive, so did his sales. He went for eight months with no income, but now things have picked up and he is back to his regular earnings. He has decided to go into chapter 13 to restructure his debts, but he remains worried about his home. After seven years of regular mortgage payments, Rhodes missed six in a row and now has racked up $500 in penalties and costs under the contract. What must his plan provide? See §1322(b)(2), (b)(5).

10.6. Michael Troncoso owns a three-bedroom house in Modesto, California, which he purchased for $550,000 in 2006. He took out a first mortgage of $440,000 and a second mortgage of $120,000. (He rolled the closing costs into the second mortgage, so the total debt exceeded the property value on his first day as a homeowner.) Today, the house is worth $300,000, and Michael owes $400,000 on his first mortgage and $100,000 on his second mortgage. He has stayed current on payments, but his job as a firefighter could be cut by the struggling city and his credit card debt is steadily climbing each month as his wife remains out of work. Michael wants to keep the house because he is zoned for the city's only blue-ribbon elementary school. He tells you that he filed for chapter 7 bankruptcy about three years ago to deal with credit card debts related to a gambling problem, for which he successfully sought treatment. He remembers at that time chatting with another bankruptcy debtor who was filing to get rid of a home equity loan. What are Michael's options to address his mortgages? See §§362(c), 1322, 1325, and 1328.

Assignment 11.

Unsecured Creditors in Chapter 13

The requirements for secured creditors in chapter 13 are only one of a myriad of requirements that a chapter 13 plan must meet for confirmation. The Bankruptcy Code prescribes treatment for unsecured creditors as well as directing judges to evaluate the chapter 13 plan against other benchmarks. These requirements burden debtors and their counsel, and they increase the amount of litigation and negotiation in chapter 13, especially as compared to the typical chapter 7 case. The final decision rests with the court at a confirmation hearing. §1324. In chapter 13—unlike the chapter 11 system covered later in the book—creditors do not cast ballots on the plan, but any creditor, the chapter 13 trustee, or the U.S. Trustee can file an objection to confirmation. The judge is accorded wide latitude in whether to sustain or deny most of these objections, which in turn leads to wide divergences in outcomes that creditors and debtors achieve in chapter 13. In this assignment, we focus on the entitlements of unsecured creditors in chapter 13 by studying the grounds on which they can object to plan confirmation.

A. UNSECURED CREDITORS' PROTECTIONS GENERALLY

A chapter 13 case involves a debtor's proposal of a plan to the creditors. To deal with the secured creditors and prevent repossession of the debtor's property subject to the security interests, the chapter 13 plan must make payments that satisfy the statutory requirements for the present value of each allowed secured claim. If the plan so provides, a secured creditor's objection will be denied. See §1325(a)(5). The general unsecured creditors do not have similarly individualized protection for their claims. Instead, they are pooled together for pro rata treatment. (Priority unsecured creditors still get priority, of course, which we will discuss below.) Think of the debtor as paying into a pot a certain amount of money over the life of the plan. An unsecured creditor's objection boils down to "We want a bigger pot." Because of the free-rider potential (who wants to pay the lawyer to file this objection on behalf of all unsecured creditors?), the trustee is often the objecting party.

The Code's protection of unsecured creditors in chapter 13 is a minimum floor on what the debtor *must* pay into this pot over the course of the plan. Unsecured creditors can of course accept less than this floor, but if the debtor meets the statutory minimum plan contributions, any objection to the plan by an unsecured creditor who wants more money will be denied. (Creditors have more diffuse protections, such as the requirement that chapter 13 plans be filed in good faith, §1325(a)(3), as we will see in one of the cases below, just as they are entitled to equal treatment, §1322(a)(3), but for now we focus on the most important safeguards.)

The floor for unsecured creditors is found in three provisions of section 1325. Each creates a minimum payment requirement for a chapter 13 plan, assuming the trustee or a creditor objects to less favorable treatment. The first provision is that debtors must pay priority creditors in full, although without interest. The second provision, the "best interests" test, requires that each creditor receive at least as much as that creditor would have received if the debtor had gone into chapter 7. §1325(a)(4). The theory presumably is that if the creditor is better off in chapter 13 than it would be if the debtor chose chapter 7 it should just shut up. The third is that debtors must devote all their "disposable income" to funding the pot for unsecured creditor payments over the life of the chapter 13 plan. §1325(b).

The practical effect of these tests differs given the realities of most consumers' situations. The priority-creditor provision can be a meaningful obstacle to confirmation, although not all debtors have priority claims. The best interests test is not likely to prove a constraint in many chapter 13s. After all, most chapter 7s involve debtors with no unencumbered, non-exempt assets, which means the ordinary chapter 7 dividend for a general unsecured creditor is zero; requiring a chapter 13 plan to pay at least zero over the life of the plan daunts few debtors. (It matters more in chapter 11 reorganizations, as we will see later in the course.) However, the disposable income test has real bite.

B. PRIORITY CREDITORS AND THE "FULL PAYMENT" REQUIREMENT

Secured creditors are ensured minimum payments based on the value of their collateral, and unsecured creditors are ensured minimum payments based on pro rata distribution from the debtors' monthly disposable income (see below). The payment rule for priority creditors takes a third approach. Creditors with claims that would receive a priority under section 507(a) are entitled to payment in full in chapter 13 over the course of the plan. §1322(a)(2). Priority claims, however—unlike allowed secured claims—are not paid in present value dollars. Instead, the debtor is required to pay only the nominal amount of the claim, without interest. The language in sections 1325(a)(4) and (a)(5) (emphasis added) requires payment to unsecured and secured creditors, respectively, based on "the *value*, as of the effective date of the plan," which the courts uniformly understand to mean present value and hence requiring interest payments to compensate for the multi-year duration of a plan. But the language in section 1322(a)(2) (emphasis added), governing the payment of priority debt, refers only to "*full* payment, in deferred cash payments," conspicuously different text that the courts have interpreted as not requiring the payment of interest over the multi-year plan. See, e.g., In re Pitt, 240 B.R. 908 (N.D. Cal. 1999) (discussing Bruning v. United States, 376 U.S. 358 (1964)); In re Pardee, 218 B.R. 916 (9th Cir. BAP 1998). At the end of the plan, the simple sum of the payments made to a priority creditor must equal the amount of its filed priority claim. So the good news for a priority creditor is that it will be paid in full; the bad news is that it will receive no interest, so the present value of its claim will be worth significantly less than what the creditor is owed.

Because repayment in full of all priority debts is a requirement for confirmation of the plan, priority creditors are no longer placed in the competitive position they sometimes suffer in chapter 7. Unless the party entitled to repayment waives this right, each and every priority debt must be paid in full—whether it is a first priority or a fifteenth priority debt. This may be one reason why a debtor chooses a longer than three-year plan: the plan cannot be confirmed unless it proposes to pay the priority creditors 100% of their claims. If those debts are big enough, some families in serious financial trouble cannot find relief in chapter 13.

Of course, many debtors have no priority claims other than attorneys' fees. For them, chapter 13 is defined by the required treatment of secured and unsecured creditors. But some debtors are obligated to pay debts that would qualify as section 507(a) priorities and must therefore adjust their plans to account for these obligations. The most common categories of priority claims—administration claims, domestic support, and taxes—are discussed in the sections below. Each has a special advantage of its own.

1. *Administrative Expenses*

Some debtors pay section 507(a) administrative expenses in their chapter 13 plans. A debtor who did not have enough cash to pay the filing fee, for example, may pay the filing fee as a priority repayment in chapter 13. (Under Bankruptcy Rule 1006(b), the filing fee must be paid within 120 days of filing, which means that the filing fee is to be paid in installments in the first four post-filing payments.) Also, most debtors pay at least a portion of their attorney's fees in chapter 13, although the amount of the fee, and the fraction of it that is typically paid pre-petition, varies widely from jurisdiction to jurisdiction.

Under section 330(a)(4)(B), services necessary for representing the debtor in connection with a bankruptcy case are compensable; this rule applies only to individuals in chapter 12 or 13 cases (typically to be an administrative expense a benefit must inure to the *estate*, as opposed to the *debtor*, and so section 330(a)(4)(B)'s provision for payment to the debtor's individual lawyer might be considered anomalous—perhaps a congressional carrot to encourage filing in chapter 13 vs. chapter 7).

2. Domestic Support Obligations

Some debtors owe alimony or child support, both back amounts and going-forward obligations. Because domestic support obligations are entitled to priority repayment in §507(a)(1), they also enjoy full repayment priority in chapter 13. §1322(a)(2). Indeed, many chapter 13 trustees point with pride to an unexpected benefit of having an ex-spouse in bankruptcy: The trustee will take over the function of collecting domestic support and distributing it to the intended recipients.

The bankrupt ex-spouse who owes support obligations may face a different set of incentives after a bankruptcy filing. To get a plan confirmed, the debtor must show he or she is current on all domestic support obligations that became due after filing. §1325(a)(8). After confirmation, the failure to make plan payments will involve potential dismissal of the chapter 13 case, §1307(c)(11), which can mean loss of a car or resumption of various other creditor collection actions. The option of paying everyone else and stiffing the ex will no longer be available. A debtor who continues plan payments will, by necessity, have to be current on all support obligations. That said, the Code recognizes the need to balance support obligations against a fresh start. Unlike other priority claims that always must be paid in full, large government support debts can be given only partial repayment in a plan if the debtor commits to five years of repayment and commits all disposable income. §1322(a)(4).[8]

3. Tax Claims

In addition to administrative and support claims, some consumer debtors face substantial tax debts. If the debtor gets into bankruptcy before the IRS files a lien, the tax claims will be unsecured. And even if the IRS does get a lien, the tax claims can still be partially unsecured, such as when the tax debt exceeds the value of the collateral bearing the lien, or when the lien secures some but not all taxes. The automatic stay will prevent the IRS from taking any further collection actions—including securing a new lien on the debtor's property. As we saw in the earlier assignment on section 507, this unsecured tax claim will often get priority.

---

8. Agencies that help a person who has not received domestic support payments recover often take assignment of the person's support rights; that claim has priority under §507(a)(1)(B) but may receive only partial payment under §1322(a)(4).

Once a priority tax claim is determined by reference to section 507(a)(8), the debtor can then propose a plan to pay the amount of the tax claim in nominal dollars over the length of the repayment plan. This means that when the interest payments on tax debts stop at the time of filing, they really stop; they do not recommence under a present value analysis in the chapter 13 plan as with non-priority unsecured claims and secured claims.

Recall that because taxes are nondischargeable under §523(a)(1), a debtor with a tax problem rarely receives much direct relief in his dealings with the taxing authorities from a chapter 7 filing. As such, chapter 13 offers three advantages: (1) letting the debtor pay the taxes over a time that can be as long as five years, with the automatic stay holding off the IRS throughout (Remember the stay lasts until discharge, which in chapter 13 isn't until the plan is completed. §362(c)(2)(C)); (2) denying post-petition interest on unsecured claims, which will lock the tax claim at its value as of the date of the bankruptcy filing, §502(b)(2); and (3) allowing that (locked) claim to be paid in nominal, not real, dollars over the length of the plan, which is especially helpful to the debtor in inflationary times. The chance in chapter 13 to pay off the taxes over time without interest makes chapter 13 a valuable tool for taxpayers; savvy accountants often send certain clients to bankruptcy lawyers if negotiations with taxing authorities break down.

As a reminder, taxes, like most domestic support obligations, are both priority claims and nondischargeable. But the overlap is not perfect. This illustrates the interconnected nature of the Bankruptcy Code and the importance of addressing both issues in a case to provide maximum relief to a debtor.

C. UNSECURED CREDITORS AND THE "DISPOSABLE INCOME" REQUIREMENT

The robust unsecured creditor protection is the requirement that the debtor must pay all "disposable income" for the length of the chapter 13 plan. §1325(b)(1)(B). This requirement embodies both legal and factual complexities. While of course the minimum payment requirements only arise if the trustee or an unsecured creditor objects to the plan, as a practical matter such an objection to plan confirmation will nearly always be filed unless the chapter 13 trustee is satisfied that the debtor is paying all disposable income to unsecured creditors. An exception is if the unsecured creditors are receiving 100% payment. In such a situation, disposable income does not come into play as the unsecured creditors are deemed to have accepted the plan. §1325(b)(1)(A).

Recall that the 2005 amendments were based on an industry claim that there were many debtors who could pay, but took the easy way out by filing bankruptcy. To this end, Congress changed the disposable income requirement. The law now imposes a different requirement for determining disposable income on "can pay" and "can't pay." Thus, the minimum payment requirements vary not only with the type of objecting creditor (e.g., priority versus general unsecured), but also with the income of the debtor, below- or above-median.

The basic mechanism for sorting into "can pay" and "can't pay" is the debtor's income before most expenses. Based on its size and state of residence, a household is categorized as either below-median income or above-median income. As part of the legislative compromise in revising the approach to disposable income, the Code imposes a fairly simple (if sometimes opaque) payment requirement on below-median income debtors that examines a debtor's actual expenses. About two-thirds of chapter 13 filers fall into this category. For above-median debtors, Congress imposed a statutory budget. This is discussed in section 3 of this assignment, Special Rules for Above-Median Debtors.

Note at the outset we say the below-median-income debtor's disposable income must be paid over "the course of the plan," language that is not used in the Code. Instead, it eschews common English and says the debtor's disposable income must be devoted to the pot for the "applicable commitment period," §1325(b)(4)(A); we still like to think of it as plan length. But how long is a plan (the "applicable commitment period")? For a below-median debtor, the plan must be a minimum of three years and a maximum of five years (with an exception for cases paying 100% of claims, which can be shorter than three years, §1325(b)(4)(B)). The above-median chapter 13 debtor has no choice. A five-year plan is mandatory.

The idea of a minimum length is intuitive; if the debtor gets to earn a discharge *and* keep non-exempt property under chapter 13, then the unsecured creditors need some minimum amount of repayment effort to fund their pot; otherwise debtors would propose four-day plans and go home. But why a maximum? Isn't longer paying into the pot better for the creditors? Perhaps Congress doesn't want individuals under the supervision of the bankruptcy courts for too long, or perhaps it thinks eventually enough is enough, even if the debtor wants to keep going. Or maybe it is difficult enough to project income and expenses over five years. (Nothing stops voluntary repayment post-discharge after chapter 13.) Thus, plans can generally vary between three and five years in length, with that length often determined by the debtor's factual situation—e.g., what is the amount of mortgage arrearage and how long does the debtor need to stretch such payments out to find enough money in the monthly budget to "cure" it? Indeed, some debtors *want* to make longer plans than the three-year minimum because there are certain carrots within the Code (e.g., debtors paying more than 70% of their unsecured debts are not barred from refiling bankruptcy for a certain interval of time, §727(a)(9)).

1. Permissible Expenses

Whatever the length of the plan, the debtor must devote all "disposable income" to the unsecured creditors' pot. For the below-median debtor, "disposable income" is defined in the Code as all income "less amounts reasonably necessary to be expended . . . for the maintenance or support of the debtor or the dependent of the debtor. . . ." §1325(b)(2)(A)(1). *Reasonably necessary?* That sounds like a squishy standard, doesn't it? Well, that's what bankruptcy judges are for (creditors, too, in an adversarial system).

—————— **IN THE MATTER OF WYANT** ——————
217 B.R. 585 (Bankr. D. Neb. 1998)

MINAHAN, Bankruptcy Judge.

This case is before the court to consider confirmation of the debtor's Amended Plan, Debtor's Counsel's Application for Attorney Fees, and the Resistance by the Chapter 13 Trustee. The plan is not confirmed; the debtor shall file an amended plan within 21 days hereof.

The amended plan is not confirmed because the debtor does not propose to pay disposable income to the trustee as required by §1325(b)(1)(B) [§1325(b)(2) in post-2005 Code.—Eds.]

[The court reviewed various expenses, commenting critically on the debtor's "pre-bankruptcy planning," before turning to the last item.]

I further conclude that the debtor's proposed expenditures on veterinary expenses and livestock feed are unreasonable. The debtor is in the unfortunate position of owning several horses and dogs, which are elderly and which require extraordinary veterinary expenses. It is commendable that the debtor is willing to care for these animals and to attend to their feed and medical needs. On the other hand, this is a bankruptcy case in which the debtor is seeking to be discharged from his obligations to pay creditors. As between the debtor's elderly horses and dogs and his creditors, I think that the creditors should be paid first. The proposed expenditures on these animals are excessive, unreasonable, and not necessary for the maintenance or support of the debtor or his dependents.

On the other hand, the debtor should be encouraged to proceed in Chapter 13 in order that his creditors will receive payments over time. The disposable income analysis should not be so strict as to deprive the debtor of all discretionary income. Accordingly, I conclude that it is appropriate for the debtor to expend $100.00 per month for feed and veterinary expenses. This means that the proposed payments under the plan shall be increased and that for the 36 months of the plan, the debtor shall pay the trustee $1,300.00 per month. This sum represents proposed payments of $850.00 a month, plus disallowed expenses of $450.00 ($375.00 plus $75.00) . . .

By separate order, the proposed Amended Plan is not confirmed, the Chapter 13 Trustee's Objection to Confirmation is sustained, and the Application for Attorney Fees is denied.

─────────────

Was confirmation at the Pet Cemetery? Did the Visa representative volunteer to waive payment in favor of Rover? Is Mr. Wyant a cynical manipulator or a man struggling as he loses the core pieces of his life? Judges are forced into intensely personal moral decisions by a provision that appears merely financial. How about one's commitment to religion?

──────── **In re CLEARY** ────────
357 B.R. 369 (Bankr. D. S.C. 2006)

DUNCAN, Bankruptcy Judge.

The chapter 13 trustee objects to confirmation on the basis that expenditures for private school tuition are not reasonable and necessary expenses and thus that the plan does not provide "that all of the debtor's projected disposable income to be received in the applicable commitment period ... will be applied to make payments to unsecured creditors under the plan." 11 U.S.C §1325(b)(1)(B).

Findings of Fact
1. Kevin Paul Cleary ("Debtor") filed a voluntary petition for relief under chapter 13 of the Bankruptcy Code on July 31, 2006.

2. Debtor is married, although his spouse did not join in the petition. Mr. and Mrs. Cleary have six children, the youngest age 7.

3. Debtor is employed as a driver for a nationwide parcel delivery service, and has been so employed for 21 years. His current net monthly take home pay, after deduction for taxes, union dues, and a 401k contribution, is $4,522.00.

4. Mrs. Cleary was not employed outside the home for approximately 15 years of the marriage. She has been employed as a teacher's aide at a parochial school for the past 2 years. Her net take home pay, after taxes and a small 401k contribution, is $918.50. An additional $813.00 is deducted from her pay check for tuition for three of the couple's children who attend the school. Mrs. Cleary's actual take home pay is $105.50.

5. The family's gross annual income is reported on Form B22C in the amount of $86,283.60.

6. The applicable median income for a South Carolina family of 8 is $86,918.00.

7. The family currently spends $1,165.00 for the mortgage payment, including taxes, insurance and home maintenance; $265.00 for utilities; $1,500.00 for food; $85.00 for automobile taxes and insurance; $465.00 for miscellaneous expenses (clothing, laundry, medical, recreation and personal); and $100.00 for transportation. The family spends $1,513.00 for private school (elementary and secondary) tuition each month.

8. Five of the six children attend private school. The sixth child attended private school until the current school year when he asked to attend public school for the experience. The testimony was that the sixth child would like to return to private school next year. Mr. and Mrs. Cleary receive assistance from the private high school in the form of reduced tuition because of their income and family size.

9. Mr. and Mrs. Cleary own an "$150,000" 3 bedroom ranch style home and modest furnishings. They also own three vehicles; a late model van, under lien, and two older cars. The home is subject to two mortgages and has little equity if Debtor's statements of the current market value and mortgage balances are correct.

10. In addition to the mortgages and automobile loan the Debtor has two purchase money furniture accounts, two loans secured by avoidable liens on household goods, and less than $18,000 in unsecured debt, mostly from credit cards.

[Conclusions of Law]

For a below median income debtor, as we have here, the amounts reasonably necessary to be expended for the maintenance or support of the debtor or a dependent of the debtor are determined in the context of the estimated average monthly expenses reported on Schedule J.

These expenses must undergo judicial analysis, in the face of an objection, as to reasonableness and necessity; or as some might say, "the old fashion way." This Court considers Schedules I and J in the confirmation process for both above and below median income debtors. *See In re Edmunds,* 350 B.R. 636 (Bankr. D.S.C. 2006). . . .

The debtor bears the burden of showing that an expense is reasonable for confirmation purposes. *In re Watson,* 403 F.3d 1 (1st Cir. 2005); *Lynch v. Tate (In re Lynch),* 299 B.R. 776, 779 (W.D.N.C. 2003). . . . The majority of the cases reject private school tuition as a reasonable and necessary expense; at least in the absence of educational necessity or special needs. Earlier decisions expressed the "view that a debtor's creditors should not pay tuition for the debtor's children." *In re McNulty,* 142 B.R. 106 (Bankr. D.N.J. 1992); *See also In re Jones,* 55 B.R. 462 (Bankr. D. Minn. 1985) (Expressing the view, no longer held in many circles, that the public education was of high quality[]). The fulcrum was to balance "creditor's rights against the appropriate basic needs of the debtors and their dependents." *Watson* at 8. . . .

While the Debtor is retaining real estate, paying a 1% dividend to general unsecured creditors, and the children have no special education needs other than the fact that they are bright and need to be challenged; these factors are outweighed by others. The Debtor and his family have shown long term enrollment at parochial schools. All of the children attend private school, save one—who plans to return to private school next year. The Debtor's wife attended private school. The Debtor and his wife have strongly held religious convictions. The Debtor's wife would not work outside the home (and did not do so for many years) except to provide additional income to pay for private school tuition. In fact, Mrs. Cleary's pay check is reduced by the amount of tuition for the couple's children who attend the elementary school where she works.

The family's sacrifice of other basic expenses to fund private school tuition is noteworthy and, in this case, the deciding factor for the Court in approving the necessity and reasonableness of the expense for private school tuition. *See In re Grawey,* 2001 WL 34076376 (Bankr. C.D. Ill. 2001) (private school tuition and belt-tightening in the context of the dischargeability of student loans—sacrifices other basic necessities such as health care insurance). Debtor, if his testimony and schedules are truthful, could file a chapter 7 petition and it is very likely that he would lose no assets to administration for creditors. He is curing a small arrearage on his home loan through the chapter 13 plan, but the amount is *de minimis.* Debtor is giving up furniture secured by purchase money loans. For these reasons the Court finds that private school tuition is a reasonable and necessary expense of the debtor.

This aspect of the decision is limited very narrowly to the facts of this case. Mrs. Cleary is not a co-debtor. Her income would likely not be available if the children withdrew from private school because she would not work outside the home. It is only because of her religious convictions that she works outside the home and sends her children to private school. Debtor and his family sacrifice significantly in the purchase of food and clothing and in the areas of recreation and transportation expense. The expense of $1,513.00 for private school tuition is a reasonable and necessary expense.

The objection of the trustee is overruled. The plan will be confirmed by separate order.

For reasons we will see in the next assignment, a plausible argument that school fees are more entitled to statutory protection can be made post-BAPCPA, and so maybe the law has changed. For an "old school" perspective on an old school case, consider Univest-Coppel Village, Ltd. v. Nelson, 204 B.R. 497 (E.D. Tex. 1996). Mr. and Mrs. Nelson paid $395 a month to keep their 15-year-old daughter in Liberty Christian School. When they filed for chapter 13, one of their creditors objected to the expense, saying that this money should be counted as disposable income. Dad pointed out that the girl was "adamant" about not changing schools, and, in what he thought would be the clincher argument, he noted that she was the "only freshman to make the cheerleading squad." The bankruptcy court allowed the expense, but the district court said no, send the kid to public school. We wondered if there would be a protest from the pompom crowd.

The disposable income test for below-median debtors has thus been fraught with arguments to judges over various expenses, some of which serve as a reminder that people live varied lives—even if they are bankrupt. Over time, chapter 13 trustees and local lawyers develop a sense of what is likely to be acceptable to the judges in the district. The shorthand rules are often repeated, "Don't drive a car nicer than the judge" or "Get rid of the cable; the judge doesn't watch TV." One price of flexibility is to put the judge's values right in the middle of the choices.

2. *Available Income*

OK, so maybe "reasonably necessary . . . for maintenance and support" is a squishy standard that puts the debtor at the mercy of a bankruptcy judge for which expenses can be deducted from the monthly budget in determining "disposable income," but at least the first half of the calculation—income—sounds pretty straightforward. Just look at the debtor's W2, right? Were only it so. This is the Bankruptcy Code we're talking about.

────────── **In re WAECHTER** ──────────
439 B.R. 253 (Bankr. D. Mass. 2010)

HOFFMAN, Bankruptcy Judge.

This matter came before me for hearing on the objection of Denise M. Pappalardo, the standing Chapter 13 Trustee, to confirmation of the Debtor's amended Chapter 13 plan. The Trustee argues that the amended plan fails to provide for the unsecured creditors to receive the Debtor's entire projected disposable income and that in any event the plan is not proposed in good faith. The Debtor disagrees.

The parties' dispute stems from a premarital agreement entered into on April 7, 2008 by the Debtor and her then fiancé, Joao Da Silva, in which the couple agreed to keep their property and financial obligations entirely separate throughout their marriage. Subsequently, on November 2, 2009, the Debtor, but not her now husband Mr. Da Silva, filed a voluntary petition for relief under Chapter 13 of the Bankruptcy Code. . . . [T]he Debtor lists combined monthly income after payroll deductions for herself and Mr. Da Silva of $7,453.46, which includes Mr. Da Silva's net income of $1,348. . . . [T]he Debtor lists her monthly expenses including a line item of $1,309.46 described as "Spouse's prerogative, pursuant to premarital agreement, not to share income." This expense has the practical effect of offsetting all but $38.57 of Mr. Da Silva's income . . . thus leaving the Debtor with only $119 per month in disposable income to fund her Chapter 13 plan. The plan provides no dividend to general unsecured creditors.

Bankruptcy Code §1325(b)(1)(B) provides that if a trustee objects to plan confirmation the court may not confirm the plan unless the plan provides for all of the debtor's projected disposable income received during the life of the plan to be applied to make payments to unsecured creditors under the plan. The Trustee argues that the disposable income figure which is the basis for the Debtor's proposed plan payment is significantly understated, and thus violative of Section 1325(b)(1)(B), because while the Debtor includes her husband's income in Schedule I, she backs virtually all of it out in Schedule J, effectively giving her husband a free ride on all marital living expenses.

To rule on the Trustee's objection that the Debtor fails to dedicate her true projected disposable income to her plan, I turn first to the Bankruptcy Code, which defines "disposable income" as the "current monthly income received by the debtor ... less amounts reasonably necessary to be expended" for the maintenance or support of the debtor or a dependent of the debtor, charitable contributions, and other items. Bankruptcy Code §1325(b)(2). "Current monthly income" is defined as "the average monthly income from all sources that the debtor *receives* ... without regard to whether such income is taxable income ..." (emphasis added). Bankruptcy Code §101(10A). Courts are generally in agreement that in order to be considered part of the debtor's current monthly income, and, therefore, included in the disposable income calculation, income from a non-filing spouse to help cover household expenses must actually be received by the debtor. *See, e.g., In re Quarterman,* 342 B.R. 647 (Bankr. M.D. Fla. 2006).

In a typical case where spouses pool some or all of their income to pay for joint household expenses, courts look at the amount of pooled household expenses and assume that the non-filing spouse contributed a proportional amount of his or her income to the debtor for paying such expenses. *See, e.g., In re Mathenia,* 220 B.R. 427, 431 (Bankr. W.D. Okla. 1998). In the present case, however, the Debtor concedes that her husband does not contribute anything to the household expenses. Accordingly, since the Debtor does not actually receive any income from Mr. Da Silva, her plan satisfies the requirements of §1325(b)(1)(B).

The inquiry does not end there, however, and as the Trustee correctly points out, the Debtor must still satisfy the separate good faith requirement of Bankruptcy Code §1325(a)(3). The majority of courts in this circuit apply a "totality of the circumstances" test in evaluating whether a plan is proposed in good faith. *In re Torres Martinez,* 397 B.R. 158, 166 (1st Cir. BAP 2008).

Where questions of good faith arise with respect to a non-filing spouse's contribution, or lack thereof, to a debtor's disposable income in Chapter 13 cases, some courts have investigated the lifestyle choices of the non-filing spouse. Thus, for example, if the debtor received income towards household expenses from her non-filing spouse while at the same time enjoying the benefits of excessive luxury household expenses paid for exclusively by the spouse, courts have denied plan confirmation on the basis of bad faith. *See In re McNichols,* 254 B.R. 422, 430 (Bankr. N.D. Ill. 2000). On the other hand, if it is clear that the non-filing spouse is using his surplus income substantially to pay his own obligations, and is not otherwise subsidizing the debtor's luxury lifestyle while the debtor's creditors take it on the chin, then courts will find the debtor's plan to be filed in good faith. *See In re Nahat,* 278 B.R. 108 (Bankr. N.D. Tex. 2002).

Section 1 of the premarital agreement provides that each party will pay his or her own debts and that neither party is to be held liable for the debts of the other in any way. Given this restriction, the Debtor may in good faith propose a plan in which she is solely responsible for the mortgage payment on the marital home, title to which remains solely in the Debtor's name. This analysis, however, does not extend to a plan in which the Debtor purports to pay all other joint household expenses while her husband pays nothing.

Unlike the Debtor's mortgage payment, nothing in the premarital agreement requires that the couple not share general household expenses of the marital home. While the agreement clearly requires that the couple not share their income, it does not address how they will divide the joint day-to-day expenses of their married life. Therefore, the Debtor may not rely on the premarital agreement as justification for taking full responsibility for paying household expenses, effectively subsidizing her husband's income at the expense of her creditors.

According to Schedule J, the Debtor pays a total of $520 per month for utilities, water, sewer, cable, telephone and internet expenses. As the co-occupant of the marital home, Mr. Da Silva benefits from each of these expenses. In addition, the Debtor pays $649 per month for home maintenance and food, further benefitting Mr. Da Silva. In order to interpret Schedule J in a manner most favorable to the Debtor, I will assume that the Debtor's expenses for an additional telephone (presumably a mobile phone), clothing, transportation and health care costs, are solely for her benefit. This results in monthly household expenses which benefit both spouses of $1,169. If Mr. Da Silva were to contribute a proportional share of his income towards these expenses from which he benefits, the Debtor's projected disposable income would increase to $330 per month. If he were to contribute a full 50% share of these expenses, the Debtor's disposable income would jump to $703.50. In either circumstance, the Debtor could propose a plan providing for a significant dividend to her general unsecured creditors.

While I do not have the authority to order Mr. Da Silva to pay his share of the marital expenses, I can, and do, find that based on the totality of the circumstances, the Debtor's plan, in which she proposes to pay a disproportionate amount of the couple's shared household expenses, is not proposed in good faith. I will sustain the Trustee's objection to confirmation of the plan.

Another ambiguity about the scope of income for bankruptcy purposes concerns the exclusion in §101(10A)(B) for "benefits received under the Social Security Act." Unemployment compensation has its legal basis in that law, but the majority of courts has concluded that such benefits must be counted as income—and paid out to creditors. See In re Washington, 438 B.R. 348 (M.D. Ala. 2010) (collecting cases on both sides of issue).

Taken together, this case law of permissible expenses and available income provides judges with a basis for determining a below-median debtor's "disposable income" that must be committed to the pot for unsecured creditors over the plan's "applicable commitment period." If an unsecured creditor does not believe the debtor is paying this amount, it is a basis for objecting to plan confirmation. But remember that chapter 13 is not income-generating. That is, if a debtor's monthly mortgage bill, car payment, food, and all other reasonable expenses *exceed* monthly income, the debtor does not get any reprieve in chapter 13. On the contrary, this means that the debtor will be unable to confirm a plan. §1325(a)(6) ("the debtor will be able to make all payments under the plan and to comply with the plan"). Thus some debtors may have such financial distress that they cannot proceed in chapter 13 with a plan of repayment, even if they want to do so. Because their expenses are already reasonable and necessary, debtors may have difficulty downsizing further (although perhaps a cheaper car or house is an option), or, if they are eligible, filing for chapter 7.

3. Special Rules for Above-Median-Income Debtors

In the 2005 BAPCPA amendments, Congress decided to graft two important additional requirements onto chapter 13 plans regarding the disposable income test for certain higher-income debtors. Its conception of higher income—merely being above the pertinent state median income—takes what might be considered a deeply communitarian view toward identifying a high roller. (Recall BAPCPA was animated by a deep concern in Congress that many debtors could afford to pay much more of their debts and were using the perceived cakewalk of bankruptcy as a way to stiff their creditors.) The first requirement is that these above-median-income debtors have a minimum "applicable commitment period" of five years for their chapter 13 plans. The idea is that unless a debtor is paying 100% of unsecured creditors' claims, the plan must be five years.

The second and more complicated add-on for above-median-income debtors in chapter 13 is that Congress decided to pre-specify, by statute, just what these debtors would be allowed as their "reasonable and necessary expenses" in calculating the disposable income test. This was a congressional repudiation of the case-by-case adjudication of the bankruptcy judge's exercise of discretion, which continues to be the sole determination of income for below-median-income debtors. But for those above-median folks, Congress substituted multiple pages of dense statutory text on what may be deducted from income as a permissible expense. Confusingly, this statutory budget for repayment plans is not in chapter 13. Instead, it is found in §707(b), which has to do with eligibility to file chapter 7. §1325(a)(3).

Because the entire upcoming assignment looks at section 707(b)—often called "the means test"—we will defer exploring the statutory budget that applies to above-median-income chapter 13 debtors. Just recognize that for any chapter 13 filer with above-median income, "reasonable and necessary" is not nearly so free-wheeling as it sounds; it is in fact quite the opposite. You may wonder since above-median-income debtors have to endure five-year plans and calculate their minimum contributions to the unsecured creditor pot using a statutory budget that may not resemble their actual expenses, why they would file chapter 13. The simple answer is sometimes they want the advantage of legal tools unavailable in chapter 7—such as the ability to de-accelerate and cure a defaulted home mortgage. The more complicated answer is that sometimes they are *forced* to; that's what soon-to-be-explored section 707(b) is about.

Before you get carried away thinking this above-median statutory budget is going to apply to half of debtors—after all, above-median means everyone above the 50th percentile—remember that people who go bankrupt tend to have much lower incomes than the general population when they file. Indeed, median income for debtors in chapter 13 was only about $35,700 in the national sample of the 2007 Consumer Bankruptcy Project. Two-thirds of chapter 13 filers had income below the applicable median for their households and will only need to satisfy the traditional disposable income test. They never have to worry about the statutory budget explained in more detail in Assignment 12.

D. MODIFICATION OF CHAPTER 13 PLANS

A chapter 7 involves only the liquidation of already-acquired assets. By contrast, a chapter 13 plan relies on payment out of future income. Often debtors in chapter 13 bankruptcies already have had significant financial disruptions, and projections of income and expenses frequently are not borne out. In short, "disposable income" can change. If so, the debtor, the trustee, or a creditor may move to have the plan modified. §1329(a). Most often, the debtor seeks modification because of decreased income or increased expenses that have made payment of the originally promised amounts much more difficult.

An obvious limit on modification is whether the debtor has any disposable income at all; the more nuanced problem is whether the debtor's income at the time of modification will permit the debtor to continue making payments on secured debts. Modification can reduce payments to unsecured creditors but it doesn't change the statutory minimums owed to secured and priority creditors.

Modification is constrained by the statutory limit on plan length at five years. §1322(d)(1). When a plan is modified, it must still meet all the chapter 13 requirements, including this five-year limit. Most debtors, however, are already in a five-year plan. 2007 Consumer Bankruptcy Project; see also Scott F. Norberg & Andrew J. Velkey, Debtor Discharge and Creditor Repayment in Chapter 13, 39 Creighton L. Rev. 473, 526 & Tbl. 36 (2006) (reporting that 60% of cases proposed five-year plans). This wipes out significant flexibility in reworking a plan if a debtor falls behind, even for those below-median-income debtors whose plans do not have an "applicable commitment period" of five years. This means the debtor has to find a way somehow to make up for the missed payments, despite an income for which all spare change has already been fully committed.

Sometimes trustees work around this by waiting a couple of months before filing a motion to dismiss for missing plan payments as an informal "grace period" for struggling debtors. By that point, some debtors have resumed payments, and the trustee and court simply tack on the non-payment months to the end. Indeed, one trustee reports that most successfully completed plans are now 62 or 63 months in length, an outcome that one will find explicitly contemplated nowhere in the Code with its cap on chapter 13 plans at 60 months—and yet the world still spins.

Of course, modification goes both ways. That is, some debtors will get a raise, work a little overtime, or have a kid get a job and move out of the basement. This good news may be short-lived for the debtor. Creditors or the trustee may trumpet the debtor's changed circumstances and argue that the plan should be modified to permit higher payments. This monetary joy that has touched the debtor's life is even better news for the creditors, who can ask to take it all. Because the debtor is already in "disposable income" territory, any new income would seem to flow directly to them.

———————— **In re DREW** ————————

325 B.R. 765 (Bankr. N.D. Ill. 2005)

SQUIRES, Bankruptcy Judge.

[B]oth matters involve a common issue: whether the Debtors' confirmed plans can be amended under §1329 to increase the dividends payable to the pre-petition unsecured creditors as a result of the Debtors refinancing their respective real properties and receiving lump sum cash payments as part of the refinancing. . . . The Trustee contends that the cash payments should be added to the total pot that the Debtors should be required to pay under the terms of their confirmed plans.

The Drews filed their Chapter 13 petition on December 16, 2002. On March 12, 2003, their plan was confirmed. Pursuant to the plan, the Drews were to pay $350.00 per month to the Trustee for a minimum term of thirty six months (totaling $12,600.00) in order for unsecured creditors' allowed claims to receive a minimum ten percent dividend. The order confirming the plan provided that if the unsecured creditors would receive one hundred percent of their allowed claims, they could pay less than the aggregate sum of $12,600.00. At the time the Trustee's motion was filed, January 24, 2005, the Drews had not made thirty-six months of payments under the confirmed plan. Rather, they paid a total of $9,380.00. In January 19, 2005, the Court granted the Debtors' motions to obtain credit in order to refinance their properties. In the Drews' case, the Trustee alleges that at the time of confirmation, their real estate was valued at $90,000.00, and they refinanced it for $105,000.00.

In the Debtors' responses, they concede the valuations of the subject properties that were scheduled at the time of confirmation, but assert that the Trustee is now estopped from challenging those valuations at this point. They contend that the higher valuations, for refinancing purposes, show that the real properties have appreciated over the passage of time since confirmation. The Debtors argue that they should be able to keep the surplus equity and should not be required to pay those funds to the unsecured creditors and increase their dividends. The Debtors contend that granting the Trustee's motions would effectively discourage other debtors from seeking relief under Chapter 13. . . . According to the Trustee, the motions to modify the plans satisfy the requirements of §1329(b)(1), §1325(a)(1), §1325(b)(1) and §1325(a)(3).

The debtor, the trustee or any holder of an allowed unsecured claim has standing to seek modification of a plan after confirmation. *See* 11 U.S.C. §1329(a). Section 1329(a)(1) expressly permits post-confirmation plan modifications to increase the amount of payments on claims of a particular class. The Trustee has standing under §1329 to seek post-confirmation modification of the plans in order to increase the dividends to the unsecured claim holders. . . .

[The] specific issue at bar [is] whether the Court can modify the confirmed plans to increase the dividends payable to the unsecured creditors as a result of the Debtors receiving lump sum cash payments from the refinancing of their real properties. It is undisputed that the Debtors have appropriately sought and received approval to refinance the mortgages on their homes that they are attempting to keep and save in the context of their confirmed Chapter 13 plans. . . .

The interplay of 11 U.S.C. §1327(c), §541 and §1306(a)(1) deals with and provides an interesting interaction with the expanded definition of property of the estate in a Chapter 13 case. This is because §541 broadly defines property of the estate to include "all legal or equitable interests of the debtor in property as of the commencement of the case." 11 U.S.C. §541(a)(1). In addition, §1306(a)(1) includes "all property of the kind specified in [§541] that the debtor acquires after the commencement of the case but before the case is closed, dismissed or converted...." 11 U.S.C. §1306(a)(1). Thus, property that a Chapter 13 debtor acquires post-petition, like the refinancing proceeds the Debtors received in the cases at bar, becomes property of the estate pursuant to §1306, in contrast to the post-petition acquisitions that do not become part of a Chapter 7 or Chapter 11 estate. Accordingly, it has been held that a Chapter 13 estate can include gifts, inheritances and windfalls that are acquired by the debtor post-petition. *See, e.g., In re Euerle,* 70 B.R. 72 (Bankr. N.H. 1987) (inheritance); *In re Koonce* 54 B.R. 643 (Bankr. D.S.C. 1985) (lottery winnings); *Doane v. Appalachian Power Co. (In re Doane),* 19 B.R. 1007 (W.D. Va. 1982) (money loaned to the debtor by a relative).

There exists a statutory tension between §1306(a)(1) and the vesting provisions of §1327(c). Although §1327(c) notes that property vesting in the debtor includes all property acquired after the petition is "free and clear of any claim or interest of any creditor provided for by the plan," some courts have left room for the re-creation of the Chapter 13 estate after confirmation and hold that the estate continues and can be refilled with property acquired after confirmation. *See, e.g., In re Nott,* 269 B.R. 250 (Bankr. M.D. Fla. 2000) (although property of the estate at confirmation vested in debtor pursuant to §1327(b), a $300,000.00 inheritance one year after confirmation is property of the estate pursuant to §1306(a)).

The Seventh Circuit has stated that §1306(a)(2) provides that upon confirmation, the plan returns so much of the estate to the debtor's control as is not necessary for the fulfillment of the plan. *Black v. United States Postal Serv. (In re Heath),* 115 F.3d 521, 524 (7th Cir. 1997). Under that dictum, the portions of the refinancing proceeds intended by the Debtors to be paid to complete their confirmed plans are part of the continuing estates under §541 and §1306(a)(1).

Thus, the Court holds that the refinancing proceeds are part of the Debtors' bankruptcy estates post-confirmation because those proceeds were acquired by the Debtors for use in making payments under their confirmed plans. . . .

Section 1329(a)(1) can be invoked by trustees or unsecured creditors who timely move to increase a debtor's payments under a confirmed plan where the debtor's financial situation has improved. In his treatise, Judge Lundin aptly stated that:

> There is obvious fairness to requiring debtors to share good fortune with creditors. This is the same fairness that permits Chapter 13 debtors to reduce payments to creditors when circumstances disable the debtor from completing the original plan.... It is of more than academic interest that were the debtor to

convert to Chapter 7 after winning a lottery or realizing new income, the postpetition assets and income belong to the debtor and would not be available for distribution to creditors in the Chapter 7 case. Perhaps the sharing of postpetition good fortune is seen by some courts as the cost of the Chapter 13 discharge. . . . [C]ases support the proposition that an allowed unsecured claim holder [or the trustee] can force the debtor with improved financial condition to a choice: accept an increase in payments to creditors or get out of Chapter 13.

3 Lundin, §266.1 at 266–14 (footnotes omitted). *See also id.* at 266–1–5 (collecting cases for the proposition that courts have aggressively allowed trustees and unsecured claim holders to modify plans to increase payments—often over the strong opposition of debtors). It is "not the design of the Bankruptcy laws to allow the Debtor to lead the life of Riley while his creditors suffer on his behalf." *In re Bryant,* 47 B.R. 21, 26 (Bankr. W.D.N.C. 1984). . . .

Although the refinancing by the Debtors in these cases involved new debt incurred by them, the refinancing transactions were not necessarily "washes" where the increased values of the subject properties were completely offset by the new loans. The record here is not at all comprehensive, but the Court doubts that the new loans made to these Debtors were at a one hundred percent loan to value ratio. Indeed, most real estate lenders in this District lend at a much lower loan to value ratio to provide some residual cushion in the event of subsequent default by the debtor with resultant foreclosure of the new mortgage. Thus, although the record is not at all clear, it is probable that each property's value has increased substantially more than the amounts loaned. Hence, there is likely additional equity in each property that the Debtors enjoy and will retain because the properties are not being sold. The Trustee's motions effectively seek to compel the Debtors to contribute so much of that equity to the unsecured creditors' dividends as the Debtors are cashing out via the refinancing. Section 1329 permits this result. . . .

Section 1329 provides a mechanism for the Trustee to "up the ante" for the benefit of the unsecured creditors if she so moves in time, just as the statute is more frequently invoked by debtors whose situations have worsened post-confirmation and appropriately seek to effectively reduce the unsecured dividends. The statute can work either way. . . .

There has been no evidence proffered to support the speculative argument that increasing the dividends to unsecured creditors will somehow discourage debtors from either filing Chapter 13 petitions or serve as a disincentive for debtors to seek to exit the system sooner. . . . [T]he possibility of relief under §1329 only occurs after a Chapter 13 debtor's plan has achieved the major hurdle of being confirmed in the first instance, and many Chapter 13 cases never get to that point. Moreover, of those that do, the Court has anecdotally observed over the past seventeen years that the vast majority of §1329 motions are brought by debtors who seek to lower the dividend to unsecured creditors because of their subsequent adverse circumstances. . . .

Although the Code now permits judges or any party in interest to request annual financial updates, §521(f)(4), the common practice is to scrutinize the tax returns each year instead. This is likely the only practical means for creditors to learn of positive changes to a debtor's financial situation. When these matters do get to litigation, some courts have held that a putatively modifying creditor must show a "substantial and unanticipated post-confirmation change," whereas others see no such requirement in the Code. See, e.g., In re Eckert, Case No. 5-10-bk-09573 (M.D. Penn. Jan. 14, 2013) (discussing cases) (denying modification to 59-year-old debtor whose new job had mandatory overtime where debtor testified "I'm hoping to get away from overtime, 50 hours a week on my feet is a lot for me").

E. STATUTORY BARS ON CHAPTER 13 ELIGIBILITY

We close our general discussion of chapter 13 with a caution that this repayment option, even with its hefty requirements, is not open to everyone. Section 109(e) restricts who can use chapter 13. A filer must be an individual. This means no entities, even if they are affiliated with the human debtor. As a practical matter, this does not mean that businesses do not get help in chapter 13. Many self-employed people run businesses but are not incorporated or otherwise organized as legal entities. Much of these folks' business debt creates personal liability, for example, because it is charged to a credit card used for both personal and business expenses or because of a personal guarantee or home mortgage to secure a business line of credit. See Robert M. Lawless and Elizabeth Warren, The Myth of the Disappearing Business Bankruptcy, 93 Calif. L. Rev. 3 (2005).

Another bar to chapter 13 is the requirement of regular income, which comes from the history of chapter 13 being a "wage-earner's plan." By moving from wage-earners to regular income, Congress was trying to expand the relief available (to housewives, contractors, trust fund babies, etc.), so the lingering effect today of this clause as a restriction is minimal: blocking those with no income from chapter 13 and shunting them to chapter 7 or out of the bankruptcy system altogether. Courts have broadly interpreted the provision, and so today litigation is infrequent. For a discussion from the nation's top expert on chapter 13, see Judge Lundin's opinion in In re Murphy, 226 B.R. 601 (Bankr. M.D. Tenn. 1998) (stay-at-home stepmother eligible for chapter 13; had regular income even though not married to children's father who paid bills such as debtor's car payment).

A third restriction—secured and unsecured caps on noncontingent, liquidated debt—has more bite. §109(e). It seems designed to keep "the rich" from chapter 13 (they can file for an individual's plan in chapter 11 as we will see later on), consistent with chapter 13's populist origins. It's an odd tool to do so, however, because it focuses on debts not income. Poor people can have loads of debt; they tend to lack income.

In a world of home mortgages, it's easy to see why the secured debt cap is higher than the unsecured one. The debt caps do a lot more work in jurisdictions with high-cost housing, such as coastal California, or urban centers. Setting these caps at the "correct" level, however, is hard, and Congress really hasn't tried. The numbers were set back in 1978 and were not adjusted for decades thereafter. Post-2005, the debt limits adjust every three years, as with many other figures in the Code. 11 U.S.C. §104(b).

The conjunctive requirements of noncontingency and liquidation are conceptually difficult. Examples may help. A *noncontingent* debt is one that is not dependent on future events. For example, if I run over your foot and you claim I owe you two million dollars for my negligence, I may counter that your wearing black clothes and lying in the middle of the road at nighttime was contributory. Even if you think you have a winner, your claim against me is contingent because liability has not been determined. This contingent debt does not count against the chapter 13 debt limit. Think too of your parents, who may have guaranteed your student loans. If they file for bankruptcy, those obligations, while real, are contingent, as you may never default.

Liquidated means we know what the actual amount is. If I admit negligence in the car vs. foot hypo but claim there is no way—*No. Way.*— a broken foot is worth two million dollars, then we have to go to court to liquidate my negligence debt. Imagine also a losing defendant who has just been found to have violated the antitrust laws: noncontingent liability (lost case), but no idea what amount of damages will be awarded (unliquidated). Many debts can be both contingent and unliquidated: car manufacturers' warranty claims are a good example. The cars may never be defective (contingent), and if they are, the amount of the repair claims is unknown (unliquidated). These characteristics of the claims don't make them any less real—the creditors line up and file their bankruptcy claims—it just means they don't count against the chapter 13 eligibility cap.

Assuming that chapter 13 should be limited to middle class debtors and that a debt restriction is a sensible way to do so (both arguable propositions), the question still remains why restrict debts to noncontingent, unliquidated ones? Consider what happens if a specious debt is alleged by an angry creditor; wouldn't you be troubled if that could block you as a debtor from chapter 13 relief? For a good discussion of this worry, see In re Huelbig (Bankr. R.I. 2003), (discussing and disagreeing with Ho v. Dowell (In re Ho), 274 B.R. 867 (9th Cir. BAP 2002) in determining that uncertain, even unlikely liability, does not prevent a claim from being liquidated.)

Problem Set 11

11.1. You are filing your first chapter 13 case since entering practice. In your jurisdiction, judges are randomly assigned as cases are filed. The three bankruptcy judges seem to have rather different views about the requirements for confirmation of a chapter 13 plan—two are very strict and one is quite lenient. All three permit the debtor to propose an amended plan if the initial plan is not confirmed. Your client, Maria Jackson, is a single parent who supports herself and three children on the $23,000 annual salary she earns as a department store clerk in Atlanta. She is left with $60 per week after she has paid her rent, utilities, insurance, food, and gas. This amount would give her creditors about 50 percent of their outstanding debt over three years or 80 percent over five years, but it would also leave her without any cushion of any kind. Giving $60 to the trustee would also require termination of the piano lessons one child has already begun and prevent another child from starting much-needed orthodontic treatment. What kind of a plan do you propose for her? Does your malpractice insurer have an opinion on what you should do? See §§1322, 1325, 1329.

11.2. Christoph Paulus lives in a nice apartment in Milwaukee with his girlfriend Manuela, who works as a physical therapist and shares the rent and other household expenses. When he first got out of college he went a little nuts with his credit cards, so he now has $40,000 in credit card debt. He has settled down now, and, until recently, he was steadily reducing the debt by living frugally, driving the old family car his parents gave him, eating at home, shopping at Costco, and so on. Unfortunately, his elderly dad got very ill and even with Medicare coverage had substantial out-of-pocket medical expenses. Chris co-signed for the necessary charges the day his dad died and now finds himself with $60,000 in medical debt in addition to the credit cards, so he is contemplating some form of bankruptcy filing.

In the last year, Chris earned a total of about $24,000 as a temporary and contract worker, but the work has been a bit up and down and hard to predict from month to month. He recently finished his part-time MBA program and has been offered a job selling financial packages to executives. The salary would be about what he made last year, but he thinks that if he worked very hard he could make a great deal more. He values his easy going life, but is worried about his debts and can't decide whether to take the sales job or not. Chris wants to know what his options are to deal with his debts and what a chapter 13 plan would look like. What can you tell him? §§1322, 1325.

11.3. Myrtle Tundra owes over $120,000 to banks, credit card issuers, and stores, and she has a $250,000 mortgage on her house. She has about $50,000 in non-exempt personal property. Her legal practice is doing well, and she makes about $100,000 a year. Myrtle has come to see you as a bankruptcy expert because she is nervous about a debt that she guaranteed for her former law firm.

The debt was the mortgage on the small office building that the firm owned and in which it maintained its office. Her former partner, John Ice, kept the building as part of their agreed wind-up of the former firm's affairs. The mortgage is presently about $775,000, payable over 18 more years. The building is currently worth about $600,000, but it is in a rapidly developing area. A reliable real estate agent has told Myrtle that when a nearby freeway and shopping center are completed in about six months, the property will easily be worth $900,000.

John is having some trouble making the payments and may have missed this month's payment already. The mortgage is held by Loraine Ice, John's former wife, who hates both John and Myrtle for reasons Myrtle does not wish to discuss. Myrtle says Loraine would viciously exploit any default in an effort to hurt John and Myrtle. What is your advice? See §109(e).

11.4. You are completing preparation of a chapter 13 plan for Justin D'Angelis. He wants to file but his wife, who is not employed outside the home, does not. Their income is $45,000. After you have computed his expenses, it appears that he will have about $425 a month that would be available for distribution to his creditors. Mr. D is very reluctant to pay anyone, and he keeps asking if he can't claim some more expenses. Finally, he looks at the expense list and says, "I want to make contributions to my church." You ask the amount, and he says, "$425 a month." You ask if he has made regular contributions in the past, and he says, "No, but I'm turning over a new leaf." Can Mr. D confirm a plan that pays nothing to his unsecured creditors? What do you advise him? §1325(b)(2)(A).

11.5. Last year you represented Doris Frankel in her chapter 13 bankruptcy. You regard it as one of your most satisfying cases. When you met Doris she was a recently widowed, middle-aged woman who had never worked outside the home. At her husband's death, she was left with huge bills incurred during his final illness and a load of debts from his business for which she was jointly liable. After she used all the insurance and sold the business, she was still $120,000 in debt. Her creditors included some hostile and aggressive former business partners of her deceased husband. Doris took a job as a clerk at the local Mega-Lo-Mart, and she asked for your help in keeping her creditors from taking everything she and her husband had built up.

You took her into a chapter 13, and she insisted on a 25 percent repayment of her unsecured debt. You thought that amount was too high and that she would have nothing left over, but she said it was important to her self-esteem.

Today, Doris is back in your office. She hardly looks like the same woman. While she worked at the Mega-Lo-Mart and another part-time, evening job, she began real estate classes. She has passed her exams, quit her other jobs, and has been selling commercial real estate for four months.

She has come to share some wonderful news with you. Last night she got a call from a well-known real estate developer. It seems that he had met Doris and liked her quiet, sincere style. He checked her background and decided she was just the woman he wanted to be in charge of the completion and leasing of his latest office building. She recognizes the enormous work that she will have to do. She must supervise all finishing work, find tenants, negotiate leasing arrangements and customizing work, etc. Doris estimates that she will be working 60 hours a week, at least. But if she can pull it off, the bonuses for 95 percent leasing in the first year could be as much as $50,000. You are delighted for her, but do you have any free advice? See §1329.

Section 4:
The Consumer Bankruptcy System

Now that you understand the provisions of chapters 7 and 13 of the Code, this final consumer section of the textbook puts it all together. It starts with the all-important decision about the chapter under which to file the debtor's petition and then proceeds to consider the theoretical and policy issues underlying the consumer bankruptcy system that judges, scholars, lawyers, and law students should all think about in analyzing the Code. The myriad factors to consider in choosing the best chapter of the Code under which to file a consumer petition was already a complicated affair before Congress jumped in and passed BAPCPA; after BAPCPA, it is enough to test one's sanity. To make things digestible, we break out chapter choice into two assignments: the first on the BAPCPA means test—which acts as an eligibility bar to chapter 7, the same way section 109(e) acts as an eligibility bar to chapter 13. This means test is the central tool Congress has adopted to identify the debtors who could (or should) pay their debts and force them into chapter 13, where they will face a statutory budget immune from judicial intermeddling. The second part of this section discusses the other statutory and extra-statutory considerations that influence chapter choice once eligibility has been established. The exploration of theory and policy constitutes the third assignment and concludes our study of consumer bankruptcy.

Assignment 12.

The Means Test

In passing BAPCPA, Congress accepted the position that too many debtors were walking away from their debts through the perceived easy discharge of bankruptcy. To rectify this, it designed what is called the "means test" as a statutory bar to filing a chapter 7 petition, forcing those caught by its screen to face a series of less palatable options. ("Means test" is once again a term found nowhere in the Code and used everywhere in the bankruptcy world.) Barred consumer debtors would have to (1) file under chapter 13, where now mandatory five-year plans and statutory budgets await higher-income debtors, (2) file under some other chapter of the Code, such as chapter 11, which is a weird outcome for consumer debtors as that chapter is traditionally for business-based reorganizations, or (3) give up on a federal bankruptcy discharge and have to face their creditors with state exemptions but little more.

Courts and Congress have always been concerned about abusive use of the Bankruptcy Code, and so the means test was just the latest and most dramatic step in a long history of debtor policing. (Bankruptcy courts are often called courts of equity and so fairness considerations are intrinsic. Adam Levitin, Toward a Federal Common Law of Bankruptcy: Judicial Lawmaking in a Statutory Regime, 80 Am. Bankr. L.J. 1 (2006).) We start this assignment with the historical provisions for controlling debtor abuse to situate properly the means test's radical transformation of the Bankruptcy Code, then confront the means test in all its glory, and finally close with a discussion of its operation in chapter 13. Fasten your seatbelts.

A. THE HISTORICAL BAR TO CHAPTER 7: DISCRETIONARY DISMISSAL FOR SUBSTANTIAL ABUSE

There is no right to bankruptcy. Indeed, chapter 7 has always had some statutory bar or another, even before chapter 13 came along, and so the initial eligibility bars were complete exclusions from the system. For example, the first bankruptcy laws were available only to traders, an early recognition that debt relief was essential to encouraging entrepreneurial undertakings. By the mid-nineteenth century, bankruptcy laws accommodated both troubled businesses and families in financial distress. When Congress enacted the 1978 Bankruptcy Code, it kept broad access to chapter 7 with only the smallest exceptions. Indeed, the Code does not even require a showing of debtor insolvency as a precondition of filing, a requirement of many other legal systems. See, e.g., Insolvency Act, 1986, c. 45, §272 (U.K.) Bankruptcy and Insolvency Act, R.S.C., 1985, c. B-3, s. 2 ("insolvent person") (Austl.).

On the other hand, Congress has since the 1978 Code evinced a policy of wanting more people in financial distress to use chapter 13. The pro-13 policy could stem from a number of factors, ranging from Protestant work ethic sensibilities to a belief that creditors get higher returns in chapter 13 than in chapter 7. Today's restrictions on chapter 7, therefore, are less bars to bankruptcy than "encouragements" for debtors to file in chapter 13. The 1978 Code used carrots, such as a (now-diminished) super-discharge for certain debts that weren't dischargeable in chapter 7, and perhaps more importantly, a right to cure a defaulted home mortgage. Some might say these statutory carrots worked, but we suspect that a massive campaign to educate lawyers and judges to use a "new and improved" chapter had an equal if not greater effect. See Katherine Porter, The Pretend Solution, An Empirical Study of Bankruptcy Outcomes, 90 Tex. L. Rev. 103 (2011). By the mid-1980s, about one-third of all families in bankruptcy filed chapter 13 cases.

In the eyes of some, however, two problems then emerged with the consumer bankruptcy system. The first was that Congress overshot the mark in making bankruptcy relief more available resulting in "too many" people now filing for bankruptcy, and the second was that not enough of these bankrupt people were choosing chapter 13, whose uptake rate stabilized during the 1980s and 1990s at around one-third (albeit with wide variation among judicial districts). In response to these concerns, the credit industry lobbied to tighten bankruptcy relief.

In 1984, Congress gave bankruptcy judges the discretion to dismiss chapter 7 cases if the filing involved "substantial abuse." §707(b) (1984). Judges responded by dismissing the cases of debtors who had committed bad acts, criminal activities, or otherwise irked a sense of fair play, even though the technical eligibility requirements for bankruptcy had been met. Case law developed the contours of "substantial abuse" and came to cover, at least in some districts, debtors who had the ability with a modest amount of sacrifice to repay their creditors but were filing in chapter 7 instead of chapter 13. Circuit court precedents abounded, see, e.g., In re Green, 934 F.2d 568 (4th Cir. 1991), and so bankruptcy judges became the primary gatekeepers of chapter 7 eligibility, leaving the dismissed debtors typically with a "choice" of chapter 13 or remaining outside the bankruptcy system.

Ironically, many courts deciding a 707(b) motion for substantial abuse in a chapter 7 case undertook the same sort of consideration that underlies the scrutiny of a chapter 13 debtor's proposed budget: is the debtor scrimping enough to earn the privilege of a discharge? But as *Green* and other precedents made clear, "substantial abuse" was intended for the rogue outlier—a sort of safety valve to preserve system integrity. Indeed, a procedural presumption in section 707(b) clarified that the debtor enjoyed a presumption of *non-abuse*. Dismissal of chapter 7 was reserved for egregious exceptions rather than routine sorting. The case below illustrates the discretionary, judicially administered bar on chapter 7 that operated before 2005.

——————— **In re SHAW** ———————

311 B.R. 180 (Bankr. M.D.N.C. 2003)

CARRUTHERS, Bankruptcy Judge.

The Debtors are a married couple in their early 50s with two grown children, ages 21 and 24. . . . The Debtors have been continuously employed for at least the past five years. The Debtors' 2001 Federal tax return shows adjusted gross income of $138,554.00, with an increase in 2002 to $157,024.00.

Despite their consistent income during the last several years, the Debtors have been unable to make a dent in the repayment of their debts and have consistently spent more money than they were able to earn. The Debtors contend that they need a fresh start in a Chapter 7 so that they can retain their home and three vehicles [while discharging $130,000 in unsecured credit card debt—Eds.].

The Debtors' proposed [monthly] family budget as listed on Schedule J in the amount of $6,312.52 is excessive and unreasonable. First, the Debtors' mortgage payment expense is clearly unwarranted. The Debtors purchased the home in 1993. At the hearing, the Debtors explained that they needed a large [half-million dollar –Eds.] home so that there would be sufficient space for Mrs. Shaw's mother to live with them and yet not interrupt their children's lives. Mrs. Shaw's mother passed away in 1998. The Debtors currently pay $3,349.28 to maintain a home with approximately 3200 square feet as well as a finished basement. The Debtors' children are now grown, however, their 24-year-old son lives at home and contributes nothing to the monthly housing payment. If the Debtors wish to take advantage of the protections afforded by the Bankruptcy Code, they simply must obtain less expensive housing.

In addition, the court finds that the vehicle lease payments of $349.00 per month and college expenses of $520.00 per month for the Debtors' daughter are not reasonable and necessary expenses under these circumstances. While supporting a daughter in college is an admirable goal, the Debtors propose to do so at the expense of their creditors. Therefore, the Debtors' budget can be further reduced by $869.00 per month. Further reductions can be made by trimming the Debtors' telephone expenses for two home lines and two cell phones and by eliminating the ongoing expenses for the swimming pool. The court finds that the transportation cost, exclusive of car payments and insurance, is unreasonable and excessive. With just these adjustments alone, the Debtors could be able to contribute approximately $2,000.00 per month to a Chapter 13 plan. The Chapter 13 Trustee estimates a dividend of 29% over 36 months [and obviously much higher under a five-year plan—Eds.].

The Debtors admit that their bankruptcy was not the result of a sudden illness, calamity, disability, or unemployment. . . . While the Debtors have experienced some short period of unemployment, their road to financial distress was the result of lifestyle choices they made. . . . The Shaws have been living beyond their means for years. The Debtors made purchases in anticipation of future bonuses and were unable to pay off those purchases when bonuses were not received or were smaller than expected. For example, Mrs. Shaw testified that she purchased a bedroom suite less than two years ago for approximately $4,000.00 with the expectation that Mr. Shaw would get an anniversary bonus. Mr. Shaw did not receive that bonus.

The Debtors contend that they have never incurred debt maliciously or with an intent not to pay, and that their enormous debt has accumulated over a period of years. The fact that these debts accumulated over a long period of time makes it all the more difficult for the court to understand why the Debtors did not change their spending behavior years ago. According to the Debtors' testimony, they have been struggling to make payments on their debts for years, and yet continued to make expensive decisions, such as purchasing a 2002 Oldsmobile Bravado and a 2001 Oldsmobile Alero, and a $4,000.00 bedroom suite and contributing over $1,000.00 per month towards their daughter's college expenses. Thus, the Debtors have clearly been aware of their inability to pay their ever-increasing debt for years, and continued to incur cash advances and consumer purchases beyond their ability to pay.

The Debtors elected to file a Chapter 7 petition to maintain their present lifestyle. They have the ability to repay a substantial portion of the debt with their high income. The Debtors incurred cash advances and made consumer purchases far in excess of their ability to repay and their proposed family budget is both excessive and unreasonable given their current circumstances.

The court concludes that based upon the totality of the circumstances these debtors do not satisfy the criteria to be Chapter 7 debtors. To allow such would be a substantial abuse of the bankruptcy system and goals; and therefore, this Chapter 7 case should be dismissed under 11 U.S.C. §707(b) of the Bankruptcy Code.

———

Despite the courts' willingness to crack down in cases such as *Shaw*, most debtors didn't have high incomes and big discretionary expenses to cut back on. Empirical studies, including our own, showed that most people filed for bankruptcy following job losses, serious medical problems, and family break-ups, and that very few of them could repay any meaningful amount to their creditors. Good studies, however, may not best good lobbying, and creditors continued to point to a "problem" with consumer bankruptcies. In 2005, nine years after a bill drafted by the credit industry was first introduced, Congress passed BAPCPA, which made bankruptcy less accessible for all individuals. The centerpiece of these amendments was a new statutory screen, the means test, to determine who could file chapter 7.

B. THE CURRENT BAR TO CHAPTER 7: MANDATORY DISMISSAL UNDER THE MEANS TEST

1. The Overview

Perhaps blaming bankruptcy judges for the continuing rise in filings, Congress in BAPCPA removed them as the primary gatekeepers of chapter 7 access. Instead, it imbedded a fixed statutory formula to determine "abuse" and hence who can remain in chapter 7. This test runs several single-spaced pages of text, and frankly is difficult for anyone, much less students, to read. The overview below gives you a reader's guide to the statute, but there is no substitute for your working through it yourself. Technically, the heart of the means test is section 707(b)(2), but the broad structure of 707 is crucial to seeing how 707(b)(2) does its work. Section 707(a) allows courts to dismiss cases generally for "cause," including the reasons specifically stated therein. Section 707(b) adds an additional dismissal screen on *consumer debtors*, presumably in the belief that they might be especially prone to abuse the bankruptcy system.

BAPCPA renumbered the substantial abuse section that was section 707(b) in 1984 (the one discussed in *Shaw*) as new section 707(b)(1), and made two modifications. First, it deleted "substantial" before "abuse," presumably to signal that courts should now be able to throw debtors out of chapter 7 for mere garden-variety abuse without it rising to the level of being substantial. Second, it deleted the important procedural presumption of nonabuse previously enjoyed by the debtor. These were changes, to be sure, but nothing radical; they are extensions of the approach of prior amendments.

The actual "means test" of paragraph (2) of section 707(b), however, was radical. The key point of the multi-page paragraph is to create a "presumption" of abuse if the debtor can repay more than a certain minimum amount to creditors based on a complex statutory calculation. The presumption can nominally be "rebutted," but only by showing "special circumstances" that can meet the further test of section 707(b)(2)(B)(i). (For everyone else, the presumption is irrebuttable.) Finally, paragraph (3) allows additional grounds on which the court *may* dismiss a consumer debtor's petition for abuse beyond the mandatory grounds for which dismissal *shall* be ordered under paragraph (2)'s means test. (We turn to paragraph (3) in the next assignment; paragraph (2)'s means test will keep us busy enough for now.)

For newcomers, it is hard to discern the degree to which BAPCPA was a transformative event in the bankruptcy system's evolution. When chapter 13 was rolled out in the 1930s and thereafter in various districts, debtors were offered free choice between 7 and 13. Then in the 1978 Code, carrots were added to encourage debtors toward 13. In 1984, judge-administered sticks were added to underscore that encouragement. Now there is an extremely detailed formula that screens each and every debtor to determine whether chapter 7 is or is not an "abuse," the outcome of which relegates judges to the sidelines.

This judge-supplanting statutory screen on eligibility is called a "means test" because it depends upon the debtor's means, which is measured by a particularized definition of income. Other federal statutes, such as Medicaid, have means-based eligibility screens, so this is not unheard of; it was just unprecedented in the United States to evaluate people to make sure they were "poor enough" to be bankrupt. The numerical test of section 707(b) uses two approaches to measure a debtor's income: *gross* and *net* (these are our terms; you will find them nowhere in the statute). Debtors can pass either way; some have gross incomes so low they never have to undergo all the scrutiny of expenses involved in the net income screen. Higher income filers must endure intense disclosure and scrutiny of their expenses to determine their net income is not so high as to make their chapter 7 case a presumed abuse. Not surprisingly, given the workload of bankruptcy judges, the primary party to use the means test is the U.S. Trustee. Thus, BAPCPA has the effect of giving a big boost in responsibility to this administrative branch of the federal government, while signaling reduced confidence in the bankruptcy courts to police access to chapter 7.

2. The Gross Income Bypass

In what surely makes the short list for worst statutory drafting ever, buried away in paragraph (7) of section 707 is what looks like a dry standing rule. It is actually a bypass of the means test. In fact, it serves to exempt more than 90% of filers. Rephrased in English, section 707(b)(7) says that if the debtor's "current monthly income" is less than the applicable median state income, nobody can raise the means test presumption.[9] Functionally, an unraisable means test is a passed means test. Of course, this bypass doesn't stop the debtor from having to file a complicated means test calculation worksheet, see Form B22, but it does mean that the means test is just another piece of paperwork for most families. The 2007 Consumer Bankruptcy Project data show that 92% of chapter 7 filers had incomes below the applicable median for their state and household. The U.S. Trustee Program's data show a similar figure. (Median income is the same

---

9. Paragraphs six and seven read together are an Eighth Amendment violation. On first reading, they seem to say the same thing, but on closer inspection paragraph six is a standing rule that allows only judges and trustees – not individual creditors – to raise objections against below-median-income debtors on non-means test grounds (e.g., the discretionary dismissal power of paragraph (3)), whereas paragraph seven is a categorical bar on anyone – judges, trustees, the whole lot – from bringing a means test objection (i.e., paragraph (2)) against below-median-income debtors.

measure used to trigger a mandatory five-year plan and statutory budget in chapter 13.)

Section 101(10A)'s definition of "current monthly income" has little at all to do with current monthly income. Instead, it uses a six-month retrospective approach. It includes income from all sources, not just wages, such as interest on checking accounts, unemployment compensation, income tax refunds, or, in the case of a debtor who runs a small business, revenues and possibly accounts receivable (depending on accounting practices). It also includes amounts paid by others toward household expenses, §101(10A)(B). Out of the gates, we see the Code has nothing to do with what the IRS might think about as income, where we bet at least some of you were hoping to look for interpretative guidance. Sorry.

Making matters worse, neither does the Census Bureau give us any help. You might assume that because the Code directs comparison of the debtor's current monthly income with the state median income measured by the Census, those two measures of income would be comparable. Nope. The Census approach to determining income does not include sources such as capital gains; money received from the sale of property (unless the recipient was engaged in the business of selling such property); the value of income "in kind" as in food stamps; tax refunds; exchange of money between relatives living in the same household; gifts and lump-sum inheritances, insurance payments, and other types of lump-sum receipts, many (if not all) of which fall under section 101(10A)'s broad sweep. So what remains is a special bankruptcy definition of "income" unmoored from Census or IRS metrics. Note too that this disconnect between Bankruptcy Code income and Census Bureau income goes both ways. Recall the explicit exclusion of Social Security benefits from current monthly income (credit lobby scared by the AARP?). The Census Bureau *does* include this in its income measure, rendering the median income comparison of section 707(b)(7) all the more arbitrary.

The second challenge with the Code's gross income test is to find the right household size for purposes of identifying the comparison figure from the Census. The debtor's household size matters because usually (although not always) larger households in the general population have higher median incomes. But even with all the legislative ink spilled on the means test, Congress declined to define "household."

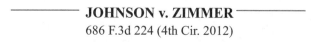

JOHNSON v. ZIMMER
686 F.3d 224 (4th Cir. 2012)

AGEE, Circuit Judge.

In this direct appeal from the United States Bankruptcy Court for the Eastern District of North Carolina, we address . . . how[] the "household" size of a debtor seeking bankruptcy relief to be calculated[.]   Upon receiving notice of the Debtor's motion for confirmation of a plan, the Debtor's ex-husband, William H. Zimmer ("the Creditor"), objected. The basis for the Creditor's objection was that the proposed plan overstated the Debtor's household size.

[T]he parties stipulated to the following facts: the Debtor and Creditor share joint custody of their two minor sons. Neither party pays child support; they share "expenses for clothing, school supplies, and other incidental expenses for their sons based on where the sons live when an expense is necessary." Out-of-pocket medical expenses are divided equally. By oral agreement, the Debtor's sons reside with her and are in her care and custody for 204 days each year. The Debtor's current husband has joint custody of three children from his previous marriage: two minor sons and a nineteen-year-old daughter. The Debtor's step-children reside with her and her husband approximately 180 days per year.

The Debtor . . . claimed a household of seven members, counting individually each person who resided in her home for any period of time within the past six months (i.e., the Debtor, her husband, her two children, and her three step-children). The Creditor asserted that the Debtor did not actually have seven members of her household because the five children and step-children did not live at her residence full-time. He contended that rather than simply counting the number of "heads on the bed" to determine household size, the Debtor's plan should use a method that better approximated the actual economic impact of each individual on the Debtor's expenses.

In examining the parties' dispute, the bankruptcy court observed that the Code does not define "household," there was no binding precedent on point, and that other bankruptcy courts followed three different approaches to define that term. As described in greater detail below, those three approaches are: the "heads-on-beds" approach that follows the Census Bureau's broad definition of a household as "all the people who occupy a housing unit," without regard to relationship, financial contributions, or financial dependency; the "income tax dependent" method derived from the Internal Revenue Manual's ("IRM") definition that examines which individuals either are or could be "included on the debtor's tax return as dependents"; and the "economic unit" approach that "assesses the number of individuals in the household who act as a single economic unit by including those who are financially dependent on the debtor, those who financially support the debtor, and those whose income and expenses are inter-mingled with the debtor's."

The bankruptcy court adopted a variation of the "economic unit" approach, first assessing the number of individuals whose income and expenses are intermingled with the Debtor's, and then calculating how much time any part-time residents were members of the Debtor's household. In adopting the "economic unit" approach, the bankruptcy court noted that the other two definitions were inconsistent with the purpose of the Code and were the least flexible in terms of adapting to an individual debtor's circumstances. In deciding that part-time residents should count as part-time members of the Debtor's "household," the bankruptcy court acknowledged that "[d]ividing children into fractions is not ideal," but concluded that this additional step in applying the economic unit approach best "capture[d] the nuances of familial support and bonds" and enabled the court to "account for dependents who reside with the debtor on a part-time basis . . . in calculating variable costs such as food, utilities, and out-of-pocket health care expenses." Accordingly, the court relied on the parties' stipulated facts to determine that each of the Debtor's two sons constituted .56 members of the Debtor's household (residing with her 204 days out of a possible 365), and that each of the Debtor's three step-children constituted .49 members of her household (residing with her 180 days out of a possible 365).

Implementing this fractional economic unit approach thus resulted in the Debtor having a total of 2.59 children in her household full-time, which the court then rounded up to three children. Thus, the Debtor, her husband, and the deemed three children yielded a "household" of five persons.

Despite the centrality of the term to the requisite analysis, the Code does not state how the size of a debtor's "household" . . . is to be calculated for determining his or her disposable income.

[W]ords that are not defined in the relevant statutory provisions are typically "interpreted as taking their ordinary, contemporary, common meaning." United States v. Lehman, 225 F.3d 426, 428 (4th Cir.2000) (quoting Perrin v. United States, 444 U.S. 37, 42, 100 S. Ct. 311, 62 L. Ed. 2d 199 (1979)). The Court "customarily turn[s] to dictionaries for help in determining whether a word in a statute has a plain or common meaning." Nat. Coalition for Students v. Allen, 152 F.3d 283, 289 (4th Cir.1998). In this instance, however, reviewing the dictionary definition of "household" does not resolve the matter because this term has multiple definitions of varying scope and consequence. For example, *Black's* defines the noun "household" as "1. A family living together. 2. A group of people who dwell under the same roof." *Black's Law Dictionary* 744 (7th ed.1999).

Context provides some guidance in this case, but ultimately does not resolve the fundamental uncertainty of what Congress intended "household" to mean. On the one hand, Congress used the word "household" as opposed to "family," "dependent child," or "dependent," all of which are used elsewhere in the surrounding and cross-referenced Code provisions. Consistent with the principle that "[t]he use of different terms within related statutes generally implies that different meanings were intended," this would often mean that Congress intended the term "household" to mean something other than what those terms mean. *See* Cunningham v. Scibana, 259 F.3d 303, 308 (4th Cir.2001) (quoting 2A Norman J. Singer, *Sutherland's Statutes and Statutory Construction,* §46.06, at 195 (6th ed.2000)). On the other hand, as set forth above, the dictionary definitions of "household" overlap with each of these terms to varying degrees, as "household" may or may not be defined to include the concept of familial connection or domestic interconnectedness.

[Section] 707(b) also refers to a debtor's "dependents" as opposed to his or her "household." Congress' use of "dependents" . . . would tend to suggest that although Congress used "dependent" and "household" at different points, they may nonetheless have related meanings. However, none of these approaches is directly required by the statutory language and is consequently based on inference and implication to one degree or another.

These are the hallmarks of statutory language that is anything but plain. Because the term "household" "lends itself to more than one reasonable interpretation," it is ambiguous. Accordingly, "our obligation is to find that interpretation which can most fairly be said to be imbedded in the statute, in the sense of being most harmonious with its scheme and the general purposes that Congress manifested." Id. Put differently, where statutory language is ambiguous, we "turn to other evidence to interpret the meaning of the provision," interpreting provisions harmoniously, where possible, or by reference to the legislative history, and always with the goal of ascertaining congressional intent. *See* New Cingular Wireless PCS, LLC v. Finley, 674 F.3d 225, 249 (4th Cir. 2012).

A handful of bankruptcy courts have adopted the heads-on-beds approach, using the Census Bureau definition of "household," although they use different—and in some cases no—reasons to explain why. Some bankruptcy courts have stated that this definition of "household" is simply its plain meaning. We are not persuaded that Congress intended for "household" to be so broadly defined. At the outset, nothing in §1325(b) directly or indirectly incorporates the Census Bureau's definition of "household." Although there is a cross-reference to the Census Bureau's median income tables, that is not sufficient to demonstrate a congressional intent to adopt the usage utilized by the Census Bureau in its wholly separate sphere of government work. Moreover, while the use of "household" as opposed to "family" or "dependents" (terms used elsewhere in [the Code] would indicate that the term means something different from those words, that does not automatically indicate that Congress intended for the term "household" to be synonymous with the Census Bureau's definition and refer to *any* person living in a particular residence. . . .

[Its definition of "all of the people, related an unrelated, who occupy a housing unit"] serves the Census Bureau's need to compile demographic information identifying the number of people in a particular geographic region. It is wholly unrelated to any bankruptcy purpose and does not serve the Code's objective of identifying a debtor's deductible monthly expenses and, ultimately, his or her disposable income. The calculation of a debtor's monthly income and expenses is aimed at ensuring that debtors pay the amount they can reasonably afford to pay to creditors. It makes little sense to allow debtors to broadly define their "households" so as to include individuals who have no actual financial impact on the debtor's expenses. This result would be entirely at odds with the stated purpose of the BAPCPA: "The heart of the bill's consumer bankruptcy reforms consists of the implementation of an income/expense screening mechanism ('needs-based bankruptcy relief' or 'means testing'), which is intended to ensure that debtors repay creditors the maximum they can afford." H.R. Rep. No. 109–31(I), *89.

Next, we consider whether the bankruptcy court erred in using the "economic unit" approach. The approach is flexible because it recognizes that a debtor's "household" may include non-family members and individuals who could not be claimed as dependents on the debtor's federal income tax return, but who nonetheless directly impact the debtor's financial situation. Thus, the entire purpose of identifying a debtor's household size is to use that number to determine his or her financial obligations and ability to pay. A definition of "household" that is also tailored to reflect a debtor's financial situation focuses directly upon the ultimate purpose of the Code.

The foregoing analysis does not end our inquiry, however, because the bankruptcy court opted to further refine the economic unit approach to account for the part-time members of the Debtor's "household." The Debtor contends that even if the bankruptcy court did not err in using an economic unit analysis to determine her household size, it nonetheless erred in dividing individuals (the Debtor's children and stepchildren) into "fractions and percentages" of her "household" when the Code "only speak[s] in terms of whole 'person[s]' and 'individuals.' " She points to the majority of courts that have used the economic unit approach to contend that the bankruptcy court relied [an] outlier case . . . to "carve[ ] children into fractions" and thus lead to "a contrived result."

We find no error in the bankruptcy court's method of applying the economic unit approach in a manner that accounted for part-time members of the Debtor's household. We recognize . . . that dividing individuals into fractional members of a household is less than ideal. At the same time, we recognize that the Debtor's situation is increasingly common in modern American life, and that the number of individuals with a financial relationship to a debtor may well vary depending on the day of the week and other circumstances. . . . Nor did the bankruptcy court err in exercising its discretion to accommodate this reality in the debtor's situation by representing the individuals as fractional full-time members of the household and then rounding to a whole number.

Because Congress' intent will most often be best implemented through a definition of "household" that is based on whether individuals operate as a single economic unit and are financially interdependent, we conclude the bankruptcy court did not err in applying this method to determine the Debtor's "household" size. Accordingly, we affirm the order of the bankruptcy court.

WILKINSON, Circuit Judge, dissenting:

While there is much in the majority's thoughtful opinion with which I agree, I cannot approve the bankruptcy court's decision to break a debtor's children into fractions. . . . That approach contravenes statutory text, allows judges to unilaterally update the Bankruptcy Code, and subjects debtors to needlessly intrusive and litigious proceedings. The bankruptcy court's approach embraces the startling conclusion that the meaning of the terms "individuals" and "dependents" in these provisions can encompass fractional human beings.

A textual rendering of statutes may seem inconvenient and even incorrect at times, but it has the long-term benefit of pushing Congress to precision and courts to observance of enacted law. The approach below may seem to reflect the economic realities of modern domestic life where children split time between parents, but it is hardly the only approach capable of doing so. Indeed, as the majority acknowledges, bankruptcy courts have a variety of other options available that may suit the circumstances of the case without so grievous an assault upon the statutory text.

The fact that Congress did not define "household," "individuals," or "dependents" in a definitions section does not entitle bankruptcy courts to take liberties with those terms. On the contrary, "[w]hen terms used in a statute are undefined, we give them their ordinary meaning," Hamilton v. Lanning, — U.S. —, 130 S. Ct. 2464, 2471, 177 L. Ed. 2d 23 (2010) (internal quotation marks and citation omitted), and the common meaning of the words "individual" and "dependent" does not include partial people. As the Supreme Court recently observed, the word " 'individual' ordinarily means '[a] human being, a person.' " Mohamad v. Palestinian Auth., — U.S. —, 132 S. Ct. 1702, 1707, 182 L. Ed. 2d 720 (2012) (quoting 7 Oxford English Dictionary 880 (2d ed. 1989)).

My disagreement with the lower court's approach does not end with its lack of textual support. I also object to its decision to update the Bankruptcy Code to address the increase in split custody arrangements. From the start, the bankruptcy court made clear that its interpretation would be guided by the need to "address[ ] the growing number of debtors with blended families and joint custody obligations without ignoring the economic realities of a debtor's living situation." It consequently chose to employ fractional units not because of any textual analysis, but out of a belief that this approach was "the best method the court can employ to 'adapt to dynamic economic change including various types of family structures regardless of size, shape, or composition.' "

These may be laudable goals, but in our legal system, we leave the updating of statutes to Congress. . . . Thus, while it may be true that many modern "households look increasingly different from the outmoded images of the 'traditional' family," In re Robinson, 449 B.R. 473, 482 (Bankr. E.D. Va. 2011), it is not our job to amend the Bankruptcy Code to account for these social changes.

Finally, by allowing judges to treat dependents as fractions, today's decision will require courts to conduct more intrusive and more litigious proceedings. . . . Assigning dependents precise percentages will almost always demand a more searching examination of a debtor's circumstances than an approach that treats them as whole beings.

In this case, for instance, the bankruptcy court divided the number of days of the year Johnson's sons and stepsons lived with her by 365 and then rounded off the results to two decimal places. Calculations involving this degree of precision are unlikely to be simple affairs. For while the parties in this case stipulated to the number of days Johnson's sons and stepsons reside with her each year, that will not always be the case. One can easily envision estranged parents disputing the details of their custody arrangements in bankruptcy court, especially when those details were not settled in or vary from a state court order. To be sure, treating children in joint custody arrangements as whole individuals may lead to some inaccuracies redounding to the benefit of either debtors or creditors, depending on the particular case. But that problem "is the inevitable result of a standardized formula like the means test." Ransom v. FIA Card Servs., 131 S. Ct. 716, 729 (2011). The same inaccuracy would occur, for example, if a debtor bore all the costs of child support while remaining frugal, as the means test would allow him to claim standardized expenses greater than his actual costs. Kops, 2012 WL 438623, at *5 n.18. In the interest of administrability, "Congress chose to tolerate the occasional peculiarity that a brighter-line test produces." Ransom, 131 S. Ct. at 729. We have no authority to rework that formula today.

I recognize that bankruptcy courts have a degree of discretion in applying the Code, and I do not seek to needlessly constrain their flexibility. But that discretion is not unlimited. "Bankruptcy courts lack authority to . . . depart from [rules] in the Code . . . to implement their own views of wise policy," In re A.G. Fin. Serv. Ctr., Inc., 395 F.3d 410, 413–14 (7th Cir.2005), and dividing a debtor's dependents into fractions falls outside those statutory bounds. Nor is such an approach even necessary to preserve flexibility in administering the Code. Eliminating the option of carving up children for purposes of the means test does not prevent bankruptcy courts from choosing from among multiple ways to calculate a debtor's household size or from taking the economic circumstances of a debtor into account. Judges can get along just fine in this area without embracing interpretations that co-opt the legislative function. With all respect for my friends who see this matter differently, I would reverse the judgment.

———

And the gross income bypass is the *easy* part of the means test! But we can be satisfied, at least, that after we have worked through the gross income test we have made the most important determination: is the debtor above or below median? Those who are below median—which is about 80% of all consumer filers according to the 2007 CBP data—may now bid a relieved farewell to section 707(b); they are free to file in chapter 7, and if they choose chapter 13, they can be done in three years of paying their "reasonable and necessary" expenses. The above-median debtors, however, must continue their descent into the depths of section 707(b)(2).

3. *The Net Income Determination*

The policy behind exempting debtors under a certain gross income from the means test is clear: they presumably earn so little that their case is not likely to be abusive. But to find whether a debtor "needs" to file chapter 7 based on a statutory calculation ought not to rest on gross income alone. Few would contend that a debtor with $1 more than the state's applicable median income who uses the lion's share of that money to pay for a drug regimen of cancer treatment is similarly situated to a debtor with the identical income but whose expenses consist of weekly facials, restaurant dinners, and expensive wine collections. Some people have more expenses than others, but it's the nature of those expenses even more than their size that should matter for abuse. Accordingly, section 707(b) analyzes debtors' *net incomes*, after allowable expenses are deducted, to gauge eligibility for chapter 7 relief. Those expenses are found in section 707(b)(2)(A)(ii). About one in ten chapter 7 filers—those who do not escape under the gross income bypass—must run this gauntlet. Its central characteristic is that it is mechanical, designed to insure that softy judges will not permit can-pay debtors into chapter 7.

a. Permissible Expenses

What is a debtor's true net income? That depends on what expenses we think a debtor *must* incur versus those we think a debtor *wants* to incur. Food yes, yachts no. Even food is open to debate: bread yes, caviar no. "Creditors should not be expected to pay for steak, when hamburger would do." In re Felske, 385 B.R. 649, 759 (Bankr. N.D. Ohio 2008). To be sure, this is what judges do all the time in chapter 13 plans when looking at challenges to debtors' proposed budgets of "reasonable and necessary" expenses. The pickle is that the means test was premised upon creditors' dissatisfaction with how the bankruptcy judges were doing in weeding out purportedly abusive chapter 7 filers under old section 707(b). To kill two birds with one stone by scrutinizing debtors' expenses *and* cabining bankruptcy judges, Congress designed a mechanical, statutory budget that is immune from interference by sentient jurists. While many federal programs deploy net income measures and while government data reveal what families actually expend on household expenses, Congress took a curious but revealing approach for what to put in this budget of permissible expenses. It turned to the IRS.

For years the IRS has negotiated with people who fail to pay their taxes. Instead of simply prosecuting and putting these people in jail or seizing their homes via tax liens, the IRS sometimes offers its own repayment plan. If the tax delinquent pays a certain monthly amount toward past-due taxes, the IRS defers asset seizure and prosecution. Since even tax deadbeats need to eat, the IRS has to determine permissible expenses to calculate net income available for tax repayment. The Service developed guidelines to inform field offices engaged in these colorful negotiations, and these guidelines include various lists of expense allowances. The IRS calls some "National Standards," for those imposed uniformly across the country, and "Local Standards" for those that vary with the debtor's residence. The Standards sometimes use sliding scales; for example, one person is allowed $301 a month for food, while a four-person household is allowed $765. (The IRS evidently believes that there are important economies of scale in meal preparation.) The Code's means test expressly defers to these IRS Guidelines for most expenses under section 707(b)(2). Whether Congress chose a budget for tax cheats for bankruptcy debtors to send an expressive message remains an open question.[10]

The U.S. Trustee Program's website reproduces the IRS expenses. http://www.justice.gov/ust/eo/bapcpa/20120501/meanstesting.htm. Although derivative of the IRS, the site goes further, for example, by breaking out mortgage costs from home operating costs. This is required for the Official Bankruptcy Form for the means test, Form B22. Apparently, the main reason to reference the IRS's guidelines is for "Other Necessary Expenses," which the U.S. Trustee's page doesn't bother to reproduce (perhaps because they are all allowed), but Form B22 breaks out these categories so filers have to do the legwork of calculating the amounts.

The means test does confer some discretion on judges, albeit modest and residual. For example, section 707(b)(2)(A)(ii)(I)'s final sentence allows judges to round up the National Standard's food and clothing allowance by up to 5% upon the debtor's showing such actual expenses are reasonable and necessary. And some deductions are allowed that are not even in the National Standards. See §707(b)(2)(A)(ii)(II) (elder care), (IV) (private schools). All these deductions are included on Form B22.

As the court in *Zimmer* noted above, the means test is hyper-rigid and seems to allow the applicable IRS expenses without regard to whether the debtor

---

10. The sources for and strictures of the National Standards are not entirely clear. The IRS website explains that the numbers are based on the Bureau of Labor Statistics and Consumer Expenditure Survey, but that it has flexibility on how much the families can deduct in the various categories. As one court explains:

> The IRM first sets "Expectations," and in paragraph 6 of section 5.15.1.1, states:
>
> The standard amounts set forth in the national and local guidelines are designed to account for basic living expenses. *In some cases, based on a taxpayers individual fact's [sic] and circumstances, it may be appropriate to deviate from the standard amount when failure to do so will cause the taxpayer economic hardship.* (emphasis added). . . . In re Kimbro, 389 B.R. 518, 528 (BAP 6th Cir. 2008), *rev'd and remanded on other grounds*, 409 F. App'x 930 (6th Cir. 2011).

Ironically, the bankruptcy courts do not enjoy the same discretion—at least not within the structure of 707(b)(2)(ii), which directs a uniform bright-line use of the IRS "Guidelines." If this isn't bizarre enough, the IRS has tried to avoid institutional responsibility for the use of its guidelines in bankruptcy by posting a disclaimer on its site that the Guidelines are *not* for bankruptcy use!

actually incurs them. Suppose a frugal debtor regularly spends only $250 per month on food, an amount the debtor would disclose in their budget of reasonable and necessary expenses on Official Form J (the monthly expense form, which existed before the means test and continues to be required). The means test per the National Standards provides for a fixed deduction of over $300 for a single individual. Is that a loophole for the skinny?

<hr>

In re SCOTT

457 B.R. 740 (Bankr. S.D. Ill. 2011)

GRANDY, Bankruptcy Judge.

Can a debtor whose secured debt payment on a car is less than the I.R.S. Standard receive the benefit of the full deduction? . . .

The local standard for a "transportation ownership/lease expense" is found at lines 28 (vehicle 1) and 29 (vehicle 2) [of Form B22A]. The I.R.S. Standard for such an expense in this district is $496.00 per vehicle. The debtors maintain that they are entitled to claim the entire I.R.S. Standard for each of their two vehicles based on a plain language interpretation of §707(b)(2)(A)(ii)(I). Specifically, the debtors focus on the portion of the statute that provides that "the debtor's monthly expenses *shall be* the debtor's applicable monthly expense amounts *specified under the National and Local Standards....*" 11 U.S.C. §707(b)(2)(A)(ii)(I) (emphasis added). As car payments are listed under the local standards on Form B22C and not as an "Other Necessary Expense[]" (which, under the statute, is limited to a debtor's *actual* monthly expense), debtors argue that they are entitled to claim the specified standard amount, despite the fact that their actual monthly vehicle payment is less. Under the debtors' interpretation, there is no room for equivocation concerning expenses: they *shall be* the national and local standards on certain 'applicable' expenses. . . .

[T]his Court believes that allowing the debtors to take the full I.R.S. Standard likewise gives meaning and distinction to the different categories of expenses in §707(b)(2)(A)(ii)(I). Once the debtors can show that they have a secured car ownership expense, they are entitled to claim the I.R.S. Standard because that is the "applicable" expense. Had Congress intended to limit the car ownership expense to actual cost, it could have said so. . . . Under the express language of §707(b)(2)(A)(ii)(I), only "the categories specified as Other Necessary Expenses" are to use actual expenses. There is no provision in §707(b)(2)(A)(ii)(I) for "reducing the specified amounts to the debtor's actual expenses...." *In re Barrett,* 371 B.R. 855, 858 (Bankr. S.D. Ill. 2007). Congress did not tell us to use actual expenses for the categories subject to the national and local standards, although it clearly knew how, had it chosen to do so. . . .

The Trustee's other . . . argument is that the debtors' approach frustrates BAPCPA's "overall purpose of ensuring that the debtors repay creditors to the extent that they can." Adopting the Trustee's position in the cases at bar would provide a greater return to unsecured creditors, as in each case, the debtors' disposable income would be increased by more than $100.00 per month. He argues that the I.R.S. Standard is not "reasonably necessary" as the term is used in §1325(b)(2) when the actual expense is less because that would not maximize the return to unsecured creditors.

Certainly, maximizing repayment to creditors was a primary goal in enacting BAPCPA. However, this Court believes that Congress intended to advance other policy objectives through BAPCPA as well. One such objective was the removal of judicial discretion in determining disposable income. As this Court previously stated in *In re Nance*:

> [F]ocusing on repayment to creditors as Congress' ultimate goal . . . ignore[s] other potential competing goals of Congress under BAPCPA, particularly the desire to eliminate judicial discretion. It is clear from the Chapter 7 means test, the adoption of standardized expense calculations for above-median debtors, and the calculation methods for determining 'projected disposable income' that a major goal of Congress was to replace judicial discretion with specific statutory standards and formulas.

371 B.R. 358, 366 (Bankr. S.D. Ill. 2007). *See also In re Rudler,* 388 B.R. 433, 439 (1st Cir. BAP 2008) ("Congress' intent in adding the means test was to create a more objective standard for establishing a presumption of abuse and to reduce judicial discretion in the process."); *Musselman v. eCast Settlement Corp.,* 394 B.R. 801, 812 (E.D.N.C. 2008) ("In enacting BAPCPA, Congress had more than one policy goal in mind. Beyond ensuring greater payouts by Chapter 13 debtors to their creditors, Congress, in its amendments to §1325(b) also sought to impose objective standards on Chapter 13 determination, thereby removing a degree of judicial flexibility in bankruptcy proceedings."); *In re Cutler,* 2009 WL 2044378 (Bankr. S.D. Ind. 2009) ("repayment to creditors may have been one of the goals behind BAPCPA, but Congress' intent in creating the means test under §707(b)(2) was to eliminate judicial discretion and replace it with a mathematical formula to determine abuse in Chapter 7 cases."). Permitting debtors to take the I.R.S. Standard furthers this goal by reducing judicial involvement. This Court recognizes that, by using a standardized approach to determining disposable income, anomalous results may occur. . . . The approach adopted by this Court still advances the goal of maximizing the return to creditors—it simply does so *within the framework prescribed by Congress and Form B22C* [which] tells us to measure the maximum return by using the applicable I.R.S. Standard—not actual.

Adopting the Trustee's approach would essentially bring this Court back to the pre-BAPCPA practice of evaluating disposable income based on the debtors'

Schedules I and J, a practice that was eliminated by Congress with the enactment of BAPCPA and creation of Form B22C.

＝＝＝＝＝

One way to think of *Scott*'s holding is that if the debtor's frugality allows her to incur lower food expenses than the IRS allows tax delinquents, that frugality should inure to her benefit and not perversely be used as evidence of abuse in declaring bankruptcy. (Was BAPCPA really worried about the frugal?) Certainly a contrary holding would create gluttonous incentives. The corollary is that even if a debtor regularly and honestly spends $400 each month on food, and even if a bankruptcy judge were to consider such an amount "reasonable and necessary," the means test doesn't care. Congress says buy in bulk, skip the organic produce, or just slim down.

This harshness of the means test's ambivalence toward a debtor's actual expenses—in contrast to chapter 13's treatment of below-median debtors (for whom reasonable necessity suffices to permit an expense)—is softened somewhat by provisions such as section 707(b)(2)(A)(ii)(V), which augments the IRS's Local Standards for housing and utility expenses by allowing deductions for the debtor's *actual* documented reasonable heating costs, even if higher than the guidelines. *But cf.* In re Trimarchi, 421 B.R. 914, 923 (Bankr. N.D. Ill. 2010) ("The Court finds a swimming pool is not a basic need required by the average American family or this family. . . . Here, the Debtor does not need [$250 monthly] to heat the pool.").

b. Permissible Debt Service

Section 707(b)(2)(A)(ii)(I) specifically prohibits monthly payments on debts to be included in the means test budget; "credit card bills" is not a permissible monthly expense. This makes some sense because part of the test is to see how much money is left over to pay creditors, and it would be oddly recursive accounting to include payments to those creditors already in calculating that surplus. But apparently not that odd! When it adopted the means test, Congress seemed concerned that the application of the strict IRS guidelines for transportation might require many debtors to give up their cars—to the great dissatisfaction of the car lenders. (Without the support of the car lenders, the proposed amendments would likely have never made it into law. See William C. Whitford, A History of the Automobile Lender Provisions of BAPCPA, 2007 U. Ill. L. Rev. 143 (2007)).

Congress responded by making secured debt an additional permitted deduction category under the means test, resulting in the odd insistence of no deductions for debts in one breath under section (b)(2)(A)(ii)(I) but the explicit allowance of their deduction for secured debts in the next under section

707(b)(2)(A)(iii). Note the omission of the "reasonable and necessary" qualifier so prevalent in the rest of the means test when it comes to the debtor's car. Well lobbied, Detroit. Home mortgage lenders also jumped aboard this gravy train (gravy car?). See id. The kicker is that section 707(b)(2)(A)(iii) allows deduction for "payments scheduled as contractually due," which suggests the whole secured debt contractual payment is allowed, not just the lesser value of the allowed secured claim if the loan is underwater.

——————— In re FREDMAN ———————
471 B.R. 540 (Bankr. S.D. Ill. 2012)

GRANDY, Bankruptcy Judge.

In a matter of first impression in this District, the Court is asked to decide whether above-median chapter 7 debtors, in performing the means test, may deduct mortgage payments on real estate that they intend to surrender.

The relevant facts, taken from the record of this case, are not in dispute. The debtors resided in a home in Englewood, Colorado from October 2001 until August 2009. The home was encumbered by a first mortgage of $232,479.15 held by Chase Home Finance LLC, with monthly payments of $1,782.08. . . . After Mr. Fredman suffered the loss of a lucrative employment situation and eventually settled in a lower-paying position, the debtors ceased making mortgage payments for this home in December 2010. No payments were made on the home after that date.

Approximately six months later, on June 7, 2011, when they filed a chapter 7 petition for relief, the debtors were living in a home that they owned in Marion, Illinois. With a current monthly income of $8,242.06, the debtors were considered to be above the median income for a family of their size in Illinois. 11 U.S.C. §707(b)(7). The Marion home was encumbered by a mortgage held by Chase Home Finance LLC for $48,789.19, with monthly payments of $546.32. The debtors listed both the Colorado and the Marion homes on Schedules A and D. The debtors' Statement of Intention, filed on the petition date, declared "under penalty of perjury" that they intended to surrender the Colorado home. . . . In addition, their intent to surrender the Colorado home was reflected by the absence of mortgage payments for the Colorado home on line 20B(b) of the B22A form, calling for "Average Monthly Payment for any debts secured by your home, if any, as stated in Line 42" and by their claim of a homestead exemption for the Marion home.

Nonetheless, on line 42 of the B22A form, entitled "Future payments on secured claims," the debtors included payments for the . . . mortgages on the to-be-surrendered Colorado home along with the mortgage payment for the Marion home. The inclusion of the Colorado mortgage payments on lines 42(a) and (c) allowed the debtors to include $1,973.23 in phantom monthly debt payments in the figure of $8,469.39 that they placed on line 47 of the B22A form, constituting the "[t]otal of all deductions allowed under §707(b)(2)." After further computation, the inclusion of the phantom Colorado mortgage payments resulted in the debtors having a negative "60–month disposable income under §707(b)(2)" of -$13,639.80 [and] that they were entitled to proceed in a chapter 7 case.

With the enactment of the Bankruptcy Abuse Prevention and Consumer Protection Act of 2005 (BAPCPA), 11 U.S.C. §707(b) was amended to add a screening mechanism, known as the "means test." The purpose of the means test is to weed out chapter 7 debtors who are capable of funding a chapter 13 case. The issue before the Court today centers on a provision of the means test that allows a debtor to take deductions for certain secured debts.

[T]he parties in the instant case call upon the Court to find the meaning of the phrase "scheduled as contractually due to secured creditors in each month of the 60 months following the date of the filing of the petition," which phrase appears in §707(b)(2)(A)(iii)(I). The UST contends that the phrase in question prevents the Fredmans from deducting the mortgage payments on the Colorado home that they will be surrendering because they have not shown the payments as contractually due on their schedules. Rather, according to the UST, the debtors' schedules show that they will not make the payments during the 60-month period following the date of the filing of the bankruptcy petition. The Fredmans counter that the phrase permits such a deduction because the Colorado mortgages remained contractually due on the petition date despite the debtors' expressed intention to surrender the home to the lenders. Their dispute centers upon two points: (1) the meaning of the term "scheduled as" and (2) whether the phrase at issue demands a mechanical, snap-shot approach taken on the petition date or a realistic, forward-looking approach that takes into account the inevitable surrender of the home. . . .

The Meaning of "Scheduled As"

[The Court explored whether "scheduled as contractually due" means something like "due on certain upcoming dates per the contract," as many bankruptcy courts had held, in which case the debtors' phantom mortgage payments most certainly were "scheduled as contractually due," or whether it means something like "listed on the debtor's schedules as a contractual debt to be paid out during the bankruptcy plan," in which case the to-be-surrendered phantom mortgage was surely not *scheduled* as contractually due. It went with the latter.–Eds.]

Mechanical vs. Realistic Approach

The Court turns now to the second point of contention: whether §707(b)(2)(A)(iii)(I) demands a mechanical, snap-shot approach or a realistic, forward-looking approach. The debtors urge the Court to adopt the majority view, which, historically, has applied a mechanical approach rather than a forward-looking approach in interpreting the embattled phrase "scheduled as contractually due to secured creditors in each month of the 60 months following the date of the filing of the petition." 11 U.S.C. §707(b)(2)(A)(iii)(I). Courts taking the majority view have reasoned that at the time a chapter 7 debtor files a bankruptcy petition and completes the means test calculation in form B22A, the debtor will not yet have relinquished the secured property slated for surrender on the Statement of Intention. E.g., In re Rudler, 576 F.3d at 45. According to this approach, both the B22A form and the statute ask "in the present tense" for a list of debts secured by property. Id. at 46. "The statutory provision is stated comprehensively, asking for the total of all payments scheduled during the five-year period, without reference to whether other documents filed in connection with the bankruptcy show that the payments are likely to stop during that period." Id.

Proponents of the mechanical approach argue that the means test is intended to determine a debtor's eligibility for chapter 7 relief at a specific point in time without regard to the accuracy of that determination. Id. at 48–49. "[T]he statute sets allowable expenses by means of several different methods, and, '[l]ike section 707(b)(2)(A)(iii), many other provisions of the means test appear to operate contrary to the goal of accurately determining the amount of income that would actually be available for payments to unsecured creditors in a Chapter 13 case.'" Id. at 48 (quoting In re Walker, No. 05–15010–WHD, 2006 WL 1314125, at *6 (Bankr. N.D. Ga. May 1, 2006)). This point is illustrated by the calculation of current monthly income as a six-month pre-petition window that ignores a changed state of affairs on the date of bankruptcy filing, id. at 48, and by the use of standardized deduction amounts for certain types of expenses that may not accurately reflect the amount of actual expenses. Id. at 49 (citing In re Hayes, 376 B.R. at 65; In re Randle, 358 B.R. 360, 364 (Bankr. N.D. Ill. 2006), aff'd, No. 07 C 631, 2007 WL 2668727 (N.D. Ill. Jul. 20, 2007); In re Walker, 2006 WL 1314125, at *7).

The majority viewpoint maintains that the plain language of the statute demands a rigid formula and that it does not impose an absurd methodology for assessing abuse. Rudler, 576 F.3d at 50. Rather, according to this approach, the mechanical treatment is consistent with Congress's intent to limit the bankruptcy court's discretion to determine abuse on a case-by-case basis. Id. . . .

In contrast, the minority position, historically, allows the Court to take into account a debtor's expressed intent to surrender secured property even if the act of surrender has not been completed on the bankruptcy petition date. . . . To allow deductions for payments that "would have been due, but never paid," id. at 598, ignores that "[a] primary intent of Congress in the passage of BAPCPA was to ensure that those debtors who can pay their debts do so." Id. at 600 (citing In re Hardacre, 338 B.R. 718, 725 (Bankr. N.D. Tex. 2006); 151 Cong. Rec. 2459 at 2469–70 (March 10, 2005)). . . .

[T]he Supreme Court rejected a mechanical approach while evaluating the debtor's income in the case of Hamilton v. Lanning, —— U.S. ——, 130 S. Ct. 2464, 177 L. Ed. 2d 23 (2010). In Lanning, the Supreme Court determined that, in calculating a chapter 13 debtor's projected disposable income, bankruptcy courts may use a forward looking approach to "account for changes in the debtor's income or expenses that are known or virtually certain at the time of confirmation." Id. at 2478. Ms. Lanning's predicament began with a one-time buyout from her former employer that greatly inflated her income in the six-month period preceding her bankruptcy filing and that resulted in her having monthly disposable income of $1,114.98 on form B22C.

The Supreme Court rejected the trustee's mechanical approach to determining "projected disposable income" as "unpersuasive," id. at 2474, because it failed to take into account the undisputed fact that Ms. Lanning's "actual income was insufficient to make payments in that amount." Id. at 2470. Instead, after analyzing the text of §1325 and recognizing that pre-BAPCPA practice allowing discretion had not been discarded with the BAPCPA amendments, the Court adopted the "forward looking approach" as the "correct" approach in calculating a debtor's "projected disposable income." Id. at 2469. The Court determined that "the Code does not insist upon rigid adherence to the mechanical approach in all cases." Id. at 2477.

Following Lanning, in Ransom v. FIA Card Services, N.A., —— U.S. ——, 131 S. Ct. 716, 178 L. Ed. 2d 603 (2011), the Supreme Court examined the expense side of the means test in arriving at a chapter 13 debtor's disposable income [for an above-median income debtor—Eds.] Id. at 721-23. The Court held that a chapter 13 debtor who owned his or her vehicle outright, without a loan or lease payment, was not entitled to claim an ownership expense under §707(b)(2)(A)(ii)(I) since the expense was not "applicable" to that debtor. The lack of a vehicle payment disqualified Mr. Ransom from taking the I.R.S. standard deduction on form B22C because the deduction was not "appropriate, relevant, suitable, or fit" for him. Id. at 724. The Court reasoned that "a deduction is so appropriate only if the debtor has costs corresponding to the category covered by the table—that is, only if the debtor will incur that kind of expense during the life of the plan." Id. Turning to the statutory purpose, the Court instructed:

> Congress designed the means test to measure debtors' disposable income and, in that way, "to ensure that [they] repay creditors the maximum they can afford." H.R. Rep., at 2. This purpose is best achieved by interpreting the means test, consistent with the statutory text, to reflect a debtor's ability to afford repayment. Cf. Hamilton, 560 U.S., at ——, 130 S. Ct., at 2475-2476 (rejecting an interpretation of the Bankruptcy Code that "would produce [the] senseless resul[t]" of "deny[ing] creditors payments that the debtor could easily make").

Ransom, 131 S. Ct. at 725.

Having pointed out that chapter 13 means testing is derived from that of chapter 7, the Supreme Court did not draw a distinction between the chapters in denying the deduction set forth in §707(b)(2)(A)(ii)(I) for vehicle-ownership costs. If a debtor did not have a loan or lease payment on a car, that debtor could not claim a phantom car ownership expense under either chapter 13 or chapter 7 means testing. Id. at 723 & n.4. A fictitious expense should not be allowed either during the life of a chapter 13 debtor's plan or in determining the suitability of a debtor's chapter 7 case.

In chapter 7 cases . . . there continues to be a split of authority on the issue at hand, with the majority of cases adopting the mechanical approach. . . . The majority view is followed in In re Rivers, 466 B.R. 558, 566-67 (Bankr. M.D. Fla. 2012) (Lanning and Ransom do not affect the deductions that a chapter 7 debtor may claim under the means test of §707(b)(2), which functions as a screening mechanism in chapter 7 and, like eligibility under 11 U.S.C. §109, should be determined as of the petition date), In re Sonntag, No. 10-1749, 2011 WL 3902999, at *3-4 (Bankr. N.D. W.Va. Sept. 6, 2011) (after Lanning and Ransom, "[g]rafting the forward looking approach now required in Chapter 13 cases onto the means test analysis in Chapter 7 cases is not required, nor justified").

The contrasting position is adopted in *In re Clary,* No. 6:11-bk-04556-ABB, 2012 WL 868717, at (Bankr. M.D. Fla. Mar. 14, 2012) (relying on Ransom to find that "[p]ermitting debtors to claim expenses they will not actually pay frustrates legislative intent and creates an inaccurate picture of their financial reality"). . . .

[T]his Bankruptcy Court can find no basis for defining the phrase one way when it is incorporated by reference into chapter 13 means testing, 11 U.S.C. §1325(b)(3), and a different way when it is applied in chapter 7 means testing. The rules of statutory construction demand that a discrete provision be read consistently wherever it appears in the same statute. . . .

While much has been made of Congress' desire to remove judicial discretion in application of the means test, there is no indication that this goal was intended to overshadow the overall goal of directing financially able debtors into chapter 13 cases. *See, e.g.,* In re Ransom, 131 S. Ct. at 729 ("BAPCPA's core purpose [is] ensuring that debtors devote their full disposable income to repaying creditors"). . . .

Based on the above analysis, this Court holds that to harmonize the language of §707(b)(2)(A)(iii) with the intent of the drafters, and to avoid a senseless result, the Fredmans may not deduct the $1,973.23 phantom monthly mortgage payments.

A "phantom mortgage" is something only a lawyer could love (which may explain the passionate dispute over the issue). In case you thought that at least the income issue was resolved, see, e.g., Danielson v. Flores, 692 F.3d 1021 (9th Cir. 2012) (holding *Lanning* inapplicable to chapter 7 and noting circuit split) (divided opinion), *rehearing en banc granted*, 704 F.3d 1067 (2012) (en banc). In both *Lanning* and *Ransom*, incidentally, the Court's majority was large. Only Justice Scalia dissented, all by himself, but in both cases. In *Lanning*, he expressed textual incredulity that the section 1325(b)(3)'s instruction to use "current monthly income," defined in the Code with an unambiguous retrospective focus should be interpreted as meaning only use current monthly income and its six-month lookback as a mere starting presumption, capable of rebuttal by "known or virtually certain" future income. *Lanning*, 130 S. Ct. at 2478. And in *Ransom* he once again repeated that if detractors of the means test think it is overly mechanical they should direct their concerns to Congress. It would appear the "plain meaning" cohort on the Supreme Court is becoming a lonelier one.

4. The Actual Test: "Presumption" of Abuse

Now the actual means test: once the debtor's net income under section 707(b)(2)(A)(ii) has been calculated, the debtor compares it to the formula in section 707(b)(2)(A)(i). The means test is flunked and abuse is presumed if the debtor's net income is greater than a certain amount, which, maddeningly, is contingent upon the debtor's total unsecured nonpriority debt.

Here is the test for whether the debtor passes: First, take the debtor's monthly net income and multiply it by sixty months (five years), which we call the debtor's "five-year payback" (because it assumes all net income goes toward paying unsecured creditors for the maximum length of a chapter 13 plan). Abuse is presumed if the five-year payback equals or exceeds the *lower* of two figures: (1) $12,475; *or* (2) 25% of the debtor's total unsecured nonpriority debt (down to a floor of $7,475).

Let's unpack what's going on. It helps to start at the end and calculate (2) from above: 25% of the total unsecured debt. Congress thinks if your five-year payback is more than this number—a quarter of what you owe your unsecured creditors—it's abusive for you to be in chapter 7 instead of 13 and tough it out. Regarding number (1), it also thinks you're abusing the system if your five-year payback is $12,475, period. The thinking there seems to be that's just a lot of money to pay in the abstract, even if it's only a fraction of what you owe your creditors.

But don't forget the floor of $7,475 to (2), from above. Think of that floor as a safety valve. Congress seems to think that if that's really all you can scrounge up to pay over five years after you've taken all the means test deductions—less than a paltry $1,500 per year—you're just not doing that well and so can't be abusing the system by filing for chapter 7 (even if that small amount is more than 25% of your total unsecured debt). Now when you look at section 707(b)(2)(A)(i) you will see how this all falls into place. (You're welcome.)

Another way to understand this tangle is to think of means test debtors as falling into three categories: the Happy—debtors whose monthly net income is less than $124 (five-year payback of only $7,475)—who all pass the test automatically; the Sad—debtors whose monthly net income is more than $195 (five-year payback of $12,475)—who all fail the screen automatically; and the Uncertain Middle—debtors falling between these two poles—who pass *only if* their five-year payback is less than 25% of unsecured, nonpriority debt. For example, if a debtor owed $28,000 unsecured and had means test monthly net income of $125 (five-year payback of $7,500), the presumption of abuse would arise. This is because the five-year payback of $7,500, even though well under $12,475, is $500 greater than $7,000 (i.e., 25% of the total unsecured debt of $28,000) and is $25 greater than the floor of $7,475. Off to chapter 13 for this abuser—unless she can "rebut" the presumption.

Speaking of which, just how *does* one rebut the presumption? If the net income test shows merely a *presumption* of abuse, then perhaps it can by rebutted introducing evidence showing a non-abusive, legitimate reason to file for bankruptcy, such as perhaps years of struggling with debts and the incursion of those liabilities through non-extravagant means. Nope. Although nominally captioned a "rebuttal" of the means test, section 707(b)(2)(B)(i) clarifies the *only* way to rebut it is to show "special circumstances, such as a serious medical condition or a call or order to active duty in the Armed Forces . . . that justify additional expenses or adjustments of current monthly income."

The "rebuttal" thus works *only* if the debtor can prove documentable changes in income or expenses that allow the debtor to pass the means test. See §707(b)(2)(B)(iv). In other words, it's just an additional category of discretionary inputs into the means test; it is not a way of escaping the eligibility bar that is the output of the formula. Evidence of virtuous work ethic and sterling character are irrelevant to the presumption of abuse. As one of us puts it:

> The operation of the means test enables the debtors to challenge the metric, but not the merits, of their surplus income. Professors at law schools . . . that strip faculty of jurisdiction to change grades after submission to the registrar but provide an exception for mistabulated grades should find this framework familiar. . . . To say that it creates a "rebuttable presumption" that the submitted grade is the final grade when the only way of rebutting the presumption is to show that the grade was added up incorrectly is doublespeak of the highest order. It is not a *presumption*, let alone a rebuttable one, that submitted grades are final. It is a *rule* that submitted grades are final, absent calculation error.

John Pottow, The Totality of the Circumstances of the Debtor's Financial Situation in a Post-Means Test World, 71 Mo. L Rev. 1053, 1059-60. Perhaps pushing back against this straightjacket, courts have been flexible in finding "special circumstances," such as extra housing expenses for special needs children, high commuting costs, student loan payments, and repaying a 401(k) loan. Compare In re Cribbs, 387 B.R. 324, Bankr. S.D. Ga. (2008) (special circumstances for loan taken out to repay creditors in attempt to avoid bankruptcy), with In re Egebjerg, 574 F.3d 1045 (9th Cir. 2009) (pension loans are not special circumstances).

Whew! What a lot of work to shake money out of the pockets of the people who want to file bankruptcy. With more than a million consumer filings annually, attorneys and courts have routinized and computerized much of the undertaking. Nearly all attorneys use software that is programmed with the IRS expenses and spits out a red or green light on the means test (it works much like tax preparation software.) But with substantial variations around the country due both to the many open legal issues arising under the law and to the factual variation of each debtor's individual expenses, challenges still abound.

This complexity burden is not borne solely by the debtor; the U.S. Trustee's office is required to look at every case filed by an individual debtor to see if the presumption of abuse is triggered and to file a statement reporting its finding that is sent to every creditor. §704(b)(1). If the debtor is above median income, the office either files a motion to dismiss or convert the case if presumptive abuse is present or a statement explaining why it has not done so. §704(b)(2). These "declination" statements and the required review are not cheap. They subsume a substantial amount of resources of the U.S. Trustee Program and add uncertainty to the supposedly uniform means test approach.

C. CHAPTER 13 IN A MEANS TEST WORLD

Although the means test's location in section 707(b) suggests its primary function is as the eligibility screen to chapter 7, do not forget its second major role in the Code: the statutory budget for above-median income debtors in chapter 13. §1325(b)(3). Congress has determined that the surplus amount that remains from such above-median debtors' incomes after the means test expenses are deducted must be paid each month to their repayment plans, period.

Oddly, the Code dictates this compulsory means test budget is for *all* above-median chapter 13 filers, regardless of whether they passed or flunked the means test for chapter 7. In other words, the statutory budget applies to even those above-median debtors who chose to file chapter 13 voluntarily after having passed the means test and been eligible for chapter 7. It is hard to see why a

Congress that wanted to see fewer chapter 7 cases and more chapter 13 cases would impose tougher rules on above-median-income chapter 13 volunteers, creating a marginal incentive on them to choose chapter 7, but that's what the Code says. §1325(b)(4)(A)(ii). Does this seemingly clear text create "absurd" results?

Subject perhaps to this last point, the means test thus does double service to implement the intent of Congress in BAPCPA. It first of all is used as a screen to force some people into chapter 13, and it is then secondarily used as a forced budget on those conscripts to dictate what will be allowed as their permissible expenses during their five-year stay. In fact, given the data already discussed that the overwhelmingly majority of chapter 7 debtors have income under the applicable median—the gross income bypass that renders the means test irrelevant—the means test's role as a chapter 7 eligibility bar is much less relevant in actual case outcomes than its role as the required chapter 13 budget for above-median income debtors, a group that makes up more than one-third of chapter 13 filers. To see how it all fits together, the following diagram may be of some help.

Figure 1. Consumer Bankruptcy: Chapter 7, Traditional Chapter 13 or the New Chapter 13?

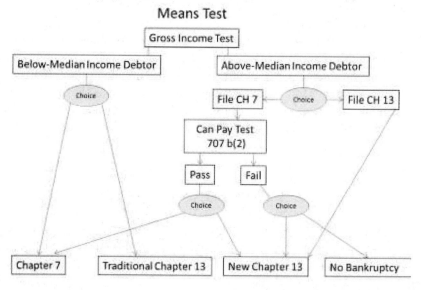

We close on a note about reality. Above-median-income debtors must live on the statutory budget for five full years (their applicable commitment period), regardless what their current monthly expenses actually are. For some, that may require some belt-tightening or relocating to different housing. For others, it may simply mean they can't make it through chapter 13, and they will convert into chapter 7 if means-test eligible. For families who can't make it on the budget in chapter 13 and who are statutorily barred from chapter 7, that may mean no relief under the federal Bankruptcy Code from creditors at all.

Indeed, the bizarreness of using a six-month retrospective figure for "current" monthly income and using fixed categories unrelated to actual expenses under the IRS National Guidelines in dictating a debtor's five-year budget likely explains the impulse of the Supreme Court cases, like *Lanning* and *Ransom*, to fudge BAPCPA's strict text. Both of those, it is no coincidence, were chapter 13 cases, in which the divergence of statutory budget from reality proved too much for the Court. As the *Fredman* court notes, these means test precedents may or may not apply when that mechanical and discretion-stripping test is used as the screen in chapter 7. In the next assignment, we turn to the other parts of the Code that courts and litigants use to reinsert flexibility and judgment into the system and the strategic choices that debtors face as a result.

Problem Set 12

12.1. Marissa Allegretti comes into your office in Detroit to see you about filing for bankruptcy. She explains that when the accounting firm she worked for closed, she scraped by on $650 a month unemployment for nearly six months, running up a pile of bills. Four months ago, she found a good job. Her base pay is $4,100 a month, but she has worked every weekend and as many late nights as she could since she joined the company, bringing in overtime that adds another $2,000 each month. She is putting everything she can into catching up on her mortgage payments, and she is making good progress. Even so, she says that she is struggling with her credit cards, with those debts multiplying at 29.99% interest.

You ask about her personal circumstances, and Marissa explains that she and her ex-husband, Tommy, share custody of their son Jamal. At the divorce five years ago, Marissa was granted $1,000 a month in child support. Her ex never paid, but he buys clothes for the boy and he has been paying $3,000 each semester for tuition at the local Catholic school, so Marissa hasn't pushed the point.

Is Marissa eligible for chapter 7? See §§101(10A), 707(b)(6), (b)(7). What advice do you give her at this point? Marissa can barely scrape together your standard $800 fee; how aggressive can she afford for you to be?

12.2. Eduardo and Sydney came to see you about filing for bankruptcy. They live near your office in Montgomery County, a suburb of Philadelphia. Both are in their mid-30s. Over the past six months, Eduardo's earnings averaged $6,600 a month as an auto mechanic, and Sydney's job as a fourth grade teacher at the nearby primary school averaged $5,200 per month (gross). They have two children, a kindergartener and an 18-month-old baby. The younger child was born with a serious heart problem. He had three major surgeries and now lives on a regimen of drugs and monitoring. Even though they have health insurance, the expenses for the baby have left them about $100,000 in debt. Some of it is medical co-pays and services, supplies and drugs that weren't covered, and some was credit card debt they ran up when Sydney took a seven-month leave from her job last year during the surgeries and recuperations and Eduardo too missed a lot of time from work. By skipping other payments and falling behind on everything else, Eduardo and Sydney have been paying about $600 a month on these bills, but that doesn't even cover the interest on the credit cards. Every month, the pile of bills gets higher.

Sydney and Eduardo live in a small three-bedroom house on a busy street. Their monthly payments are high because they had no money for a down payment, so they financed 100% of the purchase price. With their already-damaged credit, that gave them a high interest rate and a high payment. But they are proud of the fact that they have remained current on their mortgage.

You ask Eduardo and Sydney to work with your paralegal to come up with a list of their monthly expenses. They are sure about some parts, like income and taxes, because those are on their paystubs, but they are less sure about expenses. Here's what they identify:

EXPENSES	AMOUNT
Home mortgage (principal, interest, taxes & insurance)	$2,450
Utilities (water, gas, sewage, landline phone)	$190
Internet	$35
Satellite television	$75
Cell phone (basic service phones for Sydney and Eduardo)	$30
Honda Odyssey (principal, interest, required insurance)	$650
Gas and maintenance for minivan	$190
Food	$1,000
Cleaning supplies	$20
Personal care (haircuts, etc.)	$25
Clothing	$500
Laundry and dry cleaning	$10
Miscellaneous (newspapers, dog food, etc.)	$50
Lunch money for Sydney, Eduardo, kindergartener	$100
Daycare for baby, after school care for kindergartener	$1,200
Drugs, other health care supplies for baby	$250
Health insurance	$940
Social Security and income taxes	$3,394
Life insurance, Sydney and Eduardo	$200
TOTAL	$11,309

Are Eduardo and Sydney eligible for chapter 7? Do you have any additional questions or advice for them? If they rented the next-door house for the same monthly payment, would it make a difference? §707(b)(2). Use Form B22A to complete the problem, but skip line 45.

12.3. You have worked through the means test numbers for Michael Negron, a competitive skateboarder who seems to have run up $30,000 in general unsecured debt after he broke his leg last year. He rents a modest apartment and he drives an old clunker. His income over the past six months puts him above the median for a one-earner family in his state, and after allowable expenses, Michael seems to have available about $150 a month. His income has been very erratic as he tries to make a comeback, and he's not even sure if the leg is OK or will ever be. He is very reluctant to commit to a chapter 13 plan. Do you have any advice to make him eligible for chapter 7? §§707(b)(2)(B)(iv); 707(b)(2)(A)(iii); 707(b)(1); 101(12A); 526(a)(4).

12.4. Dara Faris and Katharine Roller met in law school and stayed together as a couple for seven years. Their finances were kind of a mess, partially co-mingled, partially separate. They are discussing how to divide their property as they go their separate ways. Both cars (the Subaru and the Jeep Wrangler) are in Kate's name; Dara has agreed she will take over the car payments of the Subaru she regularly drives but will leave title in Kate's name to save money on the state transfer and registration fees. That's fine with Kate, especially since they both know the Subaru is worth less than the loan on the car. The discussions are all quite amicable. Underwater on credit cards, Kate is getting ready to file chapter 13 pro se. Kate would pass the means test despite having above-median income, but chapter 7 is out because of some precious and sentimental non-exempt property she wants to keep. Recognizing she is above-median, she is OK with doing a five-year plan and with making the payments the means test requires as her budget. As Kate waves goodbye to Dara, do you see her chapter 13 as easy-peasy or will the car situation create grief? §1325(b)(3), 707(b)(2)(A)(iii); §1329.

12.5. Ken Lyarre was a phenomenally successful CEO, twice featured on the cover of *Business Week*. The first time was when his privately owned string of diet centers took the health and fitness market by storm, and the second when he lost a class-action lawsuit against him for violations of state consumer protection laws and the jury returned a verdict of a nice, round $1 billion. Ken's lawyers are planning an appeal, but they can't seem to make eye contact with him when they discuss his chances.

Ken thinks he has a better strategy: chapter 7 liquidation. He has about $1 million in assets lying around loose; the rest of his portfolio is in various spendthrift and offshore trusts, and he says he is glad to give that $1 million to deal with the verdict. His future income, drawn from the trusts, will be about $2 million annually. Is Ken eligible for chapter 7? See §707(a), (b)(1), (b)(2). *Cf.* §523(a)(2)(A), (4).

Assignment 13.
Chapter Choice

Nothing is more central to a debtor's fate than choice of the chapter under which to file a petition. That choice determines what relief the debtor can seek in bankruptcy. It also greatly affects the creditors' claims and what, if anything, the creditors can do to protect themselves. The means test of the prior assignment is a complex statutory maze, but it is only one of the puzzles that debtors and their attorneys must solve in making that all-important chapter choice.

Section 109(e) and the means test are statutory bars to eligibility to chapters 13 and 7 respectively that operate on the "front end," blocking debtors from proceeding. Yet there are also "back end" statutory constraints on relief that a debtor must consider in choosing chapters. These provisions operate much more discretionarily and hence present a trickier moving target for the attorney to gauge up front. Compounding this challenge are extra-legal concerns that bear on chapter choice, such as attorneys' fees, client counseling practices, and even local legal culture. In this Assignment we turn first to these back-end statutory restrictions and then consider the strategic choices and risk-benefit analyses of chapter choice. There's less dense statute to slog through than the means test, but don't let that lull you into thinking these issues aren't equally vital to debtors and the bankruptcy system.

A. STATUTORY CONSIDERATIONS

We begin with a look at the explicit statutory constraints on chapter choice.

1. Discretionary Dismissal From Chapter 7: Bad Faith and Totality of the Circumstances

Even if the putative chapter 7 filer survives the means test screen, there is always the risk of discretionary dismissal under section 707(b)(3). This residual standard covers all consumer debt filers, not just the above-medians. Subparagraph (A) seems straightforward, if undefined; "bad faith" is never welcome from those seeking a federal discharge of their debts. But what about (B)? This "totality of the circumstances" language seems to invite broad consideration of equitable factors, perhaps similar to the ones used to gauge "substantial abuse" in the pre-means test world. (Think back to the Shaws from last assignment and their new bedroom suite.)

This seemingly flexible, multi-prong "totality" standard must apply, however, in a straightjacketed, post-means test world. So are the old cases under former section 707(b) still good law on what constitutes "abuse" of chapter 7, or does the addition of the means test now eliminate some of the issues that courts previously got to police with the totality test? Suppose a judge thinks the means test is just too darned generous (particularly when the debtor's actual expenditures are below the IRS limits) and faces a debtor with a monthly net income of only $100, who thus passes the means test formula. Can the judge boot that debtor out of chapter 7 because $100, in that judge's mind, is a lot of money that could go toward repaying creditors and it is "abusive" for the debtor not to be making payments in chapter 13? After all, it is harder to imagine a broader swath of discretion than the "totality of the circumstances." Is such a dismissal a savvy use of statutorily-conferred discretion or a judicial arrogation of power?

——————— **In re DEUTSCHER** ———————
419 B.R. 42 (Bankr. N.D. Ill. 2009)

BARBOSA, Bankruptcy Judge.

The Debtors filed a voluntary petition for relief under Chapter 7 of the Bankruptcy Code with the Court on November 6, 2008. According to the Debtors' schedules, they have $336,752 in secured debt, $2,220 in unsecured priority debt, and $61,817 in unsecured nonpriority debt. The Debtors have admitted that their obligations are primarily consumer debts. Over half of their secured debt, or $177,782, is from a loan used to purchase a 42-foot Silverton yacht, purchased by the Debtors in September 2007. Another $11,000 is from the purchase in August 2008 of a 2006 15-foot Sea Doo Sportsliner boat, and $30,000 is from the purchase of a 2008 MKZ Lincoln SUV in June 2008. . . . The Debtors do not need the boats for work. . . . Although the Debtors' income is above the median for an Illinois household of two, there is no presumption of abuse under 11 U.S.C. §§707(a) and 707(b)(2) (the "means test"), largely because of the large secured debt payments.

As the Seventh Circuit Court of Appeals has stated, failing the means test simply means that the debtor's petition is not presumed abusive. . . . [T]he UST can still request dismissal . . . under section 707(b)(3), either for bad faith or based on the totality of circumstances (which can take into consideration a debtor's actual income and expenses). Ross-Tousey v. Neary (In re Ross-Tousey), 549 F.3d 1148, 1161-62 (7th Cir. 2008). Under the totality of the circumstances test, "a debtor's ability to pay may be the most relevant factor, but the Court must also consider: (1) whether the bankruptcy petition was filed because of sudden illness, calamity, disability or unemployment; (2) whether the debtor incurred cash advances and made consumer purchases far in excess of his ability to pay; (3) whether the debtor's proposed family budget is excessive or unreasonable; and (4) whether the debtor's schedules and statement of current income and expenses reasonably and accurately reflect the true financial condition.

The focus of the means test under Section 707(b)(2) is on whether debtors have sufficient income to repay a substantial portion of their debt, see, e.g., Eugene R. Wedoff, *Judicial Discretion to Find Abuse Under Section 707(B)(3)*, 71 Mo. L. Rev. 1035, 1036 (2006). Because this is also a factor under the totality of circumstances test, courts have struggled to define the intersection between Sections 707(b)(2) and (3). Some courts have expressed concern that a court might simply use Section 707(b)(3) to substitute its own test for the means test. See, e.g., In re Nockerts, 357 B.R. 497, 506 (Bankr. E.D. Wis. 2006) ("To apply the means test, dislike the result, and then examine the debtor's ability to fund a chapter 13 plan under §707(b)(3), renders the means test 'surplusage.'"). When addressing ability to pay under section 707(b)(3), a court must therefore be attentive to the policy choices made by Congress in drafting the means test, including the fact that it gave preferred treatment to secured creditors by allowing scheduled payments of secured debt to be listed as deductions without limitation. See, e.g., In re Le Roy, 2009 WL 357923, at *3 (Bankr. E.D. Wis. Feb. 12, 2009) ("[T]he U.S. Trustee sought to reclassify the debtors' secured debt payments as income available to pay creditors. The court determined that the Code expressly permits the deduction of secured debt payments under the Means Test, thereby providing an advantage to secured creditors over unsecured creditors. To ignore the Code's mandate and disallow secured debt expenses allowed by the Means Test would violate Congressional policy.")

. . . [W]hile a desire to reaffirm secured debt is not in itself abuse, a court can find abuse under the totality of circumstances when there is "evidence that the Debtor has manipulated the means test, purchased luxuries on credit on the eve of bankruptcy, altered his expenses in his Schedules, accrued significant debt prior to the petition, or that his budget is excessive or unreasonable." Le Roy, 2009 WL 357923, at *4.

[T]he vehicles can be characterized as luxury items, [and] the purchases seem to demonstrate a pattern of living beyond the Debtors' means. This lifestyle also seems to have been one of the main factors contributing to their financial difficulties. The Debtors have admitted that their financial situation was not caused by a "sudden illness, calamity or disability." Although much of the cause might have been the economic downturn and its impact on Mr. Deutscher's painting business, these large purchases, which took place during a period Mr. Deutscher claims to have been unemployed, clearly exacerbated the situation. Instead of learning from their mistakes, the Debtors appear to want to continue this lifestyle even after seeking a bankruptcy discharge by reaffirming their debt on these luxury items rather than follow the expectation that "when seeking bankruptcy relief, debtors may be expected to do some belt tightening, including, where necessary, foregoing the reaffirmation of those secured debts which are not reasonably necessary for the maintenance and support of the debtor and his family." In re Harter, 397 B.R. 860, 864 (Bankr. N.D. Ohio 2008). [Motion to Dismiss granted.]

Is any section 707(b)(3) decision involving a yacht likely to end well for the debtor? Yet we remain skeptical about the propriety of imposing a "judicially administered Alternative Minimum Means Test." John A.E. Pottow, The Totality of the Circumstances of the Debtor's Financial Situation in a Post-Means Test World, 71 Mo. L. Rev. 1053, 1061 (2006).

A bitter critic might say that the purpose of BAPCPA was to restrict bankruptcy relief and so any discretion exercised to dismiss one more debtor's petition is not judicial impertinence but welcome support of Congress. But the policy analysis is more complex. Consider the role of secured creditors: They don't find it remotely abusive to have debtors budget to pay secured debts in chapter 7, as Congress chose to allow with the means test; in fact, they welcome clearing the brush of unsecured debt that impedes a debtor's ability to afford secured debt payments. Secured creditors would thus claim that the "implicit policy" of the Code is to protect secured credit and judges who undermine the means test's protections are rogues. Some "totality" cases have taken just that view; the debtors who filed In re Jensen, 407 B.R. 378 (Bankr. C.D. Cal. 2009), were paying their secured creditors around $5,600 a month from about $8,600 in monthly income, including a boat payment of $760 a month. Refusing to dismiss for abuse, the court summarized the pro-secured-debt position as follows:

> Courts and commentators have struggled to define the interaction between §§707(b)(2) and (b)(3). . . . This Court certainly shares the discomfort other courts have felt at the prospect of permitting debtors to retain luxury goods in defiance of their unsecured creditors. However, the Bankruptcy Code seeks to further policies other than making unsecured creditors whole, especially in situations where unsecured creditors can be made whole only at the expense of secured creditors. Chief among these policies is advancing the availability of secured credit. See, e.g., In re Proalert, LLC, 314 B.R. 436, 441 (9th Cir. BAP 2004) ("Embodied in the Bankruptcy Code is a policy decision to protect secured credit practices."). Therefore, refusing to permit debtors to retain secured-debt property does more than punish the debtors—it also reallocates the balance of risk between secured and unsecured creditors. As one commentator has observed, in the zero-sum battle between secured and unsecured creditors, "the secured creditor's advantage is the unsecured creditor's disadvantage."

Homer Kripke, Law and Economics: Measuring the Economic Efficiency of Commercial Law in a Vacuum of Fact, 133 U. Pa. L. Rev. 929, 949 (1985).

Another perspective on BAPCPA—advanced forcefully by the consumer debtor bar—is that the legislative intent of the means test was to promote uniformity and guidance to the parties. To advance these objectives, the means test should be read to limit the ability of a court or creditor to revisit any expense deemed acceptable under the means test deductions. Revisiting a debtor's food budget under the totality standard, for example, is judicial overreaching and unravels the clarity Congress sought to confer.

Judges, scholars, and lawyers all continue to struggle with identifying the boundaries of section 707(b)(3). Discretionary dismissal remains on the books, yet almost certainly has a different function—if not statutory meaning—after the means test (can the plain meaning of a statute be altered by ex post insertion of a preceding non-referential paragraph?). Perhaps the only generalizable trend is that case outcomes seem to track "conventional sensibilities." Compare, e.g., In re Rivers, 466 B.R. 558 (Bankr, M.D. Fla. 2012) (no abuse by debtor with endometriosis surgery and two kids with severe food allergies), with, e.g., In re Roppo, 442 B.R. 888, 895 (Bankr. N.D. Ill. 2010) (finding abuse and remarking on the debtor's luxurious lifestyle: "It is baffling why the Debtor's wife acquired a Mercedes automobile the year following her [own] Chapter 7 case"). Perhaps the answer is simply greater transparency; courts should just come out and say what they think is a legitimate expense and smells of an abusively excessive lifestyle. See if this attempt to carve the distinction persuades you.

In re DURCZYNSKI

405 B.R. 880 (Bankr. N.D. Ohio 2009)

SPEER, Bankruptcy Judge.

As previously noted by the Court, bankruptcy is "meant to provide a debtor a fresh start, but not a head start. Thus, when seeking bankruptcy relief, debtors may be expected to do some belt tightening, including, where necessary, foregoing the reaffirmation of those secured debts which are not reasonably necessary for the maintenance and support of the debtor and his family." In re Wadsworth, 383 B.R. 330 (Bankr. N.D. Ohio 2007) (internal citations omitted). In this matter, the Debtors devote a significant amount of their income to maintain their home. To service the necessary obligations attendant with their home, the Debtors must allocate $2,187.21 from their monthly budget. This figure constitutes approximately 40% percent of the Debtors' net monthly income of $5,585.35. It is also 2 1/2 times the amount that is allowed under the "means test" formulation of §707(b) (2). At the time the Debtors filed their bankruptcy petition, the allowable monthly mortgage expense for a family of five when applying the "means test" of §707(b)(2) was $888.00. While the "means test" of

§707(b)(2) is not strictly applicable in this case, its standards do serve to show that a significant portion of the expenses associated with the Debtors' residence are not necessary for their basic living needs, but instead constitute a "lifestyle" choice.

The purchase of a home is a highly personal choice and is one which requires debtors to assess not only the present needs of their family, but also their long term needs. In re Kitson, 65 B.R. 615, 620-21 (Bankr. E.D.N.C. 1986). Debtors may, therefore, be afforded some latitude in their choice of a home which as opposed to a purely financial decision—for example, whether to purchase cable television—involves a moral and value based judgment on the part of the debtor. Notwithstanding, assessing a debtor's ability to pay for purposes of §707(b)(3) still requires that a court scrutinize a debtor's expenses. It, thus, cannot be avoided that an "ability to pay" inquiry under §707(b)(3) may encroach on the highly personal choices that all individuals make about how to prioritize their expenses and, on more basic level, how to live their lives. In re Fauntleroy, 311 B.R. 730, 736 (Bankr. E.D.N.C. 2004).

Within this context, it is fair to state that the more an expense involves a moral and value based judgment on the part of the debtor, the more deference that will be accorded to the debtor's decision. Conversely, the more a decision is purely financial in character, the more scrutiny that will be accorded to that decision. For example, the decision to have a child, while undoubtedly having a financial component, is largely a moral decision, and thus it would be highly unusual for such a decision to have a negative impact on a debtor in a §707(b)(3) analysis. In fact, deference to the debtor's decision to have a child may be constitutionally required. In re Edwards, 50 B.R. 933, 940 n.9 (Bankr. S.D.N.Y. 1985). On the other hand, a debtor's decision involving cable television, being largely a financial-based decision, would not be accorded much deference.

In this matter, the Court can only conclude that the Debtors' intention to retain their residence arises more from "want" as opposed to any "need." For example, no evidence was provided that the education or health of the Debtors' children would be impacted if they did not stay in their current residence. . . .

To be sure, the Debtors' have an emotional attachment to their home. However, while this is understandable, it does not justify overlooking the overall state of the Debtors' financial situation. In re DeRosear, 265 B.R. 196, 218 (Bankr. S.D. Iowa 2001). . . . Second, Mrs. Durczynski has not made a concerted effort to maximize her income, with the evidence showing that she has the ability to increase her income significantly, perhaps by 20% to 30%, if she were to work full time. . . .

Do you agree that the mother of three children's decision to work part-time was not a moral or value based judgment to which the judge should have accorded greater latitude under his own standard? If many would not agree, does that create some problems with this distinction? Despite the repeated rhetoric about "can-pay" debtors, is the means test really a normative identification of "should-pay" debtors? For example, section 707(b)(2)(D) hardly seems animated by a veteran's inability to pay.

Finally, if courts will be called upon regularly to scrutinize a debtor's budget with motions to dismiss under section 707(b)(3), have we gained any greater certainty or efficiency since BAPCPA, or have we just made matters more complicated, expensive, and painful for debtors and the court system?

2. *Discretionary Dismissal in Chapter 13: Good Faith*

A longstanding requirement for chapter 13 confirmation is that a plan be "proposed in good faith and not by any means forbidden in law." §1325(a)(3). Lest anyone have missed Congress' desire to imbue the chapter 13 system with this concept, BAPCPA added a second requirement requiring good faith in filing the petition (not just the plan). §1325(a)(7). As innocuous as "good faith" may sound, it has defied consistent and simple application. The most straightforward invocation occurs when a debtor has engaged in shady behavior or been less than forthcoming in giving financial information; those cases are fun reading but largely raise issues of fact—either the debtor did or did not do the shady behavior.

The more contested use of the good faith requirement is to challenge a creative debtor's interpretation of the other statutory requirements for chapter 13 confirmation, and this process has become more complicated post-BAPCPA. Recall that Congress was trying to encourage the use of chapter 13, and so restrictions on chapter 13 filings present some tension with the ostensible purpose of the new regime. Recall too BAPCPA was designed to remove discretion, and so re-injecting that discretion through the good faith requirement raises the same concerns described above with section 707(b)(3). Unsurprisingly, there is some overlap between the section 707(b)(3)(B) "totality of the circumstances" standard and the chapter 13 "good faith" standard, as the next case shows.

———— **In re CRAGER** ————
691 F.3d 671 (5th Cir. 2012)

HIGGINBOTHAM, Circuit Judge.

The debtor, Patricia Ann Crager, is unemployed, and her main source of income is $1,060 per month in Social Security benefits plus $16 per month in food stamps. Her main asset is her primary residence, which is valued at $55,000 and encumbered by a $40,662 mortgage. Her mortgage payments are $327.10 per month. She also has $7,855.27 in credit card debt; her minimum monthly payments total $197. Prior to filing her Chapter 13 petition, Crager was current on all mortgage and credit card payments. However, in early 2010, Crager learned that if she continued making the minimum payments on her credit cards, it would take her 17 to 20 years to pay off her balances. She contacted the loss mitigation departments of her credit card companies to seek an interest rate or monthly payment reduction but did not receive either.

Crager decided that her best course was to file for bankruptcy under Chapter 13 because it would have taken her over a year to save enough money to pay the up-front costs for a Chapter 7 bankruptcy and to do so she would have needed to stop making her minimum monthly credit card payments. She also was concerned that filing Chapter 7 would prevent her from declaring bankruptcy again for a longer period than would Chapter 13, and she believed that a Chapter 7 bankruptcy would stay on her credit report longer. Crager filed Chapter 13, with her attorney advancing the court costs of $274.

A few months after Crager filed her Chapter 13 petition and plan, the Trustee objected to confirmation of the plan. The objection asserted that Crager's petition and plan were not filed in good faith pursuant to 11 U.S.C. §1325(a)(3) and (7) and that the amount of attorney's fees sought by Crager's attorney was unreasonable. After a contested hearing, the bankruptcy court overruled the Trustee's objection and approved Crager's Chapter 13 petition and plan and the requested legal fees and advanced legal costs.

The Trustee appealed, and the district court reversed the bankruptcy court's confirmation of Crager's Chapter 13 plan and entered an order requiring the bankruptcy court to find on remand that Crager's Chapter 13 plan was filed in bad faith. Crager appealed to this court.

. . .

In this circuit, courts apply a "totality of the circumstances" test to determine whether a Chapter 13 petition and plan are filed in good faith, and the bankruptcy court applied that standard when it approved Crager's plan. In approving the plan, the bankruptcy court focused on the rising cost of medical care and suggested that Crager had a legitimate fear that a future medical problem might leave her in a situation in which she had to take on more debt and might need to file another Chapter 13 petition. The court found that it would "border on malpractice" for Crager's attorney to advise her to file a Chapter 7.

The Trustee suggests that Crager's plan is against the spirit of Chapter 13, and indeed, one of the factors a court should consider in applying the totality of the circumstances test is "whether the plan shows an attempt to abuse the spirit of the bankruptcy code." But that is only one of at least seven factors. Moreover, the bankruptcy court had the opportunity to judge Crager's credibility as a witness and found credible her proffered reasons for filing a Chapter 13 petition. It was not clearly erroneous for the bankruptcy court to find that Crager's plan was not an attempt to abuse Chapter 13, but rather a responsible decision given her particular circumstances. There is no rule in this circuit that a Chapter 13 plan that results in the debtor's counsel receiving almost the entire amount paid to the Trustee, leaving other unsecured creditors unpaid, is a per se violation of the "good faith" requirement, and the district court erred when it reversed the bankruptcy court on that ground.

Alternatively, the Trustee argues that the bankruptcy court abused its discretion when it awarded $2,800 in attorney fees to Crager's counsel.

This issue turns on the relationship between the standard for awarding compensation to the debtor's attorney set forth in 11 U.S.C. §330 and the "no-look" fee established by a Standing Order of the United States Bankruptcy Court for the Western District of Louisiana. [Eds. Note: A "no look" fee is an amount a court will approve as reasonable attorney charges without submission of a detailed fee application.]

Under 11 U.S.C. §330, the bankruptcy court may award to Crager's attorney "reasonable compensation . . . for representing [Crager's] interests . . . in connection with the bankruptcy case based on a consideration of the benefit and necessity of such services to the debtor and the other factors set forth in th[e] section." Those factors include "the nature, the extent, and the value" of the attorney's services, including

(A) the time spent on such services;

(B) the rates charged for such services;

(C) whether the services were necessary to the administration of, or beneficial at the time at which the service was rendered toward the completion of, a case under this title;

(D) whether the services were performed within a reasonable amount of time commensurate with the complexity, importance, and nature of the problem, issue, or task addressed;

(E) with respect to a professional person, whether the person is board certified or otherwise has demonstrated skill and experience in the bankruptcy field; and

(F) whether the compensation is reasonable based on the customary compensation charged by comparably skilled practitioners in cases other than cases under this title.

Under the Standing Order, a maximum no-look fee of $2,800 applies in a Chapter 13 case. The Standing Order allows the Trustee to file an objection to the presumptive fee and provides that, following notice to the debtor and a hearing, the bankruptcy court may adjust the fee. It notes that the no-look fee is not "an entitlement."

In this case, the Trustee objected to the bankruptcy court awarding the "no-look" fee on the basis that Crager's bankruptcy was "more simplistic and less complicated" than the average Chapter 13 case. Specifically: (1) the Trustee would make no disbursements to secured creditors; (2) there were only five unsecured creditors; (3) Crager's only sources of income were food stamps and Social Security benefits; (4) Crager had not filed an income tax return since 2004; and (5) Crager was judgment-proof and had no seizable assets. The bankruptcy court stated that it was the Trustee's burden not merely to raise a reasoned objection to the fee but to prove that the no-look fee should not apply, and it concluded that the no-look fee was reasonable.

The bankruptcy court was incorrect when it stated that it was the Trustee's burden to prove that the presumptive fee was unreasonable. As the Standing Order notes, the no-look fee is not an entitlement, and the Standing Order does not supplant the requirements of 11 U.S.C. §330. Therefore, the bankruptcy court was obligated to consider the factors listed in the statute if the Trustee raised a reasoned objection.

However, we see no error in the bankruptcy court's finding that the no-look fee was reasonable under the circumstances. Most importantly, the Trustee's objection was based on the false premise that Crager's case was "more simplistic" than the average Chapter 13 bankruptcy. Indeed, the Trustee's own "bad faith" challenge to Crager's plan transformed the case from a routine Chapter 13 matter into a complicated proceeding. Given this added complexity, the reasoning of the Trustee's objection was not sound, and the bankruptcy court did not err in allowing the $2,800 no-look fee.

For the foregoing reasons, we REVERSE the ruling of the district court and AFFIRM the bankruptcy court's confirmation of Crager's Chapter 13 plan.

═══════════

While the debtor—and her attorney—were winners here, the court notes the costs and risks imposed by a multi-factored examination of whether bankruptcy relief is appropriate. Clearly there is an open question in the mind of some judges whether a chapter 13 plan that pays nothing to unsecured creditors but only spreads out the debtor's attorney's fee is an appropriate use of the bankruptcy system. The next case illustrates how good faith interacts with the means test's statutory expenses to create two bites at the apple for disgruntled creditors or tough trustees.

───────── **VEIGHLAN v. ESSEX (In re Essex)** ─────────
452 B.R. 195 (W.D. Tex. 2011)

RODRIGUEZ, District Judge.

On January 5, 2010, Appellees filed a petition for relief under Chapter 13 in the United States Bankruptcy Court for the Western District of Texas. Appellant filed an Objection to Confirmation of Appellees' Original Chapter 13 Plan claiming in part that the Plan was not filed in good faith according to 11 U.S.C. §1325(a)(3). Appellees then filed an Amended Chapter 13 Plan ("Plan") that included changes necessary for the Plan to meet feasibility requirements but did not address the good faith concerns that the Appellant raised.

The Plan "calls for payments of $3,717.00 for a period of sixty months and proposes to pay approximately a 1% dividend to non-priority unsecured creditors with the dollar amount to be paid to non-priority unsecured creditors a total of no less than $1,956.41." Appellant's Br. at 10. The basis of the good faith claim relates to the fact that in the Plan, "the debtors [Appellees] were proposing to retain a homestead with a mortgage of approximately $656,000.00 ..." in which the Appellees have virtually no equity. *Id.* at 7, 24. To do so, Appellees would pay $6,770.00 towards the mortgage each month. *Id.* at 19. This amount constitutes 51% of Appellees' monthly income and represents a mortgage payment that "is over four times the amount of the IRS standard for housing *and* utilities for a family of five in San Antonio, Texas." *Id.* (emphasis included in original). In arguing that this proposal was not made in good faith, Appellant draws attention to the steep contrast between the high monthly mortgage payments and the low monthly dividend (1%) that Appellees propose to pay to unsecured creditors. Furthermore, it should be noted that before purchasing the home in 2006, Appellees had not paid income taxes for the years of 2003, 2004, or 2005 and continued this trend for 2006 as well. As a result of this failure to pay taxes, the Appellees owe the IRS $256,498.97, of which $136,681.46 is an unsecured claim. Based on the 1% dividend proposed in Appellees' Plan, the IRS will receive $1,366.82 of the unsecured debt.

Despite Appellant's objection, the Bankruptcy Court confirmed the Plan, citing the eligibility limits of 11 U.S.C. §109(e) in conjunction with the Chapter 13 purpose of allowing debtors to retain their homes during bankruptcy. As the Court stated,

> We already know that we have a statute that's designed to help people keep their homes, and we already know that Congress also, de facto, put an upper limit on

what kind of a home you can keep because they put an upper limit of how much secured debt you can take into Chapter 13. So, that's the de facto number. The de facto number for how much house can you have in Chapter 13 is set by the eligibility limits.

Ct. Tr. at 34-35. In response to the Court's Order confirming the Plan, Appellant filed an appeal and seeks reversal of the Order and denial of confirmation.

. . .

Good Faith

Many courts disagree on what constitutes a violation of Section 1325(a)(3), particularly when the section is read in conjunction with Section 1325(b). While section 1325(a)(3) concerns whether "... the plan has been proposed in good faith and not by any means forbidden by law," Section 1325(b)(3) contemplates the determination of "[a]mounts reasonably necessary to be expended" by the debtor as it essentially factors into the overall "disposable income" calculation outlined in 1325(b)(2). 11 U.S.C. §1325(a)(3), (b)(3). Section 1325(b)(3) provides that "amounts reasonably necessary to be expended" should be determined for debtors of certain income levels in accordance with 11 U.S.C. §707(b)(2)(A)-(B) which outlines the "means test" . . . Section 707(b)(2)(A)(iii)(II) places no reasonableness requirement on the monthly payments necessary to "maintain possession of the debtor's primary residence." *Id.* Rather, any amount necessary to keep the residence is allowed by Section 707 and as a result, is considered an "amount[ ] reasonably necessary to be expended" under Section 1325(b)(3). *Id.*; 11 U.S.C. §1325(b)(3).

As a result of this statutory language and the absence of a "reasonableness" component within Section 707(b)(2)(A)(iii) (II), courts have had difficulty determining whether a debtor's proposed monthly expenditures can be lawful under Section 1325(b)(3) yet constitute a violation of good faith under Section 1325(a)(3). During the confirmation hearing in this case, the Bankruptcy Court agreed that the proposed housing expenses in the Appellees' Plan comply with Section 1325(b)(3). Ct. Tr. 19. However, because the Court chose to overrule the good faith objection using Section 109(e), it did not reach the difficult question of whether the proposed plan nonetheless violated Section 1325(a)(3).

Appellant implores this Court to make that finding and to follow a line of cases from bankruptcy courts around the country holding that compliance with 1325(b)(3) is not determinative of compliance with 1325(a)(3). *See In re Sandberg,* 433 B.R. 837, 845-46 (Bankr. D. Kan. 2010) (" 'Notwithstanding the fact that the Debtors are entitled to account for the boat payments when calculating their disposable income under the means test, confirmation of a plan proposing to retain the boat is subject to the good faith test under 11 U.S.C. §1325(a)(3)....' "); . . . *In re McGillis,* 370 B.R. 720, 750 (Bankr. W.D. Mich.

2007) ("Section 1325(b) is a hazard, not a harbor. Its avoidance does not mean clear sailing. Rather, all debtors still must establish that their plans exhibit the good faith demanded by Section 1325(a)(3).").

On the other hand, Appellees urge the Court to adopt the reasoning that expenditures in compliance with Section 1325(b)(3) automatically qualify as expenditures in compliance with Section 1325(a)(3) as long as no additional instances of bad faith are alleged. *See In re Faison,* 416 B.R. 227, 231-32 (Bankr. E.D. Va. 2008) ("The Court will not find that the Debtor acted not in good faith by doing what Congress has allowed in BAPCPA, even if the expenses taken result in a lower dividend to unsecured creditors than they would receive if the Debtor were forced to relinquish property that is worth far less than the debt securing it."); . . . *In re Farrar-Johnson,* 353 B.R. 224, 232 (Bankr. N.D. Ill. 2006) ("If the reasonable necessity of a debtor's expenses is no longer relevant, then plainly the debtor's 'good faith' in claiming them cannot be relevant. Disposable income is 'determined under section 1325(b) rather than as an element of good faith under section 1325(a)(3).' ").

In light of the Fifth Circuit precedent of applying the "totality of the circumstances" test to decide questions of good faith, overruling Appellant's Section 1325(a)(3) objection solely on the basis of whether Appellees' proposed plan complies with Section 1325(b)(3) would be improper and would render Section 1325(b)(3) superfluous. However, to find that the Appellees proposed their plan in bad faith even though the housing expenses comply with Section 1325(b)(3) would also be inconsistent. In attempting to resolve this potential conflict within the statute, this Court finds the approach taken in *In re Owsley* to be persuasive. 384 B.R. 739 (Bankr. N.D. Tex. 2008). In that case, the Court concluded that "expenses deemed to be 'reasonably necessary' under subsection (b)(3) are presumed to be asserted in good faith under subsection (a)(3). The presumption of good faith can be negated by aggravating circumstances, an example of which might be a debtor's deduction of an ownership expense for a luxury vehicle purchased on the eve of bankruptcy." *Id.* at 750. Under this approach, the fact that Appellees' proposed monthly mortgage payments are lawful under Section 1325(b)(3) is important yet constitutes only one factor to be considered in addition to any "aggravating circumstances" that might arise within the overall "totality of the circumstances" test.

Appellant argues that there are aggravating circumstances in this case. Specifically, Appellant points to the fact that prior to purchasing their home, Appellees had not paid income taxes for three years. As Appellant states, "... the debtors clearly made the choice to live in a luxury home rather than pay their income taxes ... The trustee questions whether the debtors living in a $600,000.00 home while paying next to nothing on $136,681.46 of unsecured tax debt is the bargain that Congress intended between debtors and unsecured creditors." Appellant's Br. at 21. Furthermore, the Appellant points to recent cases in which bankruptcy courts have found Chapter 13 plans that allow debtors to keep highly valued homes in which they have very little equity while paying virtually nothing to unsecured creditors to be proposed in bad faith.

In the case of *In re Namie,* the debtor proposed to retain his $500,000 home even though his mortgage expenses amounted to five times more than the standard housing expenses in his community. 395 B.R. 594, 596-97 (Bankr. D.S.C. 2008). In fact, the debtor's mortgage expenses exceeded his personal net income. *Id.* The Court held that "debtor's retention of a home that consumes all of his net disposable income, to the detriment of his significant number of unsecured creditors, is not in good faith." *Id.* Although the case at issue is distinguishable from *Namie* in that Appellees mortgage does not consume the entirety of their disposable income, Appellees' proposal to pay a 1% dividend to unsecured creditors is barely more substantial than the *Namie* debtor. . . .

Considering the "totality of the circumstances," this Court finds it necessary to reverse the order of the Bankruptcy Court to confirm Appellees' Chapter 13 Plan. Although Appellees' proposed housing expenses satisfy the standards outlined in Section 1325(b)(3) and thus are presumed to have been proposed in good faith, sufficiently aggravating circumstances serve to rebut that presumption. Appellees' proposal to retain a home valued at $600,000 while paying only 1% of the $136,681.46 unsecured debt owed to the IRS is a proposal in bad faith. Furthermore, in making this proposal, Appellees have not asserted a reason why it is necessary to retain a home for which the mortgage payments are over four times the amount of the IRS standard for their area despite the extremely low dividend they seek to pay to their unsecured creditors. . . . these Appellees seem "unwilling to engage in the kind of meaningful belt tightening" necessary for individuals in bankruptcy. As Appellant states, "debtors [Appellees] have not sought to change their spendthrift ways but rather seek to maintain their pre-petition lifestyle.... There is no reason why the debtors cannot find more affordable housing and pay their unsecured creditors a reasonable dividend while still living a comfortable lifestyle." Appellant's Br. at 19.

Although the Bankruptcy Court was correct to emphasize that a purpose of Chapter 13 bankruptcy proceedings is to allow debtors to keep their homes, it is doubtful that Congress intended to protect individuals, like the Appellees, who purchased the home during a time period when they evaded their income taxes. To allow the Appellees to retain their homestead while paying only 1% of the debt owed to unsecured creditors, including the IRS, would be to allow a bargain that too greatly favors the Appellees. In light of the totality of the circumstances, the Bankruptcy Court's Order confirming Appellees' Chapter 13 Plan is reversed.

The Essex family's low five-year payback suggests a net income that would pass the means test. If so, would there be any problem with them converting to chapter 7 (or filing a new chapter 7 case) given this dismissal from 13? If they did, would they necessarily lose their home?

3. *Refiling Restrictions*

Some debtors make multiple forays into bankruptcy. (Remember the Littons and their three filings from Assignment 10.) Some refile shortly after dismissal with the same attorney, while others wait out tough circumstances or shop for a new lawyer. While the repeat filer may not attract sympathy, the largest group of refilers, especially in chapter 13, actually appears to be people simply seeking a first discharge, not scoundrels coming back for a second bankruptcy discharge with newly acquired debt. This reality does not seem to echo in the halls of Congress, however, as BAPCPA tightened the rules to prohibit a discharge in chapter 13 for any debtor who has received a discharge in a chapter 7, 11, or 12 case in the preceding four years or for any debtor who received a discharge in a chapter 13 case in the preceding two years. §1328(f). Congress also tightened the rules in chapter 7, extending the wait between chapter 7s to eight years. §727(a)(8). There are true "serial" filers out there, but they appear to be an exclusive clique. Jean Lown, New Study: Serial Bankruptcy Filers No Problem, ABI Journal (June 2007) (finding 2.7% of chapter 13 debtors had filed four or more times). These restrictions on refiling are yet another factor to balance in chapter choice. Remember they drove Ms. Crager's lawyer's decision (at least if you take the explanation at face value) to have her file under chapter 13 rather than 7.

4. *Scope of Discharge*

Chapter 13 has a somewhat more generous discharge provision than chapter 7. *Cf.* §1328 *with* §727. But the differences are now so small only Old Timers still refer to chapter 13 as offering a "super discharge." These additional debts that can only be eliminated in chapter 13 are largely limited to various government fines and penalties, amounts from divorce or separation that are in the nature of property settlements (as opposed to support), and a few other oddities. Historically the super discharge was designed to be a major carrot for filing chapter 13; the framework now is more about screening tests to check debtor's chapter choice than trying to incentivize chapter 13.

5. *Coda: Chapter 11 for Individuals*

Having waded through the pros and cons of chapter 7 and chapter 13, you may be hoping for a magical third option to address one or more of the risks of chapter 7 or chapter 13. The good news is that individuals can file chapter 11. Sure, you may think about titans like General Motors and Delta Airlines, but individuals file chapter 11 too. Indeed, 27% of all chapter 11 petitions in 2012 were filed by individuals. Bankruptcy Data Project, http://bdp.law.illinois.edu. (Nerds: Try out this interactive database!)

Little is yet known about why individuals file chapter 11. Some of them flunk the means test or have debts that exceed the chapter 13 caps. They are essentially screened out by statute from both chapter 7 and chapter 13. Their choice is 11 or nothin'. Others choose chapter 11 voluntarily over chapters 7 or 13 to deal with complicated financial issues beyond the scope of these materials; suffice it to say chapter 11 accords more flexibility and can deal with greater complexity. Precisely for these reasons, however, chapter 11 is slower and more expensive.

And there is more bad news: Congress reduced incentives for individuals to use chapter 11 with BAPCPA by incorporating many aspects of the means test. Today, chapter 11 for individuals is now much closer to chapter 13—but that increased similarity by no means suggests identity. Chapter 11 is complex and involves special fiduciary obligations we will explore in the business assignments. Consumer practitioners used to mass-managing cases with legal software cannot just cross out "13" and write "11." Judge Jaroslovsky makes the point below.

NOTICE TO BAR REGARDING INDIVIDUAL CHAPTER 11 CASES

There has been a recent spate of individual Chapter 11 cases filed by attorneys who have neither the experience nor the education nor the competence to venture into Chapter 11. I believe that there are very few bankruptcy lawyers other than State Bar certified specialists who should be contemplating representation of Chapter 11 debtors in possession.

I see rampant errors being made in issues relating to cash collateral, conflicts of interest, and compensation. . . .

A Chapter 11 is not just a big Chapter 13. If you represent a Chapter 11 debtor in possession, your client is the *estate*, not the debtor personally. Failure to understand this results in serious liability exposure.

Forget about trying to fix your compensation. You will be paid what I allow, period. I suggest you not spend retainers until your fees are allowed to avoid having to return money you have already spent.

I see frequent malpractice in individual Chapter 11 cases and I am quick to note it on the record. Your employment will not be approved unless you have substantial current malpractice insurance. If you are going "bare," don't even think about taking a Chapter 11 case.

A complete understanding of the differences between chapter 11 and chapter 13 must await the detailed study of chapter 11 later in this book. To give you an idea of a few differences: (1) chapter 11 is much more expensive, both for the filing fee ($1,046 compared to $306 (chapter 7) or $281 (chapter 13)) and for attorneys' fees; (2) the retail valuation standard, section 506(a)(2), for property encumbered by a security interest does not apply; (3) creditors vote to confirm a plan in chapter 11 while confirmation in chapter 13 is determined solely by a judge; and (4) financial education is not a condition for discharge for chapter 11 debtors, as it is for chapter 7 and 13 debtors. For further discussion, and a cogent argument that individual chapter 11s are now so distinct they warrant a separate subchapter of chapter 11, see Bruce Markell, The Sub Rosa Subchapter: Individual Debtors in Chapter 11 after BAPCPA, 2007 Ill. L. Rev. 67.

Chapter 11 remains an odd fit for individuals. While individuals are a significant fraction of all chapter 11 cases, the converse is not true. Chapter 11 cases are a bare sliver of all bankruptcies filed by individuals each year. In 2012, 98.8% of cases filed by individuals were chapter 7 or chapter 13 cases according to the Bankruptcy Data Project. It makes little sense for the average family to use chapter 11 to propose a payment plan. We flag chapter 11 in this chapter choice discussion because post-BAPCPA more individuals may now be barred from both chapters 7 and 13 and thus must turn to chapter 11 if they want any bankruptcy relief.

For space reasons, we omit any discussion of chapter 12, open only to family farmers or fishermen, a sort of chapter 11 and chapter 13 hybrid (as its number suggests) that may be more debtor friendly. The filing numbers for this chapter are also very small. The empirical point is that the consumer system is largely dichotomous between 7 and 13.

B. EXTRA-STATUTORY CONSIDERATIONS

Beyond the Code's provisions, various practice realities also influence chapter choice.

1. Attorney's Fees

It has long been the practice of lawyers filing chapter 7 cases to demand their fees in cash from their bankrupt clients before filing. "Pay me next month? Well, er, . . ." Nonetheless, some lawyers did agree to be paid by the chapter 7 estate, at least until that practice was ended by the Supreme Court's decision in Lamie v. U.S., 540 U.S. 526 (2004). That decision did not apply to the reorganization chapters (11, 12, and 13), and it is routine in many districts in chapter 13 cases to include payment of the debtor's attorney's fees as part of the monthly payments that go through the chapter 13 trustee, just like the filing fee and the trustee's fee. This difference in payment possibilities is another important distinction between the chapters.

The fee-only chapter 13 that survived challenge in *Crager* has actually fared even better in a post-BAPCPA world. The working theory seems to be that debtors who are paying even a pittance in chapter 13 are doing more to benefit creditors than if they just filed chapter 7 and so are "worthy." But as this excerpt from a First Circuit case shows, debtors who file fee-only cases do so under a watchful gaze.

In re PUFFER
674 F.3d 78 (1st Cir. 2012)

Lipez, J., Concurring.

We have observed that the Bankruptcy Code's purposes are twofold: to give the deserving debtor a fresh start and to maximize the payment to creditors. A fee-only Chapter 13 plan may accomplish little toward the goal of satisfying creditors, but such a plan may nonetheless be essential to free "the honest but unfortunate debtor" from intolerable circumstances.

Bankruptcy judges evaluating a particular fee-only plan may properly take into account whether the plan "is consistent with the spirit and purpose of [Chapter 13]—rehabilitation through debt repayment,"—but I fear that circumscribing the totality of the circumstances assessment with the requirement of special circumstances [the majority opinion's proposed test to permit a fee-only plan — Eds.] will in practical effect impose on debtors the more daunting task of disproving bad faith rather than proving good faith. I am therefore reluctant to confine what should be, in the majority's apt words, a "holistic balancing of relevant factors."

...[A]s the majority observes, the fee-only structure may leave unknowledgeable debtors vulnerable to attorneys seeking to maximize their compensation. See Kerry Haydel Ducey, Note, Bankruptcy, Just for the Rich? An Analysis of Popular Fee Arrangements for Pre-Petition Legal Fees and a Call to Amend, 54 Vand. L. Rev. 1665, 1703 (2001) (hereinafter Just for the Rich?) (noting that, "[i]n some cases, self-interest . . . compels the attorney to advise debtors to file Chapter 13 or other high percentage payment plans when Chapter 7 would actually better serve the debtor" (footnote omitted)).

Nonetheless, we must keep in mind that a struggling debtor who lacks the resources to pay a Chapter 7 attorney's fee up front has limited options. Although he theoretically could proceed pro se, I doubt that bankrupt individuals will ordinarily be able to navigate the complexities of the bankruptcy process on their own. Indeed, an empirical study indicating that the percentage of pro se debtors has increased in the aftermath of BAPCPA shows that such cases are not succeeding. See Angelia Littwin, The Affordability Paradox: How Consumer Bankruptcy's Greatest Weakness May Account for its Surprising Success, 52 Wm. & Mary L. Rev. 1933, 1938 (2011) ("[T]he high pro se failure rate since

2005 suggests that it is reasonable to equate the inability to afford a lawyer with having less than full access to the bankruptcy system."); see also Just for the Rich?, 54 Vand. L. Rev. at 1667 ("Legal counsel is indispensable if a debtor is to effectively file for bankruptcy. The bankruptcy laws are complex, and legal counsel is often crucial in helping the debtor make an informed decision based on his unique circumstances and the available alternatives." (citing William C. Hillman, Personal Bankruptcy: What Every Debtor and Creditor Needs to Know 20 (1993) ("Many mistakes people make by trying to do it on their own often cannot be corrected later. Even the simplest choices involve uncertainties and risks if you are not thoroughly familiar with the law."))). Moreover, lawyers play an important role in the bankruptcy system beyond their direct assistance to clients.

A debtor could attempt to find cheaper, or free, legal services, but I have no reason to think that counsel fees vary widely or that competent bankruptcy legal advice is readily available for free. . . .

The fee-only cases underscore the difficult reality that modern chapter 7 practice requires up-front payment for cash-starved debtors. Many years of serious empirical work have failed to reveal whence stems the chapter 7 lawyer's fee. Some claim debtors are told to skip the next mortgage payment or two to fund the fee; others assert that the debtor is given to understand that it is time to get that one last loan from Mom or your bowling buddy. Another theory is that debtors time their filings to coincide with additional cash, usually a tax refund. Ronald J. Mann & Katherine Porter, Saving Up for Bankruptcy, 98 Geo. L.J. 289, 319-20 (2010). With the substantial increase of fees after BAPCPA, price constraints may shape chapter choice even more. In one countervailing maneuver, however, Congress added in BAPCPA the ability to file *in forma pauperis*. 28 U.S.C. §1930(f). Such filings are now about 3% of all chapter 7 cases. Some have argued that anyone who needs a waiver of the filing fee should not be able to afford an attorney. Others have noted, consistent with the excerpt from *Puffer*, that pro se filings fare relatively poorly and that a debtor's attorney may be necessary for not just debtors but creditors.

Another recent study observed a further serious issue with attorney's fees – a huge regional disparity. Lois Lupica explains that the variations "go beyond big city = expensive, small town = cheap." She explains the lawyers themselves may have input into setting attorney's fees, even in chapter 13 where the Code seems to require court approval of any fees. Her study reproduces this attorney's description:

> [T]he judges get together with small filers, medium filers, and large filers
> and trustees and say, "Hey, what you guys need to do is let me know what you

need to charge. Give me a figure, kind of roughly an average case. What we're going to do is put that as an average figure, which is $3,250. Now you can go with that if you want. And that's $3,250 at confirmation. Keep track of your time afterwards and do supplemental fees. Or you can just do it hourly, right from the start. We'll just pay you hourly, or you can do $4,500 for the life of the case."

Posting of Lois Lupica to Credit Slips, Mar. 29, 2011, www.creditslips.org.

For people in such serious financial trouble that bankruptcy looms, the cost of legal assistance is a serious burden. Based on cases filed in 2007 studied in the Consumer Bankruptcy Project the average chapter 7 attorney's fee was $1,284; the average chapter 13 attorney's fee was $2,883. Attorneys' fees implicate both access to justice concerns and the cost-benefit analysis of chapter choice; they also reveal much of the nature of consumer bankruptcy practice.

2. Outcomes in Consumer Bankruptcy

A good lawyer tells clients what to expect well beyond the immediate relief of an automatic stay. Congress too hotly debates the respective outcomes of the different bankruptcy chapters, apparently holding firm to the belief that chapter 13 is just better for everyone. In this section, we offer a brief introduction to the wide literature on bankruptcy outcomes. We situate the discussion here because when making a choice on Code chapter, a fully informed debtor has to know not just the statutory rules but also what best knowledge suggests are the likely outcomes of filing under the different chapters.

a. Chapter 7 Outcomes

A 2001 study of chapter 7 filers asked families one year after discharge: "Overall, since you filed for bankruptcy, has your financial situation improved, stayed about the same, or worsened?" The results were decidedly mixed. Although 64% reported improvement, more than one-third said their financial situation was the same or worse than when they sought bankruptcy relief. Katherine Porter & Deborah Thorne, The Failure of Bankruptcy's Fresh Start, 92 Cornell L. Rev. 67, 77 (2006). The authors conclude that for "many families, the fresh start either failed to materialize or dissipated within one year of the discharge of their debts in bankruptcy." Id. at 70.

The longer term picture also showed enduring financial difficulties for debtors. Professors Jay Zagorsky and Lois Lupica compared bankruptcy filers with non-bankruptcy filers, and found that even holding many differences between the groups constant, bankruptcy filers continue to work hard but struggle with income issues. Jay Zagorsky & Lois Lupica, A Study of Consumers' Post-Discharge Finances: Struggle, Stasis, or Fresh-Start?, 16 Am. Bankr. Inst. L. Rev. 283 (2007). The average filer earns $13,000 less in annual wages; it is not until thirteen years after bankruptcy discharge that bankruptcy filers catch up with their non-bankrupt peers. Id. at 310. The findings on wealth and savings show similar gaps. Of course, these data do not necessarily impugn the bankruptcy system; these people could be much worse off without the discharge. But the findings do give pause to the rosy assumption that the fresh start accords debtors instant financial rehabilitation.

The slow recovery after bankruptcy could be a sign that bankrupt debtors are profligate and return to their old, bad habits after relief, miring themselves again in debt. While more research is needed, initial studies suggest that people are actually quite reluctant to borrow after bankruptcy—at least at the prices offered. Katherine Porter, Life After Debt: Understanding the Credit Restraint of Bankruptcy Debtors, 18 Am. Bankr. Inst. L. Rev. 1 (2010). These data are a reminder that the outcomes of bankruptcy may be more than a "radical adjustment to a debtor's balance sheet. Bankruptcy has behavioral effects that may be driven by psychological or social factors, not merely economic ones." Id. at 2. In the next Assignment, we will consider the rehabilitative aims of consumer bankruptcy, along with competing goals.

b. Chapter 13 Outcomes

The conventional wisdom—borne out by multiple empirical studies, including groundbreaking work of the Consumer Bankruptcy Project back to 1981—is that only 33% of cases end in plan completion. Although as with all things chapter 13, there is wide variation from district to district, the hard fact remains that the majority of chapter 13 filers do not discharge unsecured debts. Lack of discharge does not mean chapter 13 was useless; for example, the automatic stay may let the debtor find a new home by staving off a foreclosure and then the debtor can let her case voluntarily lapse. Still, the empirical evidence suggests that most incomplete plans reflect unhappy and difficult circumstances. Katherine Porter, The Pretend Solution: An Empirical Study of Bankruptcy Outcomes, 90 Tex. L. Rev. 103 (2011) (estimating that half of all filed chapter 13 cases are not successful when measured against debtors' self-reported goals of saving collateral or discharging unsecured debt).

The Code does permit a hardship discharge when the debtor has paid at least as much as creditors would have recovered in chapter 7, modification is not practicable, and the failure to complete the plan is outside the debtor's control. §1328(b). This section is used with some regularity by savvy debtor's counsel, but note that it does not address secured debt problems, such as a failure to catch up on missed mortgage payments, and has a different scope to the discharge.

Reconsidering our earlier discussion of good faith, section 1307(c) sets forth a non-exclusive list of "cause" that allows dismissal of a chapter 13 case. The same grounds apply to conversion of a petition from chapter 13 to chapter 7, but it is relatively uncommon, see Porter, Pretend Solution, supra at 132 (finding that conversion accounts for fewer than 20% of non-completed cases.) But again, it's not clear whether dismissal in chapter 13 reflects a bad outcome for the debtor. One key difference is between pre-confirmation and post-confirmation dismissal. The former usually occurs because the debtor never attempts confirmation, i.e., no plan is ever filed, or the debtor fails to complete a necessary step, such as pre-bankruptcy counseling or paying the filing fee. These cases likely reflect the limited options available to people at risk of losing their homes to foreclosure, cars to repossession, or other imminent collection activity. The upfront cost of chapter 7 is higher since attorneys' fees cannot be paid over time, and so many debtors come into chapter 13 only seeking a temporary respite, perhaps to seek shelter while working on a non-bankruptcy solution, such as a loan modification.

The post-confirmation dismissals reflect a different set of issues, with the cause for dismissal nearly always being the debtor's default on plan payments. Some debtors "intentionally" fail to pay the trustee, such as when a mortgage company has already lifted the stay and foreclose for missed mortgage payments on a maintained-and-cured mortgage; with the home gone, many simply exit the bankruptcy system, unconcerned or unaware they have not discharged their unsecured debts. In the study reported in *The Pretend Solution*, *supra*, one debtor offered this advice to others considering bankruptcy.

> Be prepared for a rocky road. It's not an easy thing to go through. It's a longer process than what we thought it would be and there [are] unbelievable amounts of paperwork. We had creditors telling us that bankruptcy wouldn't solve our problems. We wanted to believe it would help us, but maybe they were telling us the truth.

Thus, while lawyers can truthfully tell their clients "only about a third of you will likely get to plan completion and discharge," that statement glosses over the factual nuance of each debtor's financial distress.

c. Outcomes from the Creditor's Perspective

Creditors, of course, also care about bankruptcy outcomes, although their primary concern is getting paid as much as possible as fast as possible. It is difficult, however, to know how unsecureds really fare in chapter 13; the empirical evidence points in different directions. At an aggregate level, chapter 13 trustees distributed $1.58 billion to nonpriority unsecured creditors. U.S. Trustee Program, FY-2011 Chapter 13 Trustee Audited Annual Report. That's a lot of dough. On the other hand, in the median case, the payment to unsecured creditors is zero. This was true in post-BAPCPA cases filed in 2007, based on Consumer Bankruptcy Project data, as well as cases filed in prior years, including 2001. Scott Norberg, The Chapter 13 Project: Little Paid to Unsecureds, 26 Am. Bankr. L.J. 1, 54-56 (2007). The actual median payout seems a wee bit higher because in many districts trustees capture new postconfirmation income, primarily tax refunds in subsequent years, in a confirmed plan with zero proposed payout.

The trend in congressional amendments to the Code has long been either to encourage chapter 13, or more stridently, to limit access to chapter 7, which makes a bizarre disconnect between the data and what people lobby for. Some have argued that the purpose of the BAPCPA reforms was not to promote chapter 13 but to discourage filings generally, in order to keep families longer in a "sweat box" of debt, where they continue to make payments under increasingly difficult circumstances. Ronald J. Mann, Consumer Bankruptcy and Credit in the Wake of the 2005 Act: Bankruptcy Reform and the "Sweat Box" of Credit Card Debt, 2007 U. Ill. L. Rev. 375. If so, then the poor outcomes in chapter 13 are of no concern to these creditors.

One thing creditors may care very much about with bankruptcy outcomes is the creation of future customers. Nobody wants to lend to someone about to go bankrupt; creditors use analytical products to try to identify those on the brink of bankruptcy. But what of the recently bankrupt? Some would argue that the clean balance sheets of these consumers should make them attractive borrowers, but others would argue their track records raise red flags. We let the market—at least as it was before 2008—speak.

Bankrupt and Swamped With Credit Offers
When Chapter 7 Filers Wipe Out Their Debts, Card Firms Jump

By Caroline E. Mayer
Washington Post (April 15, 2005); Page A01

Overwhelmed by more than $60,000 in debt, Lenya Garcia filed for bankruptcy protection last July. In January, her case was completed and her debts — mostly on credit cards — were dismissed. Less than a month later, a rash of new credit card offers began arriving in the mail.

"I was very surprised," said the 36-year-old Bronx bookkeeper. "I figured my credit history had a big smear on it, and it would take a long time to get credit." Initially Garcia threw the offers away, but then she had a hard time renting a car without a credit card. So she took the next good "preapproved" offer — 14.9 percent interest and no sign-up or annual fee — and signed up at the company's Web site. "I was approved instantly."

Bankruptcy attorneys say Garcia's experience is the norm for debtors emerging from bankruptcy. "I tell my clients they will be inundated with offers," said North Carolina attorney T. Bentley Leonard. The reason is simple, he said: This group of consumers is a very attractive market to lenders because their debts have been wiped out and new debt cannot be forgiven for another six years.

"One day they owe $50,000, the next day, nothing. What better person to lend money to?" Leonard said.

That's certainly the pitch of one database firm, NewLeadsUSA, which sells lists of bankrupt consumers and businesses from publicly available data. "Opportunity knocks after life's hard knocks," the NewLeads Web site says. "Bankruptcy means a new financial life for many businesses and consumers. Be among the first to reach this unique and lucrative market."

3. The Lawyer's Role

We end on a brief note underscoring the importance of lawyers in navigating this dizzying system. "Counsel" may range from full disclosure and free chapter choice on the one hand to an ultimatum that the attorney will only file the debtor under one chapter or the other. In this framework, deciding between chapter 7 and chapter 13 may be less about strategy and more about "sorting" or "steering" by counsel. Judges, trustees, the U.S. Trustee, and creditors also make decisions that affect chapter choice; the attorneys' fees discussion above is only one example. Attitudes and experiences about things like the importance of homeownership, the morality of repaying debts, and the efficacy of one chapter or the other all come into play. Recent research suggests that even the race of the debtor is correlated with chapter choice, even after controlling for other likely explanations. Jean Braucher, Dov Cohen & Robert Lawless, Race, Attorney Influence and Bankruptcy Chapter Choice, 9 J. Empirical Legal Studies 393 (2012).

Collectively, the factors that shape chapter choice beyond a client's wishes (which may never be truly known in the presence of these other influences) are collectively called "local legal culture." See Jean Braucher, Lawyers and Consumer Bankruptcy: One Code, Many Cultures, 67 Am. Bankr. L. J. 501 (1993); Teresa Sullivan, Elizabeth Warren, and Jay Westbrook, The Persistence of Local Legal Culture: Twenty Years of Evidence From the Federal Bankruptcy Courts, 17 Harv. J. L. & Pub. Pol'y 801 (1994). To give you just a taste of the disparities, the chapter 13 filing rate in some bankruptcy districts is 3% in some districts and more than 50% in others. Indeed, some judges or trustees let it be known they will grill debtors harder if they tried chapter 7 and were bounced into 13 than if they just filed for 13 from the outset. While there is debate about the benefits of diversity versus uniformity, we close by noting that much of local legal culture, and by extension the realities of consumer bankruptcy, reflect extra-legal considerations. So much for all that time spent studying the Code!

Problem Set 13

13.1.A. You represent Angelica Ornelas, a realtor in Newport Beach, California. With bonuses and income from her share in a large real estate partnership, Angelica's total income is slightly over $200,000. She lives as if it were even higher. She has a home with a mortgage larger than the GDP of some Third World nations, three cars on which she owes more than most people owe on their homes, and a bunch of home décor, such as a hot tub, subject to purchase money liens. In short, after she pays all these fixed expenses, plus a reasonable amount for food and clothing, the means test would leave her about $222 per month for her unsecured creditors in her chapter 13 plan. She owes these creditors almost $195,000. Her total five-year payout will be $12,000, about 6% of her unsecured debt. Because most of her assets are subject to heavy liens and her state has generous exemptions, the unsecured creditors would get nothing in chapter 7. What questions do you have to ask before advising Angelica about her choices under the Bankruptcy Code? Can you get Angelica's plan confirmed? What are the weaknesses in your case? See §1325.

13.1.B. In an alternative universe you represent two of Angelica's creditors. Perfection Motors, the Mercedes dealer who holds a $35,000 purchase-money security interest on one of her cars, has called you for a consultation. The lender is very concerned because the car market has slowed abruptly due to the real estate crash and the car is "not worth more than $25,000, tops." Divine Cuisine, her caterer, hired you several months ago to collect the $15,600 that it is owed for a series of receptions Angelica gave for bosses and coworkers. What position will you take on their behalf regarding Angelica's plan?

13.2. Mr. and Mrs. Poltz are a small, neat couple who have sat in front of your desk for an hour and a half without a single smile. They are hoping you can save their home. Mr. Poltz was an inventory control clerk for the Chicago school district, but was hurt about two years ago and has been "on disability" since that time. Because the school district has good disability benefits, he is receiving about $2,900 a month. They have only modest personal possessions worth about $4,000, all of which would be exempt. The small equity they have in their house would also be exempt.

Mrs. Poltz is not employed. After paying their spartan expenses and their mortgage, they have about $150 a month left over. After Mr. Poltz was injured, they ran up credit card bills and borrowed some money unsecured from a local finance company, "always thinking Mr. P. would be back to work in just a little time." They have $10,750.42 in unsecured debts. They missed three payments on the house when Mr. Poltz's disability checks were stopped because of a computer error. The bank filed a foreclosure suit and an answer is due tomorrow, but the bank officer called last week and said they would be willing to work things out. The Poltzes say they can pick up the current payments on the mortgage and pay the arrears within three months. They have heard about chapter 13 being used for saving a home, and they are willing to pay the full $150 a month to a plan "for as long as you say." You have no doubt you could get their chapter 13 plan confirmed. What is your advice?

13.3. Noah Zinner has labored tirelessly as a community organizer and social worker. To show for it, he has two advanced degrees, a slew of awards from foundations and government and a lot of personal debt. Despite a very frugal lifestyle—he drives a beater, has used furniture, buys his clothes secondhand—he just can't seem to make ends meet on the $32,000 that he earns. He lives in Baltimore with his wife Emily, who stays at home with their four young kids. With the arrival of twins a couple of years ago, Noah started using credit cards for basic expenses, and paying just over the minimum each month. At this point, he owes $70,000 on his cards and his marriage is frayed from bickering over the bills. He wants to be an example to his community, many of whom struggle for years with low incomes and debts, and frankly is afraid of a tarnished reputation if he files bankruptcy. As a result, he adamantly insists on chapter 13 during your initial free consultation with him. What do you tell him at the end of the consultation? §§1307, 1325(a), 1328, 1329.

13.4. Maggie Smith recently won a prestigious fellowship for young lawyers to develop innovative practices. She has purchased a "taco truck" and plans to drive the truck to streets near factories that employ large numbers of low-income workers. She and a paralegal will offer commonly needed legal services, including consumer bankruptcy, at a reduced cost based on a person's ability to pay (i.e., "low bono"). You were two years ahead of Maggie in law school and have escaped from the litigation division of your large firm into a niche practice in legal professional responsibility and malpractice. Maggie has asked you to donate time on a pro bono basis to helping her draft the disclosures that she should give her bankruptcy clients. Besides a retainer agreement, what else will she need? What disclosures should she make and what language will you advise her to include? Are there additional disclosures that you would recommend based on norms of ethical practice? §§526, 527, 528, 707(b)(4).

13.5. You are a member of a law reform commission that is tasked with reform of the consumer bankruptcy system. The Congressperson who funded the commission became interested in the issue after reading this passage in an article:

> I strongly believe that the current consumer bankruptcy system is unjust. I do not use that term lightly; the debate on whether and how much income contribution should be required in the context of debt relief is powerful evidence that "justice" in bankruptcy reflects very different normative beliefs. But the existing system of chapter 7 and chapter 13 is truly built on sand; its very foundation of informed consumer choice is not supported by any evidence. For thirty years, we have known that the sorting between chapter 7 and chapter 13 does not occur based on debtors having different financial circumstances or having different normative preferences. The research consistently shows that the

selection of chapter—which itself determines the burdens of filing and the relief received—is determined by local legal culture, attorney steering, and often outright misinformation.

Assume that Congress is resolute that the two-chapter system must go. Your task is clear: recommend either solely a chapter 7 option or solely a chapter 13 option. Be prepared to vote on your position and offer reasons—based on law or policy—to support your position.

Assignment 14.
The Consumer Bankruptcy System

The Bankruptcy Code is more than just a complex law; it is an expression of social policy. It reflects political compromise over conflicting theories of debt relief. While some view relief as morally compelled, others see it as a necessary evil, with a range of opinions in the middle on the risks and benefits of forgiving legal obligations. This assignment introduces some of the contested and competing goals of the consumer bankruptcy system. It discusses the major justifications for helping families in financial distress and the most prevalent countervailing concerns with such a system. These theories and counter-theories are diverse, with economic, moral, and social considerations all in play. Although you had a brief introduction in the first assignment, we have saved this academic exploration until after you learned how the nuts and bolts of the system work in practice. This way you can reflect back critically on what does, and does not, jibe with the theories you find most compelling.

No system is driven purely by theory. Congress is a political animal and succumbs to fads, lobbying, and fecklessness. BAPCPA was animated by a belief that bankruptcy was "too easy" because many debtors "can pay" but just choose to file bankruptcy instead. The Great Recession has led many bankruptcy experts to urge dramatic reform and overhaul of that very young law. Others fear that more change can only worsen perceived problems of the current system. As the United States wrestles with these issues, countries around the world are adopting consumer bankruptcy laws—often for the first time in their nation's history—that are frequently based on the basic U.S. model of debt relief.

For better or worse, we have chosen a judicial model of debt relief in this country, run by bankruptcy judges, trustees, and, of course, attorneys. We therefore close this reflective assignment with a hard look at the lawyer's role in consumer bankruptcy, with special emphasis on the ethical perils it brings.

A. THEORIES OF CONSUMER BANKRUPTCY RELIEF

1. Introduction: The Fresh Start

The most ubiquitously deployed justification of consumer bankruptcy is that it is necessary to facilitate a debtor's "fresh start." This concept is usually traced to Local Loan Co. v. Hunt, 292 U.S. 234, 244 (1934), but therein the Court cited an earlier case in which it recited that a primary purpose of bankruptcy is to "relieve the honest debtor from the weight of oppressive indebtedness, and permit him to start afresh free from the obligations and responsibilities consequent upon business misfortunes." Williams v. U.S. Fidelity & Guaranty Co., 236 U.S. 549, 554-55 (1915). The idea seems to be one of general forgiveness: honest but unfortunate debtors get a second chance and should not be consigned to a life of debt servitude. As we shall see, however, many disagree as to whether the source of that forgiveness is economic incentivization, moral duty, or something else. Indeed, many try to elide this question-begging nature of the fresh start concept. "Some scholars just reiterate the term *fresh start* in their justifications, saying, for example, that debtors should have an 'opportunity to begin anew' or a 'chance to start over.'" Karen Gross, Failure and Forgiveness: Rebalancing the Bankruptcy Code 91 (1999). Accordingly, while there is no serious challenge in this country to the fundamental idea of the discharge of debt, there has been hot debate over its scope. Because that debate turns in substantial part on the justification for a fresh start, we turn to the major theories of consumer bankruptcy relief.

2. Rehabilitation and Human Capital

Some scholars focus on the individual benefit accorded by the bankruptcy discharge, identifying rehabilitation as the animating concept of the fresh start. In this literature, the focus is on returning the debtor to "productive economic participation." Margaret Howard, A Theory of Discharge in Consumer Bankruptcy, 48 Ohio St. L.J. 1047, 1088 (1987). As one of us put it more colorfully, "[S]ociety as a whole also loses when moping bankrupt debtors are distracted from working at their highest and best use level of productivity because they are instead coping with financial ruin." John A.E. Pottow, Private Liability for Reckless Consumer Lending, 2007 U. Ill. L. Rev. 405, 412. This productivity notion of bankruptcy allows the individual debtor to keep future wages and sufficient property so as to stay off the public dole and to maximize society's labor resources.

An offshoot of this productivity theory of bankruptcy is research on entrepreneurship. Particularly in the United States, with its strong cultural norm of small business capitalism, restyling "consumer" bankruptcy as a necessary component of supporting self-employment and economic innovation is popular.

Empirical research consequently has tried to capture the benefits of providing a "cushion for the increased level of risk of financial failure associated with entrepreneurship." Rafael Efrat, The Rise & Fall of Entrepreneurs: An Empirical Study of Individual Bankruptcy Petitioners in Israel, 7 Stan. J.L. Bus. & Fin. 163, 167 (2002).

This theory is deeply utilitarian, expressed in language centered on "the redeployment of the debtor's human capital" through a discharge of debt. Ronald J. Mann, Making Sense of Nation-Level Bankruptcy Filing Rates, in Consumer Credit, Debt and Bankruptcy: Comparative and International Perspectives 225, 242 (Johanna Niemi, Iain Ramsay & William Whitford eds., 2009). Debt relief may be humane for the individual, but that help is given for the greater service of the collective, not out of a moral or social duty to relieve an individual's human suffering.

3. Social Insurance

Some argue that consumer bankruptcy is best understood as a form of social insurance. Sometimes honest but unfortunate debtors hit financial cataclysm, and bankruptcy's fresh start ensures they will not spend the rest of their lives suffering from this faultless economic shock. Barry Adler, Ben Polak, and Alan Schwartz, Regulating Consumer Bankruptcy: A Theoretical Inquiry, 29 J. Leg. Stud. 585 (2000) (discussing social insurance theory). This theory rests in significant degree on empirical assumptions about the fraction of bankruptcies caused by "accidents" or similar misfortunes outside the debtor's control.

> Thus, at least in theory, bankruptcy should be thought of as a potential wage insurance, health insurance, disability insurance, workers' compensation, and divorce insurance program rolled into one. . . . Moving from the realm of theory to that of observation, it appears that bankruptcy does in fact serve the social insurance functions described above. . . . According to one prominent empirical study of consumer bankruptcy filings, nearly two-thirds of debtors cite job interruption or job loss, while 22% of individuals in bankruptcy cite family-related problems—including divorce—in the months leading up to their filing for bankruptcy. That same study found that nearly 20% percent of debtors cite medical problems, which in some cases were likely to be related to injury or disability. . . . It is important to note that some scholars are skeptical of these findings, however, and debate over the determinants of bankruptcy continues to be robust. Some writers have suggested that the causes of bankruptcy are likely to be more endogenous than recent empirical studies suggest. If so, recent studies may underestimate the extent to which over-consumption causes people to become insolvent.
>
> . . . [E]ven the critics of recent empirical studies acknowledge that the causes of many bankruptcies are exogenous to some significant extent. In doing

so, they acknowledge the underlying insight of the empirical data—that bankruptcy does function, at least in part, as a form of wage insurance, divorce insurance, disability insurance, and health insurance. To the extent it does so, it is important to bear in mind that bankruptcy serves the same social insurance functions as unemployment insurance, Medicare, disability insurance, workers' compensation, and spousal support laws.

Adam Feibelman, Defining the Social Insurance Function of Consumer Bankruptcy, 13 Am. Bankr. Inst. L. Rev. 129, 158-160 (2005).

Research suggests that families today are saddled with more exogenous financial risks than in the 1950s or 1970s when filing rates were much lower. See Jacob Hacker, The Great Risk Shift (2006) (describing the higher likelihood of a significant income drop in recent decades); *Two-Income Trap* (explaining link of that financial risk to bankruptcy). Discharging or reorganizing debt can help families right themselves from the financial consequences of job loss, family break-up, or medical problems—factors commonly considered the "big three" of consumer collapse. See *Fragile Middle Class* (documenting the primary explanations that people give for their bankruptcy filings). Compounding the complexity of these empirical studies is uncertainty regarding causation: something may be both a cause and a consequence of financial distress. For example, does poor health cause unmanageable debt because of medical bills and lost wages, or do people in debt suffer poor health because of stress and foregone preventative care? See Melissa B. Jacoby, Does Indebtedness Influence Health? A Preliminary Inquiry, 30 J.L. Med. & Ethics 560 (2002).

A social insurance theory of bankruptcy is more descriptive than normative. That is, adherents may, in theory, be just as happy disposing with the bankruptcy discharge and implementing a "financial crisis" government assistance program. Those of a more mercantile bent note the Aflac duck is squawking away about such insurance being provided by the private market. Second-order debate then ensues about whether such insurance should be optional for the prudent, like fire insurance, or mandatory for the disorganized, like automotive liability coverage. Those of a libertarian leaning chafe at mandatory insurance and they join those of a finger-wagging disposition to say that consumers should have the foresight to plan for their own distress (and their failure to do so should not be bailed out by those smart enough to do so). The argument is that an unwaivable bankruptcy discharge spares the rod to spoil the child.

But others contend that laws have to deal with real humans, not rational actors, and the error rates of individuals' predictive capabilities may militate toward compulsory insurance. Indeed, even with a draconian remedy for not paying debts in the U.S. in colonial times, debtor's prisons were at capacity. Imbedded in the tension about these approaches are empirical questions about the relative foreseeability of adverse events and whether their magnitude is of such degree that one could reasonably insure or save. For example, we are unaware of "birth defect insurance" that covers the lifetime costs of raising a severely disabled child and we are skeptical that private actors can self-insure with actuarial precision. By contrast, the financial harms from the death of a spouse and the loss of earning power can be covered with term insurance at a cost that many families can afford. In this view, the bankruptcy discharge insures a residual class of "uninsurable" disaster.

Part of the debate is purely empirical. How many filings fit the description of "uninsurable" disaster, and how many filings are better described as the result of profligate spending or overconsumption? Figuring out how to measure the "cause" of bankruptcy is itself hotly debated. For present purposes, it is worth noting that any data on causation comes from academic studies. Many debtors leave 341 meetings or confirmation hearings shocked that the trustee or judge is fundamentally uninterested in *why* they filed bankruptcy. (Look at the schedules for requirements that debtors explain how and why they incurred the debts; your search will be fruitless.) The lack of data allows the debate to flourish because both sides make assertions about the frequency, magnitude, and foreseeability of adverse events and profligacy.

Even the staunchest free marketer, however, is willing to embrace government intervention in the face of market failure or externality problems. Negative externalities, in the economic parlance, are costs that result from an activity that affect an otherwise uninvolved party who did not choose to incur those costs. If bankruptcy inflicts negative consequences on others beside the debtor, the mandatory insurance function served by the bankruptcy discharge may be defensible. So does it? Many have argued that the recent housing market collapse has shown that when financially distressed homeowners lose a home to foreclosure, even those who are timely, diligent mortgage-payers get hurt when prices collapse across whole neighborhoods. That said, empirical research is scant, and "the case for negative bankruptcy externalities is more intuitive than empirical at this juncture." John A.E. Pottow, Private Liability for Reckless Consumer Lending, 2007 U. Ill. L. Rev. 405, 412. Indeed, it is not even clear what we would try to measure as the "harm" of consumer debt problems. Katherine Porter, The Damage of Debt, 69 Wash. & Lee L. Rev. 979 (2012).

European countries, with the United Kingdom in particular, are much further ahead on the research front. There, financial distress has been subdivided into a distinct problem of "overindebtedness," which is defined as arising when existing and foreseeable resources are insufficient for a household to meet its financial commitments without lowering its living standards below what is regarded as a minimum acceptable threshold. Researchers are now trying to measure when the consequences of debt, both for an individual and society, impose unacceptable harms that warrant forgiveness as a policy prescription. This scholarly field is evolving.

4. Moral Obligation

Bankruptcy has always been laden with moral overtones. The fresh start of the discharge finds analogue in the Biblical Jubilee, just as the conception that a promise to repay someone a debt has moral, not just legal, purchase—even in a world where mass marketing of credit and computer programs for underwriting have taken the place of a strong handshake and look in the eye of a loan officer. These diametric moral duties are on display in the following two excerpts.

> [B]ankruptcy should not merely be a means of violating promises willy-nilly. A promise to repay money is an important legal and moral obligation, neither lightly to be undertaken nor lightly cast away. Filing bankruptcy represents a decision to repudiate promises made in exchange for goods, services, and other promises. Of such promises and reciprocity is the fabric of civil society woven.

Edith H. Jones & Todd J. Zywicki, It's Time for Means-Testing, 1999 BYU L. Rev. 177, 181 (1999).

> Rehabilitation is a goal that says something about American society. In part, society assists debtors on humanitarian grounds. Rehabilitating debtors is part of the responsibility to treat members of society humanely. It promotes values of human dignity and self respect. It also enables people and business to be a part of the ongoing credit economy. As was stated in an 1822 letter to Congress on the desirability of a bankruptcy law, bankruptcy can be seen as an "essential attribute of active and humane society.... [It is necessary] in vindication of the national humanity." A New York Times editorial made a similar point, albeit in a different context, when it observed that a "community is only as strong as the care and respect it gives its weakest members." Debtors are among the weak members of a credit society. If our treatment of them were motivated by retaliation or retribution, we would not be showing care or respect.

Karen Gross, Failure and Forgiveness: Rebalancing the Bankruptcy System 102-03 (1997).

Both approaches reflect strong normative convictions about debt and debt problems. But the former would counsel toward tougher requirements for good faith screens and repayment mandates in a bankruptcy law, whereas the latter would focus on the need to protect the discharge for those suffering from debt problems. Note that the humanitarian approach as expressed above does not concern itself with the borrower's role in accumulating the debt or the nature or the kind of debt. (Notice this similarity with the utilitarian approach.) The promise-keeping approach, however, might find such distinctions quite relevant.

(Contrast debts from a voluntary credit card agreement to medical bills for life-saving treatment for injuries caused by being hit by an uninsured drunk driver.)

As a matter of virtue ethics, forgiving debt can be seen as character-enhancing. Professor Heidi Hurd argues that releasing debtors from debts owed to us that the debtor cannot pay is an aretaic obligation, an act that cultivates a generous and forgiving character. She argues that "a desire to enforce obligations when doing so would impose upon debtors significant hardship and distress manifests attributes of character that are rightly condemned, rather than admired. Put inversely, the virtuous person does not press his rights against someone when doing so will inflict genuine suffering and psychological despair." Heidi Hurd, The Virtue of Consumer Bankruptcy, 221-22 in A Debtor's World: Interdisciplinary Perspectives on Debt (eds. Ralph Brubaker, Robert Lawless & Charles Tabb 2012). Can you connect this theory of consumer bankruptcy with the decision of JPMorgan Chase to charge off millions of dollars of consumer debt each quarter? Do you think Jamie Dimon feels virtuous when he reports the losses to the Board and shareholders, or do you think a hardened profit-seeker simply recognizes that blood cannot be drawn from a stone?

5. *Social Peace*

As Simone Weil noted in the excerpt reproduced earlier, modern societies necessarily have a distinctly mixed, and complex, view of debt. For an economy to function properly, most debt must be paid; for a society to function properly, debt must sometimes be forgiven. This point has arisen in civilizations for millennia. The reforms of Solon arose from a tumultuous time in the history of Athens when debtors revolted against their chains of debt, just as the reforms of the Bankruptcy Act arose from periodic financial panics in the United States. David A. Skeel, Debt's Dominion (2003). The social interest in debt rehabilitation is not just keeping people off the public dole, it's also keeping them off the parapets (or out of the polls).

The United States has embraced forgiveness of debts in its social culture nearly from its inception. The idea of a new beginning is woven into the fabric of our historical narrative. Bruce H. Mann, Republic of Debtors (2002). Think of immigrants fleeing creditors to the new colonies in the United States, leaving behind the old classes, the old religion, the old ideas—and the old debts. The same pattern repeated itself with the Conestoga wagon setting off for Oregon, and the farmers fleeing the Dust Bowl. With such a rich history of financial fresh starts, it is no accident that the United States was and remains the most debtor-friendly nation.

6. Creditor Conduct

Creditors' concerns also shape theories of bankruptcy. We've already pointed to some of these issues back in Assignment 1 (and a bit in Assignment 6 about claims), so we only give a quick reminder here, mainly because these concerns are more dominant in the business context. Recall that bankruptcy is a collective process, binding all creditors together in an orderly—and equal—distribution. Diligent or sophisticated creditors may hate the fact that they have to share in bankruptcy the spoils they could get with a state-law levy with lazy or unsophisticated creditors who would not pursue such collection activity. But such is the consequence of bankruptcy's deliberate restraint of creditor conduct. The overarching idea of bankruptcy under this theory is to prevent the destruction of value by precipitous and duplicative collections actions to maximize the overall recovery for everyone. Particularly for individuals, a pari passu bankruptcy distribution scheme aids creditors, such as ex-spouses owed support, from receiving nothing because larger ones, such as institutional banks, collect fast and hard, dissipating assets that if sold by a bankruptcy trustee (or held onto in a chapter 13 plan) could have produced a higher payout for all.

A related idea comes from Professor Thomas Jackson, the major proponent of the collective action argument grounding the creditor-focused theory of bankruptcy. Jackson says we need a discharge to police creditors from overleveraging debtors. If they go too far, the debtor will go bankrupt and the creditor will have the debt discharged.

> Discharge policy provides an alternative [to governmental oversight]: it leaves the determination of whether to extend credit to *creditors*, who presumably are better trained in credit policy than are legislators, and who are better able, by observing individual debtors or by employing specific contractual covenants, to monitor individuals' consumption of credit. To be sure, creditors would engage in some degree of monitoring even if the right to discharge were unavailable; they would still have an incentive to prevent an individual from falling so heavily into debt that he would lose the ability to repay. Discharge, however, heightens creditors' incentives to monitor: by providing for a right of discharge, society enlists creditors in the effort to oversee the individual's credit decisions even when the individual has not fully mortgaged his future. The availability of the right of discharge induces creditors to restrict the individual's credit intake and thus to ensure that he does not seriously underestimate his future needs. The nonwaivability of the [discharge] right forces the individual—and hence his creditors—to leave uncommitted a portion of his future wealth. Moreover, a nonwaivable discharge rule does what other laws regulating credit cannot do as effectively: it allows individuals to present their particular needs and desires to creditors, thereby permitting creditors to tailor their responses to individual circumstances.

The Fresh Start Policy in Bankruptcy Law, 98 Harv. L. Rev., 1393, 1426 (1985). Lest he be mistaken for debtor solicitude, Jackson quickly adds that this policy is driven by prudent social planning: "[T]the right to a fresh start embodied in discharge is not merely a matter of bankruptcy law, but rather a special example of the increasingly common legal requirement that individuals preserve a certain portion of their assets for the future." Id. at 1398. For a challenge to Professor Jackson's proposition that the market-based fear of charge-offs adequately polices lenders from lending to debtors who cannot repay, see, e.g., Pottow, Reckless Lending, *supra* (discussing literature on credit industry incentives).

One final benefit of the bankruptcy discharge aimed at creditors, which they may find painful but that is important to regulators and the economy, is forcing lenders to charge off losses from debtors who cannot or will not pay. Bankruptcy's reckoning promotes proper account valuation. If this concept seems nebulous, consider how the bifurcation of secured debt in bankruptcy smokes out the value of the collateral.

B. COUNTERVAILING CONCERNS

The bankruptcy discharge is a powerful tool for a debtor to deploy. As such, there are serious worries, theoretical and empirical, about how to police abuse. These countervailing concerns are not just knee-jerk opposition from a powerful credit lobby against anything seemingly pro-debtor; they are held by scholars, politicians, and the general public. Sometimes they invoke great passion, as seen in the frequently heated debates over BAPCPA.

1. Fraud

Any theory of bankruptcy needs limiting principles about when relief is justified. One of the most ancient concerns is about identifying and punishing fraud. People who hide assets from creditors to avoid repayment are bad; people who hide assets from creditors to avoid repayment and procure a discharge in bankruptcy are worse. Recall that the debtor in *Hunt* was not just "unfortunate" but also crucially "honest." A regime of forgiveness and fresh start needs honest players. The following case shows the system's approach to detecting fraud, and the holes in that system that animate protests for tighter standards.

———— **In re LANDRY** ————

350 B.R. 51 (Bankr. E.D. La. 2006)

BROWN, Judge

. . .

On December 9, 2003, the debtors filed a joint voluntary petition for relief under Chapter 7 of the United States Bankruptcy Code. At issue in this case is a 1999 Harley Davidson motorcycle owned by the debtor husband at the date of filing of this bankruptcy petition. . . The debtors did not disclose anywhere in the original schedules that he or they owned the 1999 Harley Davidson motorcycle. Claude Lightfoot, Jr. was appointed as the trustee in the case and a creditors' meeting was held on January 23, 2004 as required by §341 of the Bankruptcy Code. The trustee testified at trial that the debtors did not mention ownership of the motorcycle at the creditors' meeting.

On February 19, 2004, the trustee received an anonymous letter that indicated the debtors were abusing the bankruptcy process and concealing assets.[4] Specifically, the letter mentioned a "fancy shinny (sic) motor cycle" owned by the debtors. Because there were no objections to discharge, on March 26, 2004 the court entered the customary, routine order discharging the debtors. On August 6, 2004, the trustee sent a letter to the debtors inquiring into the anonymous report of the debtors' ownership of the motorcycle and addressing other matters relevant to the debtors' bankruptcy case. On August 17, 2004, the debtors filed amended schedules that listed the motorcycle on Schedule B. At the same time, the debtors amended their schedules to claim an exemption for the motorcycle. . . .

The trustee objected to the amendment of the debtors' schedules to claim the additional exemption for the motorcycle, and the court after an evidentiary hearing sustained that objection. The trustee also filed a motion for turnover of the motorcycle, which the court granted, and the motorcycle was sold at auction by the trustee with the proceeds going to the debtors' estate for distribution to creditors. On March 23, 2005 the trustee filed this complaint to revoke the debtors' discharge under §727(d)(1) of the Bankruptcy Code.

. . .

---

4. Exhibit 3. The court notes that the letter is brief. Its authorship was never determined even at the two trials held in this case, both involving the motorcycle. . . . Fortunately, determining the identity of the author is not necessary to a decision in this case.

The debtors in this case argue that the trustee is not entitled to proceed with this action to revoke the debtors' discharge because the trustee had knowledge of the debtors' alleged fraud before the deadline for objecting to the discharge, and that the trustee failed to act before that deadline. They further argue that even if the trustee is entitled to bring this action, their failure to schedule the motorcycle was a mistake, and they did not have the intent required to prove fraud under §727. The trustee contends that although he received the anonymous letter that contained allegations that the debtors had not scheduled the motorcycle before the debtors' discharge was entered, he did not have confirmation that the debtors did indeed own the motorcycle until after the discharge had been entered. Therefore, argues the trustee, he is entitled to bring this action under §727(d)(1). Further, the trustee argues that the debtors did act with fraudulent intent such that their discharge should be revoked.

The court first examines the requirement that the party requesting the revocation not know of the fraud until after the discharge was granted. There are two lines of cases discussing the "did not know" requirement of §727(d)(1). The minority view, which the trustee urges that the court follow, construes the knowledge requirement leniently and holds that discovery occurs when the party seeking revocation obtains actual knowledge of the facts giving rise to the action. The majority view, relied on by the debtor, construes the knowledge requirement much more strictly and holds that knowledge in a §727(d)(1) revocation action occurs when the party seeking revocation first becomes aware of facts such that he is put on notice of a possible fraud. This line of cases holds that the burden is heavily on the party seeking revocation to diligently investigate any possibly fraudulent conduct as soon as he becomes aware of facts indicating said conduct.

. . .

The rationale in these cases is that placing the burden of investigation on the party seeking revocation ensures that potentially fraudulent acts are investigated promptly. . . . This is not to say that a trustee is required to suspect that every debtor is committing fraud in his schedules. As a general rule, the trustee is entitled to rely on the truthfulness and accuracy of the debtor's schedules and is not required to assume that the debtor is lying. However, once the trustee is in possession of facts that would put a reasonable person on notice of a possible fraud, he has a duty to diligently investigate to determine if grounds exist for the denial of the Debtor's discharge and if so to timely file a complaint. . . .

The court is sympathetic to the trustee's argument that the trustee handles numerous cases in this district and receives a large volume of mail related to those cases on a daily basis [including those from "disgruntled creditors, ex-spouses or others]." Had the trustee acted promptly to follow up on the letter and been hindered in his inquiry by the debtor, or if the trustee had begun an immediate inquiry that took until after the discharge had been granted to complete, the court would be more inclined to find that the trustee had borne its burden of acting diligently to discover the alleged fraud. But because the trustee waited for what the court considers to be an extended period of time to investigate, with no explanation other than that the trustee handles a large number of bankruptcy cases, the court cannot find that the trustee acted promptly with reasonable diligence.

. . .

Complicating the facts of this case are the conflicting accounts of how the motorcycle came to be omitted from the debtors' schedules. The court notes that there are malpractice actions pending before this court involving the debtors' first and second bankruptcy attorneys, respectively Mr. Alvarez and Ms. McPherson. . . .

At trial the debtors both testified that they did not schedule the motorcycle because Mr. Alvarez, their attorney at the time of filing, told them that they could save the motorcycle by either giving it to a relative or not listing it. . . .

The court rejects the debtors' testimony that Mr. Alvarez told them to omit the motorcycle from their schedules or to give it to a relative for several reasons. First, Mr. Alvarez testified under cross-examination that not only did he not tell the debtors to omit the motorcycle from the schedules, but that he did not discuss the motorcycle with the debtors at any time prior to the filing of the bankruptcy petition. Second, the debtors' corroborating witnesses were not told that Mr. Alvarez had given the debtors this "advice" until after the debtors received the letter from the trustee requesting further information about the motorcycle. Third, the court does not accept the contention that Mr. Alvarez, an attorney who has handled several bankruptcy cases over the past five to seven years and who has been an attorney for over 40 years, would specifically advise a client—even a non-paying one—to commit bankruptcy fraud.

The court does not find that the debtors in this case acted with the requisite fraudulent intent when filling out their schedules to support a revocation of discharge. Although the other elements of §727(a)(4)(A) are met, i.e., the debtor made a statement under oath, the statement was false, the debtor knew the statement was false, and the statement related materially to the bankruptcy case, the court does not find the debtors made the statement with fraudulent intent. Specifically, the court finds that the debtors did not appear to the court to be sophisticated in their knowledge of bankruptcy. Although Mrs. Landry worked for an attorney for several years as a secretary, both she and her former employer, Mr. Gamble, testified that his office did not take any bankruptcy cases, and that Mrs. Landry did not have any understanding of how a bankruptcy case worked. The debtors' first attorney, Mr. Alvarez, testified that he did not review the completed schedules with the debtors, nor did he give them information about exemptions. Mr. Alvarez stated that he did give Mrs. Landry a blank set of schedules to fill out and told her that she needed to fill all of them out completely. He stated that because she worked for an attorney, he thought she would know how to fill out the forms. He met with her once the forms had been completed by Mrs. Landry, but assumed that they were correct and only checked them to see that something had been written on each form. Mr. Alvarez then signed the forms and filed them with the court on behalf of the Landrys. . . .

The court does not find that the debtors in this case acted with the requisite fraudulent intent when filling out their schedules to support a revocation of discharge. Although the other elements of §727(a)(4)(A) are met, i.e., the debtor made a statement under oath, the statement was false, the debtor knew the statement was false, and the statement related materially to the bankruptcy case, the court does not find the debtors made the statement with fraudulent intent. Specifically, the court finds that the debtors did not appear to the court to be sophisticated in their knowledge of bankruptcy. Although Mrs. Landry worked for an attorney for several years as a secretary, both she and her former employer, Mr. Gamble, testified that his office did not take any bankruptcy cases, and that Mrs. Landry did not have any understanding of how a bankruptcy case worked. The debtors' first attorney, Mr. Alvarez, testified that he did not review the completed schedules with the debtors, nor did he give them information about exemptions. Mr. Alvarez stated that he did give Mrs. Landry a blank set of schedules to fill out and told her that she needed to fill all of them out completely. He stated that because she worked for an attorney, he thought she would know how to fill out the forms. He met with her once the forms had been completed by Mrs. Landry, but assumed that they were correct and only checked them to see that something had been written on each form. Mr. Alvarez then signed the forms and filed them with the court on behalf of the Landrys. Additionally, according to the evidence presented at trial, the omission from the schedules concerned one item, not numerous items. When the trustee sent a letter to the debtors inquiring about the motorcycle and the tax returns, the debtors promptly consulted a new attorney and filed amended schedules within 10 to 11 days correcting the omission.

. . .

Considering all the circumstances in this case and the highly conflicting testimony . . . the trustee's complaint seeking to revoke the debtors' discharge is dismissed.

═══════════

The *Landry* case also raises issues about attorney practice, such as what to do about an undisclosed but "shinny" motorcycle, and so we turn to legal ethics considerations at the end of this assignment.

2. Declining Stigma

We open our discussion of stigma with modern humor, courtesy of *The Office*.

MICHAEL [*to all staff*]: I . . . declare . . . BANKRUPTCY!!!!!!!!!!!!!!!!!!

[*Staff all stares at him.*]

[*Scene cuts to Michael in his office, cutting a credit card in half.*]

OSCAR: [knocks on door] Hey, I just wanted you to know that you can't just say the word bankruptcy and expect anything to happen.

MICHAEL: I didn't SAY it; I DECLARED it.

OSCAR: Still. That's . . . that's not anything.

The Office: Money (NBC television broadcast Oct. 18, 2007), available at http://www.youtube.com/watch?v=hiCilTzhXrA.

Some might point to this episode as evidence of declining moral values about the importance of repaying debts and avoiding bankruptcy. After all, bankruptcy should be serious business, not sitcom humor. What has the world come to when someone would make such a declaration in front of work colleagues? Critics of the present bankruptcy system have asserted that bankruptcy has lost its stigma, with the implication that that stigma serves as a necessary social check on over-use of the bankruptcy discharge beyond the truly needy. Edith H. Jones & Todd J. Zywicki, It's Time for Means-Testing, 1999 BYU L. Rev. 177. Some perceive such a change in the stigma of bankruptcy as part of a general moral decline in our society, while others point to the laxity of the bankruptcy laws specifically as deserving the blame. (The 1978 Code intentionally sought to destigmatize bankruptcy, for example, by replacing the term "bankrupts" with "debtors.")

Scant empirical support has been offered for the declining stigma hypothesis, see, e.g., F.H. Buckley & Margaret F. Brinig, The Bankruptcy Puzzle, 27 J. Legal Stud. 187 (1998) (using Roman Catholicism and divorce rates as proxies for social disinclination to file bankruptcy), and other evidence actually suggests that bankruptcy stigma has worsened or at least remained constant. To be sure, the foreclosure crisis of the Great Recession may have reshaped some of these attitudes, but we await the studies relating home loss to general attitudes about debt relief. On balance, most of the sociological research suggests bankruptcy is a stigmatizing experience. One pre-BAPCPA study, for example, explains how debtors hid their bankruptcies from family members, friends, neighbors, and coworkers. *Two-Income Trap* at 13. Another looks at the way that one might expect stigma to change the financial characteristics of filers. Its hypothesis and findings: "If the bankruptcy ranks have been swelled even in part by the presence of significant numbers of can-pay debtors, then the median debt-to-income ratio for the group should fall. The data, however, tell a different story. The ratio has risen sharply from 1.4 to 3.0 for total debt-to-income and similarly from 0.79 to 1.5 for nonmortgage debt-to-income. . . ." Teresa A. Sullivan, Elizabeth Warren & Jay L. Westbrook, Less Stigma or More Financial Distress: An Empirical Analysis of the Extraordinary Increase in Bankruptcy Filings, 59 Stan. L. Rev. 213, 236-39 (2006). The authors note that if stigma decline explained even half of the bankruptcy increase from the mid-1980s to mid-2000s, such a result would represent a sea change in American values in a very short period. Id. at 235. Whatever the available evidence, it is clear that the BAPCPA amendments were driven by a belief that many debtors could pay their debts but just didn't want to, which aligns with a worldview of vanishing stigma.

3. *Moral Hazard*

Moral hazard is a concern that people will borrow and spend profligately because bankruptcy relief is available as an out. Jay Lawrence Westbrook, Local Legal Culture and the Fear of Abuse, 6 Am. Bankr. Inst. L. Rev. 463 (1998). One solution to moral hazard is to allow consumers to demonstrate their imperviousness to such temptation. For example, debt contracts with such remedies as "arm-breaking" would minimize borrower moral hazard. Samuel A. Rea, Arm-Breaking, Consumer Credit and Personal Bankruptcy, 22 Econ. Inquiry 188 (1984). Some believe that allowing debtors to opt out of bankruptcy discharge will help combat moral hazard. Barry Adler, Ben Polak & Alan Schwartz, Regulating Consumer Bankruptcy: A Theoretical Inquiry, 29 J. Leg. Stud. 585 (2000) (arguing that mandatory bankruptcy laws for consumers are inefficient). The broader economic point is that tougher bankruptcy laws make moral hazard less likely and so lower the cost of credit.

We have little to add to this discussion because it raises many of the same concerns of declining moral stigma, albeit articulated with an economist's dispassion. (The social insurance theory of bankruptcy naturally raises questions of fraud and moral hazard, the two big worries of insurers; diminishing stigma would only compound the moral hazard concern.) It grabbed the attention of the Congress, where repeated passages of BAPCPA's legislative history complained of bankruptcy becoming "too easy." "[T]oo many people have abused the bankruptcy laws. They've walked away from debts even when they had the ability to repay them." President George W. Bush, Remarks at the Signing of [BAPCPA] (April 20, 2005).

One point to clarify on both the declining stigma and moral hazard concerns is that there are two ways bankruptcy can be "too easy." First, debtors facing financial distress might choose bankruptcy instead of belt-tightening, negotiating deferred payments to creditors, or working harder. Second, particularly strategic and long-range planning debtors might react to bankruptcy with more "upstream" conduct, incurring debt in the first place—or choosing not to accrue a rainy day fund—secure in the knowledge a bankruptcy discharge awaits them should things turn bad. Stigma moralists probably worry more about the first problem of post-distress conduct, whereas moral hazardists fret more about the upstream effects, which economists would call the "ex ante" incentives of bankruptcy. The data on the first point seem to point in the direction that debtors in bankruptcy are in wretched financial shape and so probably couldn't pay much, BAPCPA notwithstanding. Robert Lawless et al., Did Bankruptcy Reform Fail? An Empirical Study of Consumer Debtors, 82 Am. Bankr. L.J. 349 (2008).

The data on the second point—of upstream incentive effects—are hard to come by. Natural legal experiments are rare, but some scholars have tried to weigh in. For example, the increased entrepreneurial activity linked with higher state exemptions could be used to show that debtors (at least debtors inclined toward business) do respond to legal incentives relating to collection law. See Wei Fan & Michelle J. White, Personal Bankruptcy and the Level of Entrepreneurial Activity, 46 J.L. & Econ. 543 (2003). But speculation on the ex ante effects of bankruptcy law remains in the realm of conjecture. Our own eight cents are that while some insurances bring moral hazard effects, others don't. Some may tear around in rental cars, but few likely start smoking because they have Blue Cross health insurance. Applying the social insurance model to bankruptcy, our own view of best available evidence is that few people mire themselves in debt because they think bankruptcy is an easy out.

4. Cross-Subsidization

Although lenders try to credit score, it is tough to tell in advance who will go bankrupt, especially since some bankruptcies are driven by exogenous events unrelated to debtor conduct, such as a job loss at a closed factory. This means if the bankruptcy discharge imposes losses on the lender ex post (i.e., after the credit has been extended), those costs will be recouped ex ante (lenders do this by spreading costs to the next round of borrowers, pricing it into credit terms, or at the extreme, rationing credit.) If bankruptcy correctly addresses the moral hazard concern and identifies the honest but unfortunate debtor idealized in *Hunt*, then all is as it should be: losses are distributed among all who borrow, as a cross-subsidy from the non-bankrupt to the bankrupt. While some assert this is unfair to responsible promise-keeping debtors, most accept such loss-spreading as legitimate. As the World Bank Report explains:

A society that has embraced the good of lending is in a similar position to one that has embraced the benefits of driving. Each carries inevitable risks and casualties, and some form of loss spreading is a healthy way of maximizing and smoothing the benefits for all. An insolvency regime thus represents the trade-off for deregulation of consumer lending.

World Bank, Report on the Treatment of the Insolvency of Natural Persons (2012). If the assumptions of optimal usage of bankruptcy are relaxed, however, the discussion becomes more complicated. If unneedy debtors sneak into bankruptcy and discharge, then the cross-subsidy becomes unfair, and, worse, as the ranks of the bankrupt swell, the magnitude of the (unfair) cross-subsidy grows. A debate raged during the run-up to BAPCPA about the size of this loss-spreading effect. A $400 per family annual "bankruptcy tax" emerged as a sound bite of the credit lobby that proved impervious to efforts to expose the shaky and suspect foundation for such a figure. Elizabeth Warren, The Phantom $400, 13 J. Bankr. L. & Prac. 77 (2004). Critics of the "bankruptcy tax" justification for restricting bankruptcy relief do not doubt the existence of a cross-subsidy; they doubt its magnitude, pointing to the fact that half of credit card debt is already written off as uncollectible well before bankruptcy. In other words, to the extent loan losses increase costs, the effect of bankruptcy law on that mechanism is attenuated at best.

C. CONSUMER BANKRUPTCY REFORM

1. *Comparative Lessons*

The BAPCPA amendments seemed to inflame rather than settle debates on consumer bankruptcy policy. Some assert that the Code now needs fundamental reform, while others want tweaks at the margins for topics of particular importance in today's economy, such as the nondischargeability of student loans and medically related bankruptcies. Both normative and empirical arguments inform the debate.

One point of increasingly important reference is what other countries do, particularly as consumer credit grows rapidly around the world. In 2012, the World Bank reported that two dozen nations have adopted full-fledged insolvency regimes for natural persons. World Bank Report, supra at 18. It is worth emphasizing the corollary that all other countries lack such a regime. People in debt may face relentless collection pressures, or creditors may have no effective means for preserving or recovering from assets and income. Until 1984, when Denmark adopted a consumer law, even continental Europe with its highly developed economy, had no equivalent to the longstanding chapter 7 and chapter 13 options for U.S. individuals. Comparatively, most systems are less friendly to debtors than the Code—even after BAPCPA imposed the means test. In the

Scandinavian countries, for example, someone may only have one insolvency proceeding per lifetime. (That's one way to deal with refilings!) In other places, debtors must affirmatively prove their good faith in seeking relief, an aspect presumed with U.S. petitions unless and until raised by court or creditor objection. On the other hand, the U.S. system may not be all that different from others in practice. Compare the treatment below with the approach taken in evaluating "abuse" under the Code.

Insolvency applicants who can get bus won't be allowed a car
Independent.ie, March 24, 2013

Tough lifestyle conditions to be imposed on people who attempt to write off mortgage debt under the [Irish] Government's new Insolvency regime include a warning that those living on public transport routes will not be allowed to include the running of a car as one of their expenses. The guidelines will also impose lifestyle conditions for families, who will be expected to eat healthily and cut back on leisure activities. Although those who avail of the service will be expected to drop pay-for-view television and private health care, they will be allowed enough money to at least purchase a newspaper and books. In spite of the banks' efforts to depress the level of personal expenditure allowed to those seeking an escape from mortgage arrears, the Insolvency Service has decided that while a "reasonable standard of living does not mean that a person should live at a luxury level neither does it mean that a person should only live at subsistence level." Instead, those attempting to write off mortgage debt "should be able to participate in the life of the community, as other citizens do."

Some laws are confined to encouraging renegotiation of consumer debts, with little formal relief from the courts. Other nations permit courts to discharge unpaid debts, leaving creditors to accept whatever payment is approved by the court or mandated by statute. For an excellent and concise overview of European approaches, see Jason Kilborn, Comparative Consumer Bankruptcy (2012).

Korea is an illustrative case study of the momentum toward more generous relief. After a consumer debt crisis that saw millions of South Koreans hopelessly indebted on credit cards and other consumer loans, Korea enacted a "rehabilitation" proceeding that provides for the debtor to keep paying the original debts without interest for eight years; at that point, the debtor receives a discharge. Before that regime, Korean consumer bankruptcy did not usually result in discharge but was a mechanism for enforcing and strengthening creditors' rights.

The U.S. Code's days as paragon may be waning. One particular trend of note is the development of special regimes for low-income, no-asset filings, such as the U.K.'s Debt Relief Order. New Zealand and Canada have similar summary proceedings that avoid court and are purely administrative to save time and money for all. The World Bank's Working Group on the Treatment of the Insolvency of Natural Persons, however, was careful to avoid affirmative prescriptions, stating that its purpose was merely to offer "guidance" on the "opportunities and challenges encountered in the development of an effective regime." Id. at 3-4. You might reflect on the expedited processing these countries are using for "hopeless" cases and contrast the 90+% full chapter 7 cases that yield no unsecured creditor dividend.

2. Fixing the Overfiling Problem

For decades—well before the debate over BAPCPA began—people bemoaned the increased use of bankruptcy and that "too many" people were filing. Some pointed to declines in stigma and moral hazard problems, while others argued that the social safety net, including job stability and health insurance, had eroded. We reprise consideration of these concerns in the context of filing numbers. Consumer bankruptcies rose sharply during the 1990s and early 2000s, beginning to fall in 2010. These filing rates appear to reflect macro-economic effects, the most important of which being the growth in consumer debt. The graph below, courtesy of Professor Robert Lawless, shows a pattern between bankruptcy filings and household debt (data are population- and inflation-adjusted).

U.S. Bankruptcy Filings & Household Debt, 1946 - 2010

The solid line shows the annual number of U.S. bankruptcy filings per 1,000 population. The dashed line shows the amount of "household debt" (total consumer credit plus home mortgages) per capita and inflation-adjusted to 2010 dollars. All data are from U.S. government sources (Administrative Office of U.S. Courts, Census Bureau, Bureau of Economic Analysis, and the Federal Reserve.

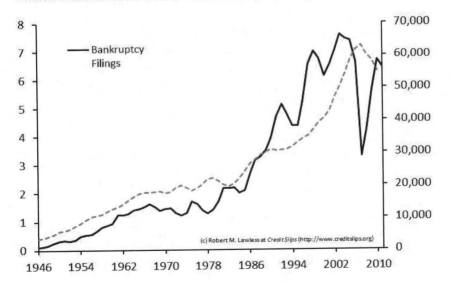

Bankruptcy filings have thus increased hand-in-hand with the amount of debt that U.S. households carry. This correlation between filings and debt has held for 65 years. Thus excoriating an "explosion" of bankruptcy filings as an intrinsic harm without consideration of the concomitant rise in debt is at best incomplete or at worst disingenuous, as this colorfully entitled blog post makes clear: http://www.creditslips.org/creditslips/2012/09/paul-ryans-bullshit-about-bankruptcy-data.html. And as Professor Lawless explains:

> Despite previous data and intuition that rising consumer debt walks hand-in-hand with rising bankruptcy filing rates, increases in consumer debt are associated with short-term decreases in bankruptcy filing rates. The effect likely stems from desperate borrowing by financially strapped consumers postponing the day of reckoning. Like many short-term effects, this one also loses in the long run, as mounting consumer debt catches up with consumers and eventually leads to higher long-term filing rates.
>
> The paradox of consumer credit – that it both decreases and increases bankruptcy filings depending on the time horizon – makes for a more complicated policy picture. Credit controls must be considered for both their short-term and long-term effects. . . . The lesson is the lesson of unintended consequence. Short-term expansions of credit may allow debtors to temporarily stave off bankruptcy filings just as marginally stringent amendments to the bankruptcy laws may actually lead to more bankruptcies. . . . Instead of decreasing the number of bankruptcy filings, the 1984 amendments are statistically associated with an increase. Amendments to curtail perceived abuses under the bankruptcy law? Sounds like a familiar (and recent) story.

Robert M. Lawless, The Paradox of Consumer Credit, 2007 U. Ill. L. Rev. 347, 371-72.

Can tightening the law affect the number of people who go bankrupt? The filings did dip precipitously in the immediate wake of BAPCPA, suggesting it packed a punch, but then they rose sharply again starting in 2007 and 2008, suggesting that law yields to the economy. This tangle makes it difficult to set policy for those who believe that empirical research should matter. Even assuming changing the bankruptcy laws affects the number of people who file for bankruptcy, the underlying normative question remains should we reduce the number of people filing? How do we know there are "too many" bankruptcies? Maybe there are too few. One criticism of BAPCPA is that it targeted a symptom—too many filings—without addressing underlying causes. Consider the radically different policy prescriptions if bankruptcy filings were explained, variously: (a) by a fraying social safety net of reduced public assistance programs; (b) by a fundamental erosion of the ethical belief that paying off one's debts is morally obligatory; (c) by a vast expansion of for-profit credit card lending that drives revenue through indecipherable fees and penalties; or (d) by an empowerment of previously marginalized consumers who have now learned through advertising or word of mouth that bankruptcy can relieve oppressive dunning.

3. The Question of Scope

Consumer bankruptcy is foremost about the treatment, not the prevention, of debt problems. While the optimal level of filings and its effects on access to credit are concerns that continue to be debated, the bankruptcy system generally does not seek to prevent financial distress. It just deals with how to clean up the pieces. BAPCPA was a bit of a departure in this regard. Consider that its full name was the Bankruptcy Abuse Prevention *and Consumer Protection Act* (emphasis added). In addition to changing the Code, it altered the Truth-in-Lending Act provisions that cover credit cards. While some would say that this twining was purely political, others would say that these most recent revisions to the Code finally started to go after the root causes of financial malaise, with requirements such as mandatory financial literacy training. (For a skeptical review of its efficacy, see Lauren Willis, Against Financial-Literacy Education, 94 Iowa L. Rev. 197 (2008).) The discussion of medical bankruptcies, still ongoing today, suggest that bankruptcy law overlaps with complex social policy areas, such as the provision of health care. While it may upset purists, as one of us suggests, bankruptcy law is excellently situated to deal with such "non-bankruptcy" matters as the strength of social assistance programs. Elizabeth Warren, Bankruptcy Policymaking in an Imperfect World, 92 Mich. L. Rev. 336 (1993).

We might go so far to say that the very scope of bankruptcy law has evolved over the Code's lifespan. The traditional conception of bankruptcy as alms to the poor is outdated. *As We Forgive.* The now-dominant view is that financial distress and bankruptcy are middle-class phenomena. Driven by scholarly studies of who files and why, such as our own in the Consumer Bankruptcy Project, the bankruptcy system today is seen as distinct in kind from other programs to alleviate poverty. This boundary means that the U.S. bankruptcy system is often framed more like social insurance than social assistance. Consider that BAPCPA greatly increased the protection of assets in retirement accounts, §§522(d)(12), 541(d), a luxury few on welfare and Medicaid even have.

A final constraint of bankruptcy law is that it is ultimately a judicial system. Bankruptcy is premised on the adversarial nature of debt collection that governs at state law; it is a system of courts, judges, and lawyers. The "bankruptcy as law" mentality can lead to undue belief that changing the Code will reflexively change outcomes. Without any change in underlying conditions, however, an institutional system dealing with overindebted consumers may simply respond to changes in formal law with offsetting changes in judicial administration. See Jean Braucher, The Challenge to the Bench and Bar Presented by the 2005 Bankruptcy

Act: Resistance Need Not Be Futile 2007, U. Ill. L. Rev. 93 (documenting bankruptcy judges' subversion of BAPCPA). In debating the future of bankruptcy law, part of the task is assessing the boundaries of bankruptcy relief and whether those boundaries should be expanded or narrowed.

D. ETHICAL ISSUES IN CONSUMER PRACTICE

The general rules of professional responsibility apply in bankruptcy, but there is an additional overlay of bankruptcy-specific rules and concerns, such as special rules for fee approval. Here, we see the consequences of those rules running up against a modern system dominated by high-volume practice.

─────── **In re SPICKELMIER** ───────
469 B.R. 903 (Bankr. Nev. 2012)

MARKELL, Bankruptcy Judge.

The hearing on this Rule 9011 Order to Show Cause did not start auspiciously. After reserving a half-day for the hearing, the court waited to call the matter to allow debtors' counsel, who was subject to the order and whose tardy arrival the court anticipated, extra time to arrive. After waiting almost ten minutes, the court took appearances, and only one lawyer–for a creditor–entered an appearance. One debtor was also present.

Without any appearance by the attorney or law firm named in the Order to Show Cause, the court indicated it would take the matter under submission and then prepared to adjourn. At this point, the debtor present asked to be heard, and the court allowed him to speak. As he was expressing his concerns about the poor quality of his counsel's representation, his attorney – Jeremy Mondejar of the law firm of Barry Levinson & Associates – finally arrived. He was approximately 15 minutes late. As he approached the lectern, he turned on his laptop computer, balanced it in one hand, and began scanning its screen apparently to determine what the hearing was about. He then made his appearance.

The lawyer's subsequent performance, as detailed below, shows that he was unaware of what had been filed in the case and ignorant of the contents of the Order to Show Cause at issue. He floundered, showing an almost complete lack of preparation. It was painful for all in the courtroom, from the client who saw his money being wasted, to the court staff who all too often had seen similar performances from the same attorney, to the court who had to endure silences – sometimes approaching 30 seconds – as Mr. Mondejar attempted to understand and answer the court's questions from information on his computer screen.

Were there ever a time to use "fail," as the contemporary vernacular permits, it is now, and in reference to this deplorable display of legal representation: it was an epic fail.

The Order to Show Cause

[The court] set an order to show cause given the circumstances under which Mr. Levinson's office submitted it. In particular, it required Mr. Levinson's office to appear and show cause why the filing of the OST [Order Shortening Time—Eds.] Motion did not violate Rule 9011. (*Id.* at 1). After the court informed counsel of its concerns, the order specifically advised counsel to be prepared to discuss the following at the hearing on the order to show cause:

(i) why he filed an OST Motion for the same motion, which was previously opposed and which this court denied on September 13, 2011,

(ii) why he has failed to disclose both the previous motion, and the order denying same, in his OST Motion; and

(iii) why he did not notify the party who opposed the previous motion in the attorney information sheet as required by Local Rule 9006(a) (and why the date of notification of the Office of the United States Trustee was in June, when the OST Motion is dated in September).

(*Id.* at 1-2). The court also warned counsel that he should be prepared to address "why the OST Motion, which does not contain any information that would help the court find a basis upon which to grant the relief requested, does not violate [Rule] 9011." (*Id.* at 2). In particular, the court requested that counsel be prepared to offer specific examples, supported by admissible evidence, of the prejudice referred to in the Levinson Affidavit. (*Id.*)

The Show Cause Hearing

The court scheduled the show cause hearing for October 12, 2011 at 9:30 a.m. (*Id.* at 1). It was the only matter on calendar, and the court had set aside a half day for it. The court, having anticipated that counsel would be late, waited to call the matter almost 10 minutes after its scheduled time. With only counsel for Bank of Nevada entering an appearance, the court took the matter under submission and prepared to adjourn. (*Id.* at 4). When one of the Debtors, Dr. James Spickelmier, asked to be heard, the court went back on the record. (*Id.*) Dr. Spickelmier expressed his dissatisfaction with the representation he had received from Mr. Levinson's office. (*Id.*) He stated that counsel had previously failed to appear in court, that counsel had twice assured him that he would appear at the show cause hearing, and that counsel had received payment of over $5,000 for services rendered in this case. (*Id.* at 4-5). At approximately 9:45 a.m., almost 15 minutes after the hearing's scheduled time, Mr. Mondejar, an attorney from Mr. Levinson's office, interrupted Dr. Spickelmier and entered an appearance as set forth in the introduction above. (*Id.* at 6).

When asked why he was 15 minutes late, Mr. Mondejar explained that he "just got caught up in traffic, and . . . was trying to look up some notes . . . on-line." (*Id.*) From that point, Mr. Mondejar continued to stare at his laptop computer as he struggled to respond to the simplest of queries by the court. As he read from his laptop, Mr. Mondejar successfully identified the matter before the court: "this is [the] order to show cause for the vacation of . . . the order to dismiss." (*Id.* at 7). But Mr. Mondejar only managed to tread water for so long; he painfully floundered through the remainder of the hearing.

When the court asked Mr. Mondejar for his response to the Order to Show Cause, eyes fixated on his computer screen, he replied:

> Okay. We were going to convert this. We're going to convert this to a Chapter 11, and he was over the debt limit for a 13. And we believe it's in the best interest, and it's just that we . . .didn't have the proper time to do all that stuff, and he's over the debt limit, so, I mean, we just need the time to do that stuff, your Honor.
> (*Id.* at 7-8).

In an attempt to shepherd Mr. Mondejar through the hearing, the court quoted portions from the Order to Show Cause. Specifically, the court directed Mr. Mondejar's attention to its request for admissible evidence demonstrating the existence of the prejudice referred to in the Levinson Affidavit, the prejudice which supposedly necessitated an order shortening time. (*Id.* at 8-9). The only evidence Mr. Mondejar was prepared to offer, after consulting with Dr. Spickelmier during the hearing, was that a notice of foreclosure had been placed on the Debtors' door two weeks before the hearing. This action, however, would have occurred *after* the filing of the OST Motion. (*Id.* at 11).

Similarly disappointing was Mr. Mondejar's explanation for why Mr. Levinson's office had filed a motion, to be heard on shortened time, that was identical to a previous motion, which the court had denied, and why the later filing contained no mention of the previous denial. (*Id.*) He had none. (*Id.*) All he had was what he could read from his computer screen. This was the lowest moment in attorney representation the court has ever witnessed.

II. ANALYSIS OF RULE 9011 VIOLATIONS

[The court examined the pleading and appearance under the standard for attorney conduct set forth in Fed. R. Bankr. P. 9011 and ruled that the firm had committed multiple violations.]

III. DISGORGEMENT OF FEES UNDER SECTION 329

Section 329(b) authorizes the court to "examine the reasonableness of a debtor's attorney fees and, if such compensation exceeds the reasonable value of any such services, the court may cancel any such agreement, or order the return of any such payment, to the extent excessive." *Hale v. U.S. Trustee*, 509 F.3d 1139, 1147 (9th Cir. 2007) (internal modifications and quotations omitted). The court's Order to Show Cause also put Mr. Levinson's office on notice of a potential disgorgement under this section. It stated that one of the sanctions the court could impose was an "order . . . to disgorge fees under the authority of 11 U.S.C. §329." (Dkt. No. 71, p. 2).

The reasonable value of services rendered by a debtor's attorney "is a question of fact to be determined by the particular circumstances of each case. The requested compensation may be reduced if the court finds that the work done was excessive or of poor quality." 3 COLLIER ON BANKRUPTCY ¶ 329.04[1] (Alan N. Resnick and Henry J. Sommer, eds., 16th ed. 2011) (citing *Hale*, 509 F.3d 1139). *See also Hale v. U.S. Trustee (In re Basham)*, 208 B.R. 926, 933 (B.A.P. 9th Cir. 1997) (affirming bankruptcy court's order to disgorge fees that were unreasonable given the lack of contemporaneous time records and the failure to provide competent and complete representation).

The work counsel performed for the Debtors in this case reflects a lack of competence and diligence that does not deserve to be compensated. Initially, Mr. Levinson's office filed a case for Debtors for which they were not eligible. Their debts clearly exceeded the debt limit for Chapter 13; although the applicable debt limit at the time of filing permitted only $360,475 of unsecured debt, the Debtors' schedules, prepared by Mr. Levinson's office, listed a total of the non-contingent, liquidated unsecured debts of $583,888.13.

After filing for Debtors a petition for relief under a chapter for which they were not eligible, Mr. Levinson's office negotiated a stipulation for conversion or dismissal with the Chapter 13 Trustee, but failed to comply with it, resulting in the dismissal of the Debtors' case. Counsel then attempted to remedy this failing by moving for reconsideration, but he did not appear at the hearing on the motion. Thereafter, counsel moved for an order shortening time on a motion identical to the one the court previously heard and denied on regular time, without citing to any legal authority that supported the filing. Worse, when the court held the hearing on the Order to Show Cause issued with respect to these filings, counsel failed to provide any support for its actions, despite being warned to come to court prepared to provide such support. Given the poor quality of the services rendered by Mr. Levinson's office in this matter, the court finds that the reasonable value of those services is zero, that is, $0.00. Pursuant to Section 329, which provides the court a separate and independently sufficient basis upon which it can order the disgorgement of fees, the court hereby orders that Mr. Levinson's office disgorge all monies paid by the Debtors in this Chapter 13 case. [The court also imposed sanctions under Rule 9011, including referral to the State Bar of Nevada.]

━━━━━━━━━

While it is hard to make money at "zero, that is, $0.00" per case, the reality is that even the highest-quality bankruptcy attorneys are working with clients who are, to put it mildly, tight for cash. One solution to reduce attorneys' fees and increase access to representation is to automate much of the routine practice. Technology ranging from software to complete the bankruptcy forms to robo-dialers to remind debtors of appointments drives down the cost per case. But such capital investments only make sense if amortized over a high-volume practice. Yet certain "bankruptcy mills" draw scorn for behavior different only in degree, but not in kind, from that lambasted in *Spickelmier*, such as attorneys wandering around section 341 meetings politely asking people if they happen to be their client.

On the other hand, presumably for fear of being overwhelmed, few legal services organizations help with bankruptcy cases, and pro se filers fare poorly, especially in chapter 13. Why should cost-saving technology be pooh-poohed in the consumer bankruptcy world when it is lauded as "efficient" and "competitive" in a high-end corporate legal practice? Both *Landry* and *Spickelmier* show the raw edges of a high-volume system. In *Landry*, the trustee pointed to workload as a justification for delay in exercising his duties. In *Spickelmier*, the debtor's counsel tried essentially the same argument. Neither sat well with the court, but the high-volume nature of the system is one of the very attributes that allows widespread representation in the first place. Is half a loaf better than none (assuming it is not filled with weevils)?

Consumer debtor representation is clearly not for the faint of heart. The attorney has the usual duties of zealous representation but also faces additional obligations under the Code regarding the scope of representation that Congress has injected into the attorney-client relationship. §§524(c), 526. Add to this the scrutiny of their fees and practices that most other lawyers never have to endure, it's a wonder anyone is drawn to the field at all. (It must be the high esteem other members of the bar hold for these colleagues.) Attorneys are often one step away from landing in hot water for failing to ask the right question ("Do you own a motorcycle, Mr. Landry?") or for standing silent when professional duty requires them to speak ("Did you list all your assets on these schedules?").

Periodically over the last fifty years have been calls to eliminate or reduce the role of debtor's counsel. Some have proposed an administrative agency that would assist consumers and adjudge relief, thereby also eliminating courts and trustees. Others have called for greater simplicity in the bankruptcy system to make it more accessible for the pro se.

The new consumer bankruptcy system should be much simpler. It is not possible to solve every problem in a high-volume legal system. Undoubtedly, a simpler system would eliminate some of the "debtor friendly" tools of the Bankruptcy Code. In its place would be a system of rough justice, but one in which the rough justice is nearly universally delivered. Policy makers need to move beyond the traditional model of sophisticated lawyers providing tailored legal advice and accept that cost concerns mean that consumers will have only very limited access to legal counsel. To make that counseling worthwhile, lawyers need to spend their time gathering factual information from clients. In the current system, counseling by a lawyer who is guided by conventional norms of professionalism likely entails mapping out the twists and turns of the Bankruptcy Code to help the client consider options.

See Katherine Porter, The Pretend Solution: An Empirical Study of Bankruptcy Outcomes, 90 Tex. L. Rev. 103 (2011). Other scholarship points to bankruptcy as unusually successful in aiding consumers in financial distress, comparing its procedures and results with public assistance systems such as disability and welfare. One big difference in bankruptcy is the presence of the debtors' lawyers, who enforce consumer protection statutes both inside and outside bankruptcy cases and lend professionalism and efficiency to the system. They even coalesce to lobby for pro-debtor legal reforms. See Angela Littwin, The Affordability Paradox: How Consumer Bankruptcy's Greatest Weakness May Account for Its Surprising Success, 52 Wm. & Mary L. Rev. 1933, 2009-2020 (2011).

We revisit ethical issues in bankruptcy practice near the end of the book in the context of business reorganization. At that time, we will consider again whether the across-the-board nature of the rules of professional responsibility, including the bankruptcy-specific provisions related to fees and conflicts, work well in a system that covers everything from individual households to the largest corporations in the world. For now, we close by noting how the current consumer bankruptcy system, whether theoretically well-grounded or an unprincipled mess of legislative compromise, is a judicial one driven by lawyers.

Problem Set 14

14.1. You were elected a few years ago as a layperson representative to a statewide ecumenical council. The council discusses cutting-edge issues of policy and has recently debated same-sex unions, gun control, and international adoption. Each council session opens with a "provocation" on a chosen topic, and you have been asked to do so for the next meeting on the topic of consumer bankruptcy. Assume that the attendees have read this assignment, that you are the only lawyer, and that the members of the council represent a wide variety of denominations and members. In your provocation, identify the most pressing points that such a council should consider in deciding whether to issue a policy statement on consumer bankruptcy and identify at least one short quotation from the assignment (text or excerpt) that you will display as your one illustrative example.

14.2. The dust has settled on BAPCPA, and the credit lobby and consumer advocates are prepared to do battle again. Congresswoman Herring opposed BAPCPA, and her district has been pummeled hard in recent years by rising unemployment and plummeting home values. She wants your recommendation for one concrete consumer bankruptcy reform that she could introduce and push through. Longer term, there is a good think tank in her state that needs more government work, and she would like to include in her bill a requirement for a consumer bankruptcy study. For that purpose, she wants to know the most important factual question that could be answered by empirical research as well as some idea of what kind of data would be necessary to answer it. She's a practical woman, so suggest something that can actually be done.

14.3. You are thinking of doing an independent study with your bankruptcy professor, who said yes on the condition that you put together an outline of your proposed topic: identifying and documenting the harms of unmanageable debt. The professor suggested that you begin by identifying the possible effects of debt that might exist and that you include individual, economic, and social harms. To get you started, the professor pointed you to the discussion of debt's effects on health in the text. Make your list of areas for research.

14.4. Milton Hulme faced imminent home foreclosure. He had heard success stories from his neighbors about how bankruptcy helped them save their homes. Choosing not to base his decision whether to file bankruptcy solely on anecdotal evidence, he scheduled a free consultation with Chaz Chadbourne, a lawyer certified by the state bar in consumer bankruptcy. During the initial consultation, Milton was very clear about his motivation for considering bankruptcy: to save his home! Chaz explained how bankruptcy works generally and that chapter 7 is the type of bankruptcy with which he is most familiar given that "most people file under that chapter." Milton engaged Chaz to prepare and file his chapter 7 petition. When Milton's mortgage company moved for relief from the stay, Chaz filed an opposition and Chaz then requested an additional fee from Milton, explaining that it is his standard practice to charge an à la carte fee for contested matters and that $100 is the going rate. The initial retainer agreement expressly stated that "contested matters and adversary proceedings" were subject to additional fees. When Milton protested that he could not afford the $100, Chaz expressed his condolences, wished him luck, and withdrew for nonpayment. Nobody appeared at the hearing, and the bankruptcy court lifted the stay; Milton's home was sold.

Milton is devastated at the loss of his home and has called you, another board-certified local bankruptcy attorney asking if you'll file a malpractice action against Chaz. What is your analysis?

14.5. Rainbow and Blue Riley are married. They jointly filed two pro se bankruptcy petitions in the past 18 months. The court dismissed both petitions for failure to complete the required credit counseling. In the order dismissing the second case, the bankruptcy court warned that if the debtors filed another bankruptcy without first completing the required credit counseling, the couple would be barred under section 105 from ever filing for bankruptcy protection again. Preparing once again to file bankruptcy to prevent the imminent foreclosure of their home, the couple chose to retain a high-volume consumer bankruptcy firm, Silverman LLC, to get things right. They provided Silverman's staff with all of the information required to file the petition and schedules. After confirming that nothing further was needed on their part, the happy couple left the country on business. When Silverman reviewed the petition and schedules, he noticed the debtors had failed to complete the required credit counseling. Per the usual procedure, his staff had helped the Rileys create a log-in and work through the counseling at computer terminals in his office dedicated to this purpose. Using the Riley's log-in, he signed in to the counseling program, which showed that the Rileys had completed 95% of the course. To ensure the petition was filed in time to prevent the foreclosure, Silverman completed the last two screens on the computer test: inputting the social security numbers and confirming that all the information was correct. The program then generated a certificate of counseling, which was filed with the court. The 341 meeting is in a week. What is Silverman's next step?